Political Regimes and the Media in Asia

This book analyses the relationship between political power and the media in a range of nation states in East and Southeast Asia, focusing in particular on the place of the media in authoritarian and post-authoritarian regimes. It discusses the centrality of media in sustaining repressive regimes, and the key role of the media in the transformation and collapse of such regimes. It questions in particular the widely held beliefs that the state can have complete control over the media consumption of its citizens, that commercialization of the media necessarily leads to democratization, and that the transnational, liberal dimensions of western media are crucial for democratic movements in Asia. Countries covered include Burma, China, Indonesia, Malaysia, Singapore, Thailand, the Philippines and Vietnam.

Krishna Sen holds the chair of Asian Media at Curtin University of Technology and is a member of the International Advisory Board of the Asia Research Centre at Murdoch University, Australia. She has published many books and articles on the Indonesian media, and other aspects of Indonesian culture and politics.

Terence Lee is an Associate Professor of Mass Communication in the School of Media Communication and Culture and a Research Fellow of the Asia Research Centre at Murdoch University, Australia. He has published widely on various aspects of the media, politics and the creative industries in Singapore.

Routledge Media, Culture and Social Change in Asia

Series Editor: Stephanie Hemelryk Donald
Institute for International Studies, University of Technology Sydney

Editorial Board
Devleena Ghosh, *University of Technology, Sydney*
Yingjie Guo, *University of Technology, Sydney*
K.P. Jayasankar, *Unit for Media and Communications, Tata Institute of Social Sciences, Bombay*
Vera Mackie, *University of Melbourne*
Anjali Monteiro, *Unit for Media and Communications, Tata Institute of Social Sciences, Bombay*
Gary Rawnsley, *University of Nottingham*
Ming-yeh Rawnsley, *University of Nottingham*
Jing Wang *(MIT)*

The aim of this series is to publish original, high-quality work by both new and established scholars in the West and the East, on all aspects of media, culture and social change in Asia.

Television Across Asia
Television industries, programme formats and globalisation
Edited by Albert Moran and Michael Keane

Journalism and Democracy in Asia
Edited by Angela Romano and Michael Bromley

Cultural Control and Globalization in Asia
Copyright, Piracy and Cinema
Laikwan Pang

Conflict, Terrorism and the Media in Asia
Edited by Benjamin Cole

Media and the Chinese Diaspora
Community, Communications and Commerce
Edited by Wanning Sun

Hong Kong Film, Hollywood and the New Global Cinema
No Film is An Island
Edited by Gina Marchetti and Tan See Kam

Media in Hong Kong
Press Freedom and Political Change 1967–2005
Carol P. Lai

Chinese Documentaries
From Dogma to Polyphony
Yingchi Chu

Japanese Popular Music
Culture, authenticity and power
Carolyn S. Stevens

The Origins of the Modern Chinese Press
The influence of the Protestant missionary press in late Qing China
Xiantao Zhang

Created in China
The great new leap forward
Michael Keane

Political Regimes and the Media in Asia
Edited by Krishna Sen and Terence Lee

Political Regimes and the Media in Asia

**Edited by Krishna Sen
and Terence Lee**

LONDON AND NEW YORK

First published 2008
by Routledge
2 Park Square, Milton Park, Abingdon, Oxon OX14 4RN

Simultaneously published in the USA and Canada
by Routledge
711 Third Avenue, New York, NY 10017

Routledge is an imprint of the Taylor & Francis Group, an informa business

© 2008 Editorial selection and matter, Krishna Sen and Terence Lee;
individual chapters, the contributors

Typeset in Times New Roman by
Taylor & Francis Books

All rights reserved. No part of this book may be reprinted or reproduced
or utilised in any form or by any electronic, mechanical, or other means,
now known or hereafter invented, including photocopying and recording,
or in any information storage or retrieval system, without permission in
writing from the publishers.

British Library Cataloguing in Publication Data
A catalogue record for this book is available from the British Library

Library of Congress Cataloging in Publication Data
Political regimes and the media in Asia : continuities, contradictions and
change / edited by Krishna Sen and Terence Lee.
p. cm. – (Routledge media, culture and social change in Asia ; 12)

ISBN 978-0-415-40297-2 (hardback : alk. paper) 1. Mass media–
Southeast Asia. 2. Mass media policy–Southeast Asia. 3. Mass media–
Censorship–Southeast Asia. I. Sen, Krishna. II. Lee, Terence, 1924-

P95.82.A785P65 2007
302.230973–dc22
2007021862

ISBN13: 978-0-415-40297-2 (hbk)
ISBN13: 978-0-203-93625-2 (ebk)

Contents

Notes on contributors		ix
Acknowledgements		xiii
1	Mediating political transition in Asia KRISHNA SEN	1
2	"Chinese Party Publicity Inc." conglomerated: the case of the Shenzhen Press Group CHIN-CHUAN LEE, ZHOU HE AND YU HUANG	11
3	The curse of the everyday: politics of representation and new social semiotics in post-socialist China WANNING SUN	31
4	The emergence of polyphony in Chinese television documentaries YINGCHI CHU	49
5	Vietnamese cinema in the era of market liberalization CHUONG-DAI HONG VO	70
6	"Not a rice-eating robot": freedom to speak in Burma NANCY HUDSON-RODD	85
7	Revolutionary scripts: Shan insurgent media practice at the Thai–Burma border JANE M. FERGUSON	106
8	Thai media and the "Thaksin Ork pai" (get out!) movement GLEN LEWIS	122
9	Framing the fight against terror: order versus liberty in Singapore and Malaysia CHERIAN GEORGE	139

viii *Contents*

10 Regime, media and the reconstruction of a fragile consensus in Malaysia 156
ZAHAROM NAIN

11 Gestural politics: mediating the "new" Singapore 170
TERENCE LEE

12 Media and politics in regional Indonesia: the case of Manado 188
DAVID T. HILL

13 Out there: citizens, audiences and the mediatization of the 2004 Indonesian election 208
PHILIP KITLEY

Index 228

Contributors

Yingchi Chu is Senior Lecturer in Media Studies based at the Murdoch Business School and a Research Fellow of the Asia Research Centre at Murdoch University (Perth, Western Australia). She holds a PhD in Communication Studies from Murdoch University and is the recipient of an Australian Research Council Discovery Grant to conduct research on Chinese documentaries. She is the author of *Hong Kong Cinema: Coloniser, motherland and self* (RoutledgeCurzon, 2003) and a series of articles in media studies. Her latest book, entitled *Chinese Documentaries: From dogma to polyphony*, published by Routledge in 2007.

Jane M. Ferguson is a PhD candidate in the Department of Anthropology at Cornell University. Prior to her postgraduate study, she worked in the documentary media-production non-government organization, Images Asia, in Chiang Mai, Thailand, as scriptwriter and English narrator for various grassroots documentary video productions. She is currently completing her fieldwork research on topics of Shan migration, popular culture, and digital media production in a Thai–Burma borderland community, where one of her ethnographic strategies includes playing bass in a Shan rock band.

Cherian George is an Assistant Professor at the School of Communication and Information, Nanyang Technological University, Singapore. He is also a Research Associate of the Asia Research Centre at Murdoch University (Perth, Western Australia). His research focuses on state–media dynamics and the alternative press. His first book, *Singapore: The air-conditioned nation* (Landmark Books), was published in 2000. His second book, *Contentious Journalism and the Internet: Towards democratic discourse in Malaysia and Singapore*, was published in 2006 by Singapore University Press and University of Washington Press.

Zhou He is Associate Professor of Communications at the City University of Hong Kong. His research on mass communication has appeared in three books/monographs and journals such as *Communication Research, Journalism Quarterly, Journal of International Public Opinion, Media*

x *Contributors*

Culture and Society, Journalism Studies and *Journal of Intercultural Communication Studies.*

David T. Hill is Professor of Southeast Asian Studies and Fellow of the Asia Research Centre at Murdoch University (Perth, Western Australia), where he teaches Indonesian studies. His recent books, co-authored with Krishna Sen, include *The Internet in Indonesia's New Democracy* (2005) and *Media, Culture and Politics in Indonesia* (2000, 2007). His earlier works include *The Press in New Order Indonesia* (1994, 1995, 2007) and *Beyond the Horizon: Short stories from contemporary Indonesia* (1998).

Yu Huang is an Associate Professor of Journalism at Hong Kong Baptist University. His research interest includes media and social transformation in post-Mao China.

Nancy Hudson-Rodd is Senior Lecturer in the School of International, Cultural and Community Studies at Edith Cowan University (Perth, Western Australia). She is a cultural geographer who has conducted research on changing place identities of small border towns of Laos, Thailand and Burma. She has a special interest in the social cultural contemporary life in Burma under a military regime, visiting the country often over the past ten years. Her research includes study of labor, housing, property and land rights in Burma, state and popular cultural ideas of heritage, changing landscapes and sustainable development. She is the Australian corresponding member for the Commission of Cultural Research in Geography of the International Geographical Union (IGU) and a member of the Technical Advisory Network (TAN) of the Burma Fund.

Philip Kitley is Professor of Communication and Head, School of Social Science, Media and Communication at the University of Wollongong (New South Wales, Australia). He has published widely on Indonesian cultural and media developments and is the author of *Television, Nation and Culture in Indonesia* (Ohio University Press, 2000), translated as *Konstruksi Budaya Bangsa Di Layar Kaca* (ISAI, Jakarta, 2001). More recent research has focused on the role of the Indonesian Broadcasting Commission and emerging patterns and practices of "publicness" in the reform period. From 1986 to 1989, he served as Cultural Attaché at the Australian Embassy in Jakarta.

Chin-Chuan Lee is Chair Professor of Communications at the City University of Hong Kong and Professor Emeritus of Journalism and Mass Communication at the University of Minnesota. His most recent works include: *Power, Money, and Media: Communication patterns and bureaucratic control in cultural China* (editor, Evanston: Northwestern University Press, 2000); *Global Media Spectacle: News war over Hong Kong* (senior coauthor, Albany: State University of New York Press,

2002); *Chinese Media, Global Contexts* (editor, London: Routledge, 2003); and *Beyond Western Hegemony: Media and Chinese modernity* [chaoyue xifang baquan: meijie yu wenhua zhongguo de xiandaixing] (Hong Kong: Oxford University Press, 2004).

Terence Lee is Associate Professor of Mass Communication and a Research Fellow of the Asia Research Centre at Murdoch University (Perth, Western Australia). He holds a PhD in Politics from the University of Adelaide, and has published widely on various aspects of the media, politics, culture and the creative industries in Singapore. Before embarking on an academic career, he worked in media and broadcasting policy in Singapore. His forthcoming book, entitled *The Media, Cultural control and government in Singapore*, is scheduled to be published in 2008 (Routledge).

Glen Lewis has lived and worked between Canberra, Australia and Bangkok, Thailand since 1997. He has taught at the University of Canberra, the University of Technology, Sydney, Bangkok University, Kansas University and the University of Queensland. His earlier books include: *Australian Communications Technology and Policy* (co-editor with Elizabeth More, Sydney: AFTVS, 1988); *Australian Movies and the American Dream* (New York: Praeger, 1987); *Real Men Like Violence* (Sydney: Kangaroo Press); and *A History of the Ports of Queensland* (Brisbane: University of Queensland Press).

Krishna Sen holds the chair of Asian Media at Curtin University of Technology and is a member of the International Advisory Board of the Asia Research Centre at Murdoch University, Australia. She has published many books and articles on the Indonesian media, and other aspects of Indonesian culture and politics. Her most recent book (co-authored with David T. Hill) is *The Internet in Indonesia's New Democracy* (Routledge, 2005).

Wanning Sun is Senior Lecturer in Media Studies at Curtin University, Western Australia. She is the author of *Leaving China: Media, migration and transnational imagination* (Rowman and Littlefield, 2002), and editor of *Media and Chinese Diaspora* (Routledge, forthcoming). Her research interests range through Chinese media, Asian media, gender, migration and social change in China.

Chuong-Dai Hong Vo is a PhD candidate in the Department of Literature at the University of California, San Diego, USA. Her dissertation examines post-1975 debates in Vietnam over the direction of literature. Her project reads these literary debates as a case study for thinking about the intersection of definitions of modernity, the relevance of the Communist state, the role of dissent and the impact of transnational capitalism and globalization.

xii *Contributors*

Zaharom Nain is Associate Professor of Communication Studies at Universiti Sains Malaysia (Penang, Malaysia) and a Research Associate of the Asia Research Centre at Murdoch University (Perth, Western Australia). He has authored numerous journal articles and book chapters on the Malaysian media as well as the political economy of national and international communications. He has been a Fulbright Visiting Professor at the University of California, San Diego and a Visiting Fellow at Sophia University, Tokyo. In 2004, he was Visiting Professor at the University of Utah, Salt Lake City, USA.

Acknowledgements

This book has its origins in an international conference held on 26–27 August 2004 at Murdoch University, Perth, Western Australia. The conference, entitled "Empire, Media and Political Regimes in Asia," was jointly convened by Krishna Sen and Terence Lee as part of a larger flagship project – entitled "Political Regimes and Governance in East and Southeast Asia: Problems and Prospects" – that was conceived and fully funded by the Asia Research Centre, Murdoch University. Six of the papers (Chapters 2, 3, 4, 9, 10 and 11) that were first presented at the conference have been significantly revised and included in this volume, supplemented by additional chapters from authors more recently invited into the project. The editors would like to express their deep appreciation to all contributors, especially those who participated at the conference, including the paper presenters whose works are not represented in this volume.

We would like to thank the Director of the Asia Research Centre, Professor Garry Rodan, whose support enabled us to host the conference and to put this volume together. We are also grateful to Tamara Dent, Administrative Officer of the Asia Research Centre, for her work in organizing the 2004 conference.

Chapter 2 by Chin-Chuan Lee, Zhou He and Yu Huang, first published in *Media, Culture and Society* 28(5), is reproduced in this volume with the permission of Sage Publications Ltd, London.

Krishna Sen and Terence Lee
March 2007

1 Mediating political transition in Asia

Krishna Sen

This volume is a collection of essays dealing with the media under authoritarian, transitional and newly post-authoritarian regimes in East and Southeast Asia at the beginning of the twenty-first century. The chapters focus specifically on the following national contexts: Burma, China, Indonesia, Malaysia, Singapore, Thailand and Vietnam (reasons for this particular selection become clear a little later in this chapter). Written in the aftermath of 9/11, and its more regionally specific reverberations the Bali bombings, in a context of increasing restrictions and surveillance in the west, the essays have necessarily departed from the simple liberal convictions that western media provide unqualified support for a free media and work against authoritarian controls all around the world.

Collectively, these essays analyze the ways in which global, national and sub-national media are embedded in national political regimes and the processes of their transformation in Asia. In so doing, these essays question three common narratives underlying popular and academic writing on the mass media in authoritarian and transitional regimes:

- that an all-powerful state can control entirely its citizens' media consumption;
- that commercialization of the media is synonymous with its democratization;
- that the western media, by its very nature, plays a liberationist role in the context of democratic movements in Asia.

Against such persistent assumptions these essays demonstrate that not even the most repressive regime, such as that in Burma (see Chapters 6 and 7 by Hudson-Rodd and Ferguson respectively) can completely control the production and consumption of media messages within their national borders. We demonstrate (see particularly Chapter 2 by Lee, He and Huang on China and Chapter 11 by T. Lee on Singapore) that privatization of media does not necessarily lead to weakening of the state's political control over the operations of the media, nor indeed (as Sun argues in Chapter 3) is there any necessary correlation between diversified media ownership

2   *Krishna Sen*

and democratization of media content in terms of whose images and voices are represented and how (although Chapter 4 by Chu provides a somewhat contrary view to Sun's on this matter). Above all, we have shown that in a post-9/11 world anti-authoritarian movements in Asia cannot necessarily depend on the support of western "democracies" or their "free" media (see especially Chapter 9 by George as well as Sun's Chapter 3).

For these essays, the medium is not the message; agency and content are all-important. A lot has been written in the last decade about the new digital media and their inherent drive, depending on one's point of view, to either democracy or totalitarianism.[1] It is our contention, however, that the engagement of the mass of the population is at the heart of both legitimizing authoritarian rule and its replacement by democratic modes of governance. In much of the region that we are looking at (with the exception of Singapore) the reach of the Internet is too limited for it to be mobilized for mass consumption. There are, however, some areas (Burma in particular) where the Internet provides one of the very few vectors of communication outside of state control, and thus becomes significant in any discussion of media and democracy in such contexts. This book does not make any technologically determined distinction between old and new media, or between broadcast and narrowcast media. We are interested instead to see the interplay of print and electronic media as they are deployed in the contradictions between authoritarianism and the struggle for democratic representation, whether at the ballot box (as discussed in Chapter 12 by Hill) or on the streets (as discussed in Chapter 13 by Kitley), or in insurgencies (see Chapter 7 by Ferguson).

The intricate tessellations between media and political regimes in Asia, as elsewhere in the world, have many strands. Any attempt to unpick these requires a degree of simplification. The rest of this introduction is an attempt to straighten out some of the main threads that run in intricate ways through the essays in this book.

Media/theory in transition

The media in Asia are a relatively new field of academic enquiry. Initial academic interest in the field emerged in the context of UNESCO debates about the cultural influence of western media in the Third World, often referred to in shorthand as the NWICO (New World Information and Communication Order) debates. The first book specifically on the media in Asia was a collection of papers from a UNESCO conference in Bangkok.[2] Since then, through to the early 1980s, a small number of volumes carrying the words "Asia" and "media" in their titles dealt largely on the issue of Asia's post-colonial transitions out of economic and cultural domination by the West, focusing either on autonomy from western media messages or on the role of media in economic development.

Mediating political transition in Asia   3

The NWICO debate was drawn across a clear line of cold war contentions: with the Eastern Bloc, the non-aligned movement (including many of the nations we discuss in this book) and the intellectual left in the West on one side and the US and its allies on the other. At an historical distance now, both sides of the argument seem convincing and flawed in equal measures. On the one hand, the American ideal of "free flow of information" across all national and cultural borders is arguably an ideological cover for creating ever larger markets for US media products. On the other hand, authoritarian and military regimes across the world, including the governments of every nation covered in this book, paid lip service to national cultural protectionism to justify keeping out the foreign media whose content they could not control, while strangling the national media's capacity for any degree of autonomy.[3]

While at the level of global governance the arguments and their proponents seemed to fall across some clear dividing lines – left–right, east–west, first world–third world, or more emotively democratic versus authoritarian and imperialist versus nationalist, at the level of national and regional politics the picture was always vastly more complicated. In the Asian nations we look at in this book, media owners and professionals, public intellectuals and academics (who in shorthand we might call the media and media policy producers) held contradictory and changing positions in relation to debates about restricting global media flows. In the entertainment media (primarily cinema, and to a lesser extent recorded music) in the 1960s and 1970s, national producers at times made common cause with the importers supporting unrestricted Hollywood imports and at other times sided with the creative artists to restrict foreign content. And cultural nationalism in the region could often focus on regional contradictions rather than on the East–West divide alone. In Indonesia, for instance, while the Sukarno government attempted to ban cultural imports from the US, and closer to home from US allies like Taiwan and Malaysia, film producers and distributors mobilized against Indian cinema on much the same grounds of cultural and economic nationalism.

In the news media (particularly the print media) the concerns were twofold. First the global stranglehold of a very small number of western news agencies produced questions about the nature of the coverage of Asia, and therefore the image of the Asian nations internationally. A second set of questions emerged around issues of relevance to Asian citizens of the news content supplied by the four major international news agencies, which fundamentally determined what was published everywhere in the world. Governments in Asia set about creating what in UNESCO forums were referred to as "news exchange mechanisms" (NEMs), to enable national communities to speak for themselves.[4] The ASEAN (Association of Southeast Asian Nations), for instance, established a repository into which the various members would deposit print and broadcast material about their own nations, on which media from the other nations in the group could draw, thus circumventing the so-called "western" bias of the news agencies.

4   *Krishna Sen*

The critique of the western media through the 1960s and 1970s was embedded in post-colonial theories about the continuing economic and cultural imperialism of the west at the end of the period of colonialism.[5] Parallel to the politics of cultural autonomy and right to representation (in "our own" terms, rather than in that of the west) ran the economic discourse of poverty alleviation in Asia, implicating the media into a role in development. Initially articulated by critical intellectuals and activists, the adoption and adaptation of the notion of "development journalism" by largely repressive governments in East and Southeast Asia (that is, the region which is the concern of this book) for their own corrupt ends led to an erosion of public support for these principles. National broadcasters were committed to shaping media content according to the needs of development policy. Even privately owned media were, under the guise of either development or nationalism, under continuous pressure throughout the region to toe the government's economic and political lines. Representing the nation and working for development in this region came to mean supporting the governments' positions uncritically.

Through much of the second half of the twentieth century, certainly until the 1990s, against the backdrop of the deep-seated western assumptions about the media as the autonomous "Fourth Estate," the easy subordination of national media in many Asian countries seemed to be surprising to observers from outside the region. But this subservience, and indeed it may in many cases be better understood as collaboration, needs to be qualified and explained in specific historical conditions. First, many of the institutions of the press and radio, which arrived in colonial Asia in the early twentieth century, including the practice of journalism, developed against the backdrop of anti-colonial struggles, colonial repressions and war. The early press – in the vernacular languages throughout the region (perhaps to a lesser extent in Thailand, even though there was a "nationalist" cause to fight for) – were deeply embedded in partisan struggles and committed to particular national and nationalist outcomes in a post-colonial world. In that context, a democratic media could easily be translated as one that was determinedly anti-colonial and by extension anti-western and therefore supportive of nationalist struggles and governments. Second, and this is commonly noted in western media, repressive governments – which employed legal and illegal means to exact obedience – emerged in all of the nations under discussion here. What needs to be remembered, however, is that even the worst excesses of governments were never enough to ensure complete subordination of the media workers. The western media's capacity to report from this region was always dependent on local informants' courage and conviction against great odds. Third, the almost single voice with which the US mainstream media spoke in the aftermath of 9/11 has given us a quite different context in which we might begin to understand how the sense of "us" under threat can modify the media's view of its autonomy from the government. The "embedded" journalist, an American creation, is being exported back now to Asia, just at the moment when the idea of an autonomous media is finally taking hold as commonsense in many parts of this region. Fourth, the post-9/11 turn in not just the western media and its language,[6] but more generally the valorization of security over democratic principles, has diminished the western media's capacity to support movements against western allied authoritarian governments, including some like Malaysia and Singapore discussed in this book. Finally, even before 9/11, the profit-seeking priorities of multinational media had long overridden concerns for rights and freedoms, with major television networks censoring their content to gain headway into the massive and ever-growing Chinese market. Even within the heartland of democracy, the United States, as McChesney (2000) demonstrates in his tellingly titled book *Rich Media, Poor Democracy*, the financial concerns of global media conglomerates systematically work against democratic principles such as minority rights and representational politics.

In the early twenty-first century, then, the simplistic identification of western media principles, whether it is an adversarial press or private media ownership, as the foundation of democracy around the world, has become clearly contestable. But the long-standing questions about the media in Asia remain – these are about transformation and transition: from poverty (underdevelopment) to prosperity (development), from authoritarianism to democracy. The essays in this volume address the old but nevertheless unresolved questions about the relationship between the media and transitional politics: how do media represent and support opposition to authoritarianism? How do political movements – whether they are fighting in the ballot boxes or streets or jungles – utilize mainstream and alternative media? How are transformations of political regimes reflected in changes in media texts? Importantly, we have tried to answer these questions in a particular moment of increasing contestation of assumptions about the western mainstream media's central role in democracies and democratization.

Asia/media in transition

Louise Williams, writing out of long experience as a working journalist in Asia, starts her review of the Asian media scene in 2000 thus:

> Information is power, or so the enduring dictators of history have understood. In so many of Asia's capitals, from Beijing to Jakarta, from Rangoon to Hanoi, the scene was the same. In obscure back rooms, rows of desks lay lined up, their surfaces rubbed smooth by years of diligent effort, as the faceless agents of authoritarian states dutifully poured over newspapers and magazines. Carefully, the swarms of censors cut out "subversive" articles from abroad, one by one, or bent low over "offensive" captions and photographs and blacked them out by hand. They laboured over their own local newspapers too, erasing hints of

6 *Krishna Sen*

rebellions and allusions to unpalatable truths tucked within reams of propaganda. The carefully edited articles that resulted were read by one and all, but believed by very few.

(Williams 2000: 1)

I quote at length because this story about Asia is repeated over and over again in the western media, and is so familiar that it has acquired the status of truth about Asia's authoritarian regimes and its subservient populations served by a relatively gutless media. This narrative has several notable premises: (1) the undifferentiated ("Beijing to Jakarta," etc.) and unchanging ("surfaces rubbed smooth by years ... ") nature of the context; (2) that the main opposition to Asian dictators comes from overseas print media (the "censors" in Williams' evocative picture are looking first and foremost, as it were, for the "articles from abroad"); and finally (3) the image of the "press" dominates the story of the media overall. Williams is one of the finest Australian journalists with linguistic skills that have afforded her extraordinary access to Southeast Asia. And yet, such broad sweeps over time and space reflect not her specialist knowledge, but a discourse which is so institutionalized as to be almost unavoidably reproduced.

On the other hand, it would not be difficult to find a quite different construction of Asia in the late twentieth century where she is represented as shining, new, glass-encased, multi-storied cities providing enormous opportunities for investment and growth. Neon lights, discos and giant television screens loom large in many descriptions of Singapore as well as many cities in China and Thailand. When we think of the post-colonial authoritarian regimes of Asia, we cover a great swathe of space and time from the 1950s onwards. Any generalization is bound to be fraught.

Both Singapore's highly sophisticated regime and Burma's brutal one keep dissent in the media in check, but by very different means. In the region we are looking at, we have on the one hand China, the nation with more television sets than any other in the world, Brunei, with one of the highest per capita ownerships (more than one set for every two of its citizens), and Burma, with one of the lowest in Asia (0.75 per 100 people) (see Sen 2004). It is this highly differentiated but also fast changing media that this book sets out to describe.

By the 1990s, an increasingly privatized television industry had overtaken the newspaper as a source of news and views in most of the region under discussion in this book. The massively expanding Chinese media industry has been diversifying since the 1980s. While state control of content clearly remains, one needs to be sceptical about how any centralized censorship could possibly be effective in a nation where, by 2000, 651 television stations were pumping out thousands of hours of programming across the major cities in China (see Hong 2004). Also, by the late 1980s, Malaysian and Indonesian private broadcasters had begun to draw viewers in droves away from state radio and television. By the early 1990s, even before the fall

Mediating political transition in Asia 7

of Suharto and his military government, the overwhelming majority of urban Indonesians had turned away from the government broadcaster to global television via satellite and even more to the emerging private channels (Sen and Hill 2000).

Questions about democracy and democratization in this region would similarly produce a picture of massive differences, between on the one hand Burma (under one of the poorest and most repressive regimes in the world), and on the other Indonesia (which in 1998 threw off one of the longest surviving authoritarian regimes in the world). In the necessarily flawed but useful numerical categorization of democratic governance, Freedom House's *Freedom in the World Country Ratings 1972–2006* (2006), the nations we discuss are categorized as being at very different points in the democratic trajectory, though none score its highest rating of 1, that is, countries which come closest to meeting democratic ideals of ensuring individual freedoms. Indonesia comes closest to a fully working democracy with a rating of 2 in "political rights" and 3 in "civil liberties," up from 3 and 4 respectively in the previous report. By contrast, Thailand's political rights score declines from 2 to 3 under Thaksin's leadership. Vietnam's "civil liberties" rating improves from 6 to 5. Malaysia scores 4 in both categories – showing no change from the previous year, but the text notes the promise of slow increase in political rights under the new government of Abdullah Badawi. Singapore scores 5 and 4 respectively, with the report suggesting almost no prospect of change in either political or civil rights. China remains unchanged on 7 and 6, but the accompanying text hovers between an optimism about the ongoing economic growth and a pessimism about worsening repression of political dissent. Burma, predictably, has the lowest possible rating of 7 in both categories – and has done so every year (Freedom House 2006). While the writers in this volume do not necessarily identify with the methods or judgments in this report,[7] the latest report has been summarized here because successive annual reports against largely the same set of political and civil liberties criteria demonstrate the highly contested, almost precarious, position of democracy and authoritarianism throughout the region.

Most current studies of the transitional nations point to the many, complex, different and often contradictory pathways out of authoritarianism. O'Donnell and Schmitter (1986: 70) refer to "uncertain" democracies, pointing to the "nonlinear" and "imminently reversible" process of change. There may be no generalized answers to the persistent question about what makes democracy possible and what makes it thrive. The connections between democracy and a free media are increasingly part of our commonsense, whether in the developed west or in the rest of the world. The Freedom House special report on *Countries at the Crossroads 2005* starts from the assumption that "independent media and independent judiciary are fundamental components of any effort at reform" (Repucci and Walker 2005). But correlation is not of course identical to causation.

8 *Krishna Sen*

The chapters that follow investigate national media in East and Southeast Asia in search of symptoms of democratization and democratic consolidation. We start with the most populous and powerful nation in the region, China. The authors of the three discussions on China see the democracy–media correlation in quite different ways. Focusing on the province of Shenzhen, Chapter 2 by Lee Chin-Chuan, Zhou He and Yu Huang takes a political economy approach to describe the emerging corporatization of the Chinese press. Against the common liberal assumptions, they suggest that the Chinese industry, while developing into a quasi-business that seeks to make huge profits, continues to operate to legitimize the Party mandate, showing no signs of developing into an independent press. Wanning Sun, looking at a range of media texts and trends, reaches a similar conclusion in Chapter 3 about the lack of any correlation between a capitalist media and progress of democracy. Indeed she goes further to suggest that the textual strategies fundamental to both the increasingly business-oriented Chinese media and the capitalist western media are responsible for keeping out the voices and images of the vast majority of China's rural and urban poor. By contrast, Yingchi Chu analyses recent documentary films in Chapter 4 to argue for the emergence of variety and diversity in the Chinese media. Similarly, analyzing films since the beginnings of economic reform in Vietnam, Chuong-Dai Vo identifies new and increasingly diverse textual form and content in Chapter 5. The difference here in the views of the scholars on these transitional communist nations underlines precisely the unequal shifts to plurality and democracy in media voices and images, even in the context of a single, if highly complex, nation in the region such as China.

In the chapters on Southeast Asia that follow, Zaharom Nain (Chapter 10) and Terence Lee (Chapter 11) find the Singapore and Malaysian media to be substantially unchanged, both textually and institutionally across the changes in political leadership. Looking mainly at media and cultural policy, they replicate to some extent the judgment of the Freedom House Report (2006) cited above, that there are few trends to suggest any move towards increasing democratization in these two countries. In Chapter 9, Cherian George addresses most directly the issue of post-9/11 politics and looks at "non-mainstream" or alternative media in Malaysia and Singapore. While the content of "alternative" media, he argues, can continue to be distinguished from that of the mainstream, he demonstrates also the constraints under which the alternative media find themselves, particularly in covering news of "Islam" and "terrorism" in ways that provide real alternatives to either the national or international mainstream media. Though starting from a very different premise, George, like Sun on China (Chapter 3), finds striking resonances in the discourses of the global mainstream media and that of the commercial media in Malaysia and Singapore.

The commonsense of media political economy has always suggested that media ownership translates into political power. However, the chapters by Glen Lewis on Thailand (Chapter 8) and David T. Hill on Indonesia

Mediating political transition in Asia 9

(Chapter 12) both demonstrate that such connections are at best tenuous. In the case of Thailand, there is no clear evidence that Thaksin's huge media empire necessarily prolonged his now-deposed government. Hill's chapter on local government elections in Manado show no direct causal connection between local media ownership and electoral success. Philip Kitley's more theoretical interrogation of the new Indonesian democracy in Chapter 13 outlines the emergence of a new kind of relationship between active and activist citizen-audiences and the national media.

Chapter 6 by Nancy Hudson-Rodd is the most pessimistic, providing a rare glimpse of Burma's extraordinary repressions against any semblance of freedom – but simultaneously the most positive reading of human agency – as it records the efforts of Burmese citizens to resist. The military junta, argues Hudson-Rodd, has reversed Burma's long history of press freedom, which as an ideal continues to hold sway among its citizens. Finally, Jane M. Ferguson, deeply embedded in the history and ethnography of the Shan in Burma, discovers the role of a tiny, vernacular media in the battle for Shan democracy and nationhood in Chapter 7.

Taken together, the chapters in this book provide a set of theoretically challenging and empirically rich pathways into understanding the media in East and Southeast Asia. They demonstrate ultimately that this region, and its specificities, offers an excellent location from which to question and revise commonsense assumptions about how media texts and institutions and the politics of democracy and democratization interweave in many, varied, contradictory and surprising ways.

Notes

1 For a critical review of the literature on both sides of the argument see essays in "Part One: Approaching Cyberculture" in Bell and Kennedy (eds) (2000).
2 See UNESCO (1960) *Development Mass Media in Asia.*
3 For a review of the debates around the NWICO and the "free flow of information," see Roach (1990).
4 For a detailed discussion of the NWICO debate on news and the failure of NEMs politically and culturally, see Boyd-Barrett and Thussu (1992).
5 The complicated development of the media imperialism thesis is not worth going into here. For a detailed and erudite account, see Tomlinson (1991).
6 For a fine critique of media's use of language, see Collins and Glover (eds.) (2002).
7 For a wealth of detail, see the Freedom House website on http://www.freedomhouse.org.

Bibliography

Bell, D. and Kennedy, B.M. (eds) (2000) *The Cybercultures Reader,* London and New York: Routledge.
Boyd-Barrett, O. and Thussu, D.K. (1992) *Contra-Flow in Global News: International and regional news exchange mechanisms* (Academia Research Monograph Series), London: John Libbey.

10 *Krishna Sen*

Collins, J. and Glover, R. (eds) (2002) *Collateral Language*, New York: New York University Press.

Freedom House (2006) *Freedom in the World Country Ratings 1972–2006*, available at www.freedomhouse.org/uploads/fiw/FIWAllScores.xls (accessed 5 October 2006).

Hong, J. (2004) "China," in H. Newcomb (ed.) *Encyclopedia of Television, Volume 1*, New York and London: Fitzroy Dearborn, pp. 510–14.

McChesney, R.W. (2000) *Rich Media, Poor Democracy: Communication politics in dubious times*, Urbana: University of Illinois Press.

O'Donnell, G. and Schmitter, P.C. (1986) *Transitions from Authoritarian Rule: Tentative conclusions about uncertain democracies*, Baltimore and London: Johns Hopkins University Press.

Repucci, S. and Walker, C. (2005) *Countries at the Crossroads 2005*, available at www.freedomhouse.org/template.cfm?page = 140&edition = 2 (accessed 5 October 2006).

Roach, C. (1990) "The movement for a new world information and communication order: a second wave?" *Media Culture and Society*, 12: 283–307.

Sen, K. (2004) "Southeast Asia," in H. Newcomb (ed.) *Encyclopedia of Television, Volume 4*, New York and London: Fitzroy Dearborn, pp. 2145–9.

Sen, K. and Hill, D.T. (2000) *Media, Culture and Politics in Indonesia*, South Melbourne, Victoria: Oxford University Press.

Tomlinson, J. (1991) *Cultural Imperialism: A critical introduction*, Baltimore: Johns Hopkins University Press.

UNESCO (1960) *Development Mass Media in Asia: Papers of UNESCO meeting at Bangkok, January 1960*, Paris and London: UNESCO/HMSO.

Williams, L. (2000) "Censors at work, censors out of work," in L. Williams and R. Rich (eds) *Losing Control: Freedom of the press in Asia*, Canberra: Asia Pacific Press, Australian National University.

2 "Chinese Party Publicity Inc." conglomerated

The case of the Shenzhen Press Group

Chin-Chuan Lee, Zhou He and Yu Huang[1]

In contrast to the pathways of post-Communist transformation in Central and Eastern Europe as well as in the former Soviet Union (Sparks 1997; Downing 1996; Splichal 1994), China seems to be turning itself into something akin to what O'Donnell (1978) described as a bureaucratic-authoritarian regime. O'Donnell was referring to right-wing capitalist dictatorships in Latin America that were intent on using economic development to quell political participation and to make up for the lack of a mandate. Authoritarian Asian regimes of South Korea (Park *et al.* 2000), Taiwan (Lee 2000) and Singapore (Sim 2001) were noted for justifying their suppression of press freedom and civil liberties on the ground that economic growth is predicated on social stability. We maintain that bureaucratic-authoritarian regime is becoming a useful concept to understand China in its contested and not always linear transition from a left-wing to a quasi-right-wing dictatorship. China's officialdom has attached highly negative connotations of chaos and failure to the Soviet political reform, claiming that its own reform policies have brought about enormous benefits to people and are once again making the Chinese nation mightily proud in the world arena. Yet China's impressive record of economic growth is achieved at the expense of social justice: peasants and unemployed urban workers have been gravely deprived of a socialist "safety net" in terms of jobs, housing, education, medical care and a decent income. Coterminous with China's embrace of the global capitalist structure and the rise of nationalistic sentiment, more and more domestic capitalists have been ordained as new Communist Party members. Preservation of power has become the very end of the Communist Party rather than a means to achieving Communism.

It is generally assumed that marketization goes against the established power, but in fact it may either work with or against the established power in shaping the function of the media. With major state institutions being bureaucratized to regulate, accommodate and partake selective elements of capitalism, official Chinese media have transformed themselves from being propaganda instruments to being what He (2000: 143–4) calls the "Party Publicity Inc.":

The new "Inc." is oriented more toward political publicity – promoting the image of the Party and justifying its legitimacy – than toward ideological brainwashing and conversion. More important, as an "Inc." that is financially responsible for its own survival ... subject to as much economic pressure as political influence. It needs to attract the ideologically disenchanted audience by softening its publicity messages ... and providing a wide range of information to respond to market demands. Although such an "Inc." owes its existence to the affiliation to the Party and is directed by Party-appointed executives, it is increasingly staffed by "hired" technocrats whose ideology, interest and loyalty may differ from those inherently demanded by the Party press.

In sum, the media have abandoned the Maoist role as ideological brainwashers, but continue to be vital ideological managers on behalf of the Party-state. Moreover, in the past decade these Incs have evolved from burgeoning quasi-business enterprises into large-scale operations, often in the form of monopolistic conglomerates. This chapter attempts to examine, through the case of the Shenzhen press, how conglomeration affects the formation and function of those Party publicity Incs and the various implications this process renders.

The making of Party Publicity Inc.

China launched massive social transformation in the late 1970s to save the Communist Party from the brink of its legitimacy crisis in the wake of the Cultural Revolution. The collapse of Communism worldwide and the accelerated globalization process in the 1990s have made media transformation seem more urgent (Lee 2003). In searching for a new source of legitimacy, the Chinese leaders have found a partial answer in the "modernization" project by opening up to the outside world and importing foreign capital and market economy. This economic drive is aimed at retaining the support of the disenchanted Chinese populace for the maintenance of Party rule. In the place of Communism has arisen a globally based ideology of developmentalism, emphasizing economic growth to promote social stability and national unity. The policy is nonetheless dualistic, pragmatic and paradoxical: while importing selective elements of capitalism (especially the capital, technology and management) to ignite economic growth, the Chinese authorities are determined to prevent their power and ideology from challenge.

After the failed political reform in the 1980s, the Chinese Party-state has been pursuing new growth-based legitimacy strategies since the 1990s. In this process, as Zheng (2004) observed, the Chinese leadership has adjusted the political order to accommodate a rising interest-based social order, and has rebuilt the state bureaucratic system and economic institutions to promote capitalistic economic development and nurture a nascent market economy. This massive modernization project approximates a crude type of bureaucratic-authoritarian state capitalism that preaches developmentalism as a new ideology. Bureaucratic capitalism is hardly a novelty in world history; it is particularly prominent in both traditional and modern China (Meisner 1996: 300). But the contemporary version is marked by tight control over the economy by a Communist Party-state that monopolizes bureaucratic apparatuses, maintains a very close relationship between state bureaucrats and businesses, and results in widespread corruption. Wang (2001: 98) argues that in China, capital is not external to the state, there is complicitous coexistence between the two, and the regime has transformed itself "from coercive to systemic regulatory instrumentality." The Party-state owns a vital part of the economy and sets up development priorities and national projects. It controls major resources and the financial system; any change in the pricing of these resources and in the allocation of capital may affect the entire economic sectors. The state regulates all economic activities and can turn economic issues into political ones. State bureaucrats turn into business dealers or collaborate with them, profiting through their connections with the apparatus. The Party-state has consolidated its power control by way of a fast-growing economy, which conceals deep distributional conflicts, widespread corruption and other social ills.

The extraordinary wealth of today's media conglomerates contrasts sharply with the abject poverty of yesteryear's Party press. The evolution took place ironically when budgetary constraints forced the Party-state to sever media subsidies in the early 1980s, thus pushing the media to strive for financial autonomy. By the end of the 1990s the majority of media outlets became not only financially self-sufficient but also profitable. This financial accomplishment is owed chiefly to the nation's phenomenal growth of advertising revenues – in a monopoly market. Commercialization has depoliticized the media and made them more responsive to the needs of the audience in an environment of fierce competition (He and Chen 1998). Consequently, the emerging prototype of Party Publicity Inc. has become more attuned to business pressure *and* political demand. Under no circumstances do the media undermine the Party-state's ideological premises, but they have, within limits, attempted to enhance market appeal by resorting to softened publicity messages. How is this seeming contradiction resolved? Based on her fieldwork, Lu (2003: 21) sums it up this way: Within a press group, the "parent" papers are, by design, oriented toward the wishes of the Party bosses while the "offspring" papers cater to the wants of the masses. Likewise, some pages of a newspaper serve the Party while other pages please the market. Party messages coexist with, but are clearly demarcated from, non-Party messages. This institutional "innovation" can be viewed as part of the state corporatist policy in which power marries money in a tacit manner.

Besides commercialization, the driving force behind the formation of Party Publicity Inc. is the fact that the Party leadership seems to have gradually viewed Maoist ideological indoctrination as a lost battle incompatible with economic reforms. While the Party-state retains tight reins on the media, it seems to demand only overt compliance from media workers; whether they identify with Party objectives or internalize Party values appears to be of secondary importance. Moreover, the media actively profit from the market with the help of the legitimizing power of the Party ideology: the media frame enterprising projects in terms of Party rhetoric, co-opt the anachronistic propaganda line into market and professional logics, and shape media discourses around the oscillating cycle of state control (Pan and Lu 2003). The Chinese public is propaganda-weary and deeply suspicious of (or at least apathetic to) Party ideology, save on the issue of nationalism that harks back to historical memories of collective victimization. Not only are younger generations unaccustomed to heavy brainwashing thanks to lessened emphasis on "thought work" in schools, they actively pursue consumerist culture that has been in ascendancy since the 1990s. For them, the "correct" political line seems less relevant than the staple of entertainment and lifestyle information.

Media conglomeration

Several years before China's entry into the World Trade Organization (WTO), which was seen as a symbol of China's coming of age in the globalizing world, Ding Guangen, then Minister of the Propaganda Ministry of the Communist Party Central Committee, had forewarned the protected Chinese media that their good old days would soon be over. Similar warnings were repeated by various officials. The Party-state took the initiative to absorb the perceived forces of globalization by organizing domestic media conglomerates, which should be made "bigger and stronger" to pre-empt anticipated foreign competition. The first conglomerate, the *Guangzhou Daily* Group, was launched in 1996. Others soon followed suit. China's media conglomerates benefited from skyrocketing media advertising revenues, which increased twenty times to RMB80 billion yuan (around US$10 billion, the exchange rate being US$1 to RMB8 yuan) in the 1990s, at an annual growth rate of 35 percent – a more profitable investment than that on tobacco (Yu 2002). In 2004, China had thirty-eight press groups, eight radio and television groups, six publishing groups, four circulation groups and three motion picture groups. The state policy is moving unmistakably toward further media consolidation.

Various accounts have been taken of the trajectory of the formation of press conglomerates in China (Chen and Lee 1998; Tang 1999; Cao 1999; Zhao 2000), but suffice it to note a few salient points germane to this discussion. First, the internal diversification of media organizations, especially within major Party newspapers, has laid the foundation of conglomeration. As the state severed its subsidies to the Party-state media in the mid-1980s, the media were under intense pressure to generate income, and Party organs began to sidestep official restrictions and publish editorially soft supplements such as "weekend editions."

Second, there was such a serious (in retrospect, perhaps also exaggerated) concern over competition from outside in the post-WTO era that media managers rushed abroad to learn how western conglomerates operate. They returned to echo the official slogan that only by making their own press groups "bigger and stronger" can they compete successfully with the western media. Having long scorned western media conglomerates, Beijing suddenly rationalized that these state media conglomerates, if armed with sufficient economy of scale, would pre-empt post-WTO foreign challenges. Foreign trips became so faddish and glorious that all of the more than twenty newspaper anniversary publications or historical accounts devoted special chapters to overseas visits of newspapers' top leaders, as did the *Chinese Journalism Yearbook* list such foreign trips as an important item (Cao 2002).

Third, much of the media conglomeration is fostered by administrative fiat. The most notorious case is the forced merger of the lucrative and popular human-interest tabloid, *Xinmin Evening News*, with the Party-controlled *Wenhui Bao* in Shanghai. Elsewhere the Party-state sought to reincorporate the core and wealthy Party papers into the state system and then shift part of the state's financial responsibility by forcing them to sub-sidize publications that were considered socially important but financially unprofitable (Chen and Lee 1998). These core outlets profited from capital accumulation by crowding out or taking over a chaotic array of "small papers" that had repeatedly defied state orders. Furthermore, as major units and enterprises rushed to own newspaper licenses in hopes of making profits, the total number of papers rose from 1,666 in 1992 to 2,163 in 1996. Many "enterprise newspapers" were internal publications circulated within work units, reliant mostly on forced subscription imposed on employees to sustain small circulations. In the next three years (1996–9), the Party-state launched a project to rationalize the nationwide allocation of press resources, and the first order of business was to take control of the perceived fragmentation (*san*) and chaos (*luan*) in the press structure. No new license would be issued. An estimated 15 percent of the total publications, many of them being "enterprise newspapers," were to be dismantled or merged into press groups. Press groups, with Party organs as the core, saw this as either an opportunity for expansion or a political duty to absorb failing operations.

Media conglomeration is a hallmark of China's bureaucratic-authoritarian state capitalism at work. The state is the largest capitalist stakeholder that monopolizes the majority of resources, authority and policy-making. Media conglomerates' economic interests are subordinated to their ideological mission; only by serving the Party-state's political interests would they be granted economic privileges (ranging from taxes, resource allocation and utilization, to political and monetary rewards). They are editorially and managerially controlled by the Party committees and are not open to private or foreign investment. But as long as the media profit enormously from a protected, distorted and anti-competitive market, they have no reason to defy the Party-state's supremacy. Media conglomerates are preferred over non-conglomerates, with the privileges to expand through takeover and to venture into non-media businesses. The media market has favored the rising constituencies of the affluent "buying" population in ways that match the logic of global capitalism and deviate from the Communist rhetoric of serving the proletariat (Zhao 2003). The extraordinary profits of Chinese press conglomerates have come largely by courtesy of state protection, not through free market competition.

The microcosm of Shenzen's press group

To examine the evolution of Party Publicity Inc. in its conglomerate form, we have studied the case of the Shenzhen Press Group. Set up as a special economic zone in 1979, Shenzhen pioneered Deng Xiaoping's lab experiment with bureaucratic-authoritarian state capitalism. The success of Shenzhen gave Deng so much confidence that he vowed in 1988 to create several more cities like Hong Kong on mainland soil. The Tiananmen crackdown in 1989, however, brought the Party to the edge of another legitimacy crisis. As a way out of stagnation, Deng decided to rekindle national fervor for marketization in his famous southern tour of 1992, during which he used the *Shenzhen Special Zone Daily* to promulgate his views, thus propelling the paper to national prominence. Shenzhen owes its "miracle" to the full support of national resources and policy, and its geographical proximity to Hong Kong gives it privileged access to capital and technology. Shenzhen draws in a massive and active inflow of investments from Hong Kong, overseas and major Chinese provinces. It ranks with Shanghai as one of China's two leading export bases and is home to one of China's two stock listings. Boasting the highest GDP per capita in the nation, Shenzhen has established itself as a major financial center brimming with strong computer, high tech and electronic industries. The city is also the country's fourth largest advertising market (6 percent of the national total), following the national centers of Beijing (25 percent), Shanghai (10 percent), and Guangzhou (10 percent). Although the newspapers in Shenzhen are not particularly innovative, the fact that they are situated in the area that served as the first and most daring lab of market economy puts them in a pace-setting position in regards to market liberalization and structural reforms.

Doing research inside China's media organizations is undoubtedly difficult. This chapter involved the use of two research methods. The first method was based on extensive depth interviews. He (2000), one of the authors, conducted a comprehensive study of the *Shenzhen Special Zone Daily* in the mid-1990s which serves as a benchmark for our longitudinal investigation. For the present study, we interviewed dozens of editorial and managerial staff at various levels of the press group, focusing on the development and impact of press conglomeration. We approached some key interviewees through personal connections (with whom we have maintained contacts over several years); others were referred to us by our friends or their colleagues. In all cases, promise of anonymity was essential. Furthermore, inasmuch as China is now seeing the emergence of two divergent "zones of discourse" in which private conversation can be less inhibited whereas public pronouncement is definitely rigid, we taped interviews only when the interviewee was comfortable. If taping was seen as too intrusive for a candid conversation, the interview team would recall the flow of the interview immediately after each session; the reconstructed texts were then taped and transcribed. Besides, to gain further insight, we also observed news operation inside the press group.

The second method was based on documentary research. We examined a sample of Shenzhen's papers. Short of having access to "confidential" documents (China regards almost everything as "confidential") or internal publications, however, we resorted to the Internet and downloaded more than thirty articles written about the Shenzhen Press Group. The first type of articles was transcripts of Internet chat sessions attended by the press group's top managers to answer questions. Though couched in self-glorifying terms, such texts revealed the top management's mindset and outlook. The second type of articles was the work of whistleblowers from within the press group berating what they saw as the top management's high-handed and unfair policy. The third type of articles was analyses of Shenzhen's press ecology by external observers. All these articles, albeit of uneven quality, provided useful background leads for framing our interview questions, though none was taken for granted. We tried to cross-check facts and identify discrepancies among different stories. Since Chinese statistics on circulation or advertising tend to be unavailable or exaggerated, we have asked insiders to provide what they considered to be the most "reliable" estimates (see Table 2.1).

In the previous study, He (2000) thoroughly examined how the political forces and economic forces stood off against each other to influence various aspects of the *Special Zone Daily*, including its management, competition, advertising operation, content and journalists. In advertising operations and competition mechanisms, market forces evidently prevailed. In management, although political control remained tight at the top level, market forces were gradually pulling the system toward profit orientations, as manifested in the financing, hiring and firing of employees, and the internal incentive system. Individual journalists were found psychologically, physically and ideologically mobile, having developed a professional norm in tandem with the market forces while seeing themselves as "hired" Party publicists. Even though political considerations, vis-à-vis the market forces, were an overriding determinant of the news content, gradual changes were visible. The scope of coverage was getting wider, while some news frames were beginning to break out of the orthodox Party lenses. Note that at that time the *Shenzhen Special Zone Daily* was a newspaper of its own, but now it is part

18 *Chin-Chuan Lee, Zhou He and Yu Huang*

of a larger press group. In the following, we shall compare the structure and function of the Party Publicity Inc. before and after conglomeration.

Conglomerating the Shenzhen press

When the Special Economic Zone was established in the early 1980s, the *Shenzhen Special Zone Daily* was the only paper in town, owned and run by the Shenzhen Municipal Party Committee. This small newspaper catered to the needs of a fledgling city built from a tiny fishing village. As the city grew, so did the newspaper. From 1982 to 1997, the paper's advertising revenue increased from US$50,000 to US$39 million, making it one of the five most profitable papers in the country. In 1991, the Municipal People's Government launched the *Shenzhen Commercial Daily* to cash in on the lucrative market. It was positioned almost exactly against the *Special Zone Daily* and targeted an identical pool of readership. The *Commercial Daily* soon grabbed a sizeable market share to become one of the top twenty revenue earners in the Chinese press (He 2000). By 1997, the city of Shenzhen had eleven newspapers, twenty-eight magazines and journals, two television stations and at least two radio stations with several channels (Cao 1999).

In 2002, the Shenzhen Party-state authorities decreed that the two major papers be merged to form the Shenzhen Press Group, presumably to "solve the problems of duplicated efforts and unruly competition" as well as to meet the post-WTO challenges with "bigger and stronger" media outlets. The Shenzhen Press Group currently controls eight newspapers and four magazines, with its total assets and capital worth about US$625 million, making it among the richest press groups in the country. It is, strictly speaking, a single-location press chain supplemented with non-media ventures, rather than a horizontally and vertically integrated conglomerate. Of the eight papers in the group, four are in the core, and four others are too new or too inconsequential to be included in this study. Of the four core papers (see Table 2.1), the *Evening Daily* used to be a subsidiary of the *Commercial Daily*, and the *Sunshine Daily* a spin-off of the *Special Zone Daily*. The new group structure puts this quartet on an equal organizational footing without the old parent–offspring relationship. The power of the *Special Zone Daily* and the *Commercial Daily* is thus centralized at the top of the press group hierarchy. A top manager who has to balance the financial books of the entire press group described this process as undesirable. "Both papers had an elemental form of conglomeration; why mess them up?" he questioned.

The glistening landmark skyscraper of the *Special Zone Daily* overlooking a lush golf course and the Shenzhen bay, in tandem with the tall building of the *Commercial Daily* two miles away, symbolizes the marriage of Communist power and capitalist wealth. The former is a forty-six-storey high tower building (worth approximately US$100 million), one third of which is used by the paper, one third on lease, and the other third sold out.

The case of the Shenzhen Press Group 19

Table 2.1 Shenzhen Press Group, 2003

	Year established	Circulation (in thousands)	% official subscription	Ad revenues (in million US dollars)	% in the press group's ad revenues
Shenzhen Special Zone Daily	1982	320	61%	92	49%
Shenzhen Commercial Daily	1989	270	64%	45	24%
Shenzhen Evening Daily	1994	300	50%	25	13.5%
Sunshine Daily (Jing Bao)	2001	400	49%	25	13.5%
Hong Kong Commercial Daily	2002*	130	24%	7.5-10	Inapplicable

Sources: Informants.
(* This pro-Beijing paper in Hong Kong was first forced to close down due to financial hardship. It was then bought over by the Shenzhen Press Group).

The imposing grandeur of these buildings conceals an acrimonious tug-of-war fought within the press group, particularly over who should get what. All incoming revenues flow into the group's central treasury before the group returns 10 percent of each newspaper's revenue as editorial fee, while the group central pays for all other expenses. Thus the *Special Zone Daily* receives an editorial budget of US$9.2 million, the *Commercial Daily* US$4.5 million, and both the *Evening Daily* and the *Sunshine Daily* each get US$2.5 million. A top manager frustratingly recounted that although the *Commercial Daily* lags five years behind the *Special Zone Daily* in management, a culture of egalitarianism requires that the gap in benefits to staff of the two papers should be wiped out, thus creating friction.

Management change

He (2000) described the management of the *Shenzhen Special Zone Daily* in the mid-1990s as operating in a mode of "political dominance with market momentum." He meant that the Party firmly controlled the top management and the general institutional structure, but leaving market economy to influence the incentive system and financing. After conglomeration, the Party's control seems to be stronger at the top. The press group is managed by a seven-member Communist Party Committee, with three from the *Special Zone Daily* and three from the *Commercial Daily* to reflect a balance of power. The seventh member comes from the Municipal Party Committee to oversee "Party discipline." The committee is headed by Wu Songying, former director of the *Special Zone Daily*. Huang Yanglue, who headed the

Commercial Daily, is next to Wu. In a twist, Huang has been made the chief editor of the press group including his former rival, the *Special Zone Daily*.

Before the merger, only the *Special Zone Daily* was the official Party newspaper. The press group has since brought a variety of publications, ranging from *Hot Travel* to *Autonews*, into the expanded Party family. We have found evidence that consolidated ownership has exerted a strong market impact on other aspects of management. In staffing, the old timers remain on the cadres' payroll but new recruits are hired on a contractual basis. The bonus system, which started in the late 1980s, is now a well-established incentive accounting for a preponderant portion of an employee's income, relative to one's meager fixed salary.

In terms of institutional structure, the *Special Zone Daily* used to be led by a team of three, with the director at the helm assisted by a chief editor and a general manager. In the new press group, the managerial side has expanded to nine, including an operation and management office, a financial center, an advertising center, a development center and a logistics management center. All these departments are supervised by the Press Group Operation and Management Committee, equal in rank to the Press Group Editorial Committee. In the mid-1990s, the editorial side of the *Special Zone Daily* was seen as more important than the managerial side. Now the administrative and managerial side (2,000) and the circulation side (2,000) have outnumbered the editorial staff (1,200) in size. The group editorial committee, comprising chief editors from the constituent papers, meets about once every fortnight to transmit Party instructions and coordinate the overall editorial policy. In April 2004, the *Evening News* and the *Sunshine Daily* each carried a story about the outlawed Falun Gong; the reporter in the former was forgiven for negligence but the reporter from the latter was arrested. At once, the group assigned "watchmen" to the printer to prevent similar incidents.

More important, the seven-member Party committee of the press group cares about the bottom line as much as about the Party line. Wu Songying, who heads the Party committee and the press group, is said to spend the bulk of his time and energy thinking about profits. It goes without saying that he has thoroughly internalized the political line, but it is equally significant to note that he is not required to devote himself fully to handling what used to be the exclusive job of a newspaper director: propaganda. If the *Special Zone Daily* strove for financial autonomy in the 1980s, the press group now pursues an ever larger profit. The press group's first anniversary brochure compares advertising revenue profiles of major media conglomerates in China, specifically highlighting in bold-face type its own achievement: RMB1.9 billion yuan (US$230 million) in 2002, ranking third in the nation. The brochure mentioned neither any journalistic awards, nor key historical events such as Deng Xiaoping's well-known southern tour in 1992 that reignited national fervor for marketization following the interruption caused by the Tiananmen crackdown. Success of the press group appears to be measured only in terms of advertising revenues.

The press group claimed to reap US$240 million in advertising revenue in 2002, up by 24.8 percent from the previous year. It has developed a bundling policy: to advertise on either of the big two, you have to place a matching ad on either of the minor two. Our informants believed that this figure might be inflated. Based on their estimates, the total advertising revenue was around US$190 million. Table 2.1 provides a breakdown as of summer 2004: the *Special Zone Daily* garnered an annual total of US$94 million, followed by the *Commercial Daily* at US$45 million. Even the *Evening Daily* and the *Sunshine Daily* each harvested US$26 million. Combined or separate, the flagship papers are still more profitable than most commercial newspapers in neighboring capitalistic Hong Kong.

Obviously, conglomeration has consolidated Party control over the ownership of the Shenzhen press and the managerial elements of an "Inc.," making it a more controllable, sophisticated and profitable publicity/business establishment. One mid-level manager observed:

> Some newspapers play the "edge ball." [This is a metaphor from ping-pong, meaning that they try to stretch their journalistic freedom to the edge of the permissible, like hitting the ball to the very edge of the table without going out.] They want to please a handful of readers and encourage individualistic heroism among some journalists. They misguide public opinion, offend the leaders, and suffer from punishment they deserve. We don't. We adhere to the political line and maximize our economic returns.

He was referring to the *Southern Weekend* and the *Nanfang Metro Daily*, which are widely seen as models of courageous reporting but often find their chief editors purged.

From duopolistic competition to monopoly

Before the merger, the two major newspapers in Shenzhen were locked in one of the severest cut-throat competitions in the country. Both employed numerous ethically dubious tactics, offering kickbacks and advertising space, running prize-drawing gimmicks, and imposing compulsory subscription on schoolchildren and their parents through the educational bureaucracy. To boost circulation figures, they printed a large volume of excess copies which were given away at a 30 percent discount or even at no charge (He 2000). This vicious competition came to a head in 1994–5 when the *Commercial Daily* took on the evening press market, a step ahead of the *Special Zone Daily*.

The merger has quelled this sibling rivalry in circulation and advertising, while putting the conglomerate in monopoly of the Shenzhen market. One immediate impact of the consolidated ownership has been to enhance its price-fixing ability. Each of the two papers previously outsmarted each other by offering deep discounts to advertisers, in the range of 40 to 50 percent and sometimes up to 75 percent of the cover price. The discount is now offered, without exception, at 10 percent, although the unit price varies with the size of circulation (*Special Zone Daily*, unsurprisingly, being the most expensive). Six months after the merger, the group had already raised the level of its real circulation to 80 percent of the printed copies, up from 50 percent previously. Instead of racing to print thicker issues, the group imposed a forty-page limit on weekdays and fifty-six pages at weekends.

Moreover, monopoly due to conglomeration has enhanced the group's revenue-generating capabilities. Half a year after the merger, the group's overall advertising revenues rose by 20 to 30 percent, and, in fact, all four papers saw vast growth in revenues. The first year into the merger, the group reaped an addition of US$6.25 million in advertising revenue and US$5 million in circulation. A top manager noted with pride: "In China, only thirty to forty newspapers have garnered more than 100 million yuan (US$12 million) in advertising, and we are the only group in which each of the four papers surpasses this mark." Shenzhen provides an annual pool of US$312 million in media advertising, of which 60 percent is accrued by the Shenzhen Press Group's four constituent papers, 30 percent goes to television, and less than 10 percent to the *Nanfang Metro Daily*. The dominance of the Shenzhen Press Group is all the more glaring if we consider that Shenzhen TV probably "steals" half of its advertising income from the popular Hong Kong-based Phoenix channel by inserting its own ads whenever Phoenix breaks for commercials.

Conglomeration has also strengthened the local press's hand in warding off outside competitors. A recent incident graphically illustrates the group's deployment of protectionist maneuvers against the *Nanfang Metro Daily*, which began to encroach into the Shenzhen market in the early 2000s. Two factors worked in favor of the *Nanfang Metro Daily*. First, because the Party exercises less stringent control over the metro papers than on the flagship Party organs, the *Nanfang Metro Daily* can afford to be journalistically more aggressive. Second, there is a well-understood rule in China prohibiting the paper from criticizing officials at the same or higher organizational level. Since the *Metro* is a member of the provincial-level Nanfang Press Group, it has greater latitude in criticizing Shenzhen's local authorities, when Shenzhen's papers can only sing the praises of their local bosses. The *Nanfang Metro* did not hesitate to exploit these advantages. As a result, its newsstand sales quickly soared to the point where they exceeded all the retail copies of Shenzhen papers combined. It lured away a significant roster of major advertisers. In May 2001, a year before the merger, the two Shenzhen papers collaborated with the Shenzhen Publications Distribution Bureau, a government office under the Ministry of Postal Service, in imposing a ban on more than 1,000 newsstands (which they owned or supervised) to sell the *Metro*. The notice warned these newsstands against "selling any non-Party newspapers from outside the city" or else they would be levied extra taxes. The two papers also blacklisted more than 100 advertisers for having carried ads on the *Metro*. The *Metro* immediately protested, waging a high-pitched public relations campaign that caught national attention. The dispute ended only after the *Metro* apologized for its "emotional" and "sensational" coverage of, and reaction to, the event; it also made other concessions to retain the right of the paper to be sold in Shenzhen. A year after the merger, in April 2003, the Shenzhen Press Group further prohibited advertisers from placing ads on the *Metro*, stating that advertisers would be denied a discount offer on the first offense, be deprived of positive media portrayal on the second offense, and face negative attack on the third. The *Metro* waged another round of protest campaigns, but to no avail. The Shenzhen Press Group dismissed the allegations as "rumors." Priding itself on "reflecting the mainstream thought with an alternative approach," the *Metro* had collected loyal readers and angry foes. Its aggressive exposé of several controversial topics (such as the official cover-up of SARS) infuriated provincial leaders, who finally retaliated by sending its top manager and chief editor to jail on flimsy charges of embezzlement. The paper's further inroad into Shenzhen has been thus blocked.

Hidden subsidy: state office subscription

It is misleading for the media to claim that they have struck full financial autonomy without state subsidies. They enjoy a variety of overt or hidden privileges. In addition to preferential taxation, the media are entitled to protectionist policies and land grant – and, it should not be overlooked, state office subscription. Within the Shenzhen Press Group, six in ten subscribers of the two flagship papers and five in ten of the two evening papers are government offices (Table 2.1). This dependence level seems higher than the national average, which had declined from around 50 percent in the mid-1990s (Tang 1999:142). In Beijing, state office subscription dwindles to 27 percent and home delivery accounts for 14 percent of the circulation, whereas the newsstands sell 60 percent of newspaper copies (Yu 2002: 47). In general, the Party papers are heavily subsidized by state office subscription, home delivery is popular with "softer" evening papers, and newsstand sale is the major venue for entertainment-oriented papers (Huang and Ding 1999: 149).

In Shenzhen, inasmuch as state bureaucracies, organizations and work units earmark a newspaper budget, they habitually subscribe to both organ papers without discrimination to avoid embarrassment or offense. Although the Shenzhen Press Group reaps 90 percent of its revenues from advertising, it is the institutional subscription that provides the flagship papers with a stable, affluent and influential clientele whom advertisers seek to reach. For this reason, the two organ papers charge advertising at considerably higher

24   *Chin-Chuan Lee, Zhou He and Yu Huang*

rates than the other two evening papers despite their comparable circulations. The big advertisers are from real estate, automobiles, information technology (IT) and electronic products, and pharmaceutical products.

To maintain revenues, journalists within the press group have been arm-twisted to solicit circulation and advertising on top of their journalistic duties. Each employee has a "responsibility quota" and is rewarded for meeting it. Some institutional clients reportedly subscribe to the papers en masse; they seek to repay personal *guanxi* (connection), obtain choice advertising space or bargain for favorable coverage – and not for the pleasure of reading. Despite protestations and criticisms, the practice continues unabated.

Journalistic norms

Ten years ago, journalists in the *Special Zone Daily* were found to be mobile and restless. The opportunities to make windfall profits in the burgeoning capitalist market proved too tantalizing for many talented journalists. Stories about how several of them left their news career to strike quick money were passed around as legends. Ideologically, journalists spread across a wide spectrum, perceiving their occupational roles differently but all beginning to think of themselves as "hired" Party publicity officers (He 2000).

Much has changed since then. Most of the journalists within the group are no longer restless, for it has dawned on them that not everybody can make it in the dangerous "commercial ocean." Because of their own substantially improved material status, many have come around to identifying with the goal of developmentalism as promoted by the Communist leadership. Typical is a remark made by a mid-level editor:

> I don't have any particular belief. I am struggling to climb the social ladder. I am a realist. I just want to make a secure living in Shenzhen, where I have no political connections. I don't care about justice or any such grand causes. No matter what happens, we benefit from staying with the system. Whether it is Jiang Zemin's theory of "Three Represents" or Hu Jingtao's new "Three People's Principles," the most important thing is to maintain stability, promote development, and improve the standard of living.

Indeed, Chinese journalists, especially those in Shenzhen, are beneficiaries of national developmentalism. A beginning reporter within the press group makes an after-tax salary of US$500–1,000 per month, a senior reporter or editor US$1,620–2,000, a chief editor US$3,750–5,000, and the top managers US$6,250–10,000. In addition, all journalists enjoy subsidies for car purchases up to half of the sale prices, free housing or housing allowances, and free medical and other fringe benefits. By China's or Shenzhen's standard, this income is extraordinarily attractive, and it is almost comparable to

The case of the Shenzhen Press Group   25

the income levels of Hong Kong journalists whose cost of living is about four times higher. A mid-level manager told us, without exaggeration, that he makes more money than he can spend. There was disparity in income and benefits among the different units before the merger, but the conglomerate has largely leveled the ground by raising the income of those in the less profitable divisions. The news group has not led to the downsizing of its workforce: since few people are willing to resign from their well-paid jobs or to take attractive early retirement packages, it is difficult to recruit new blood. Prospects for getting internal promotion also look dimmer.

Editorial division and creation of a two-tier publicity Inc.

In 1994, a top manager of the *Special Zone Daily* described his paper as a "socialist face with a capitalist body." He intimated that the front pages were devoted to Party-state publicity, whereas the inside pages catered to an audience trying to live with a burgeoning capitalist economy. According to He (2000), the paper's content was something of a mosaic, with coverage of Shenzhen's economy making up 21 percent of its total. Other major parts of the mosaic included international events and China's diplomatic endeavors (14 percent), sports (11 percent), activities in science, technology, education, arts and culture (9 percent) and events in Hong Kong, Macao and Taiwan (7 percent). Political activities accounted for only 6 percent of the items, but they were longer and placed more prominently. More than half (56 percent) of the stories took orthodox Communist "frames." Coverage of corruption was conspicuously absent; the paper abounded with themes of law, discipline and heroism.

A decade later, after conglomeration, a careful inspection of the two major papers seems to reveal little substantive change in content, notwithstanding the improvements made in layout, graphics and typology. Despite constant calls for more distinct role differentiation, the *Special Zone Daily* and the *Commercial Daily* remain quite homogeneous, while the *Evening Daily* and the *Sunshine Daily* seem to be copycats of each other. The merger of the two competitive outlets has created further inertia. As an informant puts it, "It matters little who wins, because you are only losing to one of your own." Most of our informants did not hesitate to concur that the two big rich papers are too straitjacketed and timid. As one of them noted: "Are the two papers competitors, or not? Their relationship is awkward and ambiguous." The group has managed to foster a balance of power among various forces rather than to encourage journalistic innovation. Several top officials from the press group's flagship papers participated in Internet chat sessions with readers. When asked about their editorial timidity, they defended that a "responsible" Party organ should provide nothing but "correct" and "accurate" reportage, and hence should refrain from pursuing "hot" stories.

By default or by design, conglomeration has bought, under the rubric of "subordinate newspapers/publications editorial committee," an array of "soft" publications: the *Shenzhen Times, Shenzhen Week, Autonews, Shenzhen*

Youth and *Hot Travel*. Together with the *Shenzhen Evening Daily* and the *Sunshine Daily*, they form the second tier of the press group that caters to readers' interest in entertainment, travel, automobiles and human-interest stories. As the chief editor of one of the core newspapers explained:

> Conglomeration has the advantage of providing diverse content. As Shenzhen gets increasingly diverse, readers' tastes vary. In the past, we thought we could satisfy different interests in one paper. That idea did not work. We tried to meet various interests but ended up meeting none particularly well. Now, the press group is like a super Wal-Mart, providing everything for everybody – be it a government official, a professional person or a migrant worker. We can run anything that is politically safe and financially viable. We did not realize this advantage before, but now we do.

The ideological implications are twofold. First, this illustrates how the ideological division of labor within the press group takes place (Lu 2003). Second, having softened ideological purity and fervor, the Party-state is extending its "capitalist body" to cover areas it had never before reached (or, in fact, it had once denounced as "bourgeois liberal") through ample provision of an assorted diet to the divergent audience members.

Overseas expansion

As a city adjacent to Hong Kong, Shenzhen provides the local newspapers with unique access to an "overseas" media market. In the mid-1990s, the *Special Zone Daily* experimented with a joint venture with Hong Kong's *Sing Tao Daily* in setting up the *Shen Sing Daily*, aimed at both Shenzhen and Hong Kong markets. That venture failed. In 1999, the *Special Zone Daily* bought the defunct *Hong Kong Commercial Daily* from the pro-China United Newspaper Group. The first offer had been made to, and was declined by, the *Guangzhou Daily*. The Beijing authorities' intention to keep such a pro-China voice alive in Hong Kong coincided with the *Special Zone Daily*'s business ambition to be the first paper to establish an overseas stronghold. Later incorporated as part of the Shenzhen Press Group, the *Hong Kong Commercial Daily* has continued to operate in deficit. Despite internal opposition, the press group's top brass treats it as a "pet project" and continues to pour money into the paper. The official justification is to fulfill the political mission of bolstering the Beijing-appointed, unpopular chief executive in Hong Kong; by China's rigidly assigned roles, however, this high mission is hardly the business of a "local" paper. The seemingly unwise investment can be seen as the first step in the plan, as a group manager said, to "borrow a ship to sail overseas." The group leadership wants to acquire experiences for future overseas reach and expansion. But some characterized its overseas plan as "aimless."

The ship has been "sailing" back to China instead of overseas. Having a marginal presence in Hong Kong, the paper sells most of its copies in the Pearl River Delta area. Because it is based in Hong Kong, the paper has the liberty of carrying lottery gambling and horse-racing tips, the latter being banned on the mainland. On a given Hong Kong horse-racing day, the paper may double its circulation from 150,000 to 300,000 copies to suit mainland fans who make bets through underground dealers. The central government occasionally provides funds to support the paper's perceived political role; in 2002, for example, it gave US$2.5 million to upgrade the paper's facilities and equipment. Treating it as a special operation, the Shenzhen Municipal Party Committee also decided in 2003 that the press group should continue to support the *Commercial Daily* by pumping an additional US$1.25 million into it. In 2003, the paper broke even for the first time, but went into the red soon after. A staff member noted: "We will make money someday because we have a lot of things that other mainland newspapers do not have. Even if we lose money, we will continue because the paper serves a special political function."

A top manager even quotes Lenin to say that external expansion is the best medicine to heal internal dissension that results from the merger. Even though the current policy forbids private and foreign investment in the media, he is optimistic that the restriction will eventually be lifted. "As long as the Communist Party has a controlling interest and editorially holds the final say, the more private or foreign capital, the better," he concludes. The cash-rich Shenzhen Press Group has been exploring options to buy a "shell" company and list itself on the stock market. In fact, when speculation twice hinted that the press group was taking active interest in a particular "shell," the named company saw its stock value doubled overnight. Since neither overseas expansion nor stock listing seems within reach at present, the group is investing heavily to build a fourth printing plant, which is expected to bring in greater returns by servicing other clients.

Conclusion

The post-Mao media transformation can be divided into two phases. The first was in the 1980s when the media began to introduce elementary components of advertising into their operations; the second was after 1992 when they plunged into the deep ocean of commercialism amid the Party-orchestrated march toward marketization. The dialectic of the political and the economic has transformed the Party-state from an omnipotently coercive apparatus into a less intrusive administrative instrument that seeks to manage its interests, images and national consciousness in different guises. The motif has been the "marketization of political management." Marketization does not trigger political reform but pre-empts pressure for political change in China. In absorbing the cross-pressure, the media as a "Party Publicity Inc." possess "a capitalist body" with "a socialist face" (He 2000).

Preserving the "face" is a precondition for enriching the "body." The publicity Inc. is part of – not external to – the Party-state, run by the Party committee and profiting heavily from market monopoly. But the Inc. is also identified increasingly as a profit-making business apparatus. As an informant put it, "The Party controls the press group, and the press group controls the market." The Party pulls the string and lets the press group control the market; consequently the media toe the Party line and maximize economic gains at the same time.

The Party Publicity Inc. in its conglomerate form represents a complicitous accommodation between power and money engineered by a post-Communist bureaucratic-authoritarian regime. The Shenzhen Press Group has enlarged its size and capital, waiting anxiously for further expansion. The newspaper merger has engendered a monopoly market that enhances the corporate entity's price-fixing and income-generating capabilities. Having smothered what used to be a duopolistic competition, the press group meets no more challengers. It has taken a variety of predatory measures to dictate the terms of circulation and advertising, thus making more money without improving the content. Moreover, it has flexed its political/economic muscles to protect the Shenzhen press market from external competition. Further representing a unity of contradictions, the press group is organized around two tiers to absorb political pressure and maximize economic interests. The first-tier flagship newspapers seek to publicize the Party's policies, legitimize its mandate to rule and contribute to the establishment of cultural and ideological hegemony. The second tier made up of "soft" publications seeks to entertain and inform readers while contributing to the social construction of human relationships and knowledge. Those two tiers function differently and serve different purposes. They alleviate the pains of packing a "socialist head" into a "capitalist body." This organizational "innovation" illustrates that absorbing the market logic has made the Party-state apparatuses more differentiated in terms of functions and interest. Media discourses have become less totalizing, but they do not question the Party legitimacy nor attack ranking officials.

This study confirms, however, what some critical Chinese scholars have observed: the huge media size translates into "scale management" rather than "scale economy," producing nothing but waste, inefficiency, duplication of efforts and cost burden (Yu 2002: 27). Organic integration within the Shenzhen Press Group remains problematic. In the 1980s, impoverished journalists around the nation were disillusioned with a lack of professional autonomy or momentum for political reform (Polumbaum 1990; Yu and Liu 1993). This study, in line with the result of a national sample survey (by Chen *et al.* 1998), shows that as journalists in Shenzhen became economically privileged in the 1990s, they were increasingly apolitical, depoliticized and contented with the status quo.

Media conglomeration was promoted presumably as a pre-emptive strategy to meet post-WTO challenges from abroad. Lee (forthcoming) contends that media conglomeration is a weak response to forces of globalization but domestically a strong facade for consolidating political control and reaping economic profit. The globalist claim provides a spurious but self-serving justification for press groups to enrich from market monopoly and for the Party-state to facilitate ideological and administrative control. The overall goals of the Party-state are highly overlapping with the interests of press groups, but it is the Party-state that decides that press groups should be among "the first to get rich." Multinational media giants, despite their corporate-speak, have not made impressive advances into China's market (Sparks 2003), and in all likelihood may not wish to aim at ideological fields as their priority ventures. Throughout the interviews, none of our informants displayed any concern about likely foreign competition because they know they will continue to thrive in a monopoly market and under no circumstances would the Party-state relinquish its editorial power to private or foreign capital. Our informants often cited western examples to argue that the state should lift restrictions on cross-media ownership and their conglomerate reach across regions. They never mentioned, however, that western media conglomerates are not the product of market monopoly created by the Party-state. Media conglomeration is, in sum, a case of state corporatism in its post-Communist reincarnation.

Notes

1 We gratefully acknowledge the Research Grants Committee of Hong Kong for providing a generous research grant (CERG-CityU1246/03H) to a larger project on which this paper is based. Shi Lin worked ably as a research assistant. This paper was presented at the conference on "Empire, Media, and Political Regimes in Asia," sponsored by Asia Research Centre, Murdoch University, Perth, Australia, 26–27 August 2004.

Bibliography

Cao, P. (1999) *zhongguo baoye jituan fazhang yanjiu* [A Study of the Development of Chinese Press Conglomerates], Beijing: Xinhua Press.
—— (2002) "xinwen gaige de tupo: cong baoshe dao baoye jituan" [A breakthrough in news reform: from newspapers to press groups], 28 May 2002; online, available at www.chuanmei.net (accessed 28 May 2002).
Chen, C., Zhu, J. and Wei, W. (1998) "The Chinese journalist," in D. Weaver (ed.) *The Global Journalist*, Caskill, NJ: Hampton, pp. 3–30.
Chen, H.L. and Lee, C.-C. (1998) "Press finance and economic reform in China," in J. Cheng (ed.) *China Review, 1997*, Hong Kong: Chinese University Press, pp. 577–609.
Downing, J. (1996) *Internationalizing Media Theory*, London: Sage.
He, Z. (2000) "Chinese Communist Party press in a tug of war: a political economy analysis of the *Shenzhen Special Zone Daily*," in C.-C. Lee (ed.) *Power, Money, and Media: Communication patterns and bureaucratic control in cultural China*, Evanston, IL: Northwestern University Press, pp. 111–51.

He, Z. and Chen, H.L. (1998) *Zhongguo chuanmei xinlun* [The Chinese Media: A new perspective], Hong Kong: Pacific Century Press.

Huang, S.M. and Ding, J.J. (eds) (1999) *guojihua bei jing xia de zhongguo meijie chanyehua toushi* [Industrialization of Chinese Media against a Globalized Background], Beijing: Qiye Guangli Press.

Lee, C.-C. (2000) "State, capital, and media: the case of Taiwan," in J. Curran and M.-J. Park (eds) *De-westernizing Media Studies*, London: Routledge, pp. 124–38

—— (2003) "The global and the national of the Chinese media: discourses, market, technology, and ideology," in C.-C. Lee (ed.) *Chinese Media, Global Contexts*, London: RoutledgeCurzon, pp. 1–31.

—— (forthcoming) "Globalization, state capitalism, and press conglomeration in China," in D. Finkelstein (ed.) *China's New Media Milieu: Commercialization, continuity, and reform*, Armonk, NY: Sharpe.

Lu, Y. (2003) "quanli yu xinwen shengchan guocheng" [Power and the process of news production], *Twenty-First Century*, 77: 18–26.

Meisner, M. (1996) *The Deng Xiaoping Era: An inquiry into the fate of Chinese socialism 1978–1994*, New York: Hill and Wang.

O'Donnell, G.A. (1978) "Reflections on the pattern of change in the bureaucratic-authoritarian state," *Latin American Studies*, 8: 3–38.

Pan, Z.D. and Lu, Y. (2003) "Localizing professionalism: discursive practices in China's media reforms," in C.-C. Lee (ed.) *Chinese Media, Global Contexts*, London: RoutledgeCurzon, pp. 215–36.

Park, M.-J., Kim, C.-N. and Sohn, B.-W. (2000) "Modernization, globalization, and the powerful state: the Korean media," in J. Curran and M.-J. Park (eds) *De-westernizing Media Studies*, London: Routledge, pp. 111–23.

Polumbaum, J. (1990) "The tribulations of China's journalists after a decade of reform," in C.-C. Lee (ed.) *Voices of China: The interplay of politics and journalism*, New York: Guilford, pp. 33–68.

Sim, S.-F. (2001) "Asian values, authoritarianism and capitalism in Singapore," *Javnost/The Public*, 8(2): 45–66.

Sparks, C. (1997) *Communism, Capitalism, and the Mass Media*, London: Sage.

—— (2003) "Are the Western media really that interested in China?" *Javnost/The Public*, 10: 93–108.

Splichal, S. (1994) *Media beyond Socialism*, Boulder, CO: Westview.

Tang, X.J. (1999) *baoye jingji yu baoye jingying* [Press Economics and Press Management], Beijing: Xinhua Press.

Wang, J. (2001) "Culture as leisure and leisure as capital," *Positions: East Asia Cultural Critique*, 9(1): 69–104.

Yu, G.M. (2002) *jiexi chuanmei bianju* [Analyzing Media Changes], Guangzhou: Nanfang Daily Press.

Yu, G.M. and Liu, X.Y. (1993) *Zhongguo minyi yanjiu* [Public Opinion Research in China], Beijing: People's University Press.

Zhao, Y.Z. (2000) "From commercialization to conglomeration: the transformation of the Chinese press within the orbit of the Party state," *Journal of Communication*, 50(2): 3–26.

—— (2003) "Transnational capital and China's communication industries," *Javnost/The Public*, 10: 53–74.

Zheng, Y.N. (2004) *Globalization and State Transformation in China*, London: Cambridge University Press.

3 The curse of the everyday

Politics of representation and new social semiotics in post-socialist China

Wanning Sun

In the popular sector of international media, especially visual media such as television, China is represented as embracing capitalism at a phenomenal speed, swept along by consumerism, market liberalism, globalization and technological convergence. Stories ranging from the conspicuous consumption of the "new rich," the emergence of the middle-class, the "explosive" growth of Internet users, mobile phone owners or car buyers for that matter – usually complete with figures and statistics intended to show staggering increase – to the triumphant arrival of Rupert Murdoch's News Corps, fall comfortably into this narrative framework. They have become "perennial" news stories, whose details are new and fresh but whose narrative forms and discursive strategies precede the actual news. These stories are usually framed in a way to suggest that there is only one story to tell about China's modernization project and only one way of telling this story: capitalism is the only game in town. Not only that, China in this story provides evidence that "backward" or "authoritarian" nations are welcome to join the game, as long as they play by the rules. The sporadic flare-ups in the Western media, carrying Western accusations of China's breaching or violation of intellectual property rights or copyright, encapsulate precisely the West's anxiety about possible "foul play" in this game of transnational corporatist capitalism.

On the other hand, there is the tendency for the international media to adopt a narrowly defined, simplistic and reductionist framework of covering China's human rights issues. In her analysis of the impact of the global human rights discourse on Burma, Lisa Brooten (2004) demonstrates that the global discourse of democracy and human rights, and specifically the western media, tends to emphasize individual civil and political rights while overlooking social, economic and cultural rights. The same thing can be said about how global human rights discourse informs Western media practices when it comes to covering China. This is why Falungong, political dissidents and freedom of speech have always received the Western media's attention, but an entire array of violations and disrespect for social, economic and cultural rights in everyday life have gone unnoticed. I suggest that this tendency, when coupled with China's ritualistic responses to the

32   *Wanning Sun*

West's critique, has a serious implication. This is because in spite of mutual accusations of unfair coverage, bias and selective reporting when it comes to representing China, and in spite of the different news values operating, both the Chinese and Western media display a penchant for the sensational and the spectacular. The international media's narrow definition of "human rights" has allowed Chinese authorities to "get away," at least so far, with the chronic and widespread phenomenon of discrimination, exploitation and disregard for citizens' rights of the majority of the Chinese population. This is partly because their lives are too mundane, ordinary and bereft of ostensible drama, conflict and action, and therefore do not fit the definition of "human rights" and do not make "good stories." Or in some cases, they simply do not lend themselves nicely to becoming televisual spectacle. The digital age of technological convergence and simultaneous satellite transmission has afforded the Chinese government the hitherto undreamed-of opportunity of reaching spectators outside China as well as its national audiences. One effective way to take advantage of this media technology for propaganda is, of course, to stage what Dayan and Katz (1992) call "media events" – national events, rituals and ceremonies in which national unity, strength and prosperity can be visualized for television audiences both at home and abroad.[1] These media events clearly have the intention of displaying to both the Chinese people and the world the wisdom and competence of the Chinese government. It is certainly this intention that motivated Chinese television to risk televising the outcome of Beijing's – successful – bid to host the 2008 Olympic Games in 2001, as well as China's launch – again successful – of a manned satellite into outer space in 2003. Doubtlessly, the 2008 Olympics in Beijing will be the biggest media event showcasing China's prowess on the global stage.

Here, I want to argue that a number of factors – not just the political agenda and the drive for profit, but also the institutional routines of media production, the cultural expectations of intended audiences, and the technological imperative of news-making in the era of visuality – intersect to encourage and reward a tendency of going for the sensational and the spectacular, the antithesis of the everyday. To understand the working of these intricate dynamics between various factors is, I argue, crucial to understanding how much is at stake – and how much hope one can afford to entertain – with regard to the democratization processes in China in the inhospitable and unfavorable environment of transnational alliances of capitalism and urban middle-class interests. To gain such an understanding, we need to look not only at the production of a media culture but also, equally importantly, at the culture of media production. Certain happenings become newsworthy because they are eventful; certain people become newsworthy because they are heroic or extraordinary figures; and certain topics become newsworthy because they are seen to be glamorous or sensational, thus transcending or representing a break from the everyday. Such a tendency manifests itself in the priority accorded to certain types of news stories over others in the everyday news selection and gathering practice. Action, for instance, including incidents, events and happenings that have clear beginnings and endings, is preferable to processes and issues. This prioritizing also manifests itself in certain ways of story-telling. Stories that contain strong visual impact are more appealing than the often complex, baffling and even contradictory, not to mention "boring," background data, information and interpretative knowledge. Furthermore, while successes and achievements – e.g. the Tiananmen Parade, the Hong Kong handover and Beijing winning the Olympic Games bid – can be as spectacular as conflicts (e.g. Falungong), tragedies (Tiananmen) and disasters (SARS outbreak), it is often the cultural familiarity factor which determines whether they will indeed make "good stories." Finally, "good stories" are the narrative stocks which, having proven to be "good stories" in the past, are hence likely to be recycled, albeit with fresh details. Consequently, a range of stock narratives, including the coercive one-child policy, the Tibet issue, the prosecutions of political dissidents, media censorship, have acquired their cultural resonance and become "perennial stories" about the authoritarian regime, available and ready for further deployment. These institutional, cultural and technological factors explain why student demonstrations in the Tiananmen in 1989 were as newsworthy to the Western spectators as the ceremony of Hong Kong's handover to China was to the audiences of state television. They also explain why SARS – visualized by the nameless faces wearing surgical masks, made sensational with the growing number of possible deaths – made a good story while the Chinese authorities simply wanted to wish it away.

My main contention is that mainstream media, both Chinese and international media, have failed to pay attention to the central social problems in post-socialist China. The mainstream media in the sense I deploy here include the state-controlled and/or produced media, such as the *People's Daily* and the Central Chinese Television (CCTV), as well as the popular section of the Chinese media operating as business enterprises, such as metropolitan newspapers in Beijing or Hunan Television in the provinces. I argue in this chapter that mainstream media in the reform era inevitably articulate middle-class concerns, priorities, sentiments and sensibility and, as such, have the tendency to render invisible, peripheral and silent "the little people" from "disadvantaged communities," as they are euphemistically referred to in the popular parlance. These "little people" from disenfranchised social groups are huge in numbers and inhabit vast social spaces in contemporary China, ranging from the peasants who live in rural China to laid-off factory workers in the city, and also to the millions of rural migrants who have left home to seek a better life in the city.

"Other" voices

There are, of course, exceptions to this generalization. From time to time, international media outlets such as the *New York Times* and the *Guardian*

34 *Wanning Sun*

do carry in-depth analyses of China's social issues at grass-roots level. Similarly, marginal media in China, as well as some sectors of commercial publishing, offer alternative perspectives. Marginal media as referred to here consist of a range of media outlets, including independent films, some of the so-called "sixth-generation" films made by directors like Wang Xiaoshuai and Jia Zhangke[2] and alternative documentaries (see Chapter 4 by Yingchi Chu in this volume). In addition, although we should not be too naïve about the promise of the Internet as the virtual public sphere, its potential to challenge the totality of the state positions on a range of sensitive issues is not to be dismissed. Furthermore, as I have discussed elsewhere (Sun 2004), the emergence of "compassionate journalism" among some media professionals in the urban metropolitan press is likely to create a possible democratizing space, which may present alternative positions to those of the state.[3] Already, we have seen an emergence of nascent but vulnerable farmers' and workers' unions (Zhao 2004). Last but not least, commercialization and market economy have in some ways forced the state media to diversify its markets, funding sources and content, making it difficult to maintain a totalizing voice of the state on all issues.

Note, for example, the following voice of dissonance about Chinese farmers and rural China:

> China is a huge rural country, with 1.3 billion people, 0.9 of whom are peasants [*nongmin*]. However, for a long time, how these peasants live and survive on the rural land has been unbeknownst to the absolute majority of the urban people. With the deepening of economic reforms in the city, we have heard very little about the agriculture sector [*nong ye*], the countryside [*nong cun*] and the peasants [*nong min*], except for the fact that more and more peasants, in fact millions in number, are leaving the land that was once their livelihood and entering the crowded city, in spite of the loneliness, humiliation, abuse and discrimination they know they will find there. It is therefore not exaggerating to say that the problem is no longer a simple economic issue of agricultural growth; it is a most serious social problem confronting the current government. In contrast to the spectacular face-lifts of the city on a daily basis, the countryside is clean forgotten. This is unconscionable: without the genuine improvement of the livelihood of 0.9 billion people in the country, any economic statistics of growth, however objectively arrived at, are simply meaningless!
>
> (Chen and Chun 2004: 1)[4]

These are the words which start *An Investigation of Chinese Peasants* (*Zhongguo Nongmin Diaocha*), a powerful account of the struggles – very often futile – of the Chinese peasants against abject poverty, economic exploitation, grass-roots corruption, brutalities from law enforcement, governmental neglect and urban apathy. The tone of the book is angry and emotional but the facts and information provided are sobering and irrefutable. Chen Guidi and Chun Tao, two veteran journalists who have spent many years covering rural issues in Anhui, one of the more rural and "less developed" provinces in China, knew they were taking a big risk in writing the book, which is the outcome of more than two years' ethnographic investigation of more than fifty counties. Published by the People's Literary Press in 2004, the book, a rare account of this kind, quickly became a bestseller. Unfortunately, but not surprisingly, the book soon turned out to be too popular for its own good. Within the space of a few months, it was officially banned and ordered off the shelf in every "good" bookstore, an order that was predictably defied by street vendors. Equally predictably, within a few months of the book being officially banned, online versions became available, adding to the appeal of the text. The publication of the book was a consequence of the commercial publishing industry successfully capitalizing on the need of the niche market. Ironically, urban readers embraced the book not in spite of but precisely because of the general lack of interest in the rural areas in China. In other words, its commercial appeal comes from its capacity to shame the ignorant and apathetic urban readers, prick their consciences and shock them out of their class-based complacency.

Even the so-called state media are no longer monolithic. For instance, *Rural Women Know It All* (*Nongjia nu bai shi tong*), a magazine under the auspices of *Chinese Women's Daily*, a state publication of the Women's Association, provides a rare channel of communication between women's advocacy groups and rural women, especially in areas such as domestic violence where the state is reluctant to intervene. Since 2003, *Rural Women Know It All* has had a spin-off publication, *Dagongmei* (*Migrant Women*) which was intended for rural migrant women. *Dagongmei*, now changed to *Lanlin* (literally meaning "blue bell flower"; also by implication "blue-collar"), has become one of the few publications migrant women identify with. In spite of its status as a state-sponsored publication, the magazine is relatively free from messages of indoctrination and is perceived by its readers – judging from its contents and readers' feedback – as a rare forum which gives voice to rural migrants' perspectives and experiences. In recent years, *Chinese Women's Daily*, together with *Rural Women Know It All*, has also received funding from a charitable organization in Hong Kong in hosting a series of national symposiums on the topic of protecting the rights of migrant women. Although including a cacophony of voices and positions – state, academic, journalistic and migrant individuals – these forums are nevertheless important moments in which genuine debates have taken place. *Hukou System and the Mobilities of Migrant Women*, for instance, is a book that came out of the second conference of this series. It contains a number of compelling and scathing criticisms of the discriminatory nature of the current residential registration system. These discursive spaces – created in the ongoing complicity and negotiation between the state, the market and the emerging middle class – bring hope for the possible emergence of a civic consciousness and an alternative concept of citizenship. Unfortunately, such publications are few and far between, and seldom reach the audiences at grass-roots levels. Furthermore, migrant workers are either too busy to read the few magazines targeting them or are reluctant to spend their hard-earned cash – however inexpensive from the point of view of urban residents – to buy them. During my fieldwork in the summers of 2005 and 2006, I regularly tried to purchase a copy of *Lanlin* from various street newspaper and publications vendors, only to be told that as the magazine did not sell, most vendors have stopped carrying it. "I can't manage to sell one single copy within a year!" one vendor told me.

Finally, and perhaps most importantly, while a wide range of media practices such as exposé journalism and compassionate journalism have emerged to give Chinese media practitioners a sense of professional identity, Chinese journalists have to remind themselves of the fact that their professional autonomy is conditional. The sudden ban on *China Youth Daily's* flagship column "Freezing Point" (*bing dian*) in early 2006, a column which started in 1994 and was popular with readers for its unflinching stance on a wide range of social issues such as corruption and discrimination against rural migrants, is a telling reminder.[5] Given the scarcity of competing voices, it is all the more crucial that we unravel the politics of representation in the mainstream media, both Chinese and international, in order to understand who is represented, from whose perspectives, and to whose political and social benefit and advantage.

The "specter of the rural"

Villagers living in rural China are now the most disempowered social group in China. To put it bluntly, rural China has been victimized by a systematic and structural state policy of economic development which clearly favors the city at the expense of the three "nongs" – *nongmin* (peasants), *nongye* (agriculture) and *nongcun* (the countryside) (Yan 2003). Economic reforms, while bringing economic benefits to many, especially those who can leave the country, have also spelt an end to widely available affordable – though not necessarily adequate – education, health care and welfare mechanisms which the socialist state had put in place. The chronic and widespread problems and difficulties confronting the Chinese peasants in these areas are seldom given coverage in the mainstream media. The vast area of the Chinese countryside is conspicuously missing from such television spectacles. Up to 67 percent of the Chinese population are villagers, and they make up 75.9 percent of Chinese television viewership (Huang 2005). However, television programs targeting rural areas or with rural themes constitute only 1 percent of all registered television stations. Even among provincial and county-level television stations, rural programs make up only 4 percent of the overall programs (Huang 2005; Yang 2005). Within the six years from

Social semiotics in post-socialist China   37

1996 to 2001, CCTV's documentary program *China's Documentary* produced 317 documentaries, of which only eighteen contain rural themes, making up less than 1 percent of its total production (Zhao and Li 2004). It is therefore not an exaggeration to say that if the Chinese countryside has experienced "specteralization," as Yan Hairong (2003) describes, this "emptying out" effect has also occurred in the realm of media production. When rural stories do appear in the mainstream media, they are mostly framed in "anti-corruption" narratives. For instance, since it began a few years ago, *Focal Point*, CCTV's flagship current affairs program, has consistently exposed cases of corruption and unlawful practices. Examples include: the rampant practice of village leaders selling, occupying or destroying farming land for quick profits; the pollution of rivers and creeks by small unethical township enterprises such as paper mills or tanneries; and the widespread practice of unlawfully taxing farmers. These stories have the tendency to "swat flies" by targeting local officials while "letting go of tigers," that is, not touching the big end of town nor questioning, criticizing or exposing inherent and intrinsic problems at systemic and structural levels.

In 2000, *Focal Point* broadcast a story entitled "Under the disguise of iodine supplement." The program reported on an accident involving the sudden and serious sickness of more than 400 primary school pupils in a rural school in Shandong Province. The accident was caused by Song Jianhua, the director of the county's health care center, who went to the school to promote a new product – an iodine supplement – on behalf of a local pharmaceutical company. This television story caught the attention of the then President Jiang Zemin, who upon watching the show issued instructions that the incident should be investigated, the offenders penalized and measures taken to ensure the health and safety of school children. Song was subsequently sacked from his position; the pharmaceutical company was ordered to stop production, with all its products and raw materials confiscated, and all stores and hospitals were notified to stop the sale and use of the product.[6]

These stories usually target the "guilty" local officials who violate state policies or praise regional or central officials for protecting the peasants by punishing the local officials. However, they seldom directly give voice to, or speak from the viewpoint of, the victims of such misconducts. This role of the media as the "watchdog of the Party" is both limiting and limited. It is, as Yuezhi Zhao argues, exercised carefully and delivered in popular morality tales (Zhao 2001), and as such is often realized at the expense of jeopardizing genuine democratic prospects (Zhao 2000).

Vast areas of places and spaces where these "little people" live, struggle and survive – typically marked by banality, boredom and a desperate lack of glamour – have become "shadowlands," ungraced by either the Chinese or the Western visual media. During the socialist era, films such as *Li Shuangshuang* and *Xi Ying Meng* (*House Full of Happiness*), set in rural China, became well known through their portrayals of individual rural

38 *Wanning Sun*

women who exemplified the new socialist ethos. These figures virtually disappeared in the 1980s and early 1990s, when fifth-generation art-house films such as the *Red Sorghum* and the *Yellow Earth* turned to the countryside to make comments about China's national history, and in doing so managed only to stage a series of romanticized and essentialized spectacles of the Chinese rural landscape. Today, when Chinese television is dominated by television dramas, it is difficult, if not impossible, to identify a series that is set in rural China, although the life of rural migrants – who have left the village and come to the city – have become perennial narrative fodder in the urban media.

The omission of the rural is also true of news media. Given the penchant for the sensational and the spectacular, it is logical that neither the Western news media, which prides itself on exposing China's violations of human rights, nor the Chinese news media, with its urban and middle-class clientele base, see much chance of selling pictures or headlines featuring boredom, lethargy and quiet despair, not to mention the widespread phenomenon of poverty, domestic violence against women and female suicide in the countryside (Pickowicz and Wang 2002). A wide range of issues of inequality, inequity and violation of citizens' rights daily and acutely experienced by these disenfranchised social groups and communities largely go unnoticed, for the simple and brutal fact that they cannot claim a privileged place on the stage of global capitalism. They fail to measure up to the benchmark of newsworthiness subscribed to by an urban-based middle-class media.

While the omission of the rural in the commercial sector of the Chinese media is a result of chasing glamour and profit, the lack of attention in the international media can be marked down either to the failure of the rural issues, problems and realities to cross the threshold of visibility in the radar areas of "foreign correspondents," or to their inability to register, according to the professional judgment of Western journalists, as potentially "good stories." Regardless of source, this lack of attention fits in with what Zhao (2001: 51) calls the "collusion between statist and corporate agendas" of American politics and media. As Zhao notes:

> These alliances underscored the antidemocratic nature of mainstream American political discourse on international issues and the continuing mobilization of the freedom-of-information rhetoric by the US elite in the conquest of global markets.
>
> (Zhao 2001: 51)

While China's rural problems and struggle do not make palatable narrative fodder, the "staggering" or "explosive" numbers indicating the growth and development of information technology in China always do.

This is not to say that the state, fully cognizant of the growing social stratification and the rural–urban divide, is not aware of the systemic lack of media coverage of rural China and its potential political risk. In fact, there have been a number of initiatives to promote the successes of economic reforms in rural China and give positive media coverage and exposure to rural life since 2005. For instance, in the summer of 2006, China National Radio (CNR) ran a series of special reports under the heading of "Building a socialist new countryside" (*jie she she hu zhu yi xing nong cun*) as part of its daily half-hour national news bulletin. This obvious discursive exercise to "de-specteralize" the Chinese countryside resorts to reviving the "to-get-rich-is-glorious" narrative which emerged in the early 1990s. These are often stories of individual farmers who adhered to the Party's call to get rich quick, tales which frequented the Chinese media in the early stage of economic reforms. Stories of this kind gradually lost their appeal in the 1990s when the locale of economic development shifted from rural to urban spaces, the latter producing wealth and glamour on an unprecedented scale and more far spectacular than their rural predecessors in the previous decade. Narratives of the "new socialist Chinese countryside" also studiously promote local officials who, through helping the community to develop and prosper, embody the Party's new-fangled slogan of "development for all" (*gong tong fa zhan*) and building "harmonious society" (*he xie she hui*). On 24 June 2006, the special report ran a two-minute story of a village outside Haikou City, Hainan Province. According to the story, Benli Village used to be a "poverty-stricken," "backward" and "infested with feudal practices." Recently, however, a newly elected village chief had seen the potential to transform the village into a business enterprise specializing in a range of eco-products. Incomes grew and villagers are now reportedly living a much more enriched life, both economically and culturally. While these stories do succeed in bringing rural China back to the nation's mediasphere – at least in the state media – they still operate according to the Party journalism's tradition of searching for positive stories within a prior ideological agenda, and are therefore severely limited in terms of what they can and cannot say about the problems and issues facing rural China.

The urban shadowland

Next to the peasants struggling against droughts and floods, excessive taxations, oppressive local governance and unfavorable economic policies, are the laid-off workers (*xiagang gong ren*) in the city, a casualty of the widespread restructuring and downsizing of state-owned enterprises (SOE). These are a social group that is rapidly becoming the under-class, or the urban poor. Although the misfortune of being laid off (*xiagang*, literally meaning stepping down from one's position) falls on both male and female workers, it is often women that bear the brunt. Cartier's (2001) statistics claim that as many as 70 percent of the laid-off workers are women. On the one hand, women, because of their parental and family commitments, cannot compete with men in retraining and reskilling. On the other hand, since the services and hospitality industry relies heavily on young women, middle-aged women have little prospect in seeking gainful employment in that sector. These harsh economic realities are seen to affect the quality of marriage and family life as well as women's psychological well-being. Decrease in income is seen to go hand in hand with family disputes, domestic violence and an increased divorce rate. Women workers' confidence is thus greatly undermined. Prevalent among (laid-off) workers is a general sense of insecurity and anxiety. They fear five things: their factory going bankrupt; getting sick and being unable to afford medication; the loss of the benefits entitlements at work; price increases; and being unable to find a job again once sacked (Sun 2002a).

In both state and popular publications, it is not the everyday struggle of adjusting to a new reality, brought about by retrenchment and the subsequent sense of despair and depression that dogs many laid-off workers, that makes headlines. Nor is it the reality of their lack of adequate social, medical and other benefit systems. It is more often than not stories of laid-off-workers-turned-entrepreneurs. These stories, especially those in the Women's Federation publications, tend largely to focus on women individuals as exemplifying the "positive" aspects of female entrepreneurship. In the popular consciousness and media discourses, the laid-off female factory worker who remains poor and who is in need of help is invisible. The only thing which may lift her out of the drab anonymity of unemployment is if/ when she manages to refashion herself into a successful – and thus glamorous – businesswoman. The perennial popularity of this laid-off-worker-turned-entrepreneur narrative may be understood in a number of ways. From the point of view of the human interest factor in popular news media, the success of the new worker-turned-entrepreneur promises a good read. She is a Cinderella character who not only invites sympathy and compassion but, more importantly, is seen to possess glamour and beauty – obviously important human qualities – in spite of her humble guise. From the perspective of the state and its media, stories of born-again entrepreneurs help create the illusion that everyone is equal with regard to opportunities, thus camouflaging the drastic social and economic stratification of individuals.[7]

Zhang Qi is one example of this form of much-vaunted born-again entrepreneurship. In October 2000, the *Xin'an Evening Post*, the most widely circulated provincial paper in Anhui, followed up on the story of a woman who, together with her husband in the same unit, had been laid off from a textile factory five years earlier. Life was predictably hard for Zhang's family, with Zhang doing whatever she could in order to support their child and make ends meet. In September 1998, out of desperation, she wrote to the paper appealing for help. Thanks to the paper's publicity, Zhang was offered a job in a company trading in bathroom facilities. She worked hard and learned many useful management and selling skills on the job. In late 1999, the paper ran a follow-up account of Zhang's transformation from a laid-off worker to a competent saleswoman. Zhang's story did not end there. In March 2000, Zhang decided to quit her job in the company and start her own business specializing in bathroom facilities. She employed more than a dozen laid-off workers including her husband and her brother. Business has been good. Zhang is now starting to branch out, setting up agent offices in other provinces and staking out a space in the market. In October 2000, the *Xin'an Evening Post* reported on her continuing success: "Laid-off female factory worker now a general manager" (25 October 2000).

Rather than criticizing the logic of a nationwide industrial restructuring which results in further disadvantaging of certain sectors of labor forces, or even lobbying for a fairer share of economic resources, stories like this can be read as assuming the position of an apologist for the state. It is precisely for this reason that the turn of fortune of these laid-off workers in these narratives is often made possible by the support of a certain benevolent figure among the government officials. Yu's (1999) study of the media's representation of laid-off female workers shows that official women's publications such as those by the Women's Federation were initially silent on the phenomenon of the massive sacking of female workers; and, when they subsequently acknowledged the situation, the issue was mostly approached from the angle of the government giving aid to female retrenched workers or that of laid-off workers seeking "re-employment" (*zai jiu ye*). The official discourse also encourages women to accept losing their jobs as natural and inevitable, and urges women to become "strong" (*zi qiang*) and "independent" (*zi li*), and to seek alternative ways of making a living after losing their jobs. Li Xiaojiang (1994) is right to point out that the economic difficulties facing women are constructed in the state discourse as individual, rather than social, problems. From the state's point of view, to emphasize women's rights to equality and access in employment in times of labor excess would be to obstruct the state's agenda of economic reforms. In other words, it is not in the political or economic interests of either the urban popular media or the state media, including its media outlets targeting women, to dwell on the materiality of tens of thousands of not-so-successful, non-enterprising, non-glamorous laid-off workers, since they are stark reminders of the unevenness and inequality brought about by the economic reforms. Understandably, while transnational advertising and glossy lifestyle magazines such as *Vogue* zoom in on the multicolored life of the "successful people" (*cheng gong ren shi*) – consisting mainly of "white-collars" (*bai lin*) working for private, especially transnational, companies (Wang 2000; Zhou 2000; Mei 2000); "golden-collars" (*jin lin*) whose annual income amounts to 150,000 to 400,000 yuan (Dai 2000); and, the "new rich" (*xin fu ren*) – the monochrome drabness which marks the daily struggle of the urban poor is conveniently forgotten.

Rural migrants in the city

While it may be convenient to turn a blind eye to the peasants in villages and laid-off workers in the city, it is simply impossible to ignore the presence

42 *Wanning Sun*

of almost 100 million internal migrants in the Chinese city, whose movements, work and ways of life have made a profound and, for some, intimate, impact on the life of urban residents, at the same time irreversibly changing China's urban landscapes. Most of these rural migrants are engaged in factory, construction and domestic work, with many working as cleaners and garbage collectors or security guards, or being involved in small businesses and the service and hospitality industry. Equally visible is the role rural migrants assume in the contemporary televisual narratives, especially in television dramas. These dramas include series such as *Girls From Out of Town* (*Wai Lai Mei*), *Shenzhen Working Girls* (*Shenzhen Dagongmei*), *Sisters' Ventures in Beijing* (*Jiejie Meimei Chuang Beijing*) and *Roughing it in Shanghai* (*Chuang Shanghai*), the last of which tells the story of a group of rural migrants from Henan Province trying – some successfully and others not – to become *Shanghairen* (Shanghai residents). This is not to mention television dramas which deal exclusively on the life of the maid, such as *Professor Tian and his Twenty-Eight Maids* and *Chinese Maids in Foreign Families*, in which rural migrant women are represented as aspiring to become modern and "civilized," but are ultimately judged to be wanting by the urban residents.

Less visible to the urban gaze and, by implication, to the media – but equally crucial to the economic growth of the state-sanctioned capitalist economy in China – are the "working sisters" (*dagongmei*) on the shop floor in the factories dotting the coastal lines of southern Chinese cities, especially in the Special Economic Zone (SEZ). Mostly producing electronics, toys, clothing and other assembly-line work, the labor market in southern SEZ factories consists of more women migrant workers from various parts of China than men.[8] On the factory's shop floor, they are mostly treated as objects to be "civilized," "disciplined" and "modernized," so that their "docile bodies," when combined with "nimble fingers,"[9] are the perfect condition of production for transnational capitalism. They are, on an everyday basis, subject to three kinds of control: physical controls, timed labor and the docking of wages (Lee C.K. 1997). Life outside the shop floor is no less restricting and subject to discipline. For most *dagongmei*, life is confined mostly to the workshop floor, the factory canteen and the dormitory, shared with ten other young women from rural, inland provinces. Most workers, even if they are married and their spouses work in the same factory, have to live in single-sex dormitories. Their children, if any, are mostly left behind with their families back in the village, since the factories that employ them do not provide education or childcare. Most workers work long hours, six days a week, and do not enjoy sundry employment benefits, let alone any protection by regulations and laws pertaining to workplace safety and compensations.[10] The everyday life of these *dagongmei* – including the denial of privacy, lack of citizens' rights and entitlements as an employee, and degrading treatment from management which disregards both their dignity and freedom – seldom makes news in either Chinese or foreign media. This is in spite of the fact that the exponential growth of China's GDP in statistical terms, which does make news, invariably relies on the continuous availability of such cheap labor.

While the official media, such as the Women's Federation publications, see fit to engage in propaganda work promoting positive images of the laid-off workers, they have put the lurid business of prostitution – another line of employment pursued by many rural migrants – into the "too hard" basket and left it to commercial media, which, like their counterparts in the West, are only interested in profiting from selling sex, violence and crime. Here, rural migrants – as exemplified by the figures of a maid, a prostitute or a victim of abduction – become, for the urban and mostly middle-class residents, the object of intense social scrutiny, anxiety, fascination and sometimes sympathy and compassion. They become, in other words, perennial figures in the commercial metropolitan press. Poised to transgress the boundaries of the public and the private, the waged and the unwaged, and the boundaries of the family, their lives have become perennial narrative fodder to urban Chinese, if not the foreign, media.[11] This representational excess is in contrast to the exploited and oppressed life of their "sisters" in the hands of transnational capitalist regimes on the factory shop floor, which goes largely unnoticed, except when an element of sensationalism is found in the story. It is exactly for this reason that the factory fire at the Zhili Toy Company in Shenzhen in 1993, which claimed 87 lives and injured 46, became newsworthy and caught the attention of both the media and NGOs (Chan 2002). What has gone unreported, due to a lack of sensational elements such as fire and death, are the systematically punitive measures and constraints imposed on migrant workers, the chronic violation and disregard of their rights as migrant workers, and their poor or substandard working conditions.

Neither the peasants – including those on the land and on the move – nor the urban proletariats have kept quiet about their discontent, anger and grievances. Mass protests, sporadically erupting into violent clashes, became common in China throughout the 1990s. While the media in China see fit not to print news of this type, for obvious political reasons, Western coverage of such protests is occasional (Zhao 2001). Further, when it does occur, the stories are, on the whole, about conflict and drama rather than the reality of the actual socio-economic inequalities which gave rise to these dramatic events. Nor is this coverage able to capture, or indeed interested in capturing, the sense of frustration and struggle which prevails in the everyday lives of these marginalized social groups. Bereft of drama, action and sensationalism, let alone spectacularity – all of which are essential to media attention – the everyday life of these groups, where violations of human rights and citizens' democratic rights occur in most "banal," "mundane" and individuated but most profound ways, goes unnoticed. Against the dazzle of the urban rich, a composite of "weak," "inarticulate" and "little" people, "laid-off workers, rural migrants in the city, and villagers languishing

44 *Wanning Sun*

in the bleak deserted countryside, retirees, disabled people, and anyone else whose monthly income is between 60 and 240 *yuan*, recede further and further into the dark corners of society" (Dai 2000: 3).

Conclusion

This chapter has tried to outline the issues and problems confronting some of these disenfranchised social groups in their daily struggle for equality, equity and their civil and human rights; at the same time, it has considered a number of ways in which these issues and problems fail the test of newsworthiness and hence the threshold of public visibility. By engaging with critics from a coalition between the dominant Western and Chinese polities and media in their respective statist and corporatist embrace of global capitalism, I have sought to present a critique of both the international media's narrow and simplistic approach to "human rights" and the Chinese media's love affair with the glamour of transnational capital. The discussion points to a less than optimistic view of China's processes of democratization, caught in the contradictions between local democratic aspirations and international media and politics of "regime change." I have also, in accounting for the omission, under-representation and/or misrepresentation of the disenfranchised groups, pointed to the limitations of a critique of the political economy of news-making alone. The discursive regime which I outline is, I argue, a consequence of the intersecting and interacting of an array of factors: political, economic, institutional, cultural and technological. In addition, it is the contingent and combinatory relationships among these factors that determine the ways in which the media participate in the shaping of the popular imagination of China's various social groups, be they disgruntled peasants, unemployed urban workers or rural migrants or, indeed, those urban middle-class or economic elites who possess glamour and political clout. The continued valorization of the transnational capitalist dimensions of both international media and, to some extent, Chinese urban middle-class media is not the consequence of deliberate, consistent and concerted efforts of individual media professionals, nor of conspiratorial schemes hatched between media conglomerates and its political supporters. Rather, it is the result of the dynamic interplay between political economy and the cultural practice of news-making. In other words, concepts such as democracy, democratization, citizenship, civil and human rights become meaningful and intelligible only in an analytical nexus which, on the one hand, considers power and hegemony from the points of view of ownership, finance, market, industry, censorship and the political and economic interests of both producers and consumers, and, on the other hand, also regards news-making, which like any other symbolic systems of representation is part of a general cultural practice conditioned by, and in turn reflective of, specific institutional, cultural and technological imperatives.

My discussion so far indeed points to the curse of the logic of the everyday. On one hand, in privileging the eventful, the heroic and the entertaining, the struggles of the workers and peasants remain largely outside the media spotlight due to their mundane nature and ordinariness. On the other hand, the media's tendency to focus on the eventful and the glamorous is understandable given the routine, predictability and everydayness of news-making. News-making is not only governed by the political agenda and drive for profits, but also by the routine of news production and news values, a set of unwritten rules determining the newsworthiness of events, issues and happenings on a daily basis. Very often, depending on the medium, news stories can afford as much complexity, nuance and depth as the amount of space (as in the case of the newspaper), the number of seconds of sound-bites (as in the case of radio) or the availability of visual images for satellite television. These routines and rules determine, for instance, that news should be timely – sometimes at the expense of depth and insight; sensational – hence events involving action and drama are preferred; and, above all, have the widest cultural resonance with intended audiences. This explains why "good stories" tend to be recycled and new and fresh materials are often written into pre-existing narrative structures. In the media environment of digital reproduction and live satellite transmission, what makes the headlines is often the story which lends itself easily to image and sound-bites, both of which tolerate neither ordinariness nor complexity. Spectacular visuality, dictated by the popular logic of "seeing is believing," has become a paramount determinant in the routine business of news selection. It is for this reason that media critics argue that any attempt at democratization therefore needs to tackle the "authoritarian" nature of cultural technology of visuality, which reflects only narrow, elitist, corporate and state interests (Jhally 2002: 334). It is as much due to these institutional, cultural and technological imperatives as to the desire to avoid making politically unsafe or economically unviable decisions that the media deem it unsuitable to reflect the reality of social injustice, discrimination and the violation of human and civil rights as experienced by rural migrants, the vast number of peasants and the urban laid-off workers on a daily basis. The permanent symbolic potency of the images of the Goddess of Democracy and the young man in front of the tank in the Tiananmen can also be understood with regard to this interplay of institutional, technological and cultural imperatives. Print media, such as newspapers, magazines and books, may continue to provide alternative voices, but the glamour and spectacle of transnational capitalism – including those staged by the state – are, and probably will continue to be, the objects of desire for postmodern media.

Notes

1 I have discussed the staging of media events on Chinese state television elsewhere (see Sun 2002). These media events include the celebration of Hong Kong's

return to mainland China in July 1998, and the commemoration of the 50th anniversary of the founding of the People's Republic of China on 1 October 1999. Since 1997, Central Chinese Television (CCTV) has hosted a number of spectacular media events, including the opening of the Yellow River Xiaolangdi Dam and the completion of the construction of the Three Gorges Dam Project.

2 It is conventional to refer to Chinese films made during the early period of economic reforms (1980s to early 1990s) as fifth-generation films. These films include, for instance, Zhang Yimou's *Red Sorghum* and Chen Kaige's *Yellow Earth*. Films made in the late 1990s and early 2000s are often referred to as "sixth-generation" films. Wang Xiaoshuai's *Beijing Bicycle* and Jia Zhangke's *The World* are two examples.

3 As I have discussed elsewhere (Sun 2004), the concept of compassion, as understood and practiced in the context of a reformed China, consists of three components which incidentally can be summarized into three "guans," namely *guan xin* (be concerned with), *guan zhu* (pay close attention to) and *guan huai* (show loving care for). I suggest that these three types of affect encompass various degrees of emotional involvement and work in tandem in re-shaping the social imagination of the urban residents, consumers and audiences. While showing concern is a conceptual activity, giving loving care may involve action such as sending donations to the victim or writing to the media to express moral support. Furthermore, I suggest that the role of media publicity is crucial in facilitating the public's awareness from one stage to another, and the audience's relationship to compassionate journalism may vary according to the degree of their willingness to empathize with the weak, the helpless or the victim. In other words, without the media showing concern, the attention of the public cannot be drawn to people in need of help; and without the public's knowledge, it is difficult to generate public support and mobilize loving care.

4 This is my translation from the Chinese.

5 It is not clear why the column was banned, but it was certain that "Freezing Point" had "annoyed" the Ministry of Propaganda on a range of matters, including the publication of a Chinese professor's criticism of history textbooks used in Chinese schools, and the publication of a speech by Taiwan's Minister of Culture.

6 The incident received wide media coverage. See, for instance, "An accident that alarms President Jiang Zemin" (*"Jing dong Jiang song shu ji de dian gai zhong du shi jian"*) in *Southern Weekend*, 26 October 2000, p. 16.

7 A critique of the popular and state media's representations of unemployed worker-cum-entrepreneur can be found in Zhao (2002) and Sun (2002a).

8 See Lee (1997) for a detailed discussion of the organization of the female migrant workers in this labor market.

9 Pun Ngai's ethnographic work describing the work and life of some migrant workers in a factory in southern China, for instance, supports this view (see Pun 2000 and 2005). The combination of the "docile body" and "nimble fingers" offered by the rural migrant workers has been discussed in many places, including Cartier (2001), Pun (2000 and 2005) and Lee (1997 and 1998).

10 For detailed investigations of the life of the *dagongmei* on the shop floor of Chinese factories, see Lee (1997) and Pun (2005).

11 See Sun (2004), for a detailed discussion of the representation of the migrant women in both the state and commercial sectors of the Chinese media.

Bibliography

Brooten, L. (2004) "Human rights discourse and the development of democracy in a multi-ethnic state," *Asian Journal of Communication*, 14(2): 174–91.

Social semiotics in post-socialist China   47

Cartier, C. (2001) *Globalizing South China*, Massachusetts: Blackwell.

Chan, A. (2002) "The culture of survival: lives of migrant workers through the prism of private letters," in P. Link, R.P. Madsen and C. Pickowicz (eds) *Popular China: Unofficial culture in a globalising society*, Lanham: Rowman and Littlefield.

Chen, B.-J. (2001) "Tigao tameng de nengjiandu" [Increasing their visibility], *Shuishi Bawang Shuishi Ji* [Who is the Emperor and Who is the Concubine?], Beijing: China Women's Press.

Chen, G. and Chun, T. (2004) *Zhongguo Nongmin Diaocha* [An Investigation of Chinese Peasants], Beijing: Renmin Chubanshe (People's Press).

Dai, J.-H. (2000) "Xu lun" [Preface], in J.-H. Dai (ed.) *Shu xie wenhua yingxiong* [Narratives of Cultural Heroes], Nanjing: Jiangsu Renmin Chubanshe (Jiangsu People's Press).

Dayan, D. and Katz, E. (1992) *Media Events: The live broadcasting of history*, Cambridge: Harvard University Press.

Huang, D.-Y. (2002) "Dagongmei chengshi hua guocheng zhong de jig e fa lu wenti" [Several legal issues confronting migrant women in the urbanization process], in *Huji Zhidu Yu Nuxin Liudong* [Residential Registration System and Female Mobilities], Centre for Research for Cultural Development of Rural Women, Guiyang, Guizhou Remin Chubanshe (Guizhou People's Press).

Huang, M.-G. (2005) "Jingji yinshu haishi wenhua chayi? dui nong dianshi jiemu xique de shenceng sikao" [Is it economics or is it cultural difference? A probe into the reasons behind the lack of rural programs on TV], *Dangdai Chuangmei* [Contemporary Communications Studies], 2: 27–9.

Jhally, S. (2002) "Image-based culture: Advertising and popular culture," in K. Askew and R. Wilk (eds) *The Anthropology of Media*, Massachusetts: Blackwell.

Lee, C.-C. (ed.) (2002) *Money, Power, and Media: Communication patterns and bureaucratic control in cultural China*, Evanston, IL: Northwestern University Press.

Lee, C.-K. (1997) "Factory regimes of Chinese capitalism," in A. Ong and D. Nonini (eds) *Underground Empires: The cultural politics of modern Chinese transnationalism*, London: Routledge.

—— (1998) *Gender and the South China Miracle: Two worlds of factory women*, Berkeley: University of California Press.

Li, X.-J. (1994) "Economic reform and the awakening of Chinese women's collective consciousness," in C.K. Gilmartin and G. Hershatter (eds) *Engendering China*, Cambridge: Harvard University Press.

Lu, Y. (2002) "Huji guangli Zhidu yu wailai dagongmei de quanyi baohu" [Residential registration system and the protection of the legal rights of migrant women], in *Huji Zhidu Yu Nuxin Liudong* [Residential Registration System and Female Mobilities], Centre for Research for Cultural Development of Rural Women, Guiyang: Guizhou Remin Chubanshe (Guizhou People's Press).

Mei, Y-M. (2000) "Ni ming de ying dao zhe: Shi shang za zhi de wen hua yi wei" [The anonymous trend-setter: the cultural significance of *Vogue* magazine], in J.-H. Dai (ed.) *Shu xie wenhua yingxiong* [Narratives of Cultural Heroes], Nanjing: Jiangsu Renmin Chubanshe (Jiangsu People's Press).

Pickowicz, P.G. and Wang, L. (2002) "Village voice, urban activists: women, violence, xand gender inequality in rural China", in P. Link, R.P. Madsen and P.G. Pickowicz (eds) *Popular China: Unofficial culture in a globalizing society*, Lanham: Rowman and Littlefield.

48 *Wanning Sun*

Pun, N. (2000) "Becoming *dagongmei* (working girls): The politics of identity and difference in reform China," *The China Journal*, 40: 1–18.

—— (2005) *Made in China: Women factory workers in a global workplace*, Durham, Duke University Press.

Sun, W. (2002) *Leaving China: Media, migration and transnational imagination*. Lanham: Rowman and Littlefield.

—— (2002a) "The invisible entrepreneur: the case of Anhui women," *Provincial China*, 7(2): 178–95.

—— (2004) "Indoctrination, fetishization, and compassion: media constructions of the migrant women," in A. Gaetano and T. Jacka (eds) *On the Move: Women in rural-to-urban migration in contemporary China*, New York: Columbia University Press.

Wang, X.-M. (2000) "Bai zhang lian de sheng hua" [The myth of a half-hidden face], in X.-M. Wang (ed.) *Zai Xin Yishi Xintai de Long Zhao Xia* [Under the Hegemony of a New Ideology], Nanjing: Jiangsu Renmin Chubanshe (Jiangsu People's Press).

Yan, H. (2003) "Spectralization of the rural: reinterpreting the labor mobility of rural young women in post-Mao China," *American Ethnologist*, 30(4): 576–95.

Yang, X.-D. (2005) "Meijie chuanbo he nongmingong liyi biaoda" [Mass communications and the representation of migrant workers' interests], *Dangdai Chuanmei* [Contemporary Communication], 6: 77–9.

Yu, H.-M. (1999) "Zhebi yu kejian: xinwen he wenxue zhong de xiagang nugong xinxiang fenxi," paper presented to Popular Culture of China Workshop, Beijing.

Zhao, Y.-Z. (2000) "From commercialisation to conglomeration: the transformation of the Chinese press within the orbit of the Party state," *Journal of Communication*, Spring: 3–24.

—— (2001) "Herbert Schiller, the US media and democracy in China," *Television and New Media*, 2(1): 51–5.

—— (2001a) "Media and elusive democracy in China," *Javnost/The Public: Journal of the European Institute for Communication and Culture*, 8(2): 21–44.

—— (2001b) "Dances with wolves? China's integration into digital Capitalism," *Info*, 3(2): 137–51.

—— (2002) "The rich, the laid-off, the criminal in tabloid tales: read all about it!" in P. Link, R.P. Madsen and C. Pickowicz (eds) *Popular China: Unofficial culture in a globalising society*, Lanham: Rowman and Littlefield.

—— (2004) "Between a world summit and a Chinese movie: visions of the 'information society,'" *Gazette: The International Journal for Communication Studies*, 66(3–4): 275–80.

Zhao, Z.-G. and Li, W. (2004) "Guanyu dangxia zhongguo jilupian zhong nongmin huayuquan de lixin sikao" [A rational consideration of the peasant's voice in the realm of Chinese documentaries], *Xinwen Daxue* [Journalism University], Autumn: 79–81.

Zhou, C.-L. (2000) "Shishang zazhi yu dazhong wenhua" [*Vogue* magazine and popular culture], in X. Wang (ed.) *Zai Xin Yishi Xintai de Long zhao xia* [In the Hegemony of a New Ideology], Nanjing: Jiangsu Renmin Chubanshe (Jiangsu People's Press).

4 The emergence of polyphony in Chinese television documentaries

Yingchi Chu

Introduction

There is no doubt that in spite of a rapidly expanding market economy in China today, large portions of the population, especially among the peasantry, migrant workers, "working sisters" (*dagong mei*), laid-off workers and other disadvantaged groups, have been unable to significantly raise their living standards and participate meaningfully in decision-making (see Chapter 3 by Wanning Sun in this volume). Nor should it be surprising that the Chinese mass media, especially television, have not been able to do much to bring about radical changes in this respect. However, what is not supported by evidence available about the current state of the media in China is that the "authoritarian" and its cultural "technology of visuality" expresses "*only* narrow, elitist, corporate, and state interests" and so contributes to rather than alleviates the suffering of the underprivileged (Jhally 2002: 334). [1] The current situation of the visual media in relation to social and political relations in China appears to be rather more complex in that television programming, production, ratings and policies are at present undergoing significant transformations that are beginning to impact upon viewing audiences in the millions. In this chapter, I argue that documentary films and programs in particular are a good indicator of such changes taking place in China's vast television arena.

The transformations which we are able to observe in Chinese documentary films are not merely changes in style, but generic shifts that reveal substantial modifications in the attitude of the Chinese government towards the media under market pressure, as well as in the face of radical changes in viewing expectations amongst China's mass media audiences. These changes, the chapter argues, are indicators of a society in a gradual process towards "democratization" and regime modification, a process in which the media are playing an increasingly significant role. Having said this, however, it is important to emphasize that innovation, as participatory and polyphonic modes of presentation, in documentary film cannot in themselves guarantee a sustained tendency towards democratization. They are necessary but not sufficient conditions for democracy. Other factors

50 *Yingchi Chu*

must come into play to achieve such a fundamental shift. And even within the constraints of documentary genres, the change from single voice to polyphonic styles, for example, does not in itself necessarily indicate "liberalization." I try here to identify what Bill Nichols has termed the documentary "voice": a "text's social point of view" (Nichols 2005: 18).

Media environment

Since the introduction of the market economy in the 1980s, the Chinese media have been regarded as playing a dual role: to serve the Party and to serve the market, even if the Party has remained the undisputed priority.[2] In recent years, however, and especially after 1993, we have arguably seen a loosening of this equation towards favoring the demands of the market. The most obvious features here are the transition from sender-centered media to audience-centered media, and the change from the conception of TV as serving the major function of "educational tool" to one of a multi-functional "information and entertainment provider" (Yu 2003: 6), from a local and national outlook to a global perspective, and one that aims towards competition with international mainstream media systems.

These changes are still primarily a top-down process, although there has been a shift in the government's view of the media. From being "political textbook" producers, the media have become a multiple role player, including the provision of information, and entertainment and news. After the student democracy movement in 1989, the government faced the triple problem of *meng* (boredom), *qi* (anger) and *huo* (puzzlement) in the media market.[3] As a response, the Ministry of Propaganda proposed *zhuada fangxiao* (controlling the large media institutions while relaxing control over the small stations) and *zhuazhong fangbian* (controlling the centre, while loosening the margin). A consequence of this policy is that small and medium-sized institutions on the periphery enjoyed more freedom than the mainstream media organizations in the capital cities. To meet the challenge of "public boredom" (*meng*), the government allowed the state media to enter the domain of commercial entertainment programming, such as soaps and comedies, and also partly lifted the embargo on media products from Hong Kong and Taiwan. To alleviate pent-up public anger, the government began to permit elites to explore alternative and critical views in the popular, even if politically marginal, press, such as evening and weekend newspapers. The government also encouraged Central China Television (CCTV)[4] to develop investigative programs such as *Focal Point* (*Jiaodian Fangtan*) and *News Probe* (*Xinwen Diaocha*) exposing corruption and injustice at local and marginal levels, as well as exploring a range of social concerns in order to reduce the anger of the masses (*qi*). The third stage in the government response, dealing effectively with public *huo* or puzzlement, is still evolving, with policies encouraging the provision of more and more diverse information. In this respect, a massive investment in current affairs programs, programs about the West, and programs on commerce, science and legal matters can be observed as relevant.

The change of attitude has also shown itself in the government's policies towards establishing commercially viable media groups able to compete with media entering China from the West, from Hong Kong as well as from Taiwan, after China's successful membership application to the World Trade Organization. Since 1997, media institutions have been gradually grouped together to establish new and large media conglomerates combining print, publishing, TV, film and radio in one institution. The significance of this move lies in the decision by the Chinese government to commit itself to treating the media as business enterprises rather than solely as institutions serving the ideological superstructure of the state. In 1998, Premier Zhu Rongji's description of CCTV as *qunzhong houshe* or "media as the *voice of the masses*" signaled a sharp deviation from the Party's principle of the "media as the voice of the Party." That this kind of shift has not occurred without tension within the government is well illustrated by the then Minister of Propaganda Ding Guan'gen's immediate qualification that nevertheless "first, the media should be the voice of the Party."

The years 2002 to 2003 saw at least two important reform attempts in Chinese broadcasting: the separation of broadcasting from production, and the operation of channels according to principles of profitability. As a result, a large number of semi-dependent and independent production companies have evolved. Eight channels of sports, transportation, film, arts, music, lifestyle, finance and science and technology are now in the process of establishing commercially viable systems and management. Also in late 2002, the Minister of Propaganda Li Changchun announced a principle of "*san tiejin*" (three proximities): that the media should be proximate with reality (focusing on real social issues); there should be proximity to the masses (with information and programs relevant to the population at large); and proximity to life (with topics concerning everyday life instead of grand political ideologies). This is a significant revision of the long-standing doctrine that the media is the mouthpiece of Party and government (Zhang 2003).

In 2004, more reforms took place in television. The government requested television stations to change from state-owned *shiye* (institutes) to state-owned *qiye* (enterprises), indicating that earning profits was no less important than political control. Although the government continued to control news, censorship and broadcasting rights, and key appointments, increasing numbers of television programs were increasingly produced by commercial production companies outside the state-owned stations. While retaining its censorship and broadcasting rights, China Education Television (CETV) contracted a private company for its Channel One program and advertising productions, programming as well as publicity (Lu 2005: 232). In the same year, Sichuan Broadcasting Television Group publicly recruited four deputy presidents for the Sichuan television station. All these changes suggest that

52   *Yingchi Chu*

Chinese television is moving towards accommodating popularity, and shifting the judgment of what acceptable media programming is to the consumer (Yu 2003: 19).

Market forces

As competition in the media industry increases, economic factors/forces become more important to the organization of media institutions. Competition between television stations in China has become stronger since 1993, when the first provincial television station acquired a satellite link. At present all thirty-one provincial stations have access to satellites, which means 1.115 billion viewers, 95.5 percent of the population, can now receive forty-six channels from satellites plus channels from local television stations (Yuan 2005: 261). At the same time, Hong Kong television channels – including Phoenix, Rupert Murdoch's commercial station based in Hong Kong – are broadcast into South China and other selected areas. Furthermore, cable television is on the increase, with sports programs, news and drama channels. In 2004, thirty-one channels outside China gained permission to broadcast into China. Adding to this media revolution is the rapid rise of the popularity of the internet (Chinese sources including the suffixes: cn, com, net and org list 668,900 websites), as well as a substantial increase in the availability of print media, with a total of about 2,119 newspapers and 9,074 magazines being offered in China today (Cui 2005: 31).

Advertising has become a major source of income for the broadcasting media. CCTV's advertising income increased from 44.45 million RMB in 1998 to 70 billion in 2002 (Zhongyang dianshi tai 2003: 27). That market success has become the number one criterion can be seen as official CCTV policy of "one centre, two basic points": one, meeting the demands of market; the other, responding to requests made by clients (Zhongyang dianshi tai 2003: 302). At the same time, this has permitted the government to reduce its funding to less than 10 percent of the CCTV budget, a percentage that guarantees the continuation of official policy of appointing key personnel.

This sharp increase of income from advertising is visible in the recent modification of the CCTV slogan to "TV media is the voice of the Party and government, *but also the voice of the people*" (Zhongyang dianshi tai 2003: 41). It has now become the declared aim of television stations to compete with international media outlets such as CNN (Zhongyang dianshi tai 2003: 82). In terms of programs, more and more CCTV offerings are designed as "service" to the consumers. As a result there are more programs about lifestyle and daily events, and more dialogue programs incorporating experts, concerned social groups and ordinary citizens, instead of "speeches of leaders" fare. Increasingly, ordinary people (*putong ren*), or those who are not policy-makers and have no financial power to influence policy-making – which includes parents, retirees, maids, migrant workers, experts, entrepreneurs, teachers, urban citizens, rural peasants, soldiers, public servants, cadres, university students, unemployed, policemen, beauty queens, the sick and academics – appear as program guests on CCTV, provincial satellite televisions as well as local stations, regularly raising their own concerns about daily life and social issues. Service programs such as *Life, At Your Service, Health, Business, Chinese Medicine* or *Daily Food*, provide information about housing, employment, education, cars, medicine, the stock market, food and shopping. The Party is of course not entirely forgotten. In 2005, the official media doctrine was to remain in touch with the masses while not losing sight of Party principles. Nevertheless, the dominant media profile today is no longer determined by overt monolithic government control; instead, the profile now foregrounds the four main functions of media: offering programs of news and current affairs, providing mass education, conveying information, and supplying entertainment.

Audience participation and feedback

More and more frequently, the ordinary people (*putong ren*), that is, the mass of common people without political or financial clout, have begun to appear on television as themes and subjects, as well as active participants in the exchange of information and opinions. At the same time, more programs are being produced according to ratings, with audience feedback becoming an indispensable measure of successful programming. The assumption that Chinese television audiences are largely made up of an urban middle class who have the power to consume, leaving the rural masses in televisual darkness, is no longer supportable by statistical evidence. For example, CCTV typically registers 900 million viewers at a time for its *Legal Report* program. Similar figures apply to educational programs broadcast by CETV. If the rural masses, which make up about 70 percent of the total population, were to be excluded, how would the figure of 1.115 billion television viewers be made up? During my 2005 field research among Chinese minorities, I noted that the houses in Dai villages in Yunnan and the Khazak huts in Xinjiang, though poorly furnished, all proudly displayed their television sets.

Talk shows and documentaries outside the sphere of government interference have become a dominant feature of what is being offered on television in China today. As Yang, who is in charge of the national research project for establishing a television theory with Chinese characteristics, observes:

> the mass of people have a right to be a part of the communication process by freely expressing their opinions. The mass media should be a forum for them to participate in, while at the same time, the government should protect the audience's right to do so.
>
> (Yang 1998: 175)

54　*Yingchi Chu*

"Participation" here means that the audiences play a significant role in the televised communication process by being invited to studios, being interviewed and filmed and having their feedback recorded for public consumption. Even if programs such as the *Legal Report, Focal Points, News Probe* and *Oriental Horizon* (*Dongfang shikong*) function as means of justification for government policies, these series tend to be increasingly shaped and justified by audience requests. Almost all television stations have now included audience feedback departments to answer audience mails, emails and phone-ins.

While participatory audiences signify part of the market face of Chinese television, it does not mean that a *critical* public sphere has developed. Primarily at this stage, audience participation and feedback guarantee the success and survival of television stations in the new market economy. That "audience participation in TV" in itself is "an indicator for democracy," as Yang argues, is open to challenge (Yang 1998: 379). Other factors need to be taken into consideration.

Global media pressure

Changes in the Chinese media have not occurred in isolation. No doubt, China's membership of the WTO is the biggest challenge to the domestic media. Never before has China paid so much attention to media developments in Britain, France, Germany, Italy, USA, Japan, South Korea and India, in search of a media profile able to match the international media system and suitable to the Chinese combination of state control and commercial needs. Chinese television management has evolved with an eye on, and under the pressure of, developments elsewhere. This is patently obvious when we look at the establishment of CCTV's English-language channel 9 in 2000, as well as the radical restructuring of the management of CCTV. The advantages of US-style management, for example, were not lost on the Chinese government when their media advisers recommended: (1) "increased awareness of channels"; (2) "ease of dealing with international TV stations"; (3) "congeniality to democratic decision making"; (4) "efficiency"; (5) "good use of resources"; (6) "focused programs" (Zhongyang dianshi tai 2003: 61–2). This pragmatism is also reflected in the strategies embraced by CCTV as it began to: regard content quality as an important principle; to look at the media in terms of market exploration; and, to facilitate entry into the global media market. As scholars have proposed for some time, "in the socialist market economy, Chinese television should adopt a model of co-existence of commercial and public television. By fostering the development of commercial television, Chinese television could become truly strong and so occupy a place in the world" (Wu 2004: 69).

Documentary cinema in China

In this increasingly diversified institutional context, documentary film texts provide a useful case-study for exploring the notion of an emerging polyphonic medium. Given traditional aesthetics with its emphasis on moral messages (*wen yi zai dao*) and the creation of imaginary worlds (*yijing*), documentary film is not an easily accommodated genre within a Chinese cultural context. *Wen yi zai dao* (the function of literature is to convey the Dao, which mainly refers to Confucian philosophical and moral principles) requires morality as a story ingredient, which is difficult to achieve in the documentary mode without fictionalization. *Yijing* emphasizes the invention of an imaginary world and meanings that are generated and communicated through that world which, again, contradicts the realist style of the documentary genre. Nonetheless, the influence of media policy in the Soviet Union – especially Lenin's view that film is the most powerful tool for mass education and that documentary film is a forceful form of visualized political argument – gave Chinese Communist filmmakers theoretical ground to replace *dao* (morality) with political ideology. Thus, documentary film became hugely important in China.

Since the inception of the People's Republic in 1949, documentary in China has been understood as a genre somewhere between news (*xinwen*) and a longer version of news, later called *zhuanti pian* (television series on special topics). These films are designed to embrace national achievements, political unity and the celebration of particular historical moments, as well as Communist and other national heroes. Under the Socialist planned economy which terminated private ownership and private production in 1952, Chinese films were produced by the state-owned film studios. These studios strictly implemented the rules given to them by the Central Film Bureau, which in turn was directly responsible to the Central Propaganda Department. In addition, the limitation of camera and sound technologies, as well as the closed-door policy being applied to films from outside China, resulted in documentary films driven by "voice-of-God" narration, essay style and lyrical script. These films were also characterized by intense attention to the composition of images, perfectly framed, meticulous description of details with close-ups, studio lighting, fragmented images that illustrate words, and the separation of sound from images. There were few or no interviews, nor was there location sound. There was ample use of music to foreground themes, while the cinematic events were heavily controlled by the filmmaker.

It was only in the early 1990s that Chinese filmmakers and critics were in a position to re-define and theorize the documentary film genre from a cinematic perspective. There are several reasons for this shift: the rejection by the domestic market of the propaganda content of the political documentary; the sharp increase in communication with the West, and with it acquaintance with a broad range of documentary cinematic options; a desire to produce Chinese documentary films for the Western markets; an explosion of scholarly, critical reassessments of the Chinese cinematic tradition; and the weakening of the long-standing association of documentary film and political leadership. In turn, the redefinition of documentary film had an indirect influence on documentary film production in China. The main landmark in this evolution was the 1993 transfer of the Central News Documentary Film Studio, established in 1952, to the CCTV, which made documentary film a part of television.

Notwithstanding such governmental intervention, documentary film-making has acquired its own momentum since the 1990s, encouraging the right to some public expression of opinions and the display of individual perceptions of society. These filmmakers work inside and outside the state-controlled formal sector. Outside the formal sector, inexpensive film technology enabled many youths to record things happening around them and within their environment. Not surprisingly, their films would be different from the government's grand cinematic narration of Chinese history and society. In the early 1990s, documentary filmmakers like Wu Wenguan, Duan Jinchuan, Jian Yue and Yang Linan made films about the daily, trivial and "insignificant" lives of marginal social groups, unemployed artists, monks, the neighborhood, pensioners and old people. Some of these films have drawn the attention of Western critics and audiences.

Within the formal sector, Shanghai television pioneered the first television program devoted to documentaries in 1993. The program became one of the most popular television programs, drawing about 36 percent of Shanghai viewers at its climax. *Mao Mao gaozhuang* (*Mao Mao Goes to Court*) documents a single mother and migrant "working sister" taking a disabled man, who she claims is the father of her child, to court. As the father of her child, the man, Mao Mao believes, should share the duty and the cost of supporting the child. However, the man denies that he is the father and therefore has no duties whatever. The documentary television program shows a large proportion of marginal groups in Shanghai, including the laid-off workers, the migrants, the maids, the sick, the divorced, the poor and rickshaw workers. The program also addresses common problems of the middle class, including issues relating to children's education and martial problems. In the same year, CCTV also established a documentary program, under the advertising slogan "telling stories of common people," which showed the lives of ordinary people. It is evident that for a nation fed on a state-sanctioned television diet of Communist heroes, heroic workers, patriotic peasants and soldiers over four decades, stories of the common people are not only a refreshing change but are also easier for audiences to identify with.

In this respect, Lü Xinyu has made a significant observation. In spite of indisputable Western influences, both industrial and cinematographic, Chinese documentary filmmakers and theorists postulate a generic format somewhat different from the conventions that have evolved in traditions outside China. As Lü notes:

> We should not understand the term *jilu pian* (documentary film) in the context of the West. In the West, the development of documentary film has various schools and streams, which are generated from the different

historical contexts of different societies. In China, the term documentary film gained its significance in the 1980s and 90s from the understanding of the term as resistance to the term *zhuanti pian,* "Special Topics."

(Lü 2003: 13)

No longer can documentary film be equated with *zhuanti pian* – a genre of special topics largely in expository mode. This is so because *zhuanti pian* were made within a specific historical context in which news documentary films were regarded as the visualization of political theory. Nor is the documentary film any longer a news film, or even a television art film. Documentary is now firmly defined as a genre with real people and real events at its centre, in realist style (utilizing interviews, observational mode, participatory and performative modes). More importantly, Lenin's law of documentary as the visualization of political theory no longer holds. As such, documentaries could not continue to serve exclusively as vehicles of government doctrine. As Ren states:

> Documentary is non-fiction film or a video product which reports and records accordingly on political, economic, cultural, military and historical events. Documentary film directly represents real people and real events, made-up fictional events are not permissible. The main narrative reporting includes interview and location shooting. This means the use of selection, waiting for and catching the right moment for recording real people, real events, in real environments and real time. This for "real" is the life of documentary.

(Ren 1997: 3)

In contrast with Communist heroes and idealized workers, peasants and soldiers, "real people" here means above all "ordinary people," especially people at the margins of society, presented by way of cinematic "individualization." According to Lü, "this is the most important contribution by contemporary Chinese documentary filmmakers. Their documentary film movement is about poor people in the city, country migrants, the disabled, cancer sufferers, orphans, ethnic minorities, and stories in poor areas" (Lü 2003: 691). Given the focus on this kind of subject matter and the realist techniques developed to do it justice, it should perhaps not be surprising to find that some Chinese observers of documentary film have taken the important step to claim publicly that "the emphasis on objectivity and truth in documentary filmmaking inevitably links with the idea of democracy, an open society and the freedom of speech" (Situ 2001: 186).

"Democratic" seeds in documentary film

"The reason why our films appeared untrue," suggests Liu "is mostly not because what we filmed is not real, but because *we filmed the real into the unreal*! Or because the real thing becomes unreal after being filmed" (Liu 2001: 814). This observation is arguably the result of several factors, including: the absence of words uttered by the documented subjects; the absence of interviews and location sound; and, the dominance of perfectly framed images with studio lighting, foregrounded by theme music and the authoritarian mode of the "voice-of-God" narration serving ideological dogma. That documentary film should be free of overt ideological messages and political doctrine is, however, only one way of realizing the genre's democratic potential. There are other avenues, such as the new focus on the presentation of actual social reality, the break with traditional aesthetics, and the reduction of editorial manipulation. As Andrew Basin once observed, editing is the enemy of the "perception of democracy." But perhaps the most promising avenue to bring out the democratic potential in documentary film genre is the introduction of participatory strategies, and in particular increased audience participation. This can take many forms, but as Ren (1997: 246) notes, "directing by the audience itself is the highest level of participation."

Political dogma tends to be a monological discourse, a one-way communication hostile to the democratic process. In all its forms, democracy is heavily dependent on the interplay of many and opposing voices – in short, polyphonic negotiation. According to Bakhtin (1973: 51), polyphony is a dialogic interplay of multiple voices replacing authoritarian monologism by allowing different and oppositional voices to compete with one another. In Dostoevsky's works, he argues, we are dealing with a "fully realized dialogical position which confirms the hero's independence, inner freedom, unfinalizedness and indeterminacy" (Bakhtin 1973: 51). Arguably, what holds true in the linguistic-semiotic mode of fictional narrative can be said to apply in principle to media discourse.

Although the history of documentary film in China suggests an ongoing evolution of a genre from monological towards polyphonic modes of presentation, from authoritarian to participatory cinematic conventions, not all monological films are of necessity "authoritarian," just as not all participatory documentaries could be called "democratic." Other factors have to be considered. Authoritarian styles have not quite disappeared after the introduction of interviews into documentary film in works such as *He Shang* in 1986. Authoritarian styles have been associated with governmental propaganda, no matter whether what is presented can be said to be "real" or not. Authoritarian modes are generated not only by a dogmatic "voice-of-God" narration, ideological editing and fragmented images, but also when a film, in spite of its artistic use of a range of cinematic strategies, largely reflects the single voice of the Party (Nichols 2005: 18–19).

During the Mao period, documentaries were produced according to a carefully manufactured and monitored *dogmatic mode*, a top-down orchestrated, monological presentational process. While this mode has not survived in its dogmatic purity under the pressure of more polyphonic styles, remnants of monological filmmaking can be recognized even today in a range of documentaries. For instance, *Dahuo lintou* (*Fire Incident*, 2002) is the story of how the Shenyang fire brigade battles a conflagration at an oil refinery in Shenyang. This award-winning documentary film contains interviews with the fire brigade conducted by supervisors, members of the fire fighter unit and nearby residents, describing what happened. The interviews convey one single message: that fire fighters are brave and are prepared to die in the course of their duty. Narration and interviews dominate, with images of long takes, location sound to show the uncontrollable conflagration, the fire fighters fighting against the flames and smoke, and the danger the neighboring buildings face. And yet such important information as the likely cause of the disaster remains concealed. Pressing questions are avoided: Who was or should be responsible? Have there been adequate precautions? Were the decisions made to control the fire appropriate? Could the death of the fireman been avoided? Instead, the film ends with several fire fighters receiving awards from the government: the formula of documentary heroism.

A similar example is the documentary film *Fuqin shi ben du bu wan de shu* (*My Father*, 2002) produced by Nanjing Television in the same year. The film is narrated in standard Mandarin. It features the son and daughter of the central character, the father. The film is the eulogy of a fifty-year-old man, a father, who died in an attempt to save public property in an accident. The title suggests that the story is presented from his children's point of view, and yet we do not hear a word spoken by the children, in spite the fact that some of the interviews with their father's colleagues, neighbors and friends are conducted by the son. His son and daughter are portrayed solely as the storytellers. Again, we are presented with some ingredients of advanced documentary cinematography, fragmented images, theme songs, carefully designed image frames, all dominated by the monologic voice of narration uniting everything into one single view of what the government thinks about the man: his self-reliance in supporting his in-laws, his wife and children after accepting government redundancy payout as a laid-off worker; his endurance without complaint; and his ultimate sacrifice to save government property from destruction. We look in vain for an alternative viewpoint. Was he really such an exceptional man? What made him so supportive of the government, and so ready to sacrifice his life? Do his children share the official view? Does his wife likewise concur with the government's decision to celebrate her husband as a hero? Here we miss the nuanced picture of diverse voices. What we get instead is, as Liu (2001: 814) succinctly puts it, a documentation that makes the real "unreal."

What we are looking for, then, is a combination of cinematographic features that produce a polyphonic assemblage of voices, in the broad sense, including the nonverbal aspects of film. Nor should we be satisfied with a merely quantitative measure of such an assemblage. The number of participants, the amount of feedback, the number of interviews, or the mere quantity of data of perceptual actuality, do not by themselves guarantee the

60 *Yingchi Chu*

exploration of the "democratic" potential of documentary filmmaking. What seems to be essential here, in the Bakhtinian sense of polyphony, is that the "many-voiced" film offers a rich diversity of *opposing* positions which the viewer must negotiate in order to constitute a socially realistic picture. In the next section of the chapter, I select a small number of examples from a very rich spectrum of documentary films to illustrate this claim. The majority of the following documentaries have received awards from either the China TV Documentary Academic Association or some independent documentary festivals, including Japan's Yamagata International Documentary Film Festival. The films are well known in the circles of documentary filmmakers and scholars. None of these films are produced and consumed in the so-called "underground."

Film analyses: from dogmatic to polyphonic documentation

Lao jingzi (*Old Mirror*, 2002), a Jiangxi television production, records how a local writer and a theatre company go about producing a dance drama in a remote village. The drama is based on the discovery by the writer of a ninety-year-old woman who has been waiting for her Communist husband's return for seventy years. Ten days after their wedding, her eighteen-year-old husband confesses that he is a Communist and will have to leave her to join the Red Army. He gives her a mirror as a present, and tells her that it might take him five, ten, twenty, even forty years to return, but return he will as soon as the Revolution is completed. He also asks her to learn to write while he is away. Waiting, his wife writes her diary and uses her mirror for seventy years, combing her hair, in the firm belief that her husband will return. People have told her that her husband has probably died, and suggest to her that she remarries and has children. However, she refuses all proposals, keeping her promise.

As her story unfolds in interviews, during visits to her modest hut and the filming of her impoverished existence, the director concomitantly shows the many difficulties to be overcome in transforming her story into a dance drama. The documentary highlights the current generation's critical evaluation of the old woman's life and their contrasting values. The film employs minimum narration with ample use of location sound, interviews, natural lighting and unobtrusive, chronological editing. The story could be read on the one hand as official praise for the old woman from Jiangxi, the birthplace of the Communist Red Army, who believes in her husband's return as firmly as the peasants believe in Communism. Yet on the other hand, the discussions and conflicts within the theatre group pose the question of the "morality" of a husband who makes unrealistic promises and raise the question of whether it is wise for a woman to spend her life waiting in vain. This realist ideology is productively juxtaposed to the central character's romantic selfless sacrifice. The film's structure rests on a parallel between two sets of voices: the voices of the Communists and those prepared to sacrifice their lives to ideology, as against the voices of everyday life and those of ideological agnosticism.

Chongfeng de rizi (*The Day We Meet Again*, 1998) from Shanghai Television portrays a couple who meet again after many years of separation. A Nationalist soldier who followed the Nationalist Army to Taiwan in 1948, one year after he had married, leaving behind his young wife and their son, now returns to Shanghai to see her again after forty years. In the meantime she has remarried, with children by her second husband. The reunion brings good memories as well as sadness. They decide to travel together to Taiwan to make up for the years they have missed. When they announce their intention, the woman faces pressure from her grown-up children who want their mother to stay, for her presence qualifies them to be entitled to a larger flat.

Following the events from the day the pair meet at the airport to the day they contemplate their dilemma, the director uses interviews, location sound and chronological cutting, with a minimum of narration. The film ends with the Taiwanese man deciding to stay in Shanghai to find a satisfactory solution. In contrast to the strong authorial guidance of earlier documentaries, the open-endedness of this documentary invites a range of interpretive positions as well as public debate. Should this Nationalist Taiwan soldier come to Shanghai to disturb the married woman's family? Is it his right to search for his wife since the marriage has never been formally dissolved? The earlier dogmatic mode of presentation and restriction of individuals to formulaic characters of heroism are replaced by an assemblage of many voices. Not only do we hear from the two husbands, the wife and the children, we also hear from the society in general with the expression of certain political and social views. Each of these voices functions to add personal views which, as a whole, produce a realistic picture of social interaction and leave interpretive space for individual viewers. If there is any message, it seems to be the selfishness of the new society and nostalgia for the care with which the older generation considers the needs of their family, as well as problems for reunification between Taiwan and the Mainland. Significantly, this documentary exclusively focuses on personal and domestic relations. In doing so, it silences the usually forceful role of the government.

Kaoshi (*Exams*, 1999), made by CCTV, follows the lives of four ten- to fourteen-year-old girls as they prepare for the entrance exam at the Central Music Academy in Beijing. Their parents move with them to Beijing, renting small houses close to the Academy in order to secure private tuition in preparation for their entrance examinations. The girls' mothers have quit their jobs to look after them and supervise their practices when their private teachers have left. The children are shown to face enormous pressure: if they fail, none of them will be able to pay back what their parents have given them, nor will they be able to face their schools, relatives and friends.

The film records the girls' daily routines, their music practices from early morning to late at night, according to a tight schedule. We witness their stress before the exam, the examination process, the exam itself and, after the exam, the girls' reactions to their results. Only one out of the four passes the first test, but none of them pass the second examination. One of the girls is applying for a visa to go to the United States for another test, while the other three, bowing to their ambitious parents, continue to practice so that one day they will realize their hope of entering the Music Academy.

The documentary is dominated by an interactive style, with an emphasis on interviews, observation of the subjects' activities, the use of natural lighting, a hand-held camera and location sound, with continuing chronological editing. Disturbing as this film may be as a depiction of parental ambitions regardless of their children's own wishes and abilities, its message is entirely generated by the events portrayed. The results of the examinations are unpredictable, allowing for a trajectory of events rather than fulfilling some pre-scripted message. The pressure on and disappointment of the children, and a childhood without innocence, raise questions about the traditional Chinese social expectation of children's performance, the current education system and methodology, as well as the rights of children, a new concept for China.

Hailu 18 li (*Low Tide*, 2002), a product of Shandong Television, has no narration, no interviews. It records the first eight hours of work of a fishing village, starting at dawn. Every day at low tide, the village people would walk eighteen miles out towards the ocean. They carry their nets and digging tools, pushing their bicycles to muddy spots rich in clams. The film records the work teams as they dig, collect nets packed with clams, and return to shore as the ocean tide rises. Back on shore we see the villagers sort and wash the clams at the market.

The cinematography is masterfully executed, with long shots, medium shots and close-ups, the juxtaposition of one shot over another, the location sound of digging, walking, talking, and sounds of ocean waves. Between shots we are provided with inter-titles separating the different stages of work, with the camera focusing on crowds of workers rather than on individuals. The film seems to say no more than "Look at that!" offering minimal authorial guidance and thus leaving the construction of cinematic meaning largely to the viewer.

Screened on the CCTV's *News Probe* program, *Haixuan* (*Election*, 1998) covers one week of a village election in Liaoning. A journalist visits the village as the inhabitants are told that an election will soon be held. She records the announcement at a meeting, with the reaction of the villagers, and interviews the candidates, people with leading roles in the village, as well as some peasants. She asks if the candidates are confident of winning and if so, why. The story unfolds smoothly until a new candidate comes forward. He is old, has no political and administrative background, nor any experience of leadership. His only claim to suitability is that he wants to contribute to his village, and firmly believes that he will do as good a job as the others. The new candidate promotes his own campaign by visiting the

Polyphony in Chinese TV documentaries 63

homes of peasants, asking them to support him. To the surprise of many, he makes it into the final round, a contest between him and the village Party Secretary. This is a suspenseful situation, for if the Party Secretary should lose, it is not only he who loses face but also the government. The implication would be that the Party had appointed the wrong person for many years. The film records how the two competitors prepare their election speeches, their feelings and attitudes to winning or losing, their answers to questions raised by voters. The Party Secretary gives a grand and well-prepared speech, while his opponent offers no more than a few brief statements, with hardly any policy but the assurance that he will give his very best. The film records the tension that is building between the two candidates as they wait for the final count.

The whole election process from the announcement of the election, the process of multi-stage voting, to the final vote, is largely recorded with location sound, the journalist's explanations, a hand-held camera, natural lighting, interviews, "vox-pop" style and reporting by the journalist-in-residence. In the end, the Party Secretary wins by the narrowest of margins. The film concludes with interviews gauging various reactions to the election result. Non-cinematic, democratic features include the minimally scripted format, the manner in which village life is permitted to emerge in the course of events, the way the villagers are able to voice their opinions, the openness of the election event and its unpredictable outcome, the openly voiced criticism of government policies, and the people-oriented decision-making process revealed during the election. The competing voices in this film – those who think the election was fair versus those who feel that the outcome was to be expected, and those who are cynical about the entire process – produce an impression of a multi-perspectival picture of an election in a rural area.

Lulu he wo (*Lulu and Me*, 2002) from Shanghai Television portrays a middle-aged man in Shanghai who has been given a meager redundancy pay-out by his work place. As a laid-off worker, he manages to make a living and support his family initially by repairing broken light fittings and lamps. His initiative is praised by the government and the Shanghai TV station celebrates his success in a brief documentary film. When the station revisits him several years later, they find him unemployed, divorced and closely attached to his dog Lulu. Employing interviews and an observational style, the film records his daily life, the way he unsuccessfully negotiates relations with several girlfriends, his inability to relate to his son, and the generous, even if sometimes rough, attention he grants his dog.

Lulu and Me could be said to explore the "democratic" potential of documentary film in that it presents a fairly unpleasant person whose loneliness and unattractive lifestyle is at least partly caused by the social system. Once celebrated as a hero in the new market economy, he is now abandoned to an increasingly undignified existence. The critique of the protagonist's own flawed personality and the critique of the state are inextricably intertwined

64   *Yingchi Chu*

to form an uneasy portrayal of a not-so-admirable social system. This is strengthened by the observational style of portrayal, the absence of any overt ideological doctrine, and the uninhibited performance of the central character.

Tielu yanxian (*Along the Railway*, 2000) exemplifies the "democratic" potential of documentary filmmaking in terms of production, ownership, method, stylistic strategies and ways of approaching the subject, including the absence of a pre-shooting script. Shot with a high-8 video camera, this award-winning film from China's first Independent Film Awards is shot by an independent filmmaker, a film student from the Beijing Film Academy. He made this film while on vacation at home in China, filming his subjects after he became one of their friends.

The film documents a group of people aged between nine and twenty who live on rubbish tips along the railway of Baoxi in Shaanxi province. These people are homeless either by circumstances or by choice. Some have escaped from home or lack the money to return home, or they have been driven out by their families or have no idea where their homes are. Most of them have left their villages, counties, towns or cities for a job and some are children who have run away from their parents. The filmed subjects are known by the names of the provinces they come from: Xinjiang, Henan, Sichuan or Dongbei (north-east). The film documents their daily lives along the railway; how they find food; pick up leftovers from passengers or rubbish bins; how they sleep, in the open by a camp fire or at stations; how they interact with each other, and how they are treated – for instance, the way they are abused verbally and physically by station security guards and nearby residents; and mostly how they see themselves and the society around them.

The documentary is filmed with location sound and natural lighting. It consists of many long takes as the camera is made to observe the subjects' actions. They are shown as they sing and chat around the campfire, or tell their stories in interspersed dialogues with the filmmaker. We hear the director's questions, and see his shadow on the image. While we do not see him directly, we witness an attack on him by one of the group's "big" brothers, who tries to stop him filming because he suspects him of being a policeman in disguise. *Along the Railway* presents a picture – very different from official accounts – of people who are the victims of the market economy and family tragedies: peasants who leave their land for a better life in the city but are unable to secure jobs. One of them is unable to return to his hometown because he has no money and because his identity card has been confiscated by the police; another is a young boy who cannot tolerate being beaten by his stepfather. What is intriguing to see, from the perspective of the middle class, is the filthy way the film's subjects live – the leftover food they consume, the dirty clothes they wear, the rough ground they sleep on, and the uncivilized manner in which they communicate with one another. And yet, they sing well and sometimes appear innocent, witty and charming, in spite of the implication that some of their activities may be potentially criminal. The multiple voices and perspectives employed in this documentary evoke a range of contradictory feelings, including sympathy, compassion and a good amount of discomfort, especially among middle-class viewers.

Similar to *Along the Railway, Laotou* (*Old Men*, 1999) is an independent production by a filmmaker who uses her own camera and editing machine. The documentary records the lifestyles of a group of male retirees with their routine of sitting around and chatting. Every morning after breakfast, they leave home with their little stools to meet a spot where they can sit in the sun in winter or in the shade in summer. They chat aimlessly about their lives, their difficulties, their illnesses, their views on society, their past and their families. Sometimes they fight like young men. However, gradually their numbers decrease due to death or simply a failure to turn up. The documentary also follows some of the old men to their homes, documenting the way they live, either with their wives or alone. The film is done in a typical observational mode with long takes and location sounds, natural lighting and minimum editing and director's interference. It presents a picture of cold social relations, which contrasts with mainstream presentations of respect for senior citizens. Throughout the film, there is no government presence, nor any care by social workers or organizations. The old men are a lonely group. One old man is the sole carer for his sick wife. The impression of a happy Chinese family in which grandchildren respect and support their grandparents is undermined in this film by the multi-voice presentation of the stark reality of old age.

There are hundreds of such documentaries, as well as an increasing number of debating programs in which a broad range of topics of public interest are aired.[5] Here too, the noticeable innovation is the participation of different social and professional groups juxtaposed to one another in the production of a new polyphonic discourse. Beyond the internal polyphony of the new documentary film style and talkback shows, we can also speak of polyphony in a broader sense. There are at present about forty-five channels available to the average household, including a large section of the Chinese peasantry. China has now more than 1.115 billion television consumers, well beyond the urban middle class, including peasants, the migrants and laid-off workers. That this multi-voice televisual scene is mainly market- and consumer-driven should not detract from the fact that it constitutes a significant change from the former monological and dogmatic dominance of the voice of the government.

Of course, the rise of polyphonic programs cannot blind us to the fact that the Communist Party tradition in documentary filmmaking continues to play a role in the televisual market. There certainly is a continuation of the propaganda tradition, glorifying the Communist Party, the selfless workers and peasants, and soldiers contributing to the society, as we have seen in the documentary examples of the *Fire Incident* and *My Father*. The majority of the documentaries about the Communist heroes and deceased leaders are still presented with a dominant "voice-of-God" narration. The important difference to note here, however, is the fact that these films are now in polyphonic competition with a rapidly rising number of programs in a more open presentational mode. In turn, government-sponsored documentaries themselves are undergoing changes as a result of this competition. New camera, editing and sound technologies, new interviewing styles, natural lighting and other realist presentational techniques, as well as a growing number of film critics and, above all, audience ratings are all putting pressure on the official televisual discourse. As a result, we cannot but notice a shift from a government-dominated media scene towards one that is multi-voiced and increasingly diverse.

Conclusion

The "democratic" potential of documentary television in films and other programs is beginning to be realized in China in a variety of ways. At the level of program content we observe a shift towards an increasing presence of ordinary citizens, the non-elites, the common people, marginal groups and peasants, portrayed under ordinary and not-so-ordinary circumstances, a decline in dogma and ideological abstraction and a foregrounding of events of social life, with often unpredictable incidents, and the new focus on the hitherto concealed margins of society.

At the level of media discourse and presentational mode, we note a sharply increased realization of the potential of the documentary mode. As John Frow (2006: 73) has observed of documentary, it is "not only the film stock but also the optical capacities of cameras and editing suites, the apparatus of sound recording, the set-up of a studio, the costs of production, and possible screening outlets" that characterize the documentary film genre. All these, Frow writes, "inform and constrain the representational possibilities available to the filmmaker, and thus the ways in which he or she can address a viewer" (Frow 2006: 73). There can be no doubt that in all these respects, documentary film in China is becoming increasingly professional, thus leaving behind much that binds it to official government doctrine. There is even less doubt as to the commercial success and viability of the new Chinese television documentary film. Whether such commercialization would lead to democratization cannot be answered in any simplistic way as many other factors play a role in any political process. Nevertheless, documentary film and other documentary programs are playing an important role in the democratization process by fostering the decline of monological, authoritarian guidance and the emergence of polyphonic styles. This process is assisted by the reduction in doctrinal and so non-realist voice-of-God narration, and a diminishing of message-controlled editing in favor of long takes, long shots, hand-held camera technique, and an increase in the use of interviews and other non-scripted filming styles.

While the government-sponsored, authoritarian documentary is by no means dead, it is now being challenged by the growing presence of a variety of new documentary film styles, permitting the democratic potential of the genre to come to the fore. While none of these presentational innovations can be argued to guarantee by themselves a more democratic form of film-making, in combination they do suggest that China is on the way towards embracing more open and self-critical ways of viewing the world. The rise of semi-dependent and independent filmmakers and production companies adds significantly to this trend. In particular, participatory strategies in a variety of television programs, including documentaries, are on the increase. One cannot but observe how the force of public approval by audience ratings of a polyphony of opposing voices in certain programs, is a sign that the televisual media are beginning to be used as a platform for promoting democracy. The potential is there even if the topics debated so far exclude a well-specified range of politically sensitive issues.

Notes

1 As cited in the conclusion of Chapter 3 by Wanning Sun in this volume.
2 See also Chapter 2 by Lee, He and Huang in this volume.
3 Interview with Dr Zhang Zhijun in Beijing (March 2004).
4 Central China Television (CCTV) is one of the two national television stations in China. The other is the China Education Television (CETV), which is managed by the Chinese Ministry of Education.
5 Debating programs, a new branch of television programming, are discussed in my book (2007) *Chinese Documentaries: From dogma to polyphony* (Routledge).

Bibliography

Bakhtin, M. (1973) *Problems of Dostoevsky's Poetics*, trans. R.W. Rotsel, Ann Arbor: Ardis Publications.
Chen, H. (2001) "Zhongguo dianshi jilu pian de lishi yu xianzhuang" [The history and contemporary situation of the Chinese television documentary], in W. San (ed.) *Jilu dianying wenxian* [Documentation and Fictionalization], Beijing: China Broadcasting Press, pp. 675–80.
Chu, Y. (2006) "Legal report: citizenship education through a television documentary," in V. Fong and R. Murphy (eds) *Chinese Citizenship: Views from the margins*, London: RoutledgeCurzon, pp. 68–95.
Cui, B. (ed.) (2005) *2004–2005 nian: Zhongguo chuanmei chanye fazhan baogao* [Blue Book of China's Media: Report on the development of China's media industry 2004–2005], Beijing: Social Sciences Academic Press.
Cui, B., Lu, J. and Wang, X. (2005) "Gaizhi yu zhuanzhe: 2004–5 nian Zhongguo chuanmei chanye fazhan zong baogao" [Reform and transition: general report on media development in China in 2004–5], in B. Cui (ed.) *2004–2005 nian: Zhongguo*

68 *Yingchi Chu*

chuanmei chanye fazhan baogao [Blue Book of China's Media: Report on the development of China's media industry 2004–2005], Beijing: Social Sciences Academic Press, pp. 3–33.

Frow, J. (2006) *Genre*, London: Routledge.

Habermas, J. (1974) "The public sphere," *New German Critique*, 1(3): 49–55.

—— (1982) *The Structural Transformation of the Public Sphere*, Cambridge, MA: MIT Press.

Jhally, S. (2002) "Image-based culture: advertising and popular culture," in K. Askew and R. Wilk (eds) *The Anthropology of Media,* Massachusetts: Blackwell.

Li, C. (1999) "Guanyu dangjin Zhongguo dianshi jilu pian de chuangzuo zuoxiang" [Trends of creativity in contemporary documentary film in China], in X. Li (ed.) *Guangbo yingshi lun* [Theory on Broadcasting and Television], Beijing: China International Broadcasting Press, pp. 281–304.

Li, Y. (2002) "Zhongguo jilu pian kua shiji sanda yanbian" [Three major changes in Chinese documentary films from the twentieth century to the present], in F. Zhang, S. Hung and Z. Hu (eds) *Quanqiuhua yu Zhongguo yingshi de minyu* [Globalization and the Destiny of Chinese Film and Television], Beijing: Beijing Broadcasting University Press, pp. 260–71.

Liu, D. (2001) "Jilu dianying de xin shengming" [New life of the documentary film], in W. San (ed.) *Jilu dianying wenxian* [Documentation and Fictionalization], Beijing: China Broadcasting and Television Press, pp. 809–25.

Lu, D. (2005) "2004 nian Zhongguo dianshi chanye fazhang baogao" [Report on the development of the Chinese television industry in 2004] in B. Cui (ed.) *2004–2005 nian: Zhongguo chuanmei chanye fazhan baogao* [Blue Book of China's Media: Report on the development of China's media industry 2004–2005], Beijing: Social Sciences Academic Press, pp. 221–41.

Lü, X. (2003) *Jilu Zhongguo [Documenting China]*, Beijing: Sanlian Publishing.

Nichols, B. (2005) "The voice of documentary," in A. Rosenthal and A. Corner (eds) *New Challenges for Documentary*, Manchester: Manchester University Press, pp. 17–33.

Ren, Y. (1997) *Dianshi jilu pian xinlun* [New Theory of Television Documentary], Beijing: China Broadcasting Press.

Situ, Z. (2001) "Zhongguo jilun pian chuangzuo qianjing" [Future of creativity in Chinese documentary], in W. San (ed.) *Jilun dianying wenxuan* [Documentation and Fictionalization], Beijing: Beijing Broadcasting and Television Press, pp. 186–200.

Wu, K. (2004) "Dianshi meijie jingji xue" [Economics of television], in H. Zhao and M. Jiang (eds) *TV Industry Management Series*, Beijing: Huaxia chuban she.

Yang, W. (1998) *Zhongguo dianshi lungang* [Principles of Chinese Television], Beijing: Beijing Broadcasting Publishing.

Yu, G. (2002) *Jiexi chuanmei bianju* [An Analysis of Change in the Media], Guangzhou: Nanfang ribao chuban she.

—— (2003) *Chuanmei yinxian li* [The Power of Media Influence] Guangzhou: Nanfang ribao chuban she.

Yuan, F. (2005) "Cong 'paoma quandi' dao 'jinggeng xizuo': jinnian woguo dianshi meiti bianhua saomiao ji zhanwang" [From "making territory" to "fine production": recent changes and its future in Chinese television], in B. Cui (ed.) *2004–2005 nian: Zhongguo chuanmei chanye fazhan baogao* [Blue Book of China's Media: Report on the development of China's media industry 2004–2005], Beijing: Social Sciences Academic Press, pp. 260–8.

Zhang, H. (ed.) (2001) *Dianshi Zhongguo* [China Television], Beijing: Beijing Broadcasting University Press.

Zhang, Z. (2003) "Shilun 'san tiejin' de dazhong chuanbo xue yiyi" [The significance of "three forms of closeness" in mass communication], *Dangdai Dianshi*, 1: 34–8.

Zhongyang dianshi tai taiban bangongshi shiye fazhan diaoyan chu (CCTV Editorial Office) (2003) *Chuancheng wenming kaituo chuangxin – yushijujin de zhongyang dianshi tai* [CCTV from 1958 to 2003], Beijing: Dongfang chuban she.

5 Vietnamese cinema in the era of market liberalization

Chuong-Dai Hong Vo

Located in the midst of Saigon's ritzy downtown is Diamond Plaza, which houses a mall offering anything from Vietnamese kitsch to French designer leather bags. This shopping complex is also where the hip urban crowd goes for a movie night out – usually choosing between Hollywood blockbusters and locally made Vietnamese films. In 2004, *Nhung Co Gai Chan Dai* (*Long Legged Girls*) was screened to a sold-out audience at 40,000 dong a ticket. At the equivalent of US$3.75, this is the price of a meal at a medium-scale restaurant. Not only was the film's box office success a sign of the growing disposable income of the Vietnamese middle class, it also highlighted the extent of the public's hunger for locally made films about the trials of daily life rather than grand narratives about war and revolutionary valor.

Vietnamese cinema has changed radically over the last thirty years with the end of the Indochinese wars and the opening of the market to international investments, which has brought with it a flood of cinematic influences and products from across Asia, Europe and the United States of America. With the advent of *Doi Moi* (Renovation) in the mid-1980s, Vietnamese Communist Party (VCP) Secretary General Nguyen Van Linh announced an era of liberalization in the arts and culture.[1] The move toward an open market economy signaled the VCP's implicit acknowledgment of widespread grassroots resistance to centralized state planning of industries and agriculture on the domestic front, as well as the liberalization processes that were taking place in the former Soviet Union and Eastern Europe Bloc countries (see Luong 2003; Nguyen 1992). Taking advantage of the fear among stalwart officials that the Party itself would face collapse if it did not make room for alternative voices, more progressive factions within the VCP began to push for cultural renovation (see Heng 1999; Tran 2000). They wanted to make room for alternatives to socialist realism as the sole ideological model of artistic expression in thematic concerns and film styles, which in Vietnamese cinema meant the portrayal of the working class as the vanguard in the process of nation-building. Unable to stave off the push for democratization of Vietnamese society, the conservative elements conceded ground, only on the condition that the new direction would not so much be a victory of the capitalist order over socialist ideals as it would a more

Vietnam: cinema and market liberalization 71

complex examination of the "reactionary elements." This was effectively an attempt to reconcile the development of an open market society with the Party at the helm.

Across the spectrum of cultural production, from 1987 to 1990, there were many open discussions about change and reform. There were debates about the tenets of socialism in numerous publications, such as *Thanh Nien* (*Youth*), *Nhan Dan* (*The People*) and *Quan Doi* (*The Army*); investigative reporting of government corruption and mismanagement; critiques of developmental narratives in the dissident writings of Nguyen Huy Thiep, Duong Thu Huong and others. Intellectuals debated alternative visions of modernity and the role of the state in the arts, as seen in issues of the weekly publication *Van Nghe* (*Literature and Art*) under the editorship of Nguyen Ngoc. This chapter examines the kinds of changes that mark the cultural texts of the *Doi Moi* period by offering close readings of three films: Dang Nhat Minh's *Thuong Nho Dong Que* (1995) (*Nostalgia for the Countryside*), Le Hoang's *Gai Nhay* (2003) (*Bar Girls*) and Pham Nhue Giang's *Thung Lung Hoang Vang* (2000) (*The Deserted Valley*). I focus on these films because they represent well-known works by three prominent directors who engage with thematic concerns that became common with the loosening of state regulation of the film industry. These concerns include: the definition of Vietnamese identity in a globalized economic system; the promises and social costs of rapid urbanization; and, perceptions of Vietnam by diasporic and other international audiences and visitors.

Since the mid-1980s, Vietnamese cinema has radically moved away from emphasis on the country's wars against regional and Western enemies, and turned more to stories about individual relations and the effects of market liberalization on people's lives. Viet Linh's *Ganh Xiec Rong* (1988) (*An Itinerant Circus*) portrays the exploitation of an ethnic minority village by a traveling Viet troupe, whose greed for gold symbolizes the deterioration of morals in the fetishization of wealth. Adapted from Nguyen Huy Thiep's short story of the same name, Nguyen Khac Loi's *Tuong Ve Huu* (1988) (*The General Retires*) shows the incompatibility between a patriarch's power, which lies in his access to an old social network, and his daughter-in-law's authority, which she gains through her entrepreneurial, but dehumanizing, skills. Like other *phim nghe thuat* (art film) productions, these films were made with state subsidies. Although the funds amounted to only US$60,000, state sponsorship also guarantees the films' promotion and distribution among the nation's theaters, and subsequently on broadcast television. As market liberalization picked up speed, however, the state gradually cut most spending on cultural productions, which left the already very small and under-funded cinema industry in deeper doldrums.

Vietnamese cinema in the *Doi Moi* period has grown significantly beyond the ability of the censors to control every step of production. But film producers have also had to constantly negotiate on the permissibility of various themes. The state has licensed dozens of private and state–private co-owned production studios over the past twenty years. By the early 1990s, studios such as Ding Do Video and Nha Trang were producing more than forty "instant noodle" films annually – offering a selection of locally made straight-to-video movies that critics decried as "low culture" productions. Within the media industry, the availability of cable services and the import of television shows and blockbusters from South Korea, Japan, Thailand and other Asian sites as well as from Hollywood, coupled with the wide popularity of pirated DVDs, offer viewers a huge array of entertainment options. These choices exert tremendous influence on the narrative, stylistic and technical processes of domestic filmmaking. Whereas the older generation of film professionals – from actors to directors – were largely trained in the former Soviet Union and Eastern Europe, the younger generation count among them several who have been trained in the West and Asia with support from funding organizations such as the Ford Foundation. Film producers, young and old, have taken on themes about government corruption, poverty and the social costs of economic competition, and the tricky relationships between local Vietnamese and returning diasporic subjects – topics that were once considered taboo.

This is a significant departure from the cinema of old, but it is not altogether a radical critique of the Vietnamese political structure nor of the state itself. I would argue that Vietnamese cinema is still largely subject to the watchful eyes of the state. Film producers can embed social critiques within their narratives, but those critiques are interwoven with a reiteration of the legitimacy of the state and the Communist Party. With the opening of the market to foreign investors, the government has recognized the need for new laws, and eventually passed the Investment Act of 1987, the Sales Tax Act of 1990, the Banking Act of 1990 and other legislation. But it has kept a relatively tight rein on the ideological front. The National Assembly passed the Media Act in 1989 after years of public debate, especially in the South. On the surface, the Act legalizes the rights of all citizens to basic freedoms, embracing freedom of the press and prohibiting censorship. But this "freedom" is restricted to content that "serves" the state and the people. This is particularly alarming in light of the 1986 Criminal Code that punishes those who work against the socialist system with prison sentences of up to twenty years. And throughout the decades of liberalization, the state has periodically cracked down on what it sees as threats to the cultural integrity of the arts, threats that reflect the interests of the factions in control of the VCP at any given time.

If the late 1980s marked a period of dramatic experimentation and testing of censorship restrictions, the 1990s witnessed the reassertion of state power by officials who desired to make clear that the Party would not tolerate criticism of the state as a whole. In 1991, conservatives within the Party managed to regain a majority at the Seventh Party Congress, renewing the use of revolutionary discourse to call for the "urgent reorganization of the media" and the "militant role of the socialist press in the fight against

Brief history of Vietnamese cinema

sabotage from the enemy camp" (cited in Nguyen 1992: 26). They managed to push for the renewal of the subsidy system to ensure the production of films that would present a positive image of Vietnam both domestically and internationally. But with the proliferation of film studios and the availability of countless alternatives to officially sponsored media, the state could no longer keep a tight rein on the film industry as it did in the past.

Brief history of Vietnamese cinema

The beginnings of Vietnamese cinema hark back to the French era, with the first documentary shot in Hanoi by a French observer at Ho Chi Minh's "Declaration of Independence" speech ceremony on 2 September 1945. The Vietnam Film Archives divides the history of the nation's film industry into four periods, which correspond to the major shifts in the country's revolutionary struggles and political economic directions – namely: the First Indochinese War; the Second Indochinese War; the post-1975 years; and the present era of *Doi Moi*.[2] During the first two periods, documentaries, feature films and cartoons were largely about the heroism of anti-colonial and anti-imperialist resistance against France and the US. These productions presented lessons on how to live during wartime, envisioned the construction of a socialist society and "the new socialist man," and glorified manual work in the fields and factories. The third period was defined by depictions of the country's fight against Chinese aggression in the late 1970s and an expansion of non-war themes that constructed the nation as one inclusive of the former Republic of Vietnam and the cultural diversity of the country's ethnic groups. Under *Doi Moi*, one of the main objectives of the largely state-controlled cinematic industry has been the projection of a Vietnamese nation that is modern and international.

Those films that have won national and international prizes and have been shown at film festivals worldwide with the state's approval have been of the *phim nghe thuat* (art film) genre. Shown in theatres for brief runs and then on state-controlled television channels, they tend to attract an older audience and those interested in "culture."[3] Some well-known films from the 1970s and 1980s paint Vietnamese subjects as victims of foreign aggression unwilling to relent. For instance, Hai Ninh's *Em Be Ha Noi* (1975) (*The Little Girl of Hanoi*) graphically depicts a city razed by daily air bombings and an entire way of life obliterated.[4] Another film, Tran Vu's *Chung Ta Se Gap Lai* (*We Shall Meet Again*), represents the characters' resilience despite the constant threat of death. Vu's film won the Main Prize for feature films at the Karlovy Vary International Film Festival in Czechoslovakia in 1976.[5] Yet another film, Hong Sen's *Canh Dong Hoang* (1979) (*The Wild Field*), portrays a Viet Cong couple's family life as well as their work as guerrillas in the Mekong Delta. This film took the Gold Medal for feature films at the 1981 Moscow International Film Festival. While the state touted these productions as exemplars of socialist realism, officials were divided on other films. Made by Vietnam's most well-connected and reputed director on the international stage, Dang Nhat Minh, *Co Gai Tren* Song (1987) (*The Girl on the Perfume River*) sparked intense debate upon its release for its portrayal of the post-war rehabilitated life of a prostitute betrayed by a former lover, a North Vietnamese spy who becomes a Communist Party official after the war. The film critiqued such officials' post-war lust for power and their abandonment of the ideals of collective struggle. To highlight the ignoble behavior of the male protagonist, someone who denies his past to protect his reputation, the film represents the prostitute as a figure whose moral and physical health regeneration symbolizes the incorporation of the formerly decrepit South Vietnam into the recently unified Vietnamese nation. What made the movie even more damning was that the heroine ends up with a former army officer from the Republic of Viet Nam. Now hailed as a forerunner of the industry's representation of more complex narratives that include the voices of those who had lived in and fought for the South and now had been re-educated and inducted as new socialist citizens, *The Girl on the Perfume River* is the most famous example of controversial films from the 1970s and 1980s.

While older Vietnamese who lived through at least one of the Indochinese wars are still interested in wartime narratives, these films fail to attract a sizeable audience, as evidenced by the dismal box office sales for Do Minh Tuan's *Ky Uc Dien Bien* (2004) (*Memories of Dien Bien*), which had an unprecedented budget of US$900,000 from the government. On the other hand, the younger generations have turned to "instant noodle" lower budget productions. To the government's dismay, these films – many costing just US$10,000 and predominantly shot in Saigon – have actually been much more profitable. These films tend to address issues concerning city life and what it means to be modern in Vietnam. Films by directors such as Le Hoang (*Gai Nhay/Bar Girls*, 2003; *Lo Lem He Pho/Street Cinderella*, 2004; and *Nu Tuong Cuop/Women Robbers*, 2005) and Vu Ngoc Dang (*Nhung Co Gai Chan Dai/Long-Legged Girls*, 2004) depict migrations from the countryside to the city, urban prostitution, drug use, HIV/AIDS infections, the alienation and destitution of city life, and the deterioration of traditional notions of *tinh cam* (feelings of personal relations or sentiments).

In the early to mid-1990s, the Politburo passed a series of decisions directing ministries to fund projects and missions that would dispel continuing international perceptions of the country as a backward society and war zone populated by characters who are no more than two-dimensional cut-outs representing the treacherous guerrilla, the pidgin-speaking prostitute, the simple-minded peasant or the corrupt government official. The rest of this chapter will analyze three key works that are representative of *nghe thuat* (high culture) and "low culture" films in the *Doi Moi* period that offer different perspectives on the construction of a Vietnamese national identity, the promises of the Communist Revolution, ethnic identity, the place of the returning diasporic subject and the relationship between social ties and economic development.

The gaze of the national male subject

Dang Nhat Minh's *Thuong Nho Dong Que* (1995) (*Nostalgia for the Countryside*) is considered a classic by both Vietnamese and international critics. The most famous of Vietnam's directors, Minh grew up in a family of intellectuals and worked as a writer and journalist before becoming a documentary filmmaker in 1963 – a common start for feature film directors. Over the span of four decades, he has made nine films and has served as General Secretary of the Vietnam Cinema Association for ten years. *Thuong Nho* is his seventh production and probably the most screened Vietnamese film on the international circuit, having won many prizes, including the NETPAC Special Mention at the Rotterdam International Film Festival and the Audience Prize at the Nantes and Fribourg Film Festivals.

Set in the mid-1990s and based on a short story by the famous dissident writer Nguyen Huy Thiep, *Thuong Nho* questions the linearity of economic liberalization theory and destabilizes nostalgic and Orientalist notions of the Vietnamese countryside as a pastoral escape. The film was made during an era when foreign capital venture firms and organizing bodies such as the International Monetary Fund (IMF) were pushing the "little tigers" of Southeast Asia to further liberalize their financial and capital markets and loosen investment rules. Americans flooded into Vietnam shortly after the Clinton Administration normalized ties with its former enemy, scrambling to play catch-up with corporations from Asia, Australia and Europe, whose governments had renewed diplomatic relations with Vietnam much earlier. Within this context, Vietnam was a still "untainted" hot spot for foreigners, many of whom were in their twenties and thirties, as well as diasporic Vietnamese seeking to make a quick fortune, enjoy an elite lifestyle and perhaps even "find themselves" in their "homeland."

Thuong Nho questions the ease of that trajectory by refusing to grant the diasporic gaze agency and instead offers a masculinist and ironic critique of the exploitation of the Vietnamese countryside by both local urban entrepreneurs and international market forces. The story centers on Nham, a seventeen-year-old who becomes head of the household after his father dies and his older brother leaves the village indefinitely to find work. Nham's journey into manhood requires that he leaves school and contributes his labor to support the family. That transition also involves his sexual awakening, triggered by his desires for Quyen, a fellow villager's niece who as a child left with her parents for Hanoi and then later escaped from the country by boat. Nham also develops sexual feelings for his sister-in-law Ngu, who turns to him for comfort in her husband's absence and who despairs of a life that seems to offer little more than hardship.

Aside from the camera's point of view, we see the narrative mostly through Nham's eyes. This privileging of his perspective and that of the omniscient narrator has two important functions. First, it wholly challenges the balance of power in the socio-economic disparity between the diasporic subject – who has returned for a break from her life in a First World country – and the local Vietnamese village population, which seems stuck in a backward, agrarian lifestyle. Second, it presents Nham's maturation as a masculinist *Bildungsroman*. The directorial lens gives way to Nham's gaze in several key moments, all involving his apprehension of Ngu and Quyen. In one of the first scenes, the spectator identifies with Nham as he watches his sister-in-law combing her long hair and pulling it up into a bun. This scene takes on overt sexual meaning with the motif's repetition at the train station when Nham first sees Quyen from the back, her long hair tossing gently as she turns to face him, leaving him speechless. She too puts her hair up later when she goes swimming – all the while shown to the viewer through Nham's eyes. In these scenes, neither woman seems aware of his gaze. This lack of awareness on the part of the female characters is symptomatic of the way the film privileges the male character as the figure capable of introspection and transformation. These encounters and the flashbacks to the train and swimming scenes as sexual fantasies build to Nham's physical climax when Ngu hugs him in a moment of utter loneliness and despair over her husband's absence, and he realizes, "*Toi biet tu ngay nay toi da tro thanh nguoi lon*" ("I knew from that day I had become an adult").

The film also foregrounds male consciousness with the use of the voice-over and representations of the village intellectuals as male. In contrast to Quyen's pursuit of education to obtain a well-paying job, Ong Giao Quy, a retired teacher, tells her that learning is about *intellectual* maturation: "*Di hoc de co tri thuc de song doi minh cho co y nghia*" ("One studies to acquire intellectual growth so that one can live a meaningful life"). She receives another lesson from the high school teacher, who questions her nostalgia for her childhood home and dispels her illusions about the simplicity of country life. Through the omniscient gaze, we see them end a night celebrating the village harvest with what is mostly a one-way conversation, in which he tells her of the villagers' dire circumstances: their sacrifices for past wars and continued military recruitment campaigns; the high prices they have to pay for imported fertilizers; their exploitation by urban middlemen; and the adverse effects of globalization on rice exports. But the teacher has to stop abruptly when he steps in a pile of dung, to Quyen's amusement, and the gaze moves to the perspective of Nham, hidden in the dark background. This switch conflates the camera's gaze with that of the young man, who represents Vietnam's younger generation – half of whom were born after the end of the Vietnam/American/civil war. This flourish, arguably, has two purposes. It suggests the director's desire to explore and include the voices of the younger generation, while at the same time showing the youthful naïveté of that perspective in relation to the more mature voices of the older male figures, who are stand-ins for the director-as-intellectual.

The film's privileging of Nham's perspective and that of the omniscient narrator ultimately has a second more important function – it makes possible a masculinist critique of the fetishization of the Vietnamese countryside as a place stuck in time by presenting Nham's life as a *Bildungsroman* replete with irony, an awareness of the self. In *The Predicament of Culture*, James Clifford (1988) discusses how Western anthropology created an "Other" by positing itself as an agent capable of irony while representing the Other as unaware of his/her place in history. Yet, according to Clifford (1988: 79), the Other has his/her own ironic awareness, and consciously performs culture for the Western outsider. I find this insight pertinent to Minh's critique of the diasporic gaze and his assertion of the local male subject's consciousness. In fact, the director represents the diasporic character Quyen as the one unaware of the ironic; instead, she is the one being watched. In the swimming scene mentioned earlier, Quyen has asked Nham if he has any aspirations. He tells her, "No," but in the voiceover, he says: "*Em co nhieu uoc mo lam nhung chi chang hieu*" ("I have many hopes, but you would not understand"). This gap between desires and realities – his maturation and hopes for the future and her return to childhood – undermines Quyen's easy return to a "homeland" that is no longer the place she had left. In fact, the film refuses to validate the diasporic subject's observations and instead represents the local male subject as the repository of truth, intellectual consciousness and critical perception of the socio-economic disparities developing in the globalizing of the Vietnamese economy.

The truth in the alleyways

Le Hoang's *Gai Nhay* (2003) (*Bar Girls*) was the first locally made blockbuster, grossing more than $1 million to the government's dismay and to alternative directors' delight. "High culture" film critics denounced it as trashy and sensationalistic in its depictions of sex, violence, drug use, deviant sexualities and scandalous plot twists. The story follows a female journalist's investigative reporting of Saigon's secret world of prostitution. Refusing to publish her superficial account of the city's underbelly, her male editor sharply reprimands her, saying that if she wants to find the truth she must be willing to immerse herself in the world of the dispossessed; she must become one of them. Ironically, Thu's disguise as a prostitute is too good and she gets beaten up by a group of sex workers who mistake her as competition. But in following her search for her attackers, the film reveals the complexities of the lives of sex workers – Hanh's abandonment by her mother and will to survive, Hoa's rich family background and drug addiction and their pathetic demise due to HIV/AIDS infection.

Although I am reluctant to characterize any Vietnamese film as melodramatic due to the overuse of this term by Western film critics and Orientalist

78   *Chuong-Dai Hong Vo*

assumptions about the pathology of the Other, *Gai Nhay* very much draws upon that genre. In fact, I would argue that its use of melodramatic elements is at times parodic, an exaggeration of good and evil and a self-aware staging of the sensational. The film opens with an aerial shot of two women in traditional white *ao dai* (long translucent dresses with slits on the sides and pants underneath) entering a hotel lobby. The camera swoops downward as it follows them inside, where they set up props for an international conference on HIV/AIDS. This scene introduces the directorial gaze as one capable of an overarching view and penetration into interior spaces both physical and psychic. The film seems to offer closure by taking the last scene back to the conference hall, where Hanh reveals she has contracted the deadly disease and begs officials to help those like her. She is a figure who embodies the polar excesses of good and evil, since she moves regularly between an underworld marked by the violence of male customers and exploitation by her pimp on the one hand, and the safe space of her aunt's riverbank shanty on the other, where she goes to visit her son and gather news about her handicapped mother. The film stages the contradiction between the values of these two worlds in its representation of her body in the closing scene. As she rises from her chair at the conference and walks to the podium, the camera slowly tilts from a close-up of her tight-fitting, red spaghetti strap shirt down to her black miniskirt and black high heels. Having been injured in a car accident after learning that her diasporic client may have deceived her into thinking he wanted to marry her, Hanh has to limp to the podium. This shot's linkage of excessive female sexuality and the corporeal punishment of unsanctioned romance parodically constructs her body as a site of victimhood – not one to be sympathized with, but one to be understood as a lesson. In stylistically focusing on her body as the locus of abuse, the film individualizes her victimhood and uses it as a cautionary tale rather than a vehicle for a social critique of the relationship among sex work, violence, drug use and the government's lack of a sufficient response to the socio-economic conditions that lead to prostitution and drug use. Indeed, as the film's authoritative voice on HIV/AIDS, the character representing a vice-director of a giant pharmaceutical firm tells reporters in an interview that it is the individual's responsibility to acquire the necessary drug treatment despite the astronomical costs. Ironically, he does not know that his daughter Hoa had become a prostitute to feed her illicit drug addiction and in the process had acquired HIV from her clients.

The film's depiction of the quest for truth about Saigon's underworld draws upon the technique of sensationalism as the best means of discovery, a bitter parody of investigative reporting, police crackdowns and official research. To find her attackers, Thu turns to both formal and informal networks of power and access – the police and the string of street "informants" who lead her to Hanh. But it is through the camera's sensationalization of Hanh's body, not through Thu's reporting, that the audience finally understands the pathetic consequences of her lifestyle.

The deployment of ethnicity in the construction of a liberal nation

A film that has been well praised by Vietnamese critics and officially sanctioned for international exhibition is Pham Nhue Giang's *Thung Lung Hoang Vang* (2000) (*The Deserted Valley*). The film centers on the lives of two female teachers, Giao and Minh, who came from the city to teach the Vietnamese language to a community of Hmong people in the country's northern highlands. A meditation on the tensions and negotiations between personal desires and public duty, *Thung Lung* depicts the northern highlands as a place removed from civilization, a place of desolation as well as one free of social prohibitions on women's sexualities. In representing teachers who put aside their personal problems for the sake of their economically and intellectually impoverished students, the film valorizes formal, state-sanctioned institutions as vehicles for achieving progress while also projecting an image of a Vietnamese nation characterized by multicultural harmony. At the same time, the film challenges the gendering of personal desires and a hierarchy of power whereby incompetent male leaders depend on their more qualified female subordinates.

Contemporary Vietnamese cultural production abounds with representations of ethnic minorities in an era in which the government has significantly increased funding for the arts as part of a comprehensive program to construct an image of a modern nation on both the domestic and international fronts. As part of that campaign, *Thung Lung* was included in a program of events accompanying an international exhibition in 2003 called *Vietnam: Journeys of Body, Mind and Spirit*, co-curated by the Vietnam Museum of Ethnology and the American Museum of Natural History. One can safely say that Vietnamese domestic audiences are familiar with the film's depiction of the northern highlands as a remote space whose physical distance from the metropolis also functions as a measure of its removal from civilization generally. This association of ethnicity with civilization or the lack of is embedded in the Vietnamese language. The Viet ethnic group alternatively refer to themselves as the Kinh, a word which means "city." This linguistic association of the Viet with city life dates back to dynastic days when the imperial center was portrayed in Viet culture as the site of civilization; the farther away other ethnic populations were from the center, the more uncivilized they were in the eyes of the Viet. But how would the markers of ethnic difference be understood by an international audience? And what constitutes the film's "Vietnameseness"? An international audience may not be familiar with the dichotomy set up between characters who represent Viet ethnicity and those who represent the Hmong or the figure of the ethnic minority. But in drawing clear distinctions between the Viet and the Hmong through dress as well as their attitudes toward education, the film projects an image of benevolent state representatives who ultimately sacrifice their own personal happiness to bring civilization to their less knowledgeable fellow citizens. At the same time, in showing the isolation faced by the Viet characters, the film questions the effectiveness of such a state policy and the sacrifices required.

In my examination of how *Thung Lung* represents Vietnamese identity on the domestic as well as international scenes, I would like to consider how the film reproduces the racialization of ethnicity in Vietnam and the state policy of spreading Viet culture to the edges of the national border. In 1979, the Vietnamese state codified decades-long scholarly debates on how to classify the country's ethnic groups by fixing the number at fifty-four. The clear demarcation and naturalization of ethnic differences harks back to French anthropology and Cold War recruitment of various ethnic groups to fight in the Indochinese wars. French anthropologists, military officials and missionaries wrote detailed ethnographies on the highlanders as a way to ascertain social relationships among ethnic groups and to create a divide-and-conquer strategy that maintained French colonial dominance. The process of "tribalization" and "ethnicization" was an integral part of the colonial project, which sought to create a system of surveillance that essentialized culturally and linguistically heterogeneous populations whose languages, customs, dress and other practices were the products of exchanges and overlaps rather than clearly defined differences. During the First and Second Indochinese Wars, Vietnamese Communist leaders used the analogy of brotherhood as a symbolic representation of the relationship between Viet and other ethnic groups, with the Viet as the "older brother" (*anh*) who would guide his "younger brothers" (*em*) in the anti-colonial struggle toward liberation and re-unification (see Pelley 2002).

This paternalistic metaphor took actual shape in state policies aimed at civilizing the natives. One such program was the education of ethnic minorities in the language of the Viet. The government practice of sending teachers from Viet-dominated cities up to the northern and central highlands, where the country's minority populations have lived for hundreds of years, dates back to 1954 when the newly created Socialist Republic of Vietnam sought to extend its control over the highlands through various practices, including schooling in the Vietnamese language rather than local indigenous languages. Until recently, this relocation to remote regions was also a way to punish those intellectuals who challenged the state's equating of artistic creation and the appropriation of art in support of the revolution (see Ninh 2005). In contemporary times, graduating college students are given the choice to volunteer for these remote teaching posts, which can be seen as necessary in a tight job market and can be a step in acquiring more desirable positions later in one's career.[6]

Thung Lung draws upon paternalistic and racialized images of ethnic minorities to create a context for the director's critique of the implementation of social policies, the gendered hierarchicalization of power within the state apparatus and the policing of women's sexualities. In the following analysis, I focus on the film's critique of the state's policy of sending Viet teachers up to the highlands, a practice portrayed as requiring individuals to put national duty before personal interests. I argue that while the film subtly questions state authority, it does so by drawing on normalized conceptions of the national body defined by racial notions of ethnicity and civilization. Composition and lighting are used to differentiate between the spaces of the civilized and the spaces of the primordial, with the former signifying learning and communal cooperation and the latter harboring secrets, deception, illicit sexuality and danger. The spaces of the schoolhouse and the teachers' quarters are well lit and represent sites where individual sexual desires and feelings of loneliness amid the isolation of the highlands have to be negotiated and, in the end, put aside for the construction of the national citizenry. On the other hand, the "wilderness" of the highlands, as epitomized by the forest, is where individual sexual fantasies can be fulfilled. Each evening, Giao leaves the quarters she shares with her colleague Minh and secretly goes into the forest to sleep with Hung, a Viet geologist. This premarital relationship is possible within the hidden space of the forest, and because it is an affair between two Viet characters, it does not destabilize the national body's ethnic integrity. However, even in the highlands, Viet gendered norms reassert themselves. Due to its premarital and thus officially unsanctioned status, the relationship cannot last. Of the four ethnic Viet characters – Giao, Minh, Tanh, the male school principal, and Hung, Giao's heterosexual lover – Minh knowingly turns a blind eye when her colleague leaves their quarters. But it is the principal who discovers the relationship and compels Hung to abandon Giao for fear that someone will find out. The forest that had offered the lovers a playground removed from the watchful eyes of others becomes sinister and, in the end, Giao is punished for her premarital transgressions. Shortly after Tanh, who is in love with Giao, discovers her affair, her lover Hung abandons her. In her desperate search for him, she gets lost and suffers a severe fall. Nursed back to health with the aid of Hmong herbal medicine, Giao reunites with her students and with Minh, both of the teachers having set aside their personal concerns for love and marriage. The movie ends with the camera tracking back from medium close-up shots of the Viet and Hmong characters, overjoyed in their reunion, to an encompassing long shot of the whole procession coming back to the school. This return to the space of the school symbolizes a multicultural commitment to progress and an acceptance of the authority of the state in achieving that goal. The school grounds represent the space for the implementation of state authority, a space in which the different ethnic groups will eventually overcome their individual desires to redouble their efforts to build a more equitable society along the lines of Viet norms.

However, the symbols that represent the state are devoid of any real authority or usefulness. The schoolhouse stands more as a reminder of the presence of the state in the locality rather than a serious effort to carry out official mandates. The building is isolated from both the local community and the state educational system. The slow panoramic shots of the mountains and valleys paint the surroundings as a desolate land disconnected from

82 *Chuong-Dai Hong Vo*

networks of transportation and communication with the metropolis. The work of teaching and maintaining the school is a tiresome and thankless duty to the state. The one character steadily committed to the state's mission is Tanh. He is well intentioned but clownish and incompetent; he cannot teach and he cannot manage the school without the teachers. He bribes the children to stay with sugar, an action that further points to his ineptness. The film's characterization of the state's top leader as buffoonish offers a subtle criticism of the policy of having former army officers hold government positions for which they are unqualified. One may note that of the Viet characters, he alone speaks with a central regional accent while the teachers speak in the Hanoi accent, the officially sanctioned norm for the educational system. Although the actress's Southern accent was dubbed over, the voice of the actor playing the principal was not. Speaking in an accent from Quang Tri, this character alludes to the central provinces, a place historically known for its anti-colonial rebellions and the birthplace of many future Communist government leaders.[7]

Initially distributed for domestic consumption, *Thung Lung* was also shown internationally at film festivals and as part of programs officially sanctioned by the Vietnamese government. Therefore one has to consider how it represents ethnicity in terms of what it means to be subjects of a nation and Vietnamese identity on the global stage. As a domestic product, *Thung Lung* offers audiences a critique of state leadership as incompetent and state mandates as devoid of meaning even as the film reproduces racialized categories of ethnicities. On the international stage, the film presents an image of an inclusive, multicultural society governed by a well-intentioned government, one struggling but yet committed to moving even the most marginalized populations of the nation toward modernity. I propose that the project of presenting a modern Vietnamese nation to an international community with which Vietnam can further develop economic and political ties requires that it adopt certain discourses of inclusiveness and good governance. Multiculturalism serves that purpose while at the same time presenting a nation whose ethnic make-up adds to the exotic attractiveness of the country.

Conclusion

Vietnamese cinema in the *Doi Moi* period offers important alternatives to narratives of revolutionary valor in its representations of Vietnam as a modern nation. These films were created in the context of the failure of agricultural and industrial collectivization, the fall of most Communist Bloc countries, and the state's embracing of market liberalization marked most prominently by the renewal of trade and diplomatic ties with countries where Vietnamese diasporic communities have settled after the mass exodus of 1975 following the end of the Vietnam/US war. In creating works that challenge the linearity of economic liberalization, give voice to the marginalized, showcase unsanctioned sexualities and question the authority of official channels of truth, these films subtly critique the leadership of the Vietnamese Communist Party and the validity of the state. However, directors are also aware of the history of state crackdowns on cultural productions that pursue a system-wide interrogation of the Party and the state. Furthermore, directors such as Dang Nhat Minh are very much figures of authority within the state apparatus. Such interconnections show that Vietnamese cinema in the *Doi Moi* era does not necessarily offer radical critiques of the state. Instead, these films – as well as others that will follow in the future – point to possibilities for further investigations into how regimes of power operate and how cultural producers use their discourses of truth.

Notes

1 Having officially acknowledged the failures of collectivization, the Communist Party embraced economic liberalization in 1986. Known as *Doi Moi*, this policy led to the relaxation of state management of the social sphere and opened Vietnam to foreign investment and the rebuilding of relations with other countries, including former enemies. This policy is analogous to *Glasnost* and *Perestroika* in the former Soviet Union.
2 The Vietnam Film Archives publication was written before the official policy *Doi Moi*. If one follows this periodization, the *Doi Moi* era would be the fourth period.
3 Before the 1980s and even today in rural areas, most people saw films at mobile outdoor theaters, which traveled from town and town and were tended by staff from the state cinema industry.
4 *Em Be Ha Noi* can be compared, in some ways, to *Hiroshima Mon Amour* (1959) in their use of the bird's-eye view of the results of air raids, and their focus on how survivors coped in the aftermath.
5 Vietnamese names are spelled in the following order: surname, middle name and first name. Following Vietnamese convention, I will refer to people by their given name after the first full mention.
6 I would like to thank my teacher Le Dinh Tu, Dean of the Vietnam Studies Department at the Ha Noi University of Foreign Studies, for explaining the socio-economic context for this government policy in contemporary times. Our conversation on this topic took place on 4 August 2005.
7 Conversation with Le Dinh Tu on 4 August 2005. For a recent historical account on the backgrounds of founding members of the communist movement, see Duiker (2000).

Bibliography

Clifford, J. (1988) *The Predicament of Culture: Twentieth-century ethnography, literature and art*, Cambridge: Harvard University Press.
Dang, M.N. (1987) *Co Gai Tren Song* [The Girl on the Perfume River], Vietnam: Vietnam Feature Film Enterprise.
—— (1995) *Thuong Nho Dong Que* [Nostalgia for the Countryside], Vietnam: My Van Films.
Duiker, W.J. (2000) *Ho Chi Minh: A biography*, New York: Hyperion.

84 *Chuong-Dai Hong Vo*

Heng, R.H.K. (1999) "Of the state, for the state, yet against the state: The struggle paradigm in Vietnam's media politics", unpublished PhD thesis, Canberra: Australian National University.

Luong, H.V. (ed.) (2003) *Postwar Vietnam: Dynamics of a transforming society*, Singapore and New York: Institute of Southeast Asian Studies and Rowman and Littlefield.

Le, H. (2003) *Gai Nhay* [Bar Girls], Vietnam: Tam Giac Vang Productions.

—— (2004) *Lo Lem He Pho* [Street Cinderella], Vietnam: Thien Ngan Galaxy.

—— (2005) *Nu Tuong Cuop* [Women Robbers], Vietnam: Thien Ngan Galaxy.

Ngo, L.P. (1998) "The changing face of Vietnamese cinema during ten years of renovation 1986–96," in D. Marr (ed.) *The Mass Media in Vietnam, 91–96*, Canberra: The Australian National University.

Nguyen, L.K. (1988) *Tuong Ve Huu* [The General Retires], Vietnam.

Nguyen, T.X. (1992) *The Press and Media in Vietnam*, trans. K. Pilz, ed. G. Will, Cologne: The Federal Institute for Eastern and International Studies.

Ninh, H. (1975) *Em Be Ha Noi* [The Little Girl of Hanoi], Vietnam.

Ninh, K. (2005) *A World Transformed: The politics of culture in revolutionary Vietnam, 1945–1965*, Ann Arbor: University of Michigan Press.

Pelley, P.M. (2002) *Postcolonial Vietnam: New histories of the national past*, Durham: Duke University Press.

Pham, G.N. (2000) *Thung Lung Hoang Van* [The Deserted Valley], Vietnam: Dong Do Phim.

Sen, H. (1979) *Canh Dong Hoang* [The Wild Field], Vietnam: Ho Chi Minh City General Film Studio.

Tran, D. (2000) *Doi Moi: Niem Vui Chua Trong*, Westminster, CA: Van Nghe.

Trinh, D.M., Trung, S., Le, Q. and Ngo, L.M. (1983) *30 Years of Vietnam's Cinema Art*, Hanoi: The Vietnam Film Archives.

Viet, L. (1989) *Ganh Xiec Rong* [An Itinerant Circus], Vietnam.

Vu, D.N. (2004) *Nhung Co Gai Chan Dai* [Long Legged Girls], Vietnam: Thien Ngan Galaxy.

Vu, T. (1976) *Chung Ta Se Gap Lai* [We Shall Meet Again], Vietnam.

6 "Not a rice-eating robot"

Freedom to speak in Burma[1]

Nancy Hudson-Rodd

The relentless attempts of totalitarian regimes to prevent free thought and new ideas and the persistent assertion of their own rightness bring on them an intellectual stasis which they project on to the nation at large. Intimidation and propaganda work in a duet of oppression, while the people, lapped in fear and distrust, learn to dissemble and to keep silent. And all the time the desire grows for a system which will lift them from the position of "rice-eating robots" to the status of human beings who can think and speak freely and hold their heads high in the security of their rights.

(Aung San Suu Kyi 1995: 175)

Taking my cue from Burma's most celebrated dissident, I explore in this chapter the complex ways in which the various military regimes have restricted freedom of expression and the efforts of the citizens to circumvent these restrictions. Burmese authors, scholars, musicians, actors, poets, comedians, activists and filmmakers keep words, images and ideas alive in face of oppressive rule. I pursue how spaces of free expression are created in Burma through acts of human endurance, tenacity and wit to crack the blanket of fear and intolerance perpetuated by the repressive military rulers.

There are strong reasons to believe that freedom of expression makes possible other rights to be fully realized (Lansner 2005: 250). An open and independent media can promote not just democracy and human rights but also economic development in whose name freedom of the press is often sacrificed. The lack of media freedoms facilitates corruption which increases the burden of poverty and prevents individuals from making any informed decisions. Amartya Sen (1999: 15–17) argues that development consists of the removing of a variety of "un-freedoms" that leave people with restricted options to explore and create their lives. In this chapter I show specifically how restrictions on the media reinforce the corruptions in the process of Burma's developmental policy-making. As such, the denial of freedom of expression is central not just to the regime's continued power but also to the lack of economic development in Burma.

Except for a brief post-independence period of parliamentary democracy (1948–62), the army has controlled state power through the Revolutionary

Council (1962–74), the one-party Socialist Republic of the Union of Burma (1974–88), the Burma Socialist Program Party (BSPP) and the State Law and Order Restoration Council (SLORC), reorganized in 1997 as the State Peace and Development Council (Seekins 2002: xiv–xv). For over forty years, civil, political, social or economic rights have not existed. The State Peace and Development Council (SPDC), maintains a tight grip on cultural, social, religious and economic affairs. Culture, religion and nationalism are exploited by the Tatmadaw (Burmese military) which sees itself as the central institution of the state dedicated to safeguarding the unity and integrity of the nation through dedication to the three national causes: non-disintegration of the union; non-disintegration of national solidarity; and perpetuation of national solidarity (Hudson-Rodd and Myo Nyunt 2004: 500). The media borders are policed to make it difficult even to observe Burma from the outside, and indeed dangerous for the Burmese to look out beyond their borders.

Burma is recognized as an "international pariah," a result of the military junta's human rights abuses and in particular their refusal to recognize the overwhelming victory of the National League for Democracy (NLD) in the 1990 elections (Rothenberg 2004: 10). Amnesty International (2005a: 1–3) reports continued harassment, arrests and imprisonment of members of political parties including Daw Aung Suu Kyi, General Secretary, and U Tin Oo, Vice Chairman, of the NLD held without trial. Individual men and women continue to be imprisoned for the sole reason of exercising their rights to freedom of expression, association and assembly with at least 1,100 people held as political prisoners, including elected members of parliament (Security Council 2005: 1).

The military regime has made ethnic minorities a special focus of violence and human rights abuses including torture, food and land confiscation, beatings, killings, forced labor, forced relocations and rape (Amnesty International 2005b; Hudson-Rodd *et al.* 2004; Karen Women's Organization 2004). Human rights abuses and the scale of atrocities committed in ethnic minority areas are the most important cause of conflict-induced internal displacement, which is unparalleled in Asia. Over 540,000 people are internally displaced in the eastern states of Burma alone, while human rights violations have displaced unknown numbers of civilians in other parts of Burma (Internal Displacement Monitoring Centre 2006). As a result of human rights abuses, more than two million Burmese have fled to neighboring countries, in particular Thailand, as displaced persons and irregular migrants, many of whom are undocumented as refugees (Human Rights Watch 2006: 232).

Censorship rules

The freedom of a society can be determined by the freedom of the press and the media. In Burma, severe restrictions on freedom of expression have long been justified on the grounds of maintaining stability of the country. Military regimes in power since 1962 have introduced and enforced a wide range of Acts and laws designed to maintain state control and prevent freedom of individual expression. With no independent judiciary and no meaningful rule of law, laws are applied selectively and arbitrarily by the military regime. The state rules by decree, not bound by any constitutional rights for fair public trials or any other human rights. "The only law in Burma is what the generals from day to day decide it to be" (Gutter and Sen 2001: 14). Any expression considered critical of the regime, state ideology or work of government departments is forbidden. Journalists, poets, writers, lawyers, teachers, filmmakers, cartoonists and editors are among the 1,100 people currently imprisoned for their expressed ideas (United Nations General Assembly (UNGA) 2005: 12). The possession of "books, magazines, cassettes or videotapes deemed hostile to the ruling junta is a criminal activity" (Vajpeyi 2004: 8), as is the distribution or possession of any material perceived to question the regime. In this section, I summarize the key laws and regulations, which criminalize freedom of thought, dissemination of information and freedom of expression.

The government's Official Secrets Act legislated by the British (in 1923) continues to be called upon to charge and imprison people who commit anything deemed harmful to the state. In 1994, Dr Khin Zaw Win, a dentist, was charged and sentenced for attempting to smuggle out "state secrets." Prior to his arrest, Khin had links with the National League for Democracy (NLD), worked for UNICEF (1991–3) in Rangoon, and received a scholarship from the government of Singapore to study for a Master's degree in public policy at the National University of Singapore. He returned to Rangoon in 1994 to conduct academic research for his thesis on the political situation in Burma and was arrested on 4 July 1994 while boarding a flight back to Singapore. Dr Khin was charged with "spreading or intending to spread false information in the knowledge that it was false" and "possessing or consulting state secrets." He was sentenced in a closed trial with no legal council to fifteen years in prison. While in prison, he was accused of sending "false" information concerning prison conditions to the United Nations special rapporteur on Myanmar. As punishment he was held for many months in a tiny cell built for military dogs and denied family visits. In 1997, he was transferred to a prison outside Rangoon, where he remained until his release on 8 July 2005, after serving ten years of his fifteen-year sentence (National Academy of Sciences 2005).

The Printers and Publishers Registration Act, promulgated in 1962 as the main instrument of the Burma Socialist Program Party control of the media, remains, with certain refinements. The Press Scrutiny Board, a thirty-member body established under this law, now called the Literary Works Scrutinizing Committee, determines whether particular texts are against government interests. Every aspect of the written word, including book covers, articles, song lyrics, film and video scripts needs permission prior to

88   *Nancy Hudson-Rodd*

publication. Publishers are required to submit manuscripts to the Committee after they are printed but before distribution. If the Committee orders deletions or changes, the publisher has to reprint and or rebind the book, at great cost. If the work is banned, the publisher must pulp all copies printed. The Scrutinizing Committee not only governs the text, language and subject of all books and other publications, but also determines the print runs of each publication.

A set of broad guidelines issued in 1975 set out the material not tolerated which included: "Any incorrect ideas and opinions which do not accord with the times and any descriptions which, though factually correct, are unsuitable because of the time or circumstances of their writing" (Iyer 1999: 9). A State Law and Order Restoration Council (SLORC) Law No. 16/89 amending the 1962 Printers and Publishers Registration Law enacted in 1989 allows the government to remove offending words – a list which can include: Aung San Suu Kyi, education, corruption, AIDS, Nelson Mandela and democracy (Burma Lawyers' Council 2003). Violation of this law can lead to up to seven years' imprisonment (Human Rights Documentation Unit 2001: 464). Well-know Burmese writer Ko Than Win Hlaing, editor of two journals (*Myanma Zay Gwet See Pwar Yay* and *Mya Yeik Nyo*) and author of five books published in Rangoon, fell foul of this regulation when he submitted for censor approval (2000) the second edition of his book *Historical Burmese Persons Talk Through Statues.*[2] He was arrested on 2 August 2000 and was sentenced to seven years in prison under Section 17/20 of the Act. His second edition included two new pages, which noted Aung San, independence leader, as the father of Daw Aung Suu Kyi (Assistance Association for Political Prisoners (Burma) 2006). In December 2005, the International Committee of the Red Cross (ICRC) visited Thrawaddy Prison, where Ko Than Win Hlaing is held, but were not allowed to see prisoners. Moe Moe Kyi, the wife of Ko Than Win Hlaing, states that her husband has been denied the right to read in prison (Aung Min 2006; Democratic Voice of Burma 2006).

The Television and Video Law (The State Law and Order Restoration Council Law No. 8/96) issued on 29 July 1996 further restricts freedom of expression. Under this law, a license must be purchased for possession of a television set or a videocassette recorder (Myanmar Law 1996: 4). Even foreign diplomatic missions and the United Nations agencies are required to submit all imported videos to the censor board (Myanmar Law 1996: 37). Government video censorship boards scrutinize all videotapes, local, imported and made for export, and have the power to ban, destroy, censor and restrict showing of such videos. Individuals are charged a fee to have the video inspected. The Act makes it compulsory for every video exhibited to include the censorship certificate and for that certificate to be shown at every screening (Myanmar Law 1996: 25). The Censorship Board is empowered to re-inspect any videotape previously certified and to revoke the certificate. Violators of these provisions are subject to up to three years

Freedom to speak in Burma 89

in prison and/or a fine of up to 100,000 kyat (Myanmar Law 1996: 32). Any person owning undeclared video equipment involved in the production, consumption, duplication or distribution of videos not passed by the Board is liable to a prison sentence (Human Rights Documentation Unit 2001: 463).

As Iyer explains, the law aims to promote "the emergence of video tapes which will contribute towards national solidarity and dynamism of patriotic spirit; prohibit and ban decadent video tapes which will undermine Myanmar culture and Myanmar tradition" (Iyer 1999: 15–17). In carrying out their mandate, the Ministry of Information (2004: 192) boasts that "Video Censor and Video Services have been undertaken with momentum" by listing the increasing number of local and imported videotapes released, scrutinized and banned each year. Used extensively to restrict flow of information, U Kyaw Khin, Dr Hlaing Myint and Maung Maung Wan were each sentenced (1996) to three years in prison for obtaining unauthorized recorded videotapes which reportedly contained "anti-government messages" broadcast by foreign television stations (Iyer 1999: 17).

One of the most far-reaching pieces of legislation limiting freedom of expression is the Computer Science Development Law issued on 27 September 1996. This law made the unauthorized importation, possession or use of computers with networking capacities, modems or any other means of transmitting information electronically punishable with between seven and fifteen years in prison and/or a fine. The law requires anyone who owns or uses a computer to obtain a license from the Ministry of Communications, Post and Telegraphs. The Myanmar Computer Science Council was established to decide which computer equipment was to be banned or restricted. People caught using computers without a license or with networking capabilities, which may undermine state security, law and order, national unity, national culture, or state secrets relevant to state security, face up to fifteen years in prison and/or fines. Anyone who imports or exports computer software or information banned by the Council can be imprisoned for a term of five to ten years (Human Rights Documentation Unit 2000: 234–5).

Special public order laws are widely used to restrict freedom of expression, silence any dissent and curtail any opposition movement. Under the Emergency Provision Act (1950), a person can be sentenced to up to seven years in prison for infringing "upon the health, integrity, conduct and respect of State military organizations and government employees, or spreading false news about the government" (Gutter and Sen 2001: 6–8). A more daunting sentence of life imprisonment or death is given for those who intend to cause sabotage or hinder "the successful functioning of the State military organization and criminal investigative organizations" (Human Rights Documentation Unit 2000: 232). This Act has been most frequently used to imprison poets, artists, writers and members of political parties who speak out on various political and social issues. Comedians U Par Lay and U Lu Zaw were sentenced to seven years' hard labor (1996) for spreading "false news," allegedly making a joke about the military, during a

90 Nancy Hudson-Rodd

public performance. They were forced to work breaking stone, with iron bars shackled between their legs (Human Rights Documentation Unit 1997: 272–3). Released in 2000, the men were banned from putting on costume or makeup and performing or traveling, effectively curtailing their livelihood (Hudson-Rodd 2001: 9). Chit Swe, a sixty-five-year-old political cartoonist whose work regularly appears in *Myanma Dhana*, was arrested and found guilty of defying the state in July 2005, but was released after one month of detention in Insein Prison, Rangoon (Cartoonists Rights Network 2005: Reporters Sans Frontières 2005).

The State Law and Order Restoration Council (SLORC) Law Amending the Law Safeguarding the State from the Danger of Subversive Elements was enacted (on 9 August 1991) by Saw Maung, Senior General and Chairman of the State Law and Order Restoration Council, to prevent Aung San Suu Kyi's request of appeal against her house arrest. Passed under martial law, this amendment allows the authorities to detain an "offender" without charge or trial for three years (Smith 1991:87). Although Saw Maung, an eccentric junta chief, "retired" in 1992, the law remains fully intact. In fact, detention time has since been lengthened from three to six years. Any right of appeal and review of sentence was eliminated (Aung Naing Oo 2003: 70). The accused are either sent to prison (under Section 10A) or house detained (under Section 10B). U Win Htein and Maung San Hlaing, sentenced to fourteen and seven years' prison respectively in August 1996, were accused of giving information to foreign journalists about the torture of political prisoners and denied legal representation at their closed trial (Iyer 1999: 12). Aung San Suu Kyi's house detention of May 2003 was extended another six months in November 2005. Under this law, she can be held effectively – without judicial appeal, without charges and without trial – up to May 2009.

The Law Protecting the Peaceful and Systematic Transfer of State Responsibility and the Successful Performance of the Functions of the National Convention Against Disturbance and Opposition enacted 6 June 1996 imposes prison sentences of up to twenty years and confiscation of property and funds for anyone who express their political views publicly. This law prohibits the preparation or dissemination of speeches or statements deemed to undermine or be critical of the military (Human Rights Documentation Unit 1998: 109). The military junta, refusing to permit the 485-member legislative assembly to convene in 1990, formed a National Convention to draft a new Constitution. Sporadically meeting since 1993, without the participation of the NLD and other pro-democracy political groups (The Economist 2004: 10), it last convened in 2005 without completing a Constitution. Before the May 2004 National Convention, the military junta increased suppression and sentenced two journalists to long prison terms. Ne Min, a lawyer and former reporter who worked for the BBC in the 1980s, was sentenced to fifteen years in prison on 7 May 2004 by a closed military tribunal in Insein Prison. He was charged with

Freedom to speak in Burma 91

"spreading false rumors" and for giving information to foreign-based media outlets outside Burma. On the same day Ne Min was sentenced, Nyan Htun Linn, a student activist and former office manager of a Thai-based news website, was sentenced to twenty-two years for distributing a statement criticizing the procedures of the upcoming convention (Human Rights Documentation Unit 2005: 460).

Suppression of those who read or watch anything that criticizes the authority of the military junta continues unabated despite attempts to formalize legal structures. Dr Win Aung, a township NLD leader, and Khin Maung Win, an NLD supporter, were sentenced to ten years in prison while Soe Win Aung, a high school teacher, received a three-year prison sentence. The three men were charged with possessing and consuming "unauthorized" information critical of the regime which included *Who Killed Aung San* (1993), a book by exiled Burmese author Kin Oung, and a video of Aung San Suu Kyi's 2003 tour of northern Burma (*Mizzima News* 2005; International Freedom of Expression eXchange 2005).

Communication and access to independent sources of information is further restricted as phones are limited and Burma is one of only four countries in the world that does not allow open public access to the internet (Reporters Sans Frontières 2003: 24). The few internet cafés available ban web-based emails such as Yahoo or Hotmail and access to opposition sites is blocked with technology supplied by Fortinet, a US firm. This heavy censorship extends to the recording of all internet computers every five minutes the screen is consulted (Reporters Sans Frontières 2006a). There are only seven telephone mainlines per 1,000 people (United Nations Development Program 2005: 264), and switching systems for Burma's landlines are so inadequate that local calls are impossible to complete. While mobile phones are available, they can cost up to US$4000 on the black market (*The Irrawaddy* 2006: 9).[3] It is worth noting, though, that plans are in place for new mobile phone networks that may eventually lower the exorbitant cost and shorten the current waiting list of a year. Burma's currency, the kyat, fell to an all-time low of US$1:1300 kyat in 2005, forcing up prices of daily commodities such as cooking oil, fuel and food.

State-controlled media

The military regime restricts citizens' access to independent information but imposes and reproduces their version of Burma on billboards, newspapers, radio and television broadcasts, and publications. The state:

> Informs, educates and entertains the public through print and media in conformity with the State policies and objectives, which are: a) to keep the public informed; and b) to educate and mobilize the public through mass communications.
>
> (Ministry of Information 2004: 180)

92 Nancy Hudson-Rodd

A twenty-four-member Committee for Writing Slogans for Nationals, formed in 1989, designed government slogans appearing on billboards. "Respect the law," "Only when the army is strong, the country will be strong," "The opposite of democracy is anarchy" and "People's desire" in Burmese and English languages are the most commonly seen roadside billboard slogans.

"People's desire" first appeared on a large billboard directly opposite the American Embassy in Rangoon, a junta response to US support for protestors during the widespread democracy demonstrations in 1988. In a special press conference held on 9 September 1989, and published as *The Protection Given by State Law and Order Restoration Council (Tatmadaw) for the People's Lives and Property and the Activities of Destructive Elements* (Ministry of Information 1989), the regime leveled accusations at "party organizations, rightist forces, some diplomats, some foreign broadcasting stations, some foreign publications and anti-government forces outside the country who were carrying out both underground and above-ground activities [for] using students and simple honest people" to fulfill their political agendas (State Law and Order Restoration Council Secretary (1) Brig-Gen Khin Nyunt, Ministry of Information 1989: 1).

"People's desire" also features prominently in the state newspaper, the *New Light of Myanmar* (henceforth NLM). The State Peace and Development Council in 1997 "laid down 12 political, economic, and social objectives" in order to make "a peaceful, modern and developed nation" (Ministry of Information 2005: 6). The first or second page of each book and magazine which manages to get past the censors must include the following four regime slogans:

Our three main national causes:

- Non-disintegration of the union: Our cause.
- Non-disintegration of the national solidarity: Our cause.
- Consolidation of national sovereignty: Our cause.

People's desire:

- Oppose those relying on external elements, acting as stooges, holding negative views.
- Oppose those trying to jeopardize stability of the state and progress of the nation.
- Oppose foreign nations interfering in internal affairs of the state.
- Crush all internal and external destructive elements as the common enemy.

Four political objectives:

- Stability of the state, community peace and tranquility, prevalence of law and order.

- National reconsolidation.
- Emergence of a new enduring state Constitution.
- Building of a new modern developed nation in accord with the new state Constitution.

Four economic objectives

- Development of agriculture as the base and all-round development of other sectors of the economy as well.
- Proper evolution of the market-oriented economic system.
- Development of the economy inviting participation terms of technical know-how and investments from sources inside the country and abroad.
- The initiative to shape the national economy must be kept in the hands of the state and the national peoples.

Four social objectives

- Uplift of the morale and morality of the entire nation.
- Uplift of national prestige and integrity and preservation and safe-guarding of cultural heritage and national character.
- Uplift of dynamism of patriotic spirit.
- Uplift of health, fitness and education standards of the entire nation.

Great development and progress of the nation is proclaimed in the state-owned daily newspaper *New Light of Myanmar* (English and Burmese) and on state-owned Myanmar Radio and Television (MRTV). The newspaper and the television show Tatmadaw (military) men in green uniforms travel-ing to all parts of Burma opening dams, hospitals, stretches of roads and bridges, and unveiling signboards. Generals are reported and shown in the media "instructing" Burmese men and women how to conduct their professional and spiritual lives. The following instances are cases in point:

> Engineers: Minister for Construction, Major-General Saw Tun inspected Ayeyawady Bridge project. The minister gave instructions on timely completion of the bridge, work site safety and thrifty use of construction materials. The minister also inspected the installation of iron beams at the bridge.
>
> (*NLM*, 7 December 2005: 2)

> Hydrologists: Chairman of Yangon Division Peace and Development Council Commander of Yangon Command Lt-Gen. Myint Swe and Yangon Mayor Brig-Gen. Aung Thein Lin inspected Yangon City Water Supply Project and left instructions.
>
> (*NLM*, 12 December 2005: 11)

> Bankers: Maj-Gen. Hla Tun, Minister for Finance and Revenue inspected banking services of Myanma Economic Bank and gave

instructions on smooth dealing with people. The Minister told service personnel to try to possess qualifications in discharging the duties of the State.

(*NLM*, 14 December 2005: 7)

Farmers: Lt-General Kyaw Win, member of the SPDC, oversaw running of the harvester and power-tiller and instructed farmers to extend growing of phisic nut plantations in Shan State.

(*NLM*, 11 December 2005: 16)

Academics: Senior General Than Shwe gave "guidance to faculty members of universities and colleges to produce qualitative and quantitative educated human resources who can serve the interest of the nation" at the opening of the Government Technological College in Myitkyina.

(*NLM*, 16 December 2005: 8)

Burmese people are forced to sit impassively and attentively in front of the generals who instruct. The people in the audience betray no emotion. Their bodies are held stiff. There is no sign of recognition. No questions are asked. No offhand remarks to a neighbor are made. And all notwithstanding the fact that these generals are relatively uneducated, with little knowledge of the areas in which they "instruct."

The military leaders claim "equitable development in rural and urban areas, improvement of communications and transportation, health, education and the economy" (Ministry of Information 2004: 6). The Ministry of Information published *Magnificent Myanmar (1988–2003)* in 2004 to "vividly chronicle the genuine situation of Myanmar" and to display the "magnitude of what the Tatmadaw Government has done in the fifteen year period" (2004: 6). Again in 2005, the Ministry of Information published an update of the Tatmadaw government's "achievements," including newly established publishing houses in Mandalay, Myitkyina, Lashio, Magway, Kale, Taunggyi, Kengtung, Sittway, Myeik and the opening up of 162 new television retransmission stations (Ministry of Information 2005: 372). That year, a further 373 new Information and Public Relations Department libraries and offices were established to ensure people living outside the capital received the military's words.

Needless to say, despite the increasing volume and geographic spread of state media boasting "equitable development," the people of Burma live in a different reality than the one portrayed in state newspapers, journals, radio and television. Few watch the state television or read the newspaper because it is so stultifying and unchanging day after day, and pointing out such popular disdain of state propaganda constitutes an offence in itself. When Brigadier General Zaw Tun (then Deputy Minister of Ministry of National Planning and Development) stated at a seminar (2000) that Senior General

Freedom to speak in Burma 95

Than Shwe, supreme military junta leader, was the only person in Burma who watches Myanmar television, he was fired shortly after (Tin Maung Than 2000: 89).

According to state propaganda,

Incredible success gained within a span of 15 or 16 years can be witnessed in aspects such as national stability, rule of law, education, health, economy, social advancement and culture. Feeling disgruntled at such achievements, the aboveground and underground destructive elements inside and outside the country, the colonialists and their sub-ordinates turned a blind eye to them and aired fabricated news out of shame and disgrace in collaboration with some foreign news agencies.

(Kyaw Win 2004)

A gulf exists between such official proclamations in the media and the lived realities of Burma's citizens. Exposing the social and economic conditions of life in Burma is difficult, almost impossible. Aung Pwint, a documentary filmmaker, editor and poet, was prohibited from making videos in 1996. Nyein Thit and Aung Pwint were arrested in 1999, charged with "sending news" to banned Burmese newspapers using an illegal fax machine. These two documentary filmmakers, still in prison, received the 2004 International Press Freedom Award for their dedication to exposing social and political reality of life, documenting forced labor and daily life in ruled areas of Burma, in spite of military harassment (Human Rights Documentation Unit 2005: 460).

Even reporting natural events, such as floods, is off limits. Unusually heavy rains broke the walls of a dam in central Burma in June 2001, flooding 200 villages, resulting in the death of about 1,000 people, some killed by bites of poisonous snakes that had been swept along in the water. Burmese journalists avoided reporting this event, except for one man who thought of a clever way of reporting the event to bypass censorship. He documented relief efforts of Burmese people, full of Buddhist devotion, who helped each other during this crisis. The sixteen-page photo essay was censored with no explanations given and the editor published the magazine short of those sixteen pages (Neuman 2002: 7). Lazing La Htoi, a documentary filmmaker, used his video camera to record the floods in northern Kachin State which had killed several people and damaged much property. Then he made 300 copies on compact video disc for distribution before local authorities arrested him. The Cyber Computer Centre he operated was closed down and he was ordered to recall all 300 copies. Through it all, the state newspaper did not report any flooding (Committee to Protect Journalists, 6 August 2004).

The junta moved the administrative capital from Rangoon to Pyinmana in November 2005. Civil servants were told to move at short notice despite the unfinished site. U Thaung Sein, a photojournalist, and Ko Moe Htun, a

96 *Nancy Hudson-Rodd*

journalist, were arrested and sentenced to three years in prison on 23 March 2006 for taking pictures and filming the streets of Pyinmana, the new capital of Burma. This was the first time a citizen had been given the maximum three-year sentence under the Television and Video Act promulgated in July 1996 (Reporters Sans Frontières 2006b).

International media in Burma

Media are responsible to collect the news of global reach and broadcast it as it is. When listening to news about Myanmar aired by some foreign agencies such as the British Broadcast Corporation (BBC), Radio Free Asia (RFA) and the Voice of America (VOA), it can be found that they are constantly spreading rumors about Myanmar. The invented news reports are intentionally designed to deceive the rest of the world, and Myanmar nationals living in foreign countries for various reasons (Kyaw Win 2004). As mentioned earlier, while the military regime boasts expansion of its media networks, the majority of the Burmese people do not read the military state newspapers or watch state television. People listen on their tiny transistor radios to international radio for independent news of Burma and the world. Indeed, there are some Burmese writers and professionals who dare to speak on the BBC, RFA, VOA and the Democratic Voice of Burma (DVB) radio. For Burmese citizens, even the act of reporting overseas what is stated in the *New Light of Myanmar*, the state-owned newspaper, is dangerous. Educated professionals in Burma risk their freedom for passing on the "news" in state newspapers with no commentary. As Major Aye Htun, Head of the Press Scrutiny Board (quoted in *The Irrawaddy* 2004: 3), has warned a group of writers in Rangoon:

> We know who is talking and giving interviews to Radio Free Asia and Democratic Voice of Burma. We can put any of you in prison anytime. It is illegal to talk to these radio stations. We don't recognise them as legal and they are formed by people who want to attack the government.

Military officials search continually for "informants" or people who give information to foreigners and speak on international Burmese language radio. Defense services intelligence men are trained to identify Burmese who give information to foreign media. Military security force men are taught how to identify foreign press sources. The Ministry of Information trains civil servants and warns civilians on how to identify such "informants." In addition, Burmese journalists and correspondents for foreign media are regularly summoned to respond to negative international media comments on the military junta and to give details of their Burmese contacts. People can be arrested simply on suspicion of receiving international phone calls. Journalists in exile confirm that the people with whom they speak would often have their telephone lines cut without warning. Two new mobile-phone tapping centers were established and the Military Security Force arrested two people in Moulmein for receiving "suspicious" international calls on their mobile phones (Reporters Sans Frontières 2006c: 3). Few foreign journalists are issued visas to enter Burma. Those who want to enter Burma are advised to follow the one cardinal rule: "Don't be too sympathetic with the democratic opposition or with Nobel Peace Laureate Aung San Suu Kyi" (Aung Zaw 2001: 1).

Economic consequences

Economic planning proceeds in Burma without public input, reliable economic data or official accountability. Without freedom of academic research and the ability to disseminate research findings, there can be no public debate informed by independent sources. The *Review of the Financial, Economic and Social Conditions* published under different names by the Ministry of Planning and Finance since military rule in 1962 was publicly available until 1998. This had been the main source of annual data on the Burmese economy as projected by the government itself. Since 1988, the public have been denied access to even this document. While the accuracy of data in such publications could never be fully ascertained, the publication did provide a record for comparison and evaluation by researchers.

The regime also ceased publishing annual budget estimates in 2001/2. The Central Statistical Organization (CSO) releases erratically the *Selected Monthly Economic Indicators*. The CSO claimed to have completed a *Household Income and Expenditure Survey 2000*, but the report was never released. The regime restricts access to official documents and reports conducted by international organizations. In-country researchers are not able to use information from publications available to those outside Burma. For example, the International Monetary Fund (IMF) makes regular reports on Burma, but the regime denies release of these reports within Burma. As one economist in Burma points out most cogently, "the overriding political desire to use statistics to present the country in a favourable light has compromised objectivity and credibility" (Maung Myint 2004).

In Burma, food scarcity in urban and rural areas has been shown to result from the militarization of the nation, and its accompanying lack of freedom of expression. Poverty, malnutrition and food insecurity are more acute and widespread in the non-Burman ethnic minority-populated border areas, a settlement that resulted from a forced dislocation of farmers (Asian Human Rights Commission 1999). Children are most affected, with 9 percent of those under five suffering from moderate to severe wasting, 32 percent suffering moderate and severe stunting, 7 percent are underweight, and 32 percent are moderately underweight (UNICEF 2005). Burma has one of the highest rates of infant and maternal mortality in Asia. Infant mortality rates as high as 200–300 per 1,000 live births have been estimated in the war-torn Karen and Shan states. Maternal mortality rates (between 230 and

98   *Nancy Hudson-Rodd*

580 per 100,000 live births) are among the highest in Asia. Over half of maternal deaths result from illicit abortions, attributed to women lacking access to information regarding appropriate health care (Hudson-Rodd and Myo Nyunt 2004: 126).

Increasing problems of HIV/AIDS and narcotics abuse in Burma attract international attention, but there is a dearth of accurate field research and data. Health needs of Burma cannot be addressed in face of denial of access to information, no freedom of academic research and no ability to disseminate research findings (Article 19 1996: 1). Secrecy and censorship severely impact the health of people of Burma and the work of international humanitarian agencies. The Global Fund awarded grants of US$98.4 million to combat HIV/AIDS, tuberculosis (60 to 80 percent of AIDS patients also suffer from tuberculosis) and malaria (the leading cause of mortality and the biggest cause of death of children under the age of five) in Burma over a five-year period. The Global Fund (2005: 1–2) withdrew its funding and program in August 2005 because of the military regime's restriction on access to the parts of Burma most affected, as well as the lack of public accountability, corruption, ongoing conflict in the grant environment, and the total absence of civil society participation.

Conclusion: writing the truth

The foregoing account of severe restrictions on the media needs to be read in the context of the nation's history of a free and active press. King Mindon introduced what is regarded as Southeast Asia's first indigenous Media Act of 17 articles which guaranteed press freedom and offered immunity to local journalists in 1869: "No one shall take action against journalists for writing the truth. They shall go in and out of places freely" (U Thaung 1995: 3). Historically, Burmese journalists and authors played significant roles writing about their contemporary socio-political contexts and problems. There is a long but not so well-documented history of the role played by journalists and writers in bringing alternate views to the fore for discussion and contemplation, first in opposing colonial British rule, and later in resisting socialist and military regimes (see Andrieux *et al.* 2005; *The Irrawaddy* 2004; Aung San Suu Kyi 1995; U Thaung 1995; Allott 1993; Lintner 1989). Several "popular journalists," such as Ba Pe, Ba Cho and Chit Maung, and Burma's "favorite writers" like U Nu (who became the first prime minister of independent Burma), Thein Myint and Thakhin Soe became active in Burmese politics in their struggle for complete national independence (U Thaung 1995: 10). Newly independent Burma voted for the Universal Declaration on Human Rights (1948) resolution with no reservations because it reflected the goals and language of the founding Constitution of the Union of Burma, which guaranteed to all citizens "liberty of thought, expression, belief, faith, worship, vocation, association and action" (Preamble to the Constitution of the Union of Burma, 24 September 1947).

By the day of independence, 4 January 1948, there were thirty-nine newspapers, many with wide circulation. Seven were printed in English, five in Chinese, six in Gujarati, Urdu, Tamil, Telgu and Hindi (Ministry of Information 1954).

Diversity of the press continued after independence under U Nu, the country's first prime minister. An attempt to impose severe restrictions on the press in 1954 was repulsed by the Burma Journalists' Association who organized a unified protest (Tinker 1967: 78). There were confrontations over press coverage of the insurgencies and it was over this issue that press freedom was first curtailed under the caretaker administration of General Ne Win, when in 1958 the democratically elected Prime Minister U Nu asked General Ne Win, the army's chief of staff, to head a caretaker government. When Ne Win took power in 1958, the first thing he did was build a detention centre on the remote Cocos Island. More than 40 per cent of those imprisoned were writers and journalists. As a result, Burma went from having one of the freest presses in Asia to the most restricted. Foreign journalists and publications were banned. The press was one the key targets of the Ne Win regime. One month after he seized power in March 1962, journalists formed the Burma Press Council to protect press freedoms through a voluntary code of ethics. One by one, newspaper editors were removed. By September 1964, all independent newspapers had been forced to close. From a country with thirty-nine newspapers, only six remained thereafter. Those remaining wrote "within the accepted limits of the Burmese Way to Socialism" (Allott 1981: 19). For the next twenty-four years, freedom of expression in any form was tightly suppressed. During the democracy protests in 1988 sparked by economic disaster and repression by the military junta, more people joined in seeking their right to speak.

Anna Allott (1993: 15) explores the result of press freedoms suddenly experienced in Burma as the tight censorship control was lifted for a brief moment. For three days (from 25 to 27 August 1988), no newspapers were printed in Burma. Everyone was on the street protesting and demanding the following: the resignation of the government; the formation of an interim government; the holding of multiparty elections; and, importantly, the right to publish freely. Following the days of mass protest, official newspapers began to print relatively accurately on events unfolding in the streets. From 27 August to 21 September, unofficially circulated newssheets published photographs, personal opinions and details of what was happening on the streets. Almost one hundred unofficial publications for this period are recorded and held in the British Library (Herbert 1990: 25). Government employees of state radio and television had struck for the right to speak and show accurately the actions of Burma's citizens. The unofficial newssheets carried long interviews with Aung San Suu Kyi and photos of peaceful demonstrators, while articles describing how democracies in Western nations conducted elections appeared. Burmese journalists spoke out and gave their informed opinions.

100 Nancy Hudson-Rodd

This brief period of freedom was unfortunately short-lived. On 16 September, the army attacked the civilians, killing many, and ordered all civil servants, military and police back to work. The army seized control and General Saw Maung became the chairman of the State Law and Order Council (SLORC). Despite the military crackdown, the NLD won a majority of seats in the multi-party election held in 1990. The military refused to recognize the election results, and therefore did not allow the elected members to form a government. Elected NLD members were harassed, murdered, jailed and exiled. Aung San Suu Kyi, the NLD leader, was detained under house arrest in mid-1989. After four years in detention, she explained her vision of her country – a vision founded on free speech:

> [A] country where we can sort out our problems by talking with one another ... The word parliament comes from the word talk. It is better to talk than shout, but shouting is better than shooting ... Democracy won't solve all our problems ... While it is not a perfect system, it is a necessary beginning.
>
> (cited in Walsh 1994:18)

As stated earlier, Aung San Suu Kyi remains arrested in her house and can be held without judicial appeal up to May 2009 (Hudson-Rodd 2005: 347). She has no access to the telephone and is allowed no guests, except her doctor, who can visit fortnightly. Supplies are delivered to the street outside her house. The military guards open and photograph each object before taking the package to her door. Another dissident arrested in July 1989, U Win Tin, a prominent journalist and secretary of the NLD Executive, remains in solitary confinement in Insein Prison. Yet another political prisoner, U Win Htein, who was the personal assistant to Aung San Suu Kyi, remains in solitary confinement in Myin Gyan Prison.

Given the long history of press freedom in their nation, the people of Burma without doubt would like to be able to speak openly, move freely and conduct their business without interference. Democracy songs in 1988 express these longings:

> I am not among the rice-eating robots
> Everyone but everyone should be entitled to human rights
> We are not savage beasts of the jungle
> We are all men with reason
>
> (Aung San Suu Kyi 1995: 175)

Contemporary media and cultural workers remain well aware of the political importance of a free and fair media. Tin Htar Swe, head of the Burmese Service in the BBC, when interviewed by *The Irrawaddy* (Tin Htar Swe 2005: 32), stated the aim of this Burmese language radio which is most trusted by people in Burma for offering independent news:

Our job is to give an accurate and balanced account so that people are better informed, enabling the listeners to form their own views. Our medium is not only to help keep people informed but also to give an opportunity for the listeners to express their views. This is important for people in a country where there is a lack of freedom of expression.

Against great odds, authors, filmmakers, poets, cartoonists and journalists are continually trying to write between the lines of prohibitions and to pry open spaces for the truth to be expressed in Burma. As Zin Lin, a Burmese writer living in exile in Thailand after spending seven years in Insein Prison in Rangoon, states:

> Several generations of Burmese writers and journalists have sacrificed themselves to fight against the stupidity and greed of our leaders. This is an unequal battle. They have got the strength of their weapons, but we will not give up.
>
> (Reporters Sans Frontières 2001: 4)

Secretary Lt-Gen. Thein Sein instructed the "literati to accept the fact that art is not for art sake but in the interest of the nation and its people." He urged the literati to "ward off the danger of destructive elements who make instigations with the assistance of the foreign media" and "to fend off the danger of neo-colonialists through literary might" (*NLM*, 12 December 2005: 9–10). As under any repressive regimes, Burmese authors have become allegorical and metaphorical in their writing in a quest to avoid censorship and imprisonment for publishing "unlawful ideas." And in a repressive context, readers would have to discern a political message whether or not the author him/herself intended it to be (Allott 1993: 59). Under strict censorship during Japanese occupation, and with threats of torture, a columnist by the name of Zawana created a conversation between his head and his stomach. The stomach demanded meat and the head refused as the meat was not available. His columns describing the scarcities existing in Burma under Japanese rule were welcomed by the Burmese. The Japanese censors, however, never understood the meaning of the conversation.

Notes

1 The State Law and Order Restoration Council (SLORC) military junta on 19 June 1989 decreed the country's official foreign language name be changed from Burma to Myanmar. The choice by foreign countries of whether to refer to the country as Myanmar or Burma became politically sensitive thereafter. The United Nations accepted the change of name, as did most of the neighboring Asian countries. Many governments in Europe, North America, Australia and New Zealand use the old name as a protest against the military junta's human rights abuses and the refusal to hand over power to an elected civilian government.

102   *Nancy Hudson-Rodd*

The junta also changed many names of cities, states and major geographical features. I refer to Burma in this chapter.

2 Ko Than Win Hlaing's five books are: *Handbook on Gems* (1992); *Monarch's Sunset*, (Volume 1, 1993); Monarch's Sunset (Volume 2, 1994); *Astrology for All* (1995); and *Historical Burmese Persons Talk Through Statues* (1997).

3 The following list of monthly wages in Burma highlights the prohibitive cost of owning a mobile phone: university professor US$123.00–131.00; director-general US$146.00–154.00; senior clerical officer US$25.00–29.00; and a skilled laborer's daily rate amounts to a mere US$0.30 (Sein Htay 2006: 5, 20).

Bibliography

Allott, A. (1981) "Prose writing and publishing in Burma: Government policy and popular practice," in S.C. Tham (ed.) *Essays on Literature and Society in Southeast Asia*, Singapore: Singapore University Press.

—— (1993) *Inked Over, Ripped Out (Burmese Storytellers and the Censors)*, Chiang Mai: Silkworm Books.

Amnesty International (2005a) *Myanmar's Political Prisoners: A growing legacy of injustice*, available at http://web.amnesty.org/library/print/ENGASA160192005 (accessed 29 September 2006).

—— (2005b) *Myanmar: Leaving home*, available at http://web.amnesty.org/library/print/ENGASA160232005 (accessed 29 September 2006).

Andrieux, A., Sarosi, D. and Puangsuwan, M. (2005) *Speaking Truth to Power: The methods of non-violent struggle in Burma*, No. 2, Bangkok: Non-violence International.

Article 19 (1996) *Fatal Silence? Freedom of expression and the right to health in Burma*, London: Article 19.

Asian Human Rights Commission (AHRC) (1999) *Voice of the Hungry Nation: The People's Tribunal on Food Security and Militarization in Burma*, Kowloon, Hong Kong: AHRC.

Assistance Association for Political Prisoners (Burma) (2006) "Brief biography of Than Win," 25 January, available at www.aapb.org (accessed 10 February 2006).

Aung Min (2006) "Health of political prisoner deteriorates in Burmese jail," *Naranjara News*, 26 January (online), available at www.naranjara.com (accessed 10 July 2006).

Aung Naing Oo (2003) "The State Protection Law protects the junta," *Legal Issues on Burma (Burma Lawyers' Council)*, 15 (August): 70–2.

Aung San Suu Kyi (1995) "In quest of democracy," in Aung San Suu Kyi and M. Aris (eds) *Freedom from Fear and Other Writings*, 2nd edn, Ringwood, Victoria: Penguin Books.

Aung Zaw (2001) "Journalists beware," *The Irrawaddy*, available at www.irrawaddy.org (accessed 30 November 2004).

Aye Htun (2004) cited in *The Irrawaddy*, 12(6): 3.

Burma Lawyers' Council (2003) "Law Amending the Printers' and Publishers' Registration Law, 1962 (SLORC Law No.)," available at www.blc-burma.org/html/Suppressive%20law/spl_e.html (accessed 4 July 2006).

Cartoonists Rights Network (2005) "Month-long jail sentence for cartoonist Chit Swe condemned," 10 August (online), available at www.cartoon-crn.com (accessed 8 July 2006).

Committee to Protect Journalists (CPJ) (2004) "Burma: documentary filmmaker arrested," 6 August (online), available at www.cpj.org/news/2004/Burma06-aug04na.html (accessed 24 March 2005).

Democratic Voice of Burma (DVB) (2006) "Burmese political prisoner Than Win Hlaing seriously ill," 25 January (online), available at http://www.dvb.no/english/print_news.php?id = 636 (accessed 4 July 2006).

Global Fund (2005) *Termination of Grants to Myanmar*, 18 August, Fact Sheet, Geneva: Global Fund.

Gutter, P. and Sen B.K. (2001) *Burma's State Protection Law: An analysis of the broadest law in the world*, Bangkok: Burma Lawyers' Council.

Herbert, P. (1990) *South-East Asia Library Group Newsletter*, December, 34–5: 25.

Hudson-Rodd, N. (2001) "'People's Desire': cultural expression and state oppression in Burma," Burma Media Association, available at http://english.dvb.no/e_docs/185people_desire.pdf (accessed 30 September 2006).

Hudson-Rodd, N. (2005) "Mandalay and Rangoon," in T.-C. Wong, K.C. Goh and B. Shaw (eds) *Challenging Sustainability: Urban development and change in Southeast Asia*, Singapore: Marshall Cavendish International.

Hudson-Rodd, N. and Myo Nyunt (2004) "Burma," in U. Butali (ed.) *The Disenfranchised: Victims of development in Asia*, Hong Kong: Asian Regional Exchange for New Alternatives (ARENA) Press.

—— (2005) "The military occupation of Burma," *GeoPolitics*, 10(3): 500–21.

Hudson-Rodd, N., Myo Nyunt, Saw Thamain Tun and Sein Htay (2004) *State Induced Violence and Poverty in Burma*, June, Bangkok: Federation of Trade Unions-Burma (FTUB).

Human Rights Documentation Unit (1997) *Human Rights Yearbook 1996 Burma*, Washington, DC: National Coalition Government of the Union of Burma (NCGUB).

—— (1998) *Human Rights Yearbook 1997–98 Burma*, Washington, DC: National Coalition Government of the Union of Burma (NCGUB).

—— (2000) *Human Rights Yearbook 1999–2000 Burma*, Washington, DC: National Coalition Government of the Union of Burma (NCGUB).

—— (2001) *Human Rights Yearbook 2000 Burma*, Washington, DC: National Coalition Government of the Union of Burma (NCGUB).

—— (2005) *Human Rights Yearbook 2004 Burma*, Washington, DC: National Coalition Government of the Union of Burma (NCGUB).

Human Rights Watch (2006) *World Report 2006*, available at http://hrw.org/wr2K6/wr2006.pdf (accessed 29 September 2006).

Internal Displacement Monitoring Centre (2006) *Burma*, available at www.internal-displacement.org/8025708F004CE90B/(httpCountries)/59F29664D5E69CE-F802570A7004BC9A0?open (accessed 29 September 2006).

International Freedom of Expression eXchange (IFEX) (2005) "Three men jailed for consuming 'unauthorised' information," 14 July (online), available at www.ifex.-org/eng/layout/set/print/layout/set/print/layout/set/print/content/view/fall/67965 (accessed 30 September 2006).

Iyer, V. (1999) *Acts of Oppression: Censorship and the law in Burma*, March, London: Article 19.

Karen Women's Organization (2004) "Shattering silences: Karen women speak out about the Burmese military regime's use of rape, Mae Sot, Thailand," available at www.ibiblio.org/obl/docs/Shattering-Silences.doc (accessed 29 September 2006).

104 *Nancy Hudson-Rodd*

Kin Oung (1993) *Who Killed Aung San?* Bangkok: White Lotus Press.

Kyaw Win (2004) "RFA, a rumour factory," *New Light of Myanmar*, 9/10 June.

Lansner, T. (2005) "Media and human rights," in R. Smith and C. van den Anker (eds) *The Essentials of Human Rights*, New York: Oxford University Press.

Lintner, B. (1989) *Outrage: Burma's struggle for democracy*, Hong Kong: Hong Kong Review Publication.

Maung Myint (2004) "Constraints faced by researchers," unpublished paper, 12 September, Rangoon.

Ministry of Information (1948) *Burma's Fight for Freedom*, Rangoon: Union of Burma.

—— (1954) *Rangoon: A pocket guide*, 4th edn, Rangoon: Union of Burma.

—— (1989) *The Protection Given by State Law and Order Restoration Council (Tatmadaw) for the People's Lives and Property and the Activities of Destructive Elements*, Yangon: Government of the Union of Myanmar.

—— (2004) *Magnificent Myanmar (1988–2003)*, Yangon: Printing and Publishing Enterprise.

—— (2005) *Chronicle of National Development: Comparison between period preceding 1988 and after*, August, Yangon: Printing and Publishing Enterprise.

Mizzima News (2005) "Three men jailed for consuming "unauthorized" information," 8 July (online), available at www.mizzima.com (accessed 29 July 2006).

Myanmar Law (1996) "Burma Lawyers' Council, the State Law and Order Restoration Council, the Television and Video Law," 29 July, available at www.blc-burma.orglhtm/Myanmar%20Law/lr_e_m/96?08.html (accessed 30 September 2006).

National Academy of Sciences (2005) "Long-time prisoner of conscience from Myanmar Khin Zaw Win released," Washington, DC: Committee on Human Rights, 8 July (online), available at www.7nationalacademies.org/humanrights/Khin_Zaw_Win_Released_from_Prison.html (accessed 21 October 2006).

Neuman, L. (2002) "How Burmese journalism survives one of the world's most repressive regimes," *Asia Observer*, February (online), available at www.a-siaobserver.com?Burma/Burma-storyl.htm (accessed 18 March 2004).

Preamble (1960 [1947]) *The Constitution of the Union of Burma*, Appendix 1, in Director of Information, Government of the Union of Burma, *Is Trust Vindicated? A chronicle of the various accomplishments of the government headed by General Ne Win during the period of tenure from November 1958 to February 6, 1960*, Rangoon: Government of the Union of Burma, September, p. 533.

Reporters Sans Frontières (2001) "Burma mission report: 18 media professionals still behind bars," July (online), available at www.rsf.org/rsf/uk/html/asie/rapport01/Birmanie/Report_B.pdf (accessed 1 October 2006).

—— (2003) "The internet under surveillance: obstacles to the free flow of information online: Reporters Without Borders Report 2003," available at www.rsf.org/rubrique.php3?id_Rubrique = 378 (accessed 29 September 2006).

—— (2005) "Cartoonist Chit Swe freed on completing sentence," 25 August (online), available at www.rsf.org/print.php3?id_article = 14672 (accessed 29 September 2006).

—— (2006a) "Burma is an internet black hole," available at www.RSF.org/country-50.php3?id_mot = 86 (accessed 30 September 2006).

—— (2006b) "Court upholds three-year sentences for journalists who photograph the new capital," 27 June (online), available at www.rsf.org/print.php3?id_article = 16898 (accessed 27 September 2006).

Freedom to speak in Burma 105

—— (2006c) "Military junta launches manhunt for informants of international news media," available at www.noticias.info/asp/aspComunicados.asp?nid = 1450927src = 0 (accessed 29 September 2006).

Rothenberg, D. (2004) "Burma's democratic transition: the internationalisation of justice, the legitimacy, and necessity of facing past political violence," *Human Rights Brief*, 9(2):10.

Sarpay Beikman and *New Light of Myanmar* (2004) "Frontispiece," *Magnificent Myanmar (1988–2003)*, Yangon: Ministry of Information.

Security Council (2005) *Security Council Update Report Myanmar*, 15 December, 4: 1–5. Available online at www.securitycouncilreport.org/ (accessed 29 September 2006).

Seekins, D. (2002) *The Disorder in Order: The army-state in Burma since 1962*, Bangkok: White Lotus.

Sein Htay (2006) *Burma Economic Review* (July), Washington, DC: Burma Fund and National Coalition Government of the Union of Burma.

Sen, A. (1999) *Development as Freedom*, New York: Knopf.

Smith, M. (1991) *State of Fear: Censorship in Burma (an Article 19 country report)*, London: Article 19.

The Economist (2004) *Country Profile 2004: Myanmar (Burma)*, London: The Economist.

The Irrawaddy (2004) "Chronology of the press in Burma," *The Irrawaddy News Magazine Online Edition*, 3 May (online), available at www.irrawaddy.org/aviewer.asp?a = 3533&z = 14 (accessed 12 July 2006).

—— (2006) "Burma to install new GSM phone lines," January, 14(1).

Tin Htar Swe (2005) "Maintaining the BBC standard: an interview with Tin Htar Swe," *The Irrawaddy*, January, 13(1): 32–3.

Tin Maung Than (2000) "Myanmar, misconceptions and misunderstandings," in A. Goonasekera and C.S. Chan (eds) *What the West Says and the East Wants*, Singapore: Super Skill Graphic Publication.

Tinker, H. (1967) *The Union of Burma*, Oxford: Oxford University Press.

UNICEF (2005) "At a glance: Myanmar," available at www.unicef.org/infobycountry/Myanmar_statistics.html (accessed 29 September 2006).

United Nations Development Program (UNDP) (2005) *Human Development Report 2005*, New York: UNDP.

United Nations General Assembly (UNGA) (1946) *Resolution 59 (1)*, Plenary Meeting, 14 December.

—— (2005) *Situation of Human Rights in Myanmar*, 12 August, A/60/221.

U Thaung (1995) *A Journalist, a General and an Army in Burma*, Bangkok: White Lotus.

Vajpeyi, Y. (2004) "Overview of Asian media," in W.V. Busch (ed.) *The Asia Media Directory*, Konrad Adenauer Foundation, Singapore: First Printers.

Walsh, J. (1994) *Time Magazine*, 3 October, p. 18.

7 Revolutionary scripts

Shan insurgent media practice at the Thai–Burma border

Jane M. Ferguson[1]

From gun-toting revolutionary soldiers in the mountainous Thai–Burma border to domestic workers in middle-class homes in Chiang Mai, Thailand, the Shan constitute one of mainland Southeast Asia's largest (sub-)national ethnic groups. Most of Southeast Asia's Shan people can be found in the Shan state located in the northeast of Burma (also known as Myanmar). The political landscape of the Shan state tends to be characterized as a complex patchwork of ethnic militias, political commandos and drug warlords, scattered among villages of wet-rice farmers and slash-and-burn upland ethnic tribes. Although many Shan politicians had expected political autonomy following the Second World War, for a number of reasons the Burmese military authorities have continued to rule the area, and some groups of Shan have been engaged in one of the longest-running civil wars in modern history, with the first Shan armed separatist movement dating its formation back to 1958.

Within that struggle, however, we can also find a great deal of news, literature and bureaucratic paperwork in the Shan language. I have chosen to discuss the emergence of print media production of one Shan militia, the Shan United Revolutionary Army (SURA), later the Shan State Army-South (SSA-South), and to examine the ways in which print media production is embedded in this group's ongoing political struggle. Based on content analysis of Shan insurgent media, selected articles from the Shan journal *Song Le'o* (*Freedom's Way*) and the newsletter *Kawn Hkaw* (*Independence*), as well as ethnographic research carried out among a community of Shan insurgent soldier-veterans, this chapter examines the role of Shan print media produced by affiliates of this army in the context of the Shan ethnic liberation movement against the forces of the Burmese military government.

The first section of this chapter will situate the Shan struggle in the midst of post-colonial national liberation politics in Burma (Myanmar). Next, attention will be turned to the role of insurgent media in this national liberation struggle, from the politics, economics and geographies of insurgent media production, to media content and its interrelation with its respective readership, both within the Shan state and beyond. Ethnographic analysis based on field research among Shan communities will flesh out how people understand and re-articulate discursive links between issues such as Burmese oppression, Shan culture and the Shan political movement. As I argue, in order for the media to be truly "insurgent," it must be embedded in a dialectical relationship between its consumers, its producers and their military struggle for political autonomy.[2]

Finally, I will discuss the ways in which the Burmese state has responded to this media and its producers, as well as Shan language teachers. While, on the one hand, newer publishing technologies have aided in the de-centralization of insurgent media production such that a strong-arm suppression of the media by the Burmese state is increasingly impractical, on the other hand there has been limited aperturism on the part of the state in allowing Shan publications to enter the mainstream licit market in Burma. The contemporary situation raises fundamental questions about the role of the market, ethno-nationalism and the future of print media production and literacy in the Shan struggle for self-determination.

The Shan in upland Southeast Asia: past and present

Ethnically and linguistically similar to their Thai neighbors, the Shan can trace their presence in upland Southeast Asia nearly two thousand years, as historical and archaeological evidence places Shan settlements along the Salween River as far back as the third century (Sompong 2001: 25). Although various Shan, Burmese and Chinese kingdoms have exerted political and military authority over the region throughout the centuries, it was not until the end of the nineteenth century that the British conquest of Burma signified a European bureaucratic imposition on the areas ruled by Shan princes. Rather than fully colonize this area of upland Southeast Asia, in February 1889, the British reached an agreement called the Shan State Act with the Shan princes where the Shan would be allowed to rule their subjects as part of the "frontier areas" to British "Burma proper." At this time, the Shan princes claimed a territory of 62,500 square miles and 1.3 million people (an estimated half of whom could be counted as ethnic Shan) and in exchange for being allowed to keep their positions, the Shan rulers started to pay tribute to the British authorities (Elliott 2006: 42).

With the close of the Second World War, Burmese nationalists were engaged in independence negotiations with British colonial authorities. The British specified that evidence of cooperation with the political rulers in the former "frontier areas" would be a necessary condition for Burmese independence. The accord, signed in the Shan city of Panglong in February 1947, stipulated that the "frontier areas" would join with the newly formed Union of Burma in its independence from the British. The Union would consist of seven (predominantly Burman) "divisions" and seven "ethnic states." Two of the states, the Karenni and the Shan states, would have the option to secede following ten years' initial membership in the Union (Hkö Hse'n 1996: 374). For some politicians and members of Shan's elites, this accord made it clear that the Shan are a legitimate nation (Tai Revolutionary Council [TRC] 1990: 2). The "spirit of the Panglong Agreement" will be a key recurring pattern in Shan independentist discourses throughout the following six decades of Shan separatist mobilization and political claims-making.

In the years preceding the Panglong Agreement, a group of nine Shan educators and literary enthusiasts were already at work simplifying the Shan written script so that it would more adequately reflect the spoken language. Although there already were numerous Shan scripts in circulation, literacy was not widespread, as it was limited to a handful of elites and monastic scholars. The previous Shan scripts were imprecise and represented the Shan spoken language with little consistency (Ranu 1998: 265). These nine Shan educators also drafted school textbooks, up to the fifth grade, in the aspiration that not only would this Shan script and language be taught in schools, but also that it would be the official bureaucratic language for an independent Shan nation. In the introduction to these textbooks, Sai Hsai Möng, the representative of this committee, writes that the purpose of the textbooks is to enable the people of the Shan state, through education in the Shan language, to progress toward a modern political state (Sao Hsai Möng 1962: iii). One measure of the enthusiasm and relative success of this initial endeavor is the fact that by the 1950s, there were a total of twenty Shan printing presses throughout Burma, publishing an estimated 250 kinds of publications in the Shan language (Sai Kam Mong 2004: 340). Crucial to the success of these Shan presses were the growing numbers of people in Shan cultural associations, particularly the students in Rangoon and Mandalay universities, who constituted a highly literate elite in a largely agrarian country.

However, world events soon made the Shan state the stomping ground for Chinese nationalist troops: with the 1949 revolution in China, small units of Chiang Kai-Shek's troops spilled across the Yunnan border, and before long the Kuomintang (KMT) started systematically to establish camps in order to carry out their counter-insurgency against the Maoists (Chang 1999: 22). This development greatly concerned the Rangoon government, and soon the Burmese army (or Tatmadaw) was dispatched to administer the area (Callahan 1996: 30). The consolidation and increasing presence of Burmese troops in the area throughout the 1950s, and the subsequent imposition of martial law, caused great aggravation for many Shan politicians, who were seeing the possibility for independence becoming increasingly bleak. While some Shan politicians decided to try to negotiate for a federation rather than complete independence, other Shan princes signed over their powers to the Burmese government in exchange for hefty life pensions and property rights (Hkö Hse'n 1996: 410).

Other Shan groups were not prepared to join with the Burmese so willingly, and 21 May 1958 saw the formation of Num Sük Han (Young Warriors), the first Shan armed resistance group, led by Sai Noi (TRC 1990: 3).

This group also counted among its membership numerous students from the several Shan cultural associations mentioned earlier. In 1959, the Shan State Independence Army (SSIA) officially convened, declaring that there can be no common bond between the Shans and the Burmese (in terms of language or culture) except for religion, "nor is there any sentiment of unity which is the index of a common national mind" (Smith 1999: 36). In addition to pointing to the Panglong Agreement, the Shan independence aspirations have consistently emphasized language as part of the fundamental differences between them and the Burmese, and for them *print language* becomes the key channel through which to assert Shan administrative authority, if only initially in resistance to the Burmese state.

Throughout the 1950s, a number of historical developments – the reaction to the KMT antagonism in particular – contributed to making the Burmese army the strongest political force in the country, and by 1962, General Ne Win effectively staged a coup of the fledgling civilian government. Although his rise to power was partially built on the hope that a stronger state could end the internal strife in Burma, it has also been argued that the 1962 military coup "poured oil on the flames of the country's ethnic insurgencies" (Smith 1999: 198). On 23 February 1963, Ne Win had nationalized ten of the fourteen private banks in the Union (*Kawn Khaw* 2000: 9), and in 1964 kicked out foreign (mostly Indian and Chinese) investments, and eventually, most foreign people (Smith 1999: 201). This strategy, though criticized by Shan nationalists as being a move of pure Burmese chauvinism, also signified a wresting of capital from foreign interests and into the hands of the military, which, of course, happened to be Burmese. This strong-arm military regime soon named itself the Burmese Socialist Program Party (BSPP) and called its economic plan the "Burmese Way to Socialism." What is behind the motivation, also, is a history of independence in which the ruling class is not the capital-controlling class; most of the capital was under the control of British, Indian and Chinese business people (Callahan 1996: 32) and the military's strength was sufficient to make it such that they could become both the ruling class and the capital-controlling class, if only looking out from their headquarters down the barrel of their guns. However, while the military government professed a state monopoly on commerce, this was never realized, as shadow market forces encroached (and subsumed) key sectors of commerce within the nation. While World Bank estimates have put illicit trade as accounting for about 40 per cent of Burma's economy, other estimates suggest that the black market sector could constitute as much as 80 per cent of the national economy (Chang 2004: 487).

Language, print and politics

The Burmese Way to Socialism, the inception of Ne Win's Burmese Socialist Program Party (BSPP), and the nationalization of the economy affected

110 *Jane M. Ferguson*

Shan publishing in two marked ways: on the one hand, legitimate production plummeted as a result of the scarcity of paper, due to the lack of imports and economic mismanagement, but on the other hand, the expanding black market economy which fueled the insurgent activities gave nationality groups in liberated areas the desire and funds to maintain the Shan language.

By 1969, civilian Shan presses were ordered to halt operations (Sai Kam Mong 2004: 340). Far away from the cities, in the border area east of the Salween River, the same year saw a merger of the Shan United Revolutionary Army (SURA) (led by Gon Jerg from Num Hsük Harn) with one of the KMT divisions, with both groups choosing the Thai–Shan state border town of Piang Luang for the centre of their operations (TRC 1990: 4). This alliance lasted nearly fifteen years, and the groups shared a mutual interest in benefiting from the black market economy, and a collective anti-communist stance helped ideologically to seal this marriage of convenience. The choice of the SURA/KMT headquarters on the border crossing to the Thai (sub-) district of Wieng Haeng was strategic as it meant that the SURA could take advantage of trade with Thailand, and the border crossing as a point of entry to the black market commerce in Burma, to supply the general operations of their ethnic militias. This border crossing is 196 km northwest of Chiang Mai city, and as of then had not been fully integrated under the surveillance and administration of the Thai state (Nipanporn 2006: 42).

The areas of the Shan state east of the Salween River, all the way to the Thai border, were held by various insurgent armies, although unevenly, for nearly thirty years. The Shan State Army, by the 1970s, operated over 200 schools, while the much smaller Shan United Revolutionary Army had eighteen elementary schools of their own as well (Elliott 2006: 350). During the 1970s, the SURA acquired a moveable Shan press and used it to produce a tremendous variety of articles in the Shan language. They also carried out supply projects for the local Shan villagers, which included the militia's invoice statements, and general bureaucratic paperwork, as well as wedding and funeral announcements. One woman SURA veteran I interviewed had found out that the army was accepting women recruits from a flyer that they had printed on the Shan moveable type and distributed to her village in Mong Pan. She told me how she had encountered problems in her Burmese-run high school and, together with a classmate one year her junior, left high school in Mong Pan to join the forces of the SURA. Had she not seen the flyer specifically recruiting women soldiers, one can only wonder how the path of this woman's life might have been different. In addition to sundry publications, affiliates of the SURA produced two serials: *Kawn Hkaw* (or Independence) and *Söng Le'o* (or Freedom's Way).

Understanding insurgent media

How then are we to look at such media production? To start examining such artifacts, we must not only look at its producers, their circumstances of media production, but also its consumers and the kind of politics these artifacts mediate. Insurgent media can, and often do, fall under the rubric of "indigenous" media. Many Shan often use indigenous politics in their claims-making. As the anthropologist Faye Ginsburg has pointed out, indigenous media offer a possible means "for reproducing and transforming cultural identity among people who have experienced massive political, geographic, and economic disruption" (Ginsburg 1991: 94). As the media theorist John Downing has argued, "'radical alternative media' tend to "express opposition vertically from subordinate powers directly at the power structure and against its behavior [and] to build support, solidarity ... or even against the very survival of the power structure" (Downing 2001: xi). However, in the Shan United Revolutionary Army case, the cultural reproduction capacities of these media are seen as a means toward the end goal of national liberation and the establishment of a sovereign Shan nation-state. Hence I have found "insurgent media" a more accurate term to describe the media of the Shan liberation movement.

If we are to say therefore that publications such as *Kawn Hkaw* or *Söng Le'o* constitute examples of "insurgent media," we must look at the ways in which these media forms are embedded in the politics, economics and geographies of the movement for Shan separatism. This particular kind of mediation, then, is directed toward the negation of political authority, and in the hope for the establishment of a different kind of political order – in this case, one for an independent Shan nation. While straight content analysis can bring to light themes of rebellion and ethnic resistance in such articles as these Shan publications, in order for these publications to be deemed "insurgent" the ethnographic method provides one strategy to examine the ways in which these media are part of an insurgent struggle. If a publication is truly radical, then it must play a key role in mediating insurgency between the people it claims to be fighting for, along with the political movement which mobilizes its soldiers and its villages which support those soldiers. The relationship between surrounding villages and the insurgent camps is vital to the survival of the sub-national movement in specific and crucial ways, and a paper trail of invoices and newsletters provides an interface with the hypostatized Shan state, even in its status as a sub-nation.

Where a central government holds a monopoly on the legitimate means of mass communication, the police and the military also seek to control the circulation of all forms of media within its borders. Media which do not have approval from the government censor board are therefore by definition illegal, and those engaged in unlicensed media production are often prosecuted by the Burmese government. Shan insurgent media are considered highly volatile, and those caught involved in the production, transfer or even mere possession of such articles are subject to fines and confiscation at best, and torture and/or imprisonment at worst. Among my informants who had moved to the Shan village at the Thai–Burma border where I have been

112 Jane M. Ferguson

carrying out my fieldwork, four have spent brief periods in Burmese prisons on the grounds that they were teaching the Shan language; even though their teaching materials were purposely benign elementary school textbooks. As one of these former teachers explained, the Burmese government does not know the difference: "the fact that we were teaching the Shan language, it meant we were teaching about independence politics."

However, areas in the Shan state, particularly those east of the Salween River, constitute Shan liberated areas where the soldiers of the Burmese state do not patrol. As mentioned earlier, the Shan insurgency movement, as with all other such movements, intrinsically depends on surrounding civilian populations. Within every outpost, there will be a small team of *kun pai möng* (or scouts) who will maintain contact with surrounding villages, and take supplies up to the camps. These people are quite literally the brokers of insurgency, engaging in economic transactions to supply the armies at the ground level. At the most fundamental level, it is the *kun pai möng* who transport sacks of rice up to the hilltop insurgent camps to feed the troops, or requisition other necessary supplies from surrounding Shan villages. Whether these suppliers are in an amicable relationship with the *kun pai möng* is dependent on multiple factors, not the least of which is the villagers' respective political stance toward the Burmese government, or their trust in the political leaders of the insurgent movement. Often, as well, troops from the insurgent armies are given leave to visit families or to buy things in the shops to take back to the camps. One veteran of the Shan United Revolutionary Army carefully explained to me that back in the early 1980s, the Shan armies respected the villagers:

> If you borrowed the smallest thing, even just a sewing needle from the villagers, you had to return it; if you didn't and your captain found out, you would be punished. It was because we held the Shan villagers in the highest regard, and if we were soldiers for the Shan, and we could not abuse that. That's what we were told.

In addition to the mechanics of the economy for insurgent media production, in the struggle for liberated territory, geography plays a formative role in the logistics for printing and distribution of such materials. Whereas the Burmese government was relatively successful at controlling the production of certain forms of dissident media within the urban areas, the influence that they could exert on media production could extend only as far as could its soldiers. This is why in the 1970s and 1980s Shan liberated areas and black market economies were necessary conditions for the industrial production of Shan print media. We should not forget, also, that during this period a large moveable type was the production unit; it was still a full decade before the proliferation of the personal computer and accessible desktop publishing.

Texts of an insurgent media

Having briefly outlined the historical, economic and military context for the production of Shan insurgent media, I would like to use textual analysis and ethnographic data to explain the ways in which such media operate on the ground level, or among its troops and its public. In order to measure and discuss the ways in which insurgent media operate in the political-ethic framework of Shan resistance, I will turn now to the dominant thematic patterns of these artifacts of Shan media, produced with relatively old printing technology in a highly unstable and contested political economy described above. Using a representative selection of articles from Shan publications, I will relate them thematically to the larger political picture through ethnographic analysis. This is, I would argue, the litmus test to identify whether these Shan publications can be considered "insurgent media."

Söng Le'o or *Freedom's Way* is an annual journal originally published under the direction of intellectuals affiliated with the Shan United Revolutionary Army in the town of Mai Hsung, about a kilometer inside the Shan state from the border crossing at Piang Luang, Thailand. The publication started in 1984 with the first print run of 1,000 copies. This first issue has a thin paper cover, with fifty-two pages printed in the Shan language, and sixteen in Burmese. By the late 1980s, the actual printing had been moved to Chiang Mai, Thailand, where producers could use color separation, offset printing technologies and glue-binding to create a slick, professional-looking volume. By this time, the print run had increased to 3,000 copies. Issue number four (1987) contains 119 pages, the first sixty-six of which are in Shan, and the remaining fifty-three in Burmese. Subsequent years of production saw the incorporation of articles in Tai Kun (Eastern Shan) and later articles in English. Although the importance of the use of the Shan language is repeatedly emphasized, the pluralistic approach to the printed language in these publications demonstrates that perhaps Shan insurgent writers had an open stance toward the multiplicity of languages in the region, so long as Shan remains the primary language. Furthermore, knowing that among its audiences there are Shan speakers who are literate in Burmese (but not Shan), *Söng Le'o* does not seek to isolate itself from these potential sympathizers. It is testament to the dedication of the Shan intellectuals involved in the production of this journal that, in spite of a series of dramatic changes to the Shan political movement (from the merger with the much larger Shan United Army of Khun Sa to form the Mong Tai Army (MTA) in 1985, through Khun Sa's surrender in 1996)[3] *Söng Le'o* has continually been published every year since its inception, all the way until 2002 when production had to cease because of insufficient funds.

One of the Shan articles in the first issue of *Söng Le'o* is entitled "The way to fall and the way out" (*Tang Tok Le' Tang Awk*). The article features a cartoon depiction of a man in Shan clothing being toppled by a Burman

114 *Jane M. Ferguson*

in a traditional soldier costume. The article itself starts with the assertion that "The Burmese often accuse the Shan of having shallow ideology, as we seek independence" (Mot Som 1984: 35). Later, the article details the ways in which it is the tendency of the Shan to love the Shan nation and the Shan people, and that the Shan have the right to demand independence according to the Panglong Agreement. "The Burmese," it claims, 'have not been straight with the Shan, oppressing them like cattle or buffalo. The Shan hate the Burmese, but only because the Burmese oppressed the Shan" (Mot Som 1984: 36). This article is simultaneously hitting on two fundamental issues of Shan ethno-nationalism: the first is the "spirit of the Panglong Agreement," and the second the notion of the Burmese aggressor. Although we can look at this as a repercussion of the political circumstances of the Shan state, we can also diagnose a specific way in which political problems have been filtered through an ethnic lens; pointing to the Burman enemy as alien and hostile to the Shan often leads to the discursive and problematic mobilization of the notion of an enemy "race" (Chao-tzang 2003: 31).

In a later issue of *Song Le'o,* in an article entitled "National Symbols" (*Hköng Mai Sao Sat*), the author Hse'ng Küng Möng presents the argument that all countries, whether independent or oppressed by another force, have their national symbols, examples being the American Eagle and the Russian White Bear (Hse'ng Küng Möng 1987: 19). The Shan symbol is the tiger, or the albino tiger (Hse'ng Küng Möng 1987: 21). Ultimately, the message is for people in the Shan areas to distribute and have a deeper understanding about national symbols (Hse'ng Küng Möng 1987: 22). Certainly, most movements will have their symbolic figures, the signifier which unites in the Durkheimian sense, but what is particularly interesting is that the push for a diversity of national symbols for the Shan is prefaced by a laundry-list of other nations and their respective symbols and insignia. Here is an explicit situating of the Shan nation in a wider international framework, even to the level of aspiring to have a Shan national flower, as "local sentiments acquire national significance only in the light of an international order" (Ree 1998: 83). While full international recognition of Shan as a sovereign nation is not on the immediate horizons, these important symbolic aspects add force, through their status as modern accoutrements, to claims that the Shan have the necessary components of sovereignty.

Söng Le'o also constitutes a forum for engaging in ongoing discussion about Shan political issues. In one of the articles, entitled "If you don't know how to fix things, don't place blame" (*Paw Am Maw Me' Ya Pe Ne*), the author responds to another article in the Shan monthly magazine *Kawn Hkaw* (*Independence*) which purportedly derides Khun Sa for being Chinese, and therefore not a true Shan nationalist. In response to this accusation, the author argues that many of the Shan leaders have Chinese blood and "if they don't help the political situation of the Shan, whose situation are they going to help?" The author also details that it was Khun Sa who built the Shan United Army, and that he continues to work for the Shan today. What

Shan insurgent media practice 115

is also interesting is that the author draws upon other historical examples, such as Che Guevara, an Argentinean, who helped the people of Cuba in their political struggles (Mawn Sai Hsük 1992: 65). Once more, we can see Shan print media working to situate the Shan political struggle in an international context, co-opting symbols and drawing distant illustrations into its printed domain.

Returning to the debate which the article by Mawn Sai Hsük focuses on, in the context of Shan ethno-national liberation, the issue of foreign (especially Chinese) involvement is a constant concern, and the area of insurgent media opens a key venue wherein these debates can ensue. The derision of Khun Sa as Chinese has emerged at crucial points: following the vast commerce networks established by the KMT in the Shan state, numerous Shan informants confided that they had initially supported Khun Sa because he represented a true Shan hero, and the idea of a Shan empire did appeal to them. However, other investigations suggest that Khun Sa may have been more interested in business, and was instrumental as such in his deployment of Shan (or Chinese) ethnicity to advance his personal financial interests. Most of the Chinese traders he worked with arguably accepted him as Yunnanese, and not Shan (Chang 2004: 494).

In hindsight, the machinations of ethno-nationalism which allowed Khun Sa to accumulate massive material wealth are looked upon with great bitterness among former rank-and-file Shan soldiers. Many Shan veteran soldiers and affiliates iterated the point that Khun Sa used the Shan nation as a "façade" to carry out his heroin trafficking business behind the scenes. As one informant noted:

> He was the worst dictator imaginable. What he did was actually very clever. We Shan had been tired of watching them [the KMT] get rich while the Shan villagers had to sit paying taxes and suffering when the Burmese came to our village. Khun Sa and the MTA meant a Shan nation to us, but the more power he got, the worse he became. If he just didn't like your face, he could kill you. He became a worse dictator than the Burmans, and if anyone spoke up, he'd get cut, too. Of course we were disappointed that he surrendered to the generals, but he didn't really care about the Shan villagers like he used to say he did anyway.

One can only speculate the extent to which the Shan media aided in building Khun Sa's image as a true Shan nationalist. However, as indicated above, it clearly did form part of the debate over his legitimacy around the time of his fall from power.

Shan insurgent media can, and indeed do, speak to the two overriding purposes outlined by Downing's goals of radical media. First, they articulate the movement's opposition to the Burmese military authorities; and second, they seek to build and maintain solidarity in their national project. However, it would be potentially rash to assume that insurgent media can only fulfill

116   *Jane M. Ferguson*

these aims. The number of artistic and human interest (even potentially apolitical) articles in *Söng Le'o* suggests that just because a publication is insurgent in its relationship to dominant power structures, its pages are not always used to serve those ends explicitly. The pages of the journal are graced by poems, stories and other entertaining departures from simply "toeing the line" towards Shan insurgency.

Whereas *Söng Le'o* is an annual journal, *Kawn Hkaw* is the serial newsletter published monthly. The periodical nature of *Kawn Hkaw* allows it to keep up with events relevant to Shan politics and military movements, as well as other more time-sensitive issues. On 20 May 2002, Shan State Army (South) soldiers launched an offensive on the troops of the Tatmadaw, seeking to reclaim their former headquarters in the town of Mai Soong, opposite Piang Luang (Thailand), where they had once operated the printing press, the SURA hospital and Shan elementary schools. These were part of the territories that Khun Sa had surrendered to the Burmese military in 1996 in exchange for personal concessions. By 2002, the Burmese military had already driven out most of the civilians from these areas, and had taken the temple school of Gon Jerng's Wat Fa Wiang Inn as an operating outpost. Thai soldiers had also set up a camp near the temple, a mere 400 yards from the Burmese outpost. In *Kawn Hkaw*, the headline ran: "Shan soldiers fight to capture the old capital" (*Hsük Tai Tük Him Ngao Süng Kao*). The front page article of this issue featured three photographs: the first depicting two dead Burmese soldiers, the second showing two Burmese soldiers displaying their guns in front of their base at Mai Sung, then the third a picture of a Shan soldier tying a shirtless Burmese soldier to a tree at the same camp. For the latter two photographs, the caption read: "Burmese soldiers at Mai Sung before, and now" (*Kawn Hkaw* 2002: 3). Following the news brief about the capture, the Shan newspaper detailed the history of the area, how it served as the SURA headquarters between the years of 1969 and 1984 and the alliance with the troops of Khun Sa to the eventual surrender of the territories by Khun Sa to the Burmese Tatmadaw. The article made the point that the area had been under the control of the Burmese for six years until its recapture by the Shan soldiers.

Periodicals like *Independence* are important to the Shan movements because they can relate the events and conflicts which involve the troops of the SSA through the lens of the Shan insurgency. Those who rely on the media to learn about events such as border skirmishes through the Thai commercial media are inevitably subjected to a certain type of event framing, which is different from that of the Shan writers. This is not to say that one is more accurate or just. But looking at how Shan, Burmese and Thai newspapers reported a border clash in May of 2002 is illustrative of this particular point. For Shan nation-building projects, form and content of "Shan news" is imperative. As Benedict Anderson has argued, "the very conception of the newspaper implies the refraction of even 'world events' into a specific imagined world of vernacular readers" (Anderson 1991: 63).

Kawn Hkaw is serving that very role as it articulates this "world" explicitly in the Shan print language. Indeed, one point that is (re)iterated and made explicit in every issue of these publications is that the Shan have their own language.

Maintenance of Shan literacy, on which such insurgent media depend, is a constant struggle. As one former teacher of the Shan language informed me, the Burmese army, upon re-conquest of Shan-liberated areas following Khun Sa's surrender in 1996, rounded up and incarcerated many teachers of the Shan language. For the Burmans, teaching the Shan language meant teaching separatist politics. Another overlooked obstacle to Shan literacy is that it was not uncommon for many peasants to frown upon book-learning. One of my informants commented that if it were not for her father's insistence that she attend school, she never would have been able to read or write. In multiple-children households, the main task, especially for elder sisters, was to look after younger siblings. This woman's mother had once said, "If you learn to write, all you will do is write stupid love letters to boys, and what good will that do us?" So, even for nation-building projects in a minority language, it is important not to neglect the ways in which the local cultural matrix is (or is not) receptive to such larger national ideals or even values toward literacy. Perhaps this last example shows us the character of valuing ethno-national literacy; print-capitalism somehow must presume a certain orientation for print language if it is to take hold in a given political context.

Conclusion: market and popular culture in the new century

So what has become of the Shan print media now? With the opening up of the Burmese economy to increased foreign investment in the last decade, there has also been a loosening of the government's harsh stance on minority language publications, including Shan. The market has allowed increasing space for Shan artifacts of popular culture, especially in the form of entertainment items such as Karaoke discs (or VCDs), comics and magazines. Although there are still tiny pockets of liberated areas held by the Shan State Army (South) along the Thai–Burma border, Shan publishing is increasingly de-centralized, owing largely to the increasing accessibility of desktop publishing and Internet access. However, the Burmese government censor board still strictly controls the content of publications produced within its borders, explicitly forbidding the history of opposition groups to be written about (Thanwaa 2005: 5).

However, with numerous publishers in Thailand, such works can be produced across the border and moved into hidden markets. Although the position of the Shan migrants in Thailand is economically and bureaucratically tenuous in crucial ways, the Shan have a relatively free reign in media production within the Thai state. The Thai government under the now-deposed Prime Minister Thaksin Shinawatra had staged large-scale crackdowns on media piracy for the benefit of global media groups such as

Warner and Sony, but there is little economic incentive to regulate the circulation of Shan media, even that which is explicitly political in content. One can only speculate whether the rhetoric of pluralism somehow justifies the Thai state leaving the Shan media productions to their own devices. On the Burmese side, however, Shan insurgent media remain banned, with steep penalties for the sale or transfer of items not bearing the censor board's approval sticker. Also within the past five years, the Internet has been allowed into the formerly closed country, although the censorious government tries to keep a lid on potentially objectionable or subversive content. Nevertheless, in legalized Burmese recording studios, many Shan pop records are cut, though political content remains expressly prohibited. In spite of the ban, Shan nationalist media continue to seep across the border. So, across the Thai–Burma border, one can track love songs, novels and popular culture magazines going one way, and war songs and political material going the other, into both licensed and hidden markets of Shan audiences in both the Shan state and the border towns of northern Thailand.

In the village where I have been conducting my ethnographic fieldwork since December 2004, Shan-identified people constitute the majority, and Shan tends to be the *lingua franca* in the marketplace as well. Town meetings are conducted in the Shan language, and minutes of the meetings are handwritten in the Shan script. Funeral announcements are typed in one of the myriad of Shan fonts, and whirred out through inkjet or laser printers, to be distributed to various households. For this village, what we have here is not yet a Shan print capitalist economy of scale, but perhaps a proto-capitalist print cottage industry.

In October 2005, I attended a temple fair in which a Shan monk asked the rhetorical question: "Millions of people can speak Northern Thai, but how many can read and write it?" The implicit answer to this question is: just a handful of monks and academics; although Northern Thai does have a distinct script, there was never a broad movement to make Northern Thai a modern print language, unlike Shan. At the same time, one Shan educator looked at the example of the general lack of Northern Thai literacy among Northern Thai speakers and expressed concern that the Burmese government's more open stance toward Shan print media could have a negative effect on Shan radicalism in the medium to longer term. As he said, "one of the reasons we fought so hard to keep teaching it was because the Burmese forbade it."

Nevertheless, the Shan struggle continues, as does the teaching of the Shan language. Although the impetus for the Shan language simplification and textbooks stems from groups of politicians, scholars and educators, their fragmentation, and later bonding with articulation into the ethnic politics of a national insurgent movement allowed the Shan script to be distributed and take hold in ways that could not have been predicted by the Shan or the Burmese authorities. The Shan (sub-)nation is clearly in an interdependent relationship with the regional politics of ethnicity and black market economies. Studying the media production of group such as the

Shan insurgent media practice 119

SURA provides necessary background and insight to these struggles and processes in political history. In a dynamic region where a group is fighting for sovereignty, the production of such works is essential to the establishment of their (sub-)national legitimacy, in their own hope that this movement may achieve greater political recognition in the future. One scholar of the Shan movement under Khun Sa has presented the argument that Khun Sa was able to successfully manipulate "a variety of social, ethnic, economic, political and geographical situations in order to create a shadow state that on occasion threatened to emerge as a viable national polity in its own right" (Gallant 1999: 45). Khun Sa's surrender to the Burmese forces marked a tremendous disappointment for many Shan independentists, and also a significant loss of territory to the Burmese military. But the Shan nation-building project is far from dead, as evidenced by the various Shan splinter groups still engaged in insurgency, and the monks and literary enthusiasts still teaching the Shan script on both sides of the Thai–Burma border.

Although Khun Sa is remains the most notorious persona in the history of various Shan insurgency movement leaders, the on-the-ground work of the *kun pai möng*, the brokers and suppliers of the movement, and the Shan language teachers and literacy enthusiasts must not be ignored. For this ethno-national movement, insurgency is more than just wresting the Shan state from the control of the Burmese government: it is an affirmation of a Shan nation within an international cosmopolitical order, and Shan insurgent media play a crucial role in building that history and political relationship.

Notes

1 Acknowledgements: I wish to thank Thak Chaloemtiarana, Sitthipong Kalaya-nee, Tom Kramer, Terence Lee, Kuen Sai Jaiyen, Krishna Sen, Eric Tagliacozzo, Toshiya Ueno and Andrew Willford for their careful reading and invaluable feedback on previous drafts of this paper. I am, however, solely responsible for all shortcomings of this work. The fieldwork component of this research was conducted between October 2004 and June 2006 and was supported through the International Dissertation Field Research Fellowship Program of the Social Science Research Council with funds provided by the Andrew W. Mellon Foundation, the Thailand–United States Educational Foundation of the William J. Fulbright Foundation, the Mario Einaudi Center for International Studies and the Southeast Asia Program of Cornell University. Thanks also go to the National Research Council of Thailand."

2 In his article "Insurgent media," Eric Hiltner uses the phrase as a descriptive title (Hiltner 2005: 101). I am proposing here that the phrase can be used as an analytical category for certain forms of media production.

3 Khun Sa's SUA in the mid-1980s was vastly larger than the SURA, and so some analysts look at the SURA's choice to merge as nothing less than a sheer survival decision. Khun Sa has been sensationalized as an Opium Warlord, and amassed tremendous personal wealth as the head of the MTA forces. At one point the United States Drug Enforcement Agency had put a bounty on his head, and arguably his surrender to the Burmese in 1996 was an escape which allowed him considerable concessions, mainly his own personal freedom and maintenance of his wealth within Burma.

120 Jane M. Ferguson

Bibliography

Anderson, B. (1991) *Imagined Communities: Reflections on the origin and spread of nationalism*, London: Verso.

Callahan, M.P. (1996) "The origins of military rule in Burma," unpublished PhD dissertation, Cornell University, Ithaca, New York.

Chang, W.C. (1999) "Beyond the military: the complex migration and resettlement of the KMT Yunnanese Chinese in northern Thailand," unpublished PhD dissertation, KU Leuven, Belgium.

—— (2004) "Guanxi and regulation in networks: the Yunnanese jade trade between Burma and Thailand, 1962–88," *Journal of Southeast Asian Studies*, 35(3): 479–501.

Chao-tzang Yawnghwe (2003) "The Shan: nationalism and belonging," *The Irrawaddy*, April: 30–1.

Chlaad Chai Ramitanon, Wiradaa Somswasdee and Ranu Wichasin (eds) (1998) *Tai Tai Tai*, Chiang Mai: Min Muang Press.

Downing, J. (2001) *Radical Media: Rebellious communications and social movements*, London: Sage.

Elliott, P.W. (2006) *The White Umbrella: A woman's struggle for freedom in Burma*, Bangkok: Friends.

Fang Sawm Keo (1991) "Phawm Kan Pen Aen He'ng," *Söng Le'o*, 9: 11–12

—— (1992) "Wan Lawt Le'o Kawn Hkaw Möng Hum Tum," *Söng Le'o*, 10: 77–9.

Gallant, Thomas W. (1999) "Brigandage, piracy, capitalism, and state-formation: transnational crime from a historical world systems perspective," in Josiah McC. Heyman (ed.) *States and Illegal Practices*, Oxford: Berg.

Ginsburg, F. (1991) "Indigenous media: Faustian contract or global village?" *Cultural Anthropology*, 6(1): 92–112.

Hiltner, E. (2005) "Insurgent media," *Radical History Review*, 93: 101–6.

Hkö Hse'n (1996) *Pün Kö Tai Le' Pün Möng Tai* (self-published).

Hse'ng Küng Möng (1987) "Köng Mai Sao Sat," *Söng Le'o*, 4: 19–22.

Kawn Khaw (2000) "Untitled," 17(20): 9.

—— (2002) "Hsük Tai Tük Him Ngao Süng Kao," 19(197): 1–4.

Mawn Sai Hsük (1992) "Paw Am Maw Me' Ya Pe Ne'," *Söng Le'o*, 10: 63–6.

Mot Som (1984) "Tang Tok Le' Tang Awk," *Söng Le'o*, 1: 35–6.

Nipanporn Paenkaew (2006) *Tai rop pama*, Bangkok: Open Books.

Ranu Wichasin (1998) "Sankaep phumilang khong chao Tai Yai nai rath shan," in Chlaad Chai Ramitanon, Wiradaa Somswasdee and Ranu Wichasin (eds) *Tai Tai Tai*, Chiang Mai: Min Muang Press.

Ree, Jonathan (1998) "Cosmopolitanism and the experience of nationality," in Cheah Pheng and Bruce Robbins (eds) *Cosmopolitics: Thinking and feeling beyond the nation*, Minneapolis: University of Minnesota Press.

Sai Kam Mong (2004) *The History and Development of the Shan Scripts*, Chiang Mai: Silkworm.

Sao Hsai Möng (1962) *Kwam Nam in Pap Hen Lik Tai San Si*, Taunggyi: Committee for Shan Textbook Production.

Smith, M. (1999) *Burma: Insurgency and the politics of ethnicity*, Bangkok: White Lotus.

Sompong Wittayasakpan (1998) "Tin taan khong klum chaatpan Tai nai phuen paen din yai asia tawan ok chiang tai," in Chlaad Chai Ramitanon, Wiradaa

Somswasdee and Ranu Wichasin (eds) *Tai Tai Tai*, Chiang Mai: Min Muang Press.

—— (2001) *Phrawatisart Tai-Yai*, Bangkok: Chulalongkorn University Press.

Tai Revolutionary Council (TRC) (1990) *Pün To Ke'p Le' Hkaw Pong Kwam Sao Kawn Söng*, n.p.: TRC.

Thanwaa Sirimati (2005) "Jintanakan Mi Phromdaen Nai Lok Wannakam Phama," *Salween Post*, 27 December: 2–5.

8 Thai media and the "Thaksin Ork pai" (get out!) movement

Glen Lewis[1]

On the evening of 12 March 2006, all Thai television stations replayed archival footage of a scene from "Black May" in 1992. This showed General Suchinda, leader of the military government that seized power in a 1991 coup, and Chamlong Srimuang from the pro-democracy movement, prostrated before King Bhumibol. The monarch admonished them for the recent bloody conflict, and shortly afterwards Suchinda stepped down. The replaying of this footage was taken to be a sign of the King's concern about the confrontation between then Prime Minister Thaksin Shinawatra and Sondhi Limthongkul and the PAD (People's Alliance for Democracy), which had produced the largest mass rallies in Bangkok since 1992. The anti-Thaksin daily *The Nation* described the replay of the "Black May" footage as "the King whispers" – referring to Thaksin's statement that he would step down if the King whispered in his ear (*Nation,* 13 March 2006). Considering that the ruling Thai-Rak-Thai (TRT) Party had won in a landslide in 2001, and did so again in February 2005, this reversal of Thaksin's fortunes surprised many. When he stepped aside as prime minister after a snap election on 2 April 2006, which was boycotted by the major opposition parties, the conflict briefly captured the attention of the international media.

To understand this confused period requires an appreciation of two particular factors. These are: first, the rather unique nature of Thai nationalism, and how during political conflicts different competing symbols of the nation are discursively projected through the media (Connors 2003). Second, how Thaksin has changed the construction of the Thai public sphere through the addition of several new elements to older ones. The new factors included how TRT cleverly combined populist appeals to the rural poor with techno-nationalist representations of Thaksin as the CEO/manager of a new "knowledge economy" which appealed to the Bangkok middle classes (Lewis 2006: 22). The old factors were: (1) Thailand's tradition of "strong man" leaders, which Thaksin has brought to life again; and, (2) TRT's approach to privatization building on the already commercially oriented mission of many state enterprises. This chapter will first explain how TRT's privatization policies were applied to the broadcast media. Parts Two and

Three then analyze domestic arguments about Thai nationalism and the controversial sale of Shin Corp. – Thaksin's huge holding company with leases to the Thaicom satellites, the AIS mobile phone company, the only non-state television broadcaster ITV, and its budget airline Thai Air Asia – to Singapore's Temasek Holdings. Lastly, alternative readings of the anti-Thaksin campaign in the press are considered, and a final note is made about the 19 September 2006 military coup that ousted Thaksin.

Thai media reform: preferential privatization, community radio and the NBC

Just as there are competing discourses about Thai national identity, there are competing discourses about media reform, especially since the "People's Constitution" of 1997 promised liberalization of the media (Ubonrat 2005). This Constitution required a new National Broadcasting Commission (NBC) to issue radio and TV licenses and make broadcasting regulations. Twenty percent of frequencies would be for public use, 40 percent for state agencies and 40 percent for business. Article 40 said all radio and TV stations must be supervised by an independent agency, though Channels 5 and 7 would remain under military control. Yet where civil society activists talked of people's empowerment and grassroots participation as the aim of media reform, they were opposed by the state agencies, the army and large media owners. The latter preferred a version of media reform that would maintain existing interests and extend TRT preferential privatization policies. Their language was more concerned with issues of command and control, preserving national security, and the privileging of "free market" rules interpreted in their own interests.

Ownership of Thai broadcasting has belonged historically to state agencies and the military, but many radio and TV channels became controlled by private operators through long-term leases. Radio has been administered by the Public Relations Department (PRD) from the 1930s and television was run by the Mass Communications Organization of Thailand (MCOT) after 1977. The military has owned radio stations since the 1930s and TV Channels 5 and 7 from 1955. However, the Kanasutra family company Bangkok Broadcasting leased the top-rating Channel 7 from the army, while the Maleenont family company BEC World leased the second highest-rating Channel 3 from MCOT. Large media groups, such as Grammy, also leased airtime from the army and PRD-owned radio stations (Ubonrat 1997). The only private channel, ITV (Independent Television), began in 1996 to fulfill an undertaking of the 1992 Anand ministry to create a non-state and non-military channel after television coverage of protestors during "Black May" was widely criticized as biased. ITV originally practiced investigative journalism, but in late 2000 Shinawatra companies bought a controlling interest in ITV, which then fired journalists who refused to support Thaksin in the 2001 election (Pasuk and Baker 2004: 149).

124   *Glen Lewis*

Thai media reform was important between 1997 and 2001, but was subsequently sidelined by Thaksin. TRT held a carrot-and-stick approach to media management. The carrot was the privatization of the largely state- and military-owned broadcast media and the generous concessions granted to ITV in 2004 after its takeover by the Shinawatra family (McCargo and Ukrist 2005: 61); the stick was the removal of broadcast journalists critical of the government, the withdrawal of government advertising from anti-TRT publications, takeovers of papers to increase covert government control – notably Grammy's 2005 purchase of 23 percent of the *Bangkok Post* and 20 percent of *Matichon* (*Bangkok Post*, 19 September 2005) – and the defamation actions taken against print journalists. Thaksin openly admired Singapore's one-party governance, where the PAP's use of defamation suits against its opponents is notorious (Lee 2004: 181–2).

While broadcasting traditionally had been controlled by state agencies and the army, TRT pursued a policy of preferential privatization to keep control with large media proprietors linked to TRT. After TRT's formation in 1998, Thaksin became critical of IMF-style privatization and he slammed the Democrats for selling off Thai businesses to foreigners. He had no objections in principle to privatization: he merely wanted it on terms preferential to domestic capital. TRT-style privatization was part of a larger package of public sector reform known as "New Public Management." In the Thai version, however, the "CEO Governor" scheme, budget reform and personnel restructuring meant the centralization of decision-making and patronage in the bureaucracy under the executive (Painter 2006: 27). The telecom agencies TOT (Telephone Authority of Thailand) and CAT (Communications Authority of Thailand) were corporatized in 2002 and 2003. Thaksin aimed to make the state-owned media more commercially oriented prior to their privatization.

The main candidates for privatization were MCOT's Channel 9 and the PRD's Channel 11. MCOT was the most strategically important. Since its inception in 1977 it had been a state agency under the Ministry of Finance that was expected to operate commercially. It carries advertising on its own Channel 9 as well as its thirty-six network stations, but leases out Channel 3 to the Maleenont family (Pracha Maleenont has been a TRT Deputy PM) along with other frequencies to the pay-TV operator UBC. MCOT also runs seven Bangkok FM radio stations and fifty-three provincial stations. Until 2002, when MCOT decided to operate them directly, many were contracted out to private companies (*Nation*, 23 June 2005). These changes were introduced by its new chief, Mingkwan Saengsuwan, a former PR director for Toyota Thailand. Re-branding Channel 9 as "Modernine TV," more game and entertainment shows and some pro-social "docudramas" were produced, which led to better ratings results. MCOT was eventually listed on the Stock Exchange of Thailand (SET) in November 2004. Mingkwan also promised an international English-language channel like the BBC, though critics remained skeptical as its news programs remained close to government views. Channel 9 also carried a talk show hosted by one of the "dinosaurs" of the Thai Right, former Bangkok Governor Samak Sundravej, that targeted critics of TRT (*Nation*, 22 April 2005). This was a far cry from when civic society programs hosted by Chirmsak Pinthong had broken new ground on the channel before 2001 (Ousa 2002). However in 2006, Samak went too far by criticizing Privy Councilor Prem Tinsulanond, who is often seen as an unofficial spokesperson for the King. On 19 February 2006, his show was axed. Samak was nevertheless elected as a senator on 19 April 2006.

Privatizing the PRD was more difficult as it is directly responsible to the Prime Minister's Office and not required to operate commercially. Channel 11 is also the lowest-rating channel. In 2005, when Suranand Vejjajiva was appointed PRD director, he promised Channel 11 and Radio Thailand would become like the BBC to facilitate the PRD's privatization (*Nation*, 1 May 2005). Suranand was the former TRT spokesperson and a cousin of the Democrat's leader Abhisit Vejjajiva. In practice, one of his first decisions was to threaten the closure of community stations broadcasting at more than 30 megawatts power. This was in effect harassment of stations critical of the government. In that same month, Bangkok police shut down the radio station FM95.25. More closures were then threatened for 180 provincial stations, ostensibly on the grounds that they interfered with airport radio signals (*Nation*, 19 May 2005). In December 2005, the Thai cabinet agreed to restructure the PRD into different "service delivery" units. The Campaign for Popular Media Reform (CPMR) saw this as a move to commercialize the PRD and pre-empt the decisions of the yet-to-be-appointed NBC. Suranand said the change was in the public interest and that one of its new channels would be for children's programs. However, Thepchai Yong's verdict was that the PRD could now "make propaganda and money at the same time" (*Nation*, 27 December 2005).

The other candidate for media privatization was the RTA (Royal Thai Army) holdings. The army retained some 200 radio stations, many of which were leased out to private operators, as well as TV Channel 5. Its media profits were never made public and the army always cited national security considerations in justifying its media interests. On 1 January 1998, it launched the Thai TV Global Network (TGN) to broadcast to 155 countries. Costing 180 million baht annually, the channel aimed at overseas Thais and viewers in neighboring countries. By 2003, TGN became profitable and plans were put in place to turn Channel 5 into the third SET-listed channel (after Channel 3 and ITV). However, attempts to do so were stalled. When Thaksin's cousin, General Chaisit Shinawatra, was announced as the next army chief in August 2003, Channel 5's listing seemed imminent until a series of management clashes followed. In June 2004, Chaisit dismissed three Channel 5 directors who had refused to award a thirty-year contract for Channel 5's marketing to private operators. On 15 June 2004, Thaksin ordered the suspension of the channel's listing and a subsequent investigation

126   *Glen Lewis*

found that it had debts of more than 1.8 billion baht despite having made a profit of 300 million baht a year (*Nation,* 23 June 2004). The army's SET listing plans were thus shelved.

In the absence of media reform, the community radio movement became an alternative pro-civil society force between 2002 and 2004. Illegal broadcasting had already been part of democratization movements in Indonesia and Taiwan (see Sen 2003; Ke 2000). Now it seemed that Thai reformers were following a similar path. This attempt to promote local media to counteract the Bangkok-based media was part of a wider campaign to encourage local community development as an antidote to globalization after the 1997 crisis (Hewison 2000). As required by the 1997 Constitution, in October 1998 the PRD created trial community radio services in nineteen provinces, with members from local interest groups, including women, farmers and village headmen. These were one- or two-hour daily broadcasts on PRD frequencies and this experiment was extended to sixty-five provinces in April 2000. A PRD-backed attempt was made in 2002 for the local TAOs (Tambon Administrative Organizations, or sub-district councils) to run community radio. This was initially defeated, but after new regulations made in June and July 2003 – from which the Community Radio Federation was excluded – registration of all stations with the PRD was required and six minutes hourly advertising was allowed. The numbers of stations boomed to some 1,500, but in effect local commercial radio had supplanted the reformers' vision of community radio (Uajit 2005).

Community radio had grown in the void left by the NBC's non-appointment, but the differences between the pro- and anti-community radio lobbies had resulted in a stalemate. The PRD, MCOT, private broadcasting owners and the army favored a *status quo* interpretation of media reform; reform groups such as Civicnet, the Local Development Institute and CPMR saw community radio and broader media reform as interrelated. Another problem was the diversity of their models: there was considerable vagueness even among its supporters about its purpose. Some modeled themselves on the PRD, while others followed a commercially oriented MCOT format, where the stations sold air time to private program producers (Lucksana 2004). In contrast, reformers such as Uajit Virojtraratt of Civicnet, who ran many community radio training programs (with the financial support of the Friedrich Ebert Stiftung), advocated a more activist civic role for the stations. But by 2006, many were carrying advertising and remained under PRD supervision. State harassment also continued with an Anthong radio operator being closed for criticizing local government services (*Nation,* 10 February 2006).

Though well-meaning, the community radio campaign distracted public attention from finalizing the NBC's selection. The NBC was to be appointed for six years by the Senate from nominees named by a selection committee of media academics, government agencies, media associations and consumer groups. Yet a prolonged dispute took place in 2000 over appointing the

NBC selection committee, while big media owners, notably Pracha Maleenont of Channel 3 and Grammy's Paiboon Damrongchaitham, campaigned against the NBC (*Nation*, 13 November 2000). The NBC appointment became a political football that was kicked around for five years, until in March 2003 the Administrative Court ruled it null and void due to conflicts of interest. The game started all over again in 2005 when seven new candidates were forwarded to the Senate for approval. The most votes went to Pichian Amnartworaprasert, an economics columnist in *Matichon*, while a retired general, Thongchai Kua-sakul, scored second-highest. Pichian said the NBC's aim was to prevent the monopoly of broadcasting frequencies. Thongchai, in contrast, argued that national security was the NBC's main concern and that it should establish new stations in the troubled South to broadcast in local dialects (*Bangkok Post*, 28 September 2005). In September 2005, the Commission voted for Thongchai as chair, because he was best placed to negotiate with the armed forces to reallocate air waves so as to comply with Article 40. However, on 23 November 2005, following a complaint by the Campaign for Popular Democracy, the Administrative Court annulled the new Commission, citing conflicts of interests. One of the selection committee had been Thongchai's former boss at Channel 5 (*Nation*, 29 September 2005).

Coming just a week after the Administrative Court blocked the privatization of the Electricity Generating Authority of Thailand, this seemed to signal a welcome new degree of judicial activism. The government, however, appealed the Court's NBC decision and said that the National Telecommunications Commission (NTC) could take over frequency allocation decisions. Deputy Prime Minister Wissanu Krea-ngam claimed there was urgent need to regulate the illegal community radio stations. This proposal betrayed the spirit of media reform (*Nation*, 27 September 2005). To subordinate the NBC to the NTC, appointed in 2004, would be reverting to the year 2000 plan of having one media and telecommunications regulator, which media reformers had then successfully opposed. Wissanu's solution would only benefit existing media proprietors and state agencies. In sum, although the Constitution had promised media reform, TRT had stalled this after 2001. The community radio movement had grown as an alternative to TRT's studied inaction on reforming the media, while the NBC remained in limbo, and TRT proceeded with preferential privatization policies that further entangled the broadcast media with big businesses. It was against this background that the anti-Thaksin movement developed.

Decoding the 2006 anti-Thaksin campaign – Part 1: Sondhi and the King

What triggered off the anti-Thaksin campaign was the charge made in September 2005 that Thaksin was anti-royalist. It was the owner of the Manager media group, Sondhi Limthongkul, who made this accusation.

The charge was potentially devastating as the monarchy is the centrepiece of the Thai polity. King Bhumibol is the longest reigning monarch in the world and he – with Queen Sirikit and Princess Sirindhorn – is adored by all Thais. Any public criticism of royalty is liable to prosecution under Thai *lèse-majesté* laws. The next factor that galvanized anti-Thaksin feeling was his sale of his Shin Corp. interests on 23 January 2006 to the Singapore government holding company Temasek. Thaksin's sale of what many saw as national rather than private assets to a foreign company shattered his nationalist credentials which he had previously played on so successfully. This will be examined in the next section of this chapter.

The People's Alliance for Democracy (PAD) that organized the public protests against the government was an alliance of a number of anti-Thaksin groups. The PAD's core leaders were Sondhi, former Bangkok Governor Chamlong Srimuang, union leader Somsak Kosaisuk, and the secretary of the Campaign for Popular democracy Suriyasai Katasila. Chamlong had been Thaksin's former mentor when he led the Palang Dhama Party. He had retired from politics but returned to fight Thaksin and oppose the listing of Thailand's largest liquor company on the Thai Stock Exchange. Whether Sondhi was as well suited to present himself as a champion of democracy was another question. He had been a former staunch supporter of Thaksin, notably during the 2002 AMLO (Anti Money Laundering Organization) hostile inquiry into *The Nation* and other newspapers that criticized Thaksin. Sondhi's bankruptcy resulting from the 1997 financial crisis was resolved with the aid of Thaksin's friends at the Krung Thai Bank, but he fell out with Thaksin after his own TV program on Channel 9 was canceled, and his investments in TV Channels 1 and 2 (running on extra frequencies on Channel 11) were threatened (*Nation*, 30 November 2005).

Sondhi's news talkshow *Thailand This Week* had been screened on Channel 9 since 2003. It became an alternative critical review of Thai politics in contrast to Thaksin's weekly propaganda talks on PRD radio stations. But when Sondhi's criticism of Thaksin escalated, the program was axed on 12 September 2005 (Boonrak 2005). Sondhi then moved the program to an auditorium in Thammasat University. As it became more popular he shifted to Lumpini, one of Bangkok's largest parks, and his Friday night outdoor meetings there developed a carnival-like atmosphere (*Nation*, 6 February 2006). Their format resembled a politicized version of Thai *likay* (folk theatre) performances, where the show begins in the late afternoon and runs until the early morning. As audiences grew, the meetings were shifted to Government House on Ratchadamnoen Road, and then to Sanam Luang – the public spaces where Bangkok political protests have been centered. With media outlets initially denied access, the anti-Thaksin campaign relied – by necessity – on mass public meeting, arguably the oldest form of oppositional public communication, supplemented by live internet coverage and the distribution of video disks (i.e. VCDs and DVDs).

Sondhi's charge of Thaksin being anti-royalist was one of the most damaging indictments that could be made against the Prime Minister. On 25 September 2005, Sondhi's daily paper *Phoojadkarn* (The Manager) printed excerpts from a speech by a prominent monk, Luangtua Mahabua. Luangtua formerly had been pro-Thaksin during Thaksin's assets concealment trial of 2001 when the Constitution Court narrowly absolved him with an 8:7 ruling (Pasuk and Baker 2004: 3). But Luangtua began to liken Thaksin to an ogre who was "clearly aiming for the presidency ... The monarch trampled, the religion trampled, the country trampled, by this savage and atrocious power in a few people in the government circle. That is the circle of ogres, of ghosts, of trolls, of demons" (Wikipedia 2006). Thaksin's reputation for arrogance and being "thick-faced" in ignoring criticism had alienated many. The monk's reference to ghosts also touched on the superstitions that make up part of Thai popular Buddhism: ghost (*phii*) movies are the most distinctive genre of Thai films (Lewis 2006: 164). This hatred of Thaksin, bordering on the irrational, came out in several postings on Google's "soc.culture.thai" chat group. For instance, one posting by "death to dictators" wrote:

> Thaksin wants to open the gates to hell. After he steals sham election he will destroy good clean holy power of Buddha and Phra Phrom [the Erawan shrine, smashed on 21 March 2006 by a vandal who was beaten to death immediately afterwards] and replace with dark evil force. Thaksin is Satan, prince of darkness and lies.
>
> (Google 2006)

The charges of Thaksin's disloyalty were based, first, on his presiding over a merit-making ceremony at the Temple of the Emerald Buddha in October 2005. Although royal household officials subsequently said Thaksin had been invited to do so, criticisms of Thaksin for sitting in what was normally seen as the King's chair were carried on Sondhi's Manager website, and on another website (Thailand-insider.com) run by a former rogue businessman, Ekkayuth Anchanbutr (Connors 2005: 375). Second, Thaksin was criticized for interfering in the appointment of the Grand Patriarch, the head of all Thai Buddhist monks. Thaksin reacted by suing Sondhi for 500 million baht. The monk's speech had been published in other papers but it was only Sondhi's that was sued. The case was finally defused by the King, who in his birthday speech in December 2005 said public leaders should accept criticism. Thaksin's lawyers then dropped their case against Sondhi though they continued with a defamation suit against media activist Supinya Klangnarong.

While these issues were largely invisible to the "international community," they had been building momentum since late 2005. When Shawn Crispin wrote about the anti-Thaksin campaign, he pointed out that the sub-text of the PAD's meetings was the issue of loyalty to the King. Sondhi's supporters all wore royalist yellow shirts and adopted the slogan "We fight for the

130   *Glen Lewis*

King" (*Asia Times*, 28 March 2006). Sondhi and Thaksin's groups began trading *lèse-majesté* charges while some academics appealed for an end to the use of the *lèse-majesté* laws (*Nation*, 25 April 2006). Both groups were attempting to appropriate the monarchy as the most potent symbol of Thai nationalism for their own purposes. When the largest PAD meetings were running in Bangkok in March, a smaller pro-Thaksin "Caravan of the Poor" came in from the country to hold their own meetings at Chatuchak Park. While the PAD meetings featured pictures of the King and Queen, Thaksin supporters, the Chatuchak "mob" (the word Thais use for demonstrators) did not.

It is difficult to overstate the omni-presence of the Thai monarchy. Most households feature royal family portraits, the nightly news always covers royal household activities, and everyone stands at the cinemas for the lavish national anthem, which is a photo-montage of the long life of King Bhumibol. What underlies Thai anxieties about the King's future is that he is seventy-seven years old (in 2006) and cannot live for ever. Questions of succession are never publicly discussed, but many feel that Princess Sirindhorn would be a preferable monarch to the next-in-line Crown Prince. The *farang* (foreign) scholars who have discussed the monarchy, notably McCargo (2005) and Hewison (1997), take a less sanguine view of its political influence than the daily adulatory media coverage and consider it not particularly pro-democratic. In McCargo's (2005) reading, what was distinctive about Thaksin and TRT was that they decisively challenged the entrenched networks that had dominated the polity for generations. Chatchai Choonhavan's late 1980s ministry had also done so, before being thrown out by the military coup of 1991.

Sondhi's meetings became a focus of opposition to TRT also because of many recent scandals linked to Thaksin. These included corruption allegations about procurement contracts for the new international airport, and the 2005 attempt to sideline Auditor-General Jaruvan Mantika's anti-corruption campaign (*Nation*, 13 June 2005 and 13 December 2005). There was also the issue of Thaksin's heavy-handed treatment of the Muslim South, where more than a thousand had been killed since 2001. Some attributed Thaksin's disdain for the South to its traditional loyalty to the Democrats (McCargo 2005: 514). As Sondhi's public meetings grew, they included the conservative royalist Prawase Wasi (Connors 2005: 376), former pro-civil society broadcaster Chirmsak Pinthong, outspoken Buddhist thinker Sulak Siviraksa, and public intellectual Thirayut Boonmee. Consumer activists opposed to the privatization of state enterprises, teachers unhappy with TRT's decentralization plans, southern activists, NGOs hostile to the US–Thai Free Trade Agreement, and Chamlong's "Dharma Army" all joined the anti-Thaksin crusade (*Asia Times*, 20 January 2006).

In January and February 2006, television news mostly ignored the meetings though they were reported by the press and some radio stations. By March, however, their scale could no longer be overlooked, and all channels, except Channel 11, were covering them. Even Channel 7, whose staple evening shows are soap operas, carried an insert of the meetings set into the usual program. This was a drastic change for the broadcast media. As Thepchai Yong pointed out, Thaksin had been one of the most media-savvy Thai PMs ever, with his regular Saturday morning radio broadcasts and his cowing of the broadcast media (*Nation*, 14 March 2006). In 2005, fears of TRT control of the press also had heightened, with the Grammy entertainment group's attempted takeover of *Matichon*, Thailand's largest circulation quality paper, and the *Bangkok Post*, the largest English-language daily. However, Grammy, headed by Thaksin ally Paiboon Damrongchaitham, had to water down its takeover plans after a storm of public criticism (*Bangkok Post*, 19 September 2005). It was only fitting that Sondhi could use his newspapers *Phoojadkarn* and *Thai Day*, which was published as an insert in the *International Herald Tribune* after mid-2005, his Manager website and the Hong Kong-based ASTV (Asian Satellite Television) available on the Net, to attack a prime minister who had muzzled the broadcast media and most of the press. Through his considerable media management skills, Sondhi had successfully channeled the rising tide of anti-Thaksin feeling.

Decoding the 2006 anti-Thaksin campaign – Part 2: Thaksin and the Shin Corp. sale

The sale of the Shinawatra and Damapong family holdings in Shin Corp. to the Singapore government's Temasek brought the growing anti-Thaksin movement to a head. Thaksin was seen as selling the country's key communications assets to a foreign buyer. While Thaksin has always maintained that what was good for his businesses was good for the nation, his critics point out that Thaksin's businesses had been won with leases from government agencies. Press rumors abounded prior to the sale, which was followed by Shin Corp. denials. But on 23 January 2006, Temasek Holding – via its nominees, Cedar Holdings and Aspen Holdings – bought a 46.9 percent stake in Shin Corp. for 73 billion baht, and later raised it to 96 percent. The deal took place only a working day after a legal amendment enabled an increase in foreign shareholding in Thai telecom operations (*Bangkok Post*, 21 March 2006). Sondhi had already raised the issue of Thaksin's conflict of his business interests with his office prior to the sale. Shin Corp.'s share price and market capitalization had more than doubled in the five years since Thaksin came to power (*Nation*, 16 January 2006).

Charges of conflict of interest were nothing new to Thaksin. As Pasuk and Baker (2004) argue, Thaksin saw politics merely as an extension of business. In the case of the Shin Corp. sale, however, Thaksin was seen as reneging on his nationalist credentials. Formerly he had often represented himself as a patriotic savior of the country. This was part of his first successful election campaign in 2001, when he had portrayed the Democrats

132 *Glen Lewis*

as being in league with the IMF and forcing the sale of Thai businesses to foreigners. He repeated this claim of being the savior of the nation at the conclusion of his savage 2003 "war on drugs," when more than 2,000 suspects had been killed (Pasuk and Baker 2004: 253). Thaksin also had argued that his economic policies – labeled "Thaksinomics" by the Bangkok press in 2001 – and the OTOP program (One Tambon [an administrative sub-district], One Product) were models for other Asian states, although critics dismissed them as populist, resulting in higher levels of household debt (*Newsweek International*, 27 March 2006). With Shin Corp.'s sale, however, his bland justification was that it was good business: that he had done it for his children who wished to protect their father from charges of conflict of interest. This was unacceptable to many. Anti-Singaporean protests took place in Bangkok, where placards said "Thailand is not for sale!" and "Singapore has no corruption, but is encouraging corruption in Thailand" (*Sunday Star*, 26 March 2006). Effigies of Singapore's leaders were burnt and it was publicized that the head of Temasek Holdings, Ho Ching, is the wife of Prime Minister Lee Hsien Loong (*Sydney Morning Herald*, 27 March 2006). Critics also charged that the Singaporean Air Force had benefited from a 2004 deal that gave them access to the Udon Thani air base as part of Singapore's anti-terrorism strategy (*Kom Chad Luek*, 7 March 2006). For its part, the Singapore government dissociated itself from the sale, claiming that Temasek Holdings was independent of government control.

Details of the Shin Corp. sale were complex and lacking in transparency. While the Stock Exchange cleared both Thaksin and his daughter Pinthongta of any wrongdoing, his son Panthongtae was deemed to have violated disclosure rules in his accumulation of Shin Corp. shares, but only a small fine was imposed (*Nation*, 23 February 2006). What angered many was Thaksin's apparent hypocrisy and his cursory explanations. In early February 2006, he had called for a special parliamentary session to defend the Shin Corp. sale. On 24 February, two days after the SET's clearance, he declared a snap election, pre-empting any parliamentary inquiry. He claimed to have breached no law in the sale, but his ethics were questionable. Furthermore, when Thaksin was negotiating with Temasek on the sale, he had just concluded a five-day live "reality TV" show on rural poverty in a north-eastern Thai village, where he had been advising the local poor on how to save money. At the same time, he was about to clear a personal tax-free profit of some two billion baht (*Nation*, 15 January 2006).

The mounting anti-Thaksin feeling reinvigorated the campaign for media reform. In July 2003, *Thai Post* published an interview with Supinya Klangnarong where she said Shin Corp. had unfairly benefited from government policies. In response, Shin Corp. filed a criminal suit for libel and a separate civil suit seeking 420 million baht in damages. Supinya was part of a network of civil society activists, media reformers and community radio workers. The CPMR was established in 2002, replacing the Working

Group on Monitoring Article 40, which monitored the media reforms promised by Article 40 of the 1997 Constitution. Although the case had a much lower profile than Sondhi's campaign, Supinya's prosecution attracted support from the International Federation of Journalists and Human Rights Watch. Testimony in her defense was given by the President of the CPMR, Ubonrat Siriyuvasak, a prominent media activist from Chulalongkorn University, and Shawn Crispin, former Bangkok bureau chief of the *Far Eastern Economic Review*. Another supporter was Rosana Tositrakul, head of the consumers' group which in 2005 had successfully appealed against the privatization of the Electricity Generating Authority of Thailand (*Nation*, 18 November 2005). On 16 March 2006, the Bangkok Criminal Court dismissed defamation charges against Supinya.

Shin Corp. had responded to Supinya's criticism by arguing that Thaksin and his family had no active role in the company, which had been granted many of its concessions before he became prime minister in 2001 (*Bangkok Post*, 24 February 2004). However, sympathetic Thai journalists had labeled it a "David and Goliath" case and hailed the court's ruling as a victory for free speech. Supinya celebrated her win by calling for the repeal of the 1944 Press Act, the 1955 Telecommunication Radio Act and the 1951 Broadcasting Act, which gave the state powers to coercively control the media (*Bangkok Post*, 1 May 2006). Nevertheless, *The Nation*, which had regularly supported Supinya, had in 2004 asked questions that the verdict did nothing to change, namely:

> Why does the Army still own two television stations and hundreds of radio stations? Where do their profits go? ... How come ITV, the love-child of the 1992 events, was able to rip up its charter in full public view with total impunity? How come, seven years after passage of the 1997 Constitution, its provisions for transferring control of the electronic media from the state to the people are still not implemented – to the point most people no longer have faith that they will make much difference anyway?
>
> (*The Nation*, 13 September 2004).

A post-Thaksin Thailand? The ghosts of generals past

The six months from December 2005 to April 2006 had been politically tumultuous. Key events included: Sondhi's charges of anti-royalism against Thaksin and King Bhumibol's December speech advising the Prime Minister to forgive and forget; Thaksin's sale of Shin Corp. in January; the PAD's mass public rallies against Thaksin in March and the dismissal of Supinya's libel case; Thaksin's election declaration and the Opposition boycott of the election; and Thaksin's stepping aside (but not resigning) in April. International press coverage of these events often diverged from domestic treatment.

134   *Glen Lewis*

Though some overseas reports approved of the protests that dislodged Thaksin, others fretted about whether the overthrow of a government democratically elected in 2005 was desirable. Some articles revived earlier 1990s arguments about "Asian values" that neo-authoritarian leaders such as Mahathir Mohamed and Lee Kuan Yew had used to justify their rejection of Western democracy.

One story that particularly angered local journalists was *The Economist's* report (8–14 April 2006) headlined "A blow to Thai democracy," and sub-titled "The mob has beaten the ballot box in South-East Asia." *The Economist* opined that the "correct way to oust Mr Thaksin should have been at the ballot box." *The Nation's* journalists rejected this. The current political turmoil, they said, was a plus to Thai democracy – not a "blow." Why had Thaksin called the election, asked *The Nation*. His ostensible reason was that he did not want the street protests to extend into the period prior to the celebration of His Majesty's upcoming 60th anniversary celebrations; but in fact it was because he could not defend his family's sale of Shin Corp. to Temasek Holdings. By restricting the definition of democracy to the electoral process, the *Nation* said, *The Economist* was ignoring the longer-term corruption of the independent bodies in the polity under TRT. These included the Anti-Money Laundering Office, the National Counter Corruption Commission, the Securities and Exchange Commission, the Election Commission, and the police and public prosecutors (*Nation*, 12 April 2006). Yet *The Economist's* skepticism was echoed in much other coverage. In March 2006, *The Washington Post* had said this was the wrong time for "people power." Although the paper had earlier criticized Thaksin for his human rights record, it now warned that trying to oust him through street demonstrations risked intervention by the military (*Washington Post*, 9 March 2006).

Shortly after, the British *Guardian* gave a pro-Thaksin version of the conflict. Warning that "democracy could be the loser," it argued that Thaksin's snap election was a flexible concession and the Opposition's boycott was extremely irresponsible (*Guardian*, 27 March 2006). Some Asian press commentary was also troubled by the street protests. Singapore's Janadas Devan pointed out that Thaksin's share of the April vote was much larger than that of Blair's Labor Party in the last British election (*Straits Times*, 7 April 2006). In India, *The Statesman's* Ravinda Kumar remarked that this outbreak of people power was not an advance for the cause of democracy but the opposite (*The Statesman*, 9 April 2006). A similar story by Satyabrata Rai Chowdhuri said Thailand's problems were another sign of "dysfunctional Asian democracy." He likened it to the attempted impeachment of President Roh Moo-hyun in South Korea, and President Arroyo's problems with repeated rumors of looming coups (*The Australian*, 10 April 2006). Another parallel between Philippine and Thai experience was drawn by Takashi Shiraishi, who argued that the Thai "people power" coup demonstrated that the middle class and elites upheld democracy when it was convenient, but flouted the law when it was not (*Asahi Shimbun*, 16 April 2006).

Other international press reports were more positive. The *Boston Globe* welcomed Thaksin's resignation, saying that it signified that "the Thais are showing the world that there is a crucial distinction between corporate culture and democratic culture." *The Globe* pointed out that the April 2006 election had deprived Thaksin of a mandate, and that the rallies were a revulsion against his domestic and foreign policies. His government had behaved with excessive force in the 2003 "war against drugs" and in the 2004 campaign against Southern insurgents, as well as pandering to the Burmese generals with deals that benefited Shin Corp., and granting many government contracts to his cronies (*Boston Globe*, 10 April 2006). Shawn Crispin also approved. He commented that the police's tolerance for the demonstrators was a sign of democratic maturity. Media criticism about "people power" threatening democracy was unjust, as "the crowds ... assembled precisely to defend their hard-fought democratic freedoms against an elected leader who they believed was acting to undermine them" (*Asia Times*, 10 April 2006). Pasuk Phongpaichit and Chris Baker, two of the leading analysts of Thai politics, also supported the protests. Thaksin had "left behind a mess ... that has seriously damaged the country's political institutions and climate ... Unless he and those who profited from his administration face full judicial scrutiny, political and business interests will continue to be blurred and corruption will thrive" (*New York Times*, 14 April 2006).

These international divisions of opinion reflected a similar split among Thais. In May 2006, polls suggested the nation was heavily divided about whether Thaksin should return (*Bangkok Post*, 4 May 2006). Thai democracy was left in limbo, waiting for judicial decisions, or an act from the King, or the return of Thaksin, who some saw as an "angel" and others as a "devil" – the same terms used to describe the opposing parties in 1992 (Murray 1996). On 9 May 2006, the Constitution Court annulled the 2 April election and set another for later in the year. The caretaker prime minister now had become a ghost of Thai generals past, such as Plaek Phibunsongkhram and Sarit Thanarat, both of whom have some similarities to Thaksin in their authoritarian personalities and their self-serving policies (McCargo and Ukrist 2005: 6). The need for an independent media appears greater than ever given the current difficulties of Thai democracy.

In conclusion, three factors are essential to understanding the 2006 anti-Thaksin campaign. First, the controversial place occupied by Thaksin in Thai politics was a reflection of tensions between two versions of globalization. Conservative ideologies of globalization put economics and markets first, and civic society and people's empowerment a distant second. Thaksin owed his fortune and his subsequent political influence to a telecommunications business that relied on foreign technologies. He consistently equated his business success with that of the nation, but his claims about being a true

136   *Glen Lewis*

patriot were undone by selling Shin Corp. to a foreign company. As Rosana Tositrakul said: "Thaksin is pushing Thailand into globalization too fast, which only benefits big companies and his cronies" (*Business Day*, 28 March 2006).

Second, there was the contested nature of Thai nationalism. Although Thailand is one of the few Asian countries not to have been colonized, the traditional slogan "the nation, religion and the King" often has been used by established groups to equate the national good with their own class interests. Pavin Chachavalpongpun argues that the conflict between Thaksin and Sondhi and their supporters reflected the elasticity of Thai identity. Thaksin was attempting to incorporate his version of democracy, based on buying elections, into the concept of Thai-ness; in contrast, his opponents argued that Thai-ness was closer to the values of anti-cronyism, freedom of speech and respect for human rights (*Nation,* 8 April 2006). The contest between these competing versions of internal nationalism will continue to be played out via different claims for cultural legitimacy made through the media.

Third, Sondhi and the PAD's success showed that the use of mass public meetings, the Internet and Internet television (Sondhi's ASTV) and radio, and the production of cheap VCDs and DVDs about the anti-Thaksin meetings, could challenge Thaksin's control of the mainstream media. As the size of the anti-Thaksin meetings became impossible for even the pro-TRT media to ignore, cracks in the wall of TRT's media controls appeared, encouraging more journalists to speak out. This heartened the sections of the press that had long been critics of Thaksin, such as *The Nation* and *Naew Na*, to intensify their attacks on government media control, the intentional delay in appointing the National Broadcasting Commission, and TRT's privatization policies that aimed to commercialize the MCOT Channel 9 network and its radio stations, while retaining PRD control over community radio stations and Channel 11.

Coda: the coup of 19 September 2006

On the night of 19 September 2006, when George Bush was addressing the UN in New York, BBC coverage used a split screen to show the tanks of General Sonthi Boonyarataklin rolling through the streets of Bangkok as Bush spoke. The pro-royalist section of the military had used Thaksin's absence in New York to overthrow him in the first coup in Thailand since 1991. Press coverage of the coup produced similar divisions of opinion between the foreign and the Thai press as described above. That is, most foreign commentary "tut-tutted" about the undemocratic means of ousting Thaksin, while the Thai press pragmatically said the end justified the means. Thaksin's positive legacy was the 30 baht public health scheme and a new focus on the needs of the rural poor. Yet he has also done great damage to the Thai polity. It remains to be seen how a new version of post-Thaksin

Thai media 137

democracy may be realized. Neither the prospect of a nation controlled by Thaksin and TRT *redux* nor one fashioned by the traditional alliance of the military and the monarchy is reassuring.

Notes

1 Special thanks to Ousa Biggins, Chalinee Hirano, Lucksana Klaikaew, Uajit Virojtraratt, Duncan McCargo and Peter Thompson.

Bibliography

Bangkok (2006) English lyrics to the anti-Thaksin "Square Face" song and detailed coverage of the media's treatment of the campaign, 10 April (online), available at www.2bangkok.com and www.2bangkok.com/high.shtml (accessed 15 April 2006).

Boonrak Boonyaketmala (2005) "Sondhi Limthongkul as news," *Thai Day*, 20 November.

Connors, M.K. (2003) *Democracy and National Identity in Thailand*, London: Routledge.

—— (2005) "Thailand: the facts and f(r)ictions of ruling," *Southeast Asian Affairs 2005*, Singapore: ISEAS, pp. 365–84.

Google (2006) "soc.culture.thai group" (an unmoderated online group with daily posts), available at http://groups.google.com/group/soc.culture.thai (accessed 3 April 2006).

Hewison, K. (1997) "The monarchy and democratisation," in K. Hewison (ed.) *Political Change in Thailand: Democracy and Participation*, London: Routledge, pp. 58–74.

—— (2000) "Resisting globalization," *The Pacific Review*, 13(2): 279–96.

Ke, S.-C. (2000) "The emergence, transformation, and disintegration of alternative radio in Taiwan," *Journal of Communication Inquiry*, 24(4): 412–29.

Lee, T. (2004) "Emulating Singapore: towards a model for Internet regulation in Asia," in S. Gan, J. Gomez and U. Johannen (eds) *Asian Cyberactivism: Freedom of Expression and Media Censorship*, Bangkok: Friedrich Naumann Foundation, pp. 162–96.

Lewis, G. (2006) *Virtual Thailand: The media and cultural politics in Thailand, Malaysia and Singapore*, Oxon: Routledge.

Lucksana Klaikaew (2004) "Community radio in Thailand," unpublished doctoral thesis, University of Canberra.

McCargo, D. (2005) "Network monarchy and legitimacy crises in Thailand," *The Pacific Review*, 18(4): 499–519.

McCargo, D. and Ukrist Pathmanand (2005) *The Thaksinization of Thailand*, Copenhagen: NIAS Press.

Murray, D. (1996) *Angels and Devils*, Bangkok: White Orchid Press.

Ousa Suksai (2002) "Thai television and civil society," unpublished doctoral thesis, University of Canberra.

Painter, M. (2006) "Thaksinisation or managerialism? Reforming the Thai bureaucracy," *Journal of Contemporary Asia*, 36(1): 26–47.

Pasuk Phongpaichit and Baker, C. (2004) *Thaksin: The business of politics in Thailand*, Chiang Mai: Silkworm Books.

Sen, K. (2003) "Radio days," *The Pacific Review*, 16(4): 573–89.

138 *Glen Lewis*

Uajit Virojtraratt (2005) "Community radio," in Sopit Wangvivitana (ed.) *Media Reform Going Backward?* Bangkok: Thai Broadcast Journalists Association and Friedrich-Ebert-Stiftung, pp. 34–50.

Ubonrat Siriyuvaskak (1997) "Limited competition without re-regulating the media," *Asian Journal of Communication*, 7(2): 57–75.

—— (2005) "A genealogy of media reform in Thailand and its discourses," in Sopit Wangvivitana (ed.) *Media Reform Going Backward?*, Bangkok: Thai Broadcast Journalists Association and Friedrich-Ebert-Stiftung, pp. 50–75.

Wikipedia (2006) "Sondhi Limthongkul" (online), available at http://en.wikipedia.org/wiki/Sondhi_Limthongkul (accessed 30 January 2006).

Online newspapers

Asahi Shimbun (Japan): www.asahi.com/english
Asia Times (Hong Kong): www.asiatimes.com
The Australian (Australia): www.theaustralian.news.com.au
Bankok Post (Thailand): www.bangkokpost.net
Boston Globe (USA): www.boston.com/news/globe
Business Day (Thailand): www.biz-day.com
Economist: www.economist.com
Guardian (United Kingdom): www.guardian.co.uk
Kom Chad Luek (Thailand): www.komchadluek.net
The Nation (Bangkok): www.nationgroup.com
Newsweek International: www.msnbc.msn.com/site/newsweek
New York Times (USA): www.nytimes.com
The Statesman (India): www.thestatesman.net
Straits Times (Singapore): http://straitstimes.asia1.com.sg
Sydney Morning Herald (Australia): www.smh.com.au
Sunday Star (Malaysia): www.thestar.com.my
Thai Day (Thailand): w3.manager.co.th (offline after August 2006).

9 Framing the fight against terror

Order versus liberty in Singapore and Malaysia

Cherian George

Introduction

In 1999, Amartya Sen felt able to write that democracy had attained the status of a universal value. "While democracy is not yet universally practiced, nor indeed uniformly accepted, in the general climate of world opinion, democratic governance has now achieved the status of being taken to be generally right," he noted (Sen 1999: 3). The early years of the twenty-first century, however, saw democracy's star outshone by a new premium on security, as an increasing number of states were forced to confront terrorist threats. In Singapore and Malaysia, which had never been enthusiastic about liberal democracy in the first place, the discovery of militant cells within their shores had the effect of further marginalizing the discourse on civil liberties. The two neighboring states joined the war on terrorism in earnest in late 2001, when they began arresting dozens of individuals on the grounds of belonging to Islamic terrorist cells. A militant regional movement called the Jemaah Islamiyah (JI) was discovered, with links to the Al-Qaeda network. The men were allegedly planning to bomb American targets within the region and to lay the ground for the creation of Islamic theocracies across Southeast Asia (Barton 2005).[1] The worst was yet to be: JI members would be found responsible for the October 2002 Bali nightclub bombing that killed 202 – the deadliest day of terror since the 9/11 attack on the World Trade Center and the Pentagon. The arrests in Singapore and Malaysia months earlier may have averted similar carnage in these two countries.

The news coverage of these arrests opens a window on a question of perennial interest – the media's relationship to the state. It is a particularly interesting case because it crystallizes one of the fundamental dilemmas of state–society relations, namely the search for an appropriate balance between order on the one hand and liberty on the other. Societies facing imminent threat of violent attack tilt predictably towards order, even at the expense of civil liberties. The mainstream media can be expected to reflect such shifts in priorities. After all, while the press is often associated with liberal democratic values, one of the less celebrated but equally fundamental

140   *Cherian George*

social functions of news is surveillance: people share news because it provides "a kind of security" and an awareness of "potential threats and potential rewards" (Stephens 1997: 12). In the aftermath of the 9/11 attacks, one should not be surprised, therefore, to find that the mainstream media in various countries were less concerned about any overreach of state power and trammeled individual rights, and – whether for patriotism or profit – ready to respond to their societies' fears by serving state interests in the war on terror.

The mainstream press in Singapore and Malaysia reflected these international trends. However, belying the stereotype of media in the two countries being monolithically aligned with the state, there were also segments of the media that generated a weak but significant counter-discourse, keeping liberty on the agenda. This, again, is in keeping with global patterns. If much of critical media scholarship asserts that large, commercial media corporations are uniformly conservative institutions, structurally linked to the centers of political, economic and cultural power, it is equally clear from media studies that there is invariably some resistance to such dominance, in the form of "alternative" media. They are "alternative," not in the sense that they are interchangeable with mainstream print or broadcast news products – against which they do not have the wherewithal to compete directly – but in that they remain outside of the structures of power, resisting dominant paradigms, serving distinct social purposes, and adding to the media system's diversity. The democratic role of alternative media has been recognized by several writers, including Curran (1991) and Downing (2001: v). Downing describes these media as "generally small-scale and in many different forms," expressing "an alternative vision to hegemonic policies, priorities, and perspectives." In keeping with this description, alternative media in Singapore and Malaysia – mainly small groups of media activists operating through the internet – offered distinct perspectives on the arrests of suspected terrorists.

The governments of the two countries dealt with the suspects using the Internal Security Act (ISA), which in both jurisdictions permits arrest without a warrant and lengthy detention without trial. Legacies of British colonial rule and the battle against communist insurgency, the ISA has been justified by the two governments as a necessary instrument of last resort for the preservation of security. A history of communist-provoked violence and periodic race riots has convinced successive generations of leaders that preventive detention, provided for under the ISA, is a necessary policy option for a responsible government. The ISA is part of a broader framework of powers that classify the two polities as "semi-democracies" (Case 2002) or "illiberal democracies" (Diamond 2002) – states that conduct regular elections, but where the checks on the exercise of power in between elections are weak. While some may object to preventive detention absolutely and on principle, the more common concern is over the possible abuse of such powers. Both societies have witnessed cases of ISA use against critics and activists who appeared to pose no clear and present threat to national security but instead represented ideological challenges to those in power – challenges that would seem wholly legitimate, and even healthy, in liberal democracies. Malaysia, in particular, made use of the ISA and preventive detention fairly routinely, applying it to the former deputy prime minister, Anwar Ibrahim, and other leading lights of the nascent Reformasi protest movement in the late 1990s. Not surprisingly, therefore, opposition parties and human rights groups have protested against the ISA, calling for its repeal or reform. For example, Malaysia's main opposition group, Parti Islam SeMalaysia (PAS), has adopted the Abolish ISA platform.

The discovery and arrest of the militants was therefore subject to conflicting interpretations. On the one hand, revelations of the militants' plans to inflict terror attacks increased the public's appetite for a strong government response to preserve order. On the other hand, the use of the ISA prompted inevitable comparisons to occasions in the past when authorities cast aside civil liberties to preserve the ruling parties' dominance. The news media thus had a choice of "frames" to apply when reporting the state's crackdown on the militants. Frames have been defined as "*organizing principles* that are socially *shared* and *persistent* over time, that work *symbolically* to meaningfully *structure* the social world" (Reese 2001: 11). To focus on frames is to acknowledge that the way events and issues are defined is often more important and interesting than whether those events and issues are on the public agenda or not (the focus of classic agenda-setting research). The relevant questions become: when an event or issue is discussed in the public sphere, what are its attributes that are selected for thinking and talking about it, and what are its attributes that are not selected? The same news can be framed in different ways, with different effects. Thus, Gamson (2001: ix–x) notes that the framing process is "a struggle over meaning that is ultimately expressed through texts."

Mainstream and alternative media

Faced with different ways of framing the arrests of militants, how did the media in Singapore and Malaysia perform? Communication scholarship in other contexts gives us strong hints of what we should expect to find in this case. Although the press in liberal democracies is often described as adopting an adversarial stance against the state, researchers have consistently found mainstream news media to be unsympathetic towards perceived breaches of order – not only those that result in criminal activity, but even otherwise peaceful but unruly protest actions carried out through extra-institutional channels. At least since Gitlin's classic on the 1960s anti-war movement, which critiqued the coverage of the *New York Times* and CBS News, scholars interested in what he called "the movement–media dance" (Gitlin 1980: 17) have revealed that the mainstream press tends to frame insurgent movements as deviant – sensationalizing their tactics, and under-reporting

142 *Cherian George*

their underlying beliefs. Such movements have instead had to rely on small, marginal channels that work under the broad umbrella of the alternative media. Other scholars have noted the affinity between alternative media and contentious social movements. In their study of media coverage of anarchist protests in Minneapolis, for example, Hertog and McLeod find (to their surprise) that the most powerful predictor of content differences between stories was whether the source was a mainstream or a radical one. This, they admit, was "not part of our original set of concerns" (1995: 39) – a symptom of the neglect of alternative media in much of communication research.

The mainstream news media in Singapore and Malaysia are easy enough to identify. They are the large commercial news organizations, including several that are linked to government through direct or indirect ownership, or control over management – the Singapore Press Holdings and Media-corp groups in Singapore, and New Straits Times group, Utusan, RTM and other entities in Malaysia. Less often acknowledged in surveys of the industry are the beleaguered alternative media. Print publications include *Harakah*, the popular fortnightly organ of Malaysia's main opposition party PAS, and *Aliran Monthly*, published by Aliran, Malaysia's oldest human rights organization. Opposition party newspapers in Singapore include the irregularly published *Hammer* and the *New Democrat*.

The internet has provided fertile ground for radical journalists and activists in recent years. Internet publications exploit a loophole in the two countries' media regulations. Eager to demonstrate their commitment to develop the information and communication sectors of their economies, both governments have refrained from blocking or banning political sites. Only in 2004 did Malaysia partially back down from its no censorship guarantee, with Prime Minister Abdullah Badawi stating that hate sites, such as those showing hostages in Iraq being beheaded, would not be allowed to reside on servers in Malaysia. Still, internet regulations remain markedly more hospitable than traditional media laws to free speech, as websites are not subject to the discretionary licensing policies that are applied to all print and broadcast media (George 2003). The most ambitious of the web projects is Malaysiakini, launched shortly before the 1999 general election. Malaysiakini is a standalone internet operation, with no offline publications. Founded and run by former newspapermen and hiring full-time journalists, it had more than 100,000 readers in its heyday. Since then, it has tried – with limited success – to introduce Malaysians to the notion of paying subscription fees for alternative news and views. To reduce their dependence on the publishing permits and to increase their publication frequency, both *Aliran Monthly* and *Harakah* developed their own websites, Aliran Online and Harakah Daily. At the time of the arrests in 2001–2, the most active politically oriented alternative media project in Singapore was Think Centre, the website of a small non-government organization by the same name, devoted to promoting democratic values. Staffed by volunteer activists with little or no media experience, the site has a less professional feel than Malaysiakini or Harakah Daily, and is more explicitly oriented towards advocacy. Its regular readers number in the low thousands at most. Also prominent at the time of the JI arrests (though now defunct) was Fateha, an advocacy site led by young activists and focusing on issues of concern to Singapore's Muslim minority.

The classifications of mainstream and alternative media are based on family resemblances rather than any watertight definitions. The alternative media category is internally diverse. This is true even of the handful of websites that are mentioned above as playing a prominent role in the coverage of the JI arrests. Malaysiakini, for example, adheres to international standards of independent journalism (and has duly achieved recognition from international professional bodies such as the US-based Committee to Protect Journalists), while Think Centre and Harakah Daily are unabashedly partisan. They are also organized differently, with Aliran Online, Think Centre and Fateha dependent on volunteer energy while Malaysiakini and Harakah Daily are staffed by full-time journalists. Underlying these differences, however, are commonalities that identify them as classic cases of alternative media: their relatively small size; their commitment to agendas that place them on the margins of political, economic and cultural power; and organizational features that are deliberately chosen to sustain their existence on the margins, particularly their dependence on relatively low-cost and license-free media technologies (George 2006).

As the findings of past communication research would predict, alternative media framed the war on terrorism differently from their distant cousins in the mainstream. When the authorities in Singapore and Malaysia announced the arrests of the alleged militants in early 2002, mainstream media reports in the two countries concentrated on the terrorist threat to national security, the continuing hunt for more militants, and the implications of radical Islam for inter-ethnic relations. In Singapore, the *Straits Times* reacted to the announcement with an editorial headlined "Cohesion above all," declaring that the battle against terrorism had to be fought "using whatever means necessary, including force" (*Straits Times* 2002a: 8). North of the border in Malaysia, the first *New Straits Times* editorial on the arrests called for "zero tolerance" for "religious extremism as an instrument of politics," beneath the headline, "Weed out the roots" (*New Straits Times* 2002a: 10). In their early coverage, the mainstream press gave negligible space to the questions of whether the suspects should be tried in court and how they were being treated while in detention. However, these questions were not completely excluded from the public debate. The two countries' alternative media, operating mainly through the internet, kept these issues on the agenda from the start. These media reported the perspectives of human rights groups and opposition politicians, or wrote their own editorials to argue that liberty and justice should not be abandoned in the effort to maintain order. In Singapore, Think Centre launched its coverage of the affair with an appeal that the detainees be treated well, and that they be

144   *Cherian George*

charged in open court (Balrasan 2002). Fateha said that the episode signaled a "deeper problem" – the US military presence that appeared to have provoked the Jemaah Islamiyah's alleged plans (Zulfikar 2004: 346). Malaysiakini accompanied its first news report on the arrests with a story titled, "Gov't rapped for latest ISA arrests, urged to show evidence" (Loone 2002a). This quoted a statement from the human rights NGO Aliran, which was not carried in the *New Straits Times*.

Dominant frames in the media

A closer analysis and comparison of the content of mainstream newspapers and of the alternative media suggests that these two segments deployed different frames in their coverage of the governments' anti-JI operations.[2] In articles in the mainstream newspapers (specifically *The Straits Times* and *New Straits Times*), three different themes were apparent. First, there was an emphasis on national security. Thus, in its page one article reporting the December 2001 arrests, *New Straits Times* (*NST*) quoted the inspector-general of police as saying that the men arrested "were believed to be and were engaged in actions which could threaten national security" (Lee 2002: 1). Police suggested that the militants had links with groups overseas, thus making them part of the global terror network. This national security frame continued to shape *NST*'s coverage. One editorial argued that "had the problem not been nipped in the bud this time around, there would be no telling the devastation that might have been wrought" (*New Straits Times* 2002b: 8).

A second discernable theme dealt with the militants' religious-extremist roots. The mainstream press noted that the militants believed they were carrying out an Islamic *jihad*. The newspapers also took pains to make it clear that the militants were not representative of the countries' Muslim communities, which make up the largest religious group in Malaysia and a sizeable minority in Singapore. Both governments had an interest in maintaining their countries' reputations as safe and stable societies, with Muslim communities that are peaceful and moderate in outlook. The Malaysian government in particular was anxious that the country should not be seen as a spawning ground for global terrorism, lest it invite pressure from the United States. Thus, a page one story in *NST* led with the then-premier Mahathir Mohamad indignantly denying that Malaysia was a key staging ground for the 11 September 2001 attacks on the United States (Loh 2002: 1). In subsequent reports, his deputy Abdullah Badawi assured the domestic and international public that the situation was under control. On the other hand, it was also in the Malaysian ruling party's interests to hint at links between the opposition Islamic party (PAS) and the Muslim militants. Thus, an *NST* editorial apportioned blame for militancy to "legitimizers in our society" – including PAS (*New Straits Times* 2002a: 10). The alleged links between the militants and PAS continued to be a running theme in

NST's coverage. Statements by politicians of the ruling alliance questioning these links were also picked up.

Most of the articles in the national press framed the story simply as a police operation – the third theme in the mainstream coverage. The operation involved the hunt for more militant members, followed by additional arrests and updates on their statuses. The large numbers involved and the staggered timing of the arrests meant that a good deal of newspaper space was taken up by the need to keep readers abreast of the latest figures: how many had been arrested so far, their age range, nationalities and professions, how many were alleged to have received military training abroad, and so on. The significance of frames lies as much in what they leave out as in what they include. Thus, framing the story as an on-going, forward-looking police operation left little room for discussion of the legitimacy of the actions taken. Mainstream newspapers reported police allegations as if they were established facts, and treated the denial to the detainees of a trial in open court as a virtual non-issue. Similarly, by framing the government's actions as protecting the nation's security and reputation, other possible political motives were sidestepped.

Counter-government positions were not entirely absent from mainstream coverage. *NST* ran three short stories quoting opposition leaders criticizing the use of the ISA, alleging that the arrests were an attempt to provoke fear, and asking for assurances that the anti-terrorism campaign would not be used to stifle dissent. However, in Malaysia it was left largely to the independent websites to surface these alternative ways of thinking about the events, as will be discussed shortly. In Singapore, alternative websites Think Centre and Fateha led the way in discussing the rights of the detainees, but the issue was also picked up by the national press. Three weeks after news broke of the first arrests of alleged JI plotters, the *Straits Times* carried a three-page analysis of the arrests. While the lead story focused on ethnic relations – in keeping with the second frame described above – an accompanying article discussed in fairly neutral terms the question of whether the detainees should be tried in open court. The article's second sentence credited (or blamed, depending on the reader's perspective) Think Centre and Fateha activists for raising the issue (*Straits Times* 2002b: 15). The next day, a *Straits Times* columnist raised the vexed question of detention without trial once more, again attributing it to Think Centre and Fateha. In a rare airing of liberal sentiment, the *Straits Times* piece said: "[P]ressing to bring them to court may not be popular. But it will certainly be right" (Tan 2002: 46).

For the mainstream to echo the alternative media in this manner was certainly not typical. Thus, when Think Centre activists organized the first public forum to discuss the domestic political impact of 9/11 on the JI arrests, a *Straits Times* journalist was seen taking notes at the forum but no report appeared in the national newspaper the next day. The Think Centre website, of course, reported the forum comprehensively. Think Centre used the occasion to place the legitimacy of the ISA on the agenda. Again, it

146   *Cherian George*

took pains not to deny that national security was under threat. Speaking at the event, the group's founder James Gomez suggested instead that such threats were the rightful focus of Singapore's security apparatus, which had been too concerned in the past with tracking peaceful opposition groups and individuals. Much more confrontational than Think Centre was the response of Fateha. The Muslim group's website attempted to frame the alleged militant plot as an outcome of Singapore foreign policy – in particular the Republic's hosting of American military forces (Zulfikar 2004). Not surprisingly, such statements were swiftly condemned by the government and wider establishment.

Since neither Think Centre nor Fateha had any full-time staff, these Singaporean websites were only sporadically updated. In contrast, between January and June 2002, the professionally run Malaysiakini published more than seventy articles in which the arrest of the Malaysian militants featured prominently. Many of these articles were not appreciably different from *NST*'s. They were news stories reporting the government's latest moves or statements. As a website devoted to daily news coverage as well as commentary, Malaysiakini could not really avoid the "police action" frame. In that respect, the Malaysian government succeeded in setting the agenda: it seized and held the initiative, and was the main – and often only – source of data. Still, Malaysiakini, like Think Centre and Fateha, succeeded in framing the story in ways that distinguished its coverage from the mainstream media's in critical ways.

First, the civil rights angle was amply covered. As noted earlier, Think Centre was the first Singapore organ to speak up for the detainees' rights. The writer was careful not to challenge the national security frame – conceding that those arrested were indeed dangerous men. However, the detainees should be tried in court and the facts made public as soon as possible, Think Centre argued – not only in recognition of their rights, but also because the episode risked alienating Muslim Singaporeans if mishandled (Balrasan 2002). In Malaysia, Malaysiakini reported extensively the statements on the arrests by international and domestic human rights groups, namely Human Rights Watch, Amnesty International and Aliran – none of which were mentioned by *NST*. Malaysiakini carried Amnesty's full country report, and a comment piece by the organization's Asia Pacific development officer. Even when reporting news for which the government was the main source, Malaysiakini tagged on the civil rights critique.

Second, Malaysiakini reported the detainees' points of view. Although the detainees had limited access to the media, some of them did secure public fora. One such occasion was a review panel hearing for alleged Al-Qaeda operative Yazid Sufaat, whose affidavit protesting his innocence was secured by the independent website, but not reported by *NST*. Another was the public inquiry held by the Malaysian Human Rights Commission, Suhakam. Malaysiakini, but not *NST*, reported detainees' statements denying the government's allegations.

Third, Malaysiakini reported allegations that the Malaysian government's actions were at least partly politically motivated. According to this theory, Kuala Lumpur was exploiting the war on terrorism to crack down on political dissidents, to instill fear of Islamic militancy – and, by association, fear of PAS – among non-Muslim voters, and to curry favor with the US. These views, expressed by opposition politicians and human rights watchers, were virtually ignored by *NST*, but were a running theme in Malaysiakini. For example, it, but not *NST*, quoted a member of parliament from the opposition DAP telling an international conference, "There is a tendency in the part of the ruling government to link these suspected terrorists to the legitimate opposition party PAS" (Loone 2002b). Malaysiakini also ran a story, filed by Agence France Presse, titled "Fear of militancy boosts Mahathir through by-election win." In several alternative media articles, lawyers and detainees challenged the very existence of the group (initially identified by the government as KMM or Kumpulan Militan Malaysia, that is the Malaysian Militant Group). These reports lent further credence to the view that the arrests were politically motivated (see, for example, Leong 2002a; Baki 2002). Such cynicism was not evident in the alternative media coverage of the JI arrests in Singapore. Even the Singapore government's critics and opposition leaders did not accuse it of unnecessarily crying wolf. This could be because the Singapore government had been relatively restrained in its use of the ISA in the years preceding the JI arrests – the Act had not been used against political opponents since the mid-1980s (*Straits Times* 2003: 6).

Fourth, in the alternative framing of the government's anti-terrorist campaign, the mainstream media were part of the story as participants, not just observers. Thus, Malaysiakini reported allegations of a cover-up on the part of the mainstream news media. One opposition leader, for example, was reported as criticizing what appeared to be a domestic media blackout of international news reports about terrorist cells in the region. The detainees themselves were extremely critical of the mainstream media's role in implicating them. "KMM suspects put media on trial in Suhakam inquiry," read one Malaysiakini headline. The article reported one detainee's indignant testimony and described how "he kept looking at members of the press seated in the room." It quoted another detainee telling the inquiry, "The press plays up the matter and the information is not correct. We were labeled bank robbers, assassins, then the police catch us and just conveniently label us" (Leong 2002b).

Why the different treatment

There are two broad sets of theories that help to explain mainstream media's conservatism – their tendency to defend the status quo against insurgency ranging from peaceful social movements to armed militancy. The first is structural, highlighting the political economy of the news business. Even in liberal democracies, large news organizations are invariably establishment

148   *Cherian George*

institutions with commercial and political interests aligned to those of the state, say several commentators (see, for example, Eliasoph 1988; Herman 1998; McChesney 1999). The second set of theories focuses on the professional culture and operational routines of news production: they argue that institutions with power are by definition more "newsworthy" than those without, and that the work habits of journalism are more compatible with the workings of institutional newsmakers, with their official spokesmen and clear lines of authority, than with often-anarchic movements (see, for example, Gitlin 1980; Sigal 1986; Bennett 1997). These professional norms include the ideal of "objectivity," which results in a systematic bias for the status quo. Day by day, journalists operationalize objectivity by suppressing their own opinions and relying on sources. Some sources are treated as more authoritative than others. Inevitably, these include institutional sources at the centers of political and economic power. Thus, without meaning to, mainstream media are biased against insurgents.

Alternative media tend to be more hospitable to ideas that challenge the status quo (Atton 2002; Downing 2001). First, they are typically constituted in ways that make them less susceptible to the pulls of the center. For example, a not-for-profit orientation and the use of volunteer staff and low-cost formats can make them less dependent on capital. Exploitation of technologies that do not require government licenses makes them less reliant on political patronage. Second, some may explicitly espouse radical or progressive agendas, which redefine the institutions and issues that are considered "newsworthy." They may also reject the conventional norms of objectivity, embracing advocacy as part of their journalistic missions.

Singapore and Malaysia show clearly the different dynamics that prevail within mainstream and alternative media. If mainstream media are biased towards the status quo in liberal democracies, they are even more so in Singapore and Malaysia, where the governments have used their legislative might to guarantee that the national media maintain a conservative orientation. Discretionary licensing for print and broadcast media companies serves as the ultimate check against willful media professionals. While neither government has used its powers against journalists as frequently or as brutally as many other states have, editors are in no doubt that the authorities will not countenance anything short of active support on issues that are deemed to be of high national importance. With the ruling parties having governed continuously since independence – and with generally positive results for the vast majority of citizens – the mainstream press is on most issues ideologically aligned with the state, recognizing the government of the day as the legitimate interpreter and trustee of the national interest.

In keeping with patterns around the world, the alternative media serve as foils to the dominant discourse carried by the mainstream press. Think Centre, Fateha and Malaysiakini, Harakah Daily and other political websites operate without a government license, which is not required for online media. They are not immune to prosecution under the laws that affect mainstream journalists, ranging from defamation to the Official Secrets Act. However, not requiring a license to publish means that they can at least enter the playing field without first having to prove their loyalty to the government. In addition, both Think Centre and Malaysiakini were founded on pro-democratic missions. The editors of Think Centre and Malaysiakini had no sympathy for the agenda of militant Islam, and were as concerned as other citizens about the threat of terrorism. Their concern about the ISA was part of a broader push for human rights and greater democratization. Before the arrests of the suspected Islamic militants from 2001 to 2002, the two websites were already sympathetic to the issue of individual rights, and therefore – unlike the mainstream media – considered the likes of Amnesty International to be important newsmakers. As for Fateha, it was closely aligned with Think Centre, and its particular mission, to address the marginalization of Singapore's Muslim community, gave it a different perspective on the arrests compared with the mainstream media. Harakah Daily, as the mouthpiece of the Islamic party, PAS, similarly had a vested interest in framing the arrests differently from the government-aligned mainstream media.

Limitations of the alternative media

It was noted above that the media's coverage of instability is affected by structural factors as well as by professional norms and routines. These factors together help explain some of the particularities and nuances of the coverage of the anti-terrorist crackdown. For example, it was observed that the majority of news reports, whether in the mainstream media or in Malaysiakini, framed the story as a law-and-order operation. Malaysiakini may have a human rights agenda, but it is first and foremost a daily news website, devoted to answering that most basic of journalistic questions: "What's new?" Most of the time, the answer was provided by the Malaysian authorities, as they gave updates on their operations. Tying itself to the conventional journalistic practice of relying on informed sources, Malaysiakini's room for maneuver was limited. Thus, on most days the government set the agenda and framed the story, even for Malaysiakini. As an Aliran leader noted in an analytical feature published a week after the first arrests were announced, "Public interest groups have been fairly muted, probably due to an unwillingness to question the official theory of a regional terrorist network in the absence of hard evidence to the contrary, and the sensitivity of the issue for the government" (Netto 2002).

In different circumstances, Malaysiakini might have tried to ask tough questions of officials, and thus attempt to shape the agenda. However, the site's reporters are banned from many government press conferences, including that of the Home Ministry, which is responsible for police and internal security. For this reason, and due to the constraints of its small reporting staff numbering fewer than ten, many of the news stories carried

150 *Cherian George*

on Malaysiakini, as well as Harakah Daily, were lifted from the mainstream wire agency, Agence France Presse. The wire agencies and other foreign media generally played the story "straight." In previous cases of ISA use, foreign media have been skeptical of government motives, highlighting the critical human rights angle. In this story, however, the international consensus was that governments had to do whatever it took to clamp down on terrorism. Unlike in the past, domestic and foreign mainstream media were united in adopting a dominant national security frame, and downplaying the question of the individual rights of the accused.

That is not to say that the mainstream media completely blocked this alternative discourse. In Singapore, the *Straits Times* advanced the discussion of detainees' rights to an open trial, but only after alternative websites had broached the issue. In keeping with the theory that media bias is sometimes explained by routine operating procedures rather than structural factors, Malaysia's *New Straits Times* reported the human rights critique when it came from the "right" newsmakers – institutions and individuals considered part of the elite. Thus, although *NST* chose not to report statements by human rights NGOs such as Aliran expressing concern about the detention of the alleged militants under the ISA, the paper could not so easily ignore similar comments by leaders of the country's main opposition parties. A day after the first news story on the arrests broke, *NST* carried 217-word and 80-word stories on page 6, reporting two opposition leaders' expressions of skepticism (*New Straits Times* 2002c: 6). Similarly, in May and June, *NST* ran three reports on a *habeas corpus* application filed in the courts by one of the detainees. One of its reports was headlined, "Counsel: no plausible reason for client's detention under ISA" (*New Straits Times* 2002d: 8). *NST* also reported what transpired when the officially recognized Malaysian Human Rights Commission or Suhakam (Suruhanjaya Hak Asasi Malaysia) got involved. Suhakam convened a public inquiry in June 2002 into conditions at the country's main detention camp. The forum provided an opportunity at last to hear directly from the alleged militants, as well as from run-of-the-mill political detainees.

However, comparing *NST*'s and Malaysiakini's coverage of these public fora, one gets the impression their reporters were attending different events altogether. Recounting the *habeas corpus* hearing, Malaysiakini reported that the Shah Alam High Court was critical of the police, ruling that the police had shown "bad faith" by not allowing the detainee access to lawyers. The judge, according to the website, "rained questions on the prosecution," asking "Where did the police actually get this 'god-sent' right to take away his right to counsel? The government cannot just say that they can do so." The judge's remarks were not carried in *NST*, suggesting that the mainstream news media observe an unwritten pecking order among even elite newsmakers. As for the Suhakam inquiry, *NST*'s coverage was selective, to put it mildly. One report was headlined, "We underwent Afghan military training, KMM duo tell Suhakam probe team"; only in the eighth and eleventh paragraphs of the thirteen-paragraph story are the two men quoted as denying any intention of using their Mujahidin weapons training in Malaysia (*New Straits Times* 2002e: 9).

The value of the kind of alternative journalism provided by Think Centre, Fateha, Harakah Daily and Malaysiakini is in the eyes of the beholder. It depends on the role one sees for the press. This is not just a choice between democracy and authoritarianism, since even a whole-hearted adherence to the former does not provide unambiguous answers. Is democracy about arriving at a national consensus as efficiently as possible, for the sake of order and stability? Or is it about providing the maximum opportunity for the expression of diverse interests? If it is the former, the alternative media can be regarded as destructive spoilers – which is precisely how they are seen by many within the Malaysian and Singaporean political elite. On the other hand, if one recognizes the value of what Fraser (1991) calls "multiple public spheres" – sites where alternative ideas can be aired, and from which the larger consensus can be challenged – the alternative media are valuable ingredients in the media mix. For Downing (2001: 43), they are "the chief standard bearers of a democratic communication structure" – "although flawed, immensely varied, and not necessarily oppositional, many such media do contribute in different degrees to that mission, and more truly than the mainstream media, in ways that are often amazing, given their exceptionally meager resources."

This perspective does not imply that the alternative media should replace the mainstream, even if they could. Rather, the argument made by such scholars as Curran (1991) and Baker (2002) is that the alternative sector should at least be recognized as an indispensable part of a democratic media system. Acknowledging the complexity of modern democracy, they call for greater media diversity, with different kinds of journalism co-existing in healthy tension. The mainstream press may play some important roles well, including providing a space where an overarching national consensus can be strived for. However, small alternative media are also needed to sustain alternative discourses that are under pressure from dominant ideologies. Alternative media can sustain multiple perspectives, which, as Herbert Gans (1979: 310) has pointed out, lead to "different questions and different answers, therefore requiring different facts and different news." Gans notes that even if national cohesion is the ultimate objective, "multiperspectival news and some decentralization of the national media" might be preferable, for it would allow more people to feel included as part of a larger whole. In societies threatened by extremist and exclusionary ideologies, Gans' call for multiperspectival news may sound naïve. Should the interests of groups that espouse violent methods be given space, in the name of diversity? Even many liberals would baulk at the suggestion. However, this is in any case not the kind of counter-discourse that is being offered a platform by the likes of Think Centre and Malaysiakini. These media are promoting neither the methods nor the motives of religious extremism. Instead, they have been merely trying to remind their societies that the rule of law and individual human rights require certain processes to be respected, even in the heat of the battle against terrorism.

No doubt, journalism that resists the embrace of the post-9/11 mainstream consensus for order and security will continue to be marginalized, especially in societies such as Singapore and Malaysia where national cohesion is highly prized, and enforced by powerful states. Trying to persuade people to care about the civil liberties of alleged terrorists is an uphill struggle, whether in Singapore and Malaysia or anywhere else. This is perhaps why the media that pushed this line were not stopped by their governments: the authorities knew that the vast majority of citizens would not listen the activists' liberal protestations. The only one of the aforementioned sites that was dealt with severely was Fateha, whose leader was accused of criminal defamation – in comments unrelated to the JI affair – and fled to Australia (Zulfikar 2004). The Singapore government was probably more concerned about Fateha's wide-ranging attempts to radicalize Muslims than about its critique of the JI arrests as such. Objections to the use of the ISA against the JI enjoyed little traction, especially in Singapore, where the instrument is more sparingly used and even opposition members of parliament supported the steps taken by the government (*Straits Times* 2003: 6).

To those who value order, stability and the routines of institutionalized politics, projects such as Think Centre and Malaysiakini appear unruly and misguided. Their path is also a lonely one. Traditionally, local proponents of human rights have been able to count on supporting fire from western media. However, western journalists who rise to the defense of opposition leaders when they are denied civil liberties are, predictably, less outraged when the government's targets are religious extremists and militants. The idea that human rights are indivisible and should apply to all may be understood in theory, but is rarely applied in practice by the world's media. When it comes to hot-button issues such as religious fundamentalism, they are also less likely to appreciate nuances, and more prone to see things in black-and-white. Thus, opposition to US foreign policy is conflated with support for terrorism. For example, the AFP routinely described Fateha as sympathetic to terrorist mastermind Osama bin Laden – which Fateha denied it had ever been. One academic journal even mixed up the names of Fateha and JI, carrying a footnote that members of Fateha were the ones arrested in connection with a terrorist plot (Zulfikar 2004). Such slippages have made it easier to marginalize alternative framings of the war against terror. Indeed, even Think Centre and Malaysiakini may be guilty of double standards. Their calls to secure trials for the Muslim militants have been relatively subdued, compared with their earlier anti-ISA campaigns. The reason for this arguably has less to do with a fear of government reprisal than with the shifting ideological landscape. No society that has suddenly been forced to contemplate the prospect of terrorist acts on its streets is likely to weigh order and liberty in the same manner as before. Order has become the new paradigm for such societies. Yet it is precisely this norm's strengthened status as the new common sense that may make alternative discourses more important to sustain. The alternative media's querulous attempts to keep liberty on the agenda in hegemonic media systems give them a value out of proportion to their modest means and their marginality.

Notes

1 According to Amnesty International, at least ninety people were reportedly issued ISA detention orders in Malaysia from 2000 to 2003 for alleged involvement in Islamist "extremist" groups. As at end 2003, thirty-seven men were being held in Singapore under the ISA for allegedly plotting to carry out bomb attacks (Amnesty International Report 2004, http://web.amnesty.org/report2004/index-eng).
2 The study involved qualitative textual analysis of more than 150 articles published in the *Straits Times, New Straits Times,* Malaysiakini.com and Thinkcentre.org from January to June 2002. The newspaper articles were retrieved from the Nexis database, while the two independent websites' articles were obtained from their own online archives. For the Malaysian sources, all articles containing the keyword "KMM" were analyzed, KMM being the acronym of the name given to the militants by the authorities at that time. For the Singapore publications, the analysis covered all articles containing the name Jemaah Islamiyah or JI.

Bibliography

Atton, C. (2002) *Alternative Media*, London: Sage.
Baker, C.E. (2002) *Media, Markets, and Democracy*, Cambridge: Cambridge University Press.
Baki, H. (2002) "KMM hayna ciptaan SB – Mangsa ISA," *Harakah Daily*, 19 June.
Balrasan, A. (2002) "ISD arrests: take political realities into account," *Think Centre*, 7 January (online), available at www.thinkcentre.org (accessed 9 January 2003).
Barton, G. (2005) *Indonesia's Struggle: Jemaah Islamiyah and the soul of Islam*, Sydney: University of New South Wales Press.
Bennett, W.L. (1997) "Cracking the news code: some rules that journalists live by," in S. Iyengar and R. Reeves (eds) *Do the Media Govern? Politicians, voters, and reporters in America*, Thousand Oaks, CA: Sage.
Case, W. (2002) *Politics in Southeast Asia: Democracy or less*, Richmond, Surrey: Curzon.
Curran, J. (1991) "Mass media and democracy: a reappraisal," in J. Curran and M. Gurevitch (eds) *Mass Media and Society*, London: Edward Arnold.
Diamond, L. (2002) "Thinking about hybrid regimes," *Journal of Democracy*, 13(2): 21–35.
Downing, J.D.H. (2001) *Radical Media: Rebellious communication and social movements*, Thousand Oaks, CA: Sage.
Eliasoph, N. (1988) "Routines and the making of oppositional news," *Critical Studies in Mass Communication*, 54: 313–34.
Fraser, N. (1991) *Rethinking the Public Sphere: A contribution to the critique of actually existing democracy*, Center for Twentieth Century Studies Working Paper No. 10, Milwaukee, Wisconsin.

154   *Cherian George*

Gamson, W. (2001) "Foreword," in S.D. Reese, O.H. Gandy, Jr, and A.E. Grant (eds) *Framing Public Life: Perspectives on media and our understanding of the social world*, Mahwah, NJ: Lawrence Erlbaum Associates.

Gans, H.J. (1979) *Deciding What's News: A study of CBS evening news, NBC nightly news, Newsweek, and Time*, New York: Pantheon Books.

George, C. (2003) "The Internet and the narrow tailoring dilemma for 'Asian' democracies," *The Communication Review*, 6(3): 247–68.

—— (2006) *Contentious Journalism and the Internet: Towards democratic discourse in Malaysia and Singapore*, Singapore: Singapore University Press.

Gitlin, T. (1980) *The Whole World is Watching: Mass media in the making and unmaking of the New Left*, Berkeley: University of California Press.

Herman, E.S. (1998) "The propaganda model revisited," in R.W. McChesney, E.M. Wood and J.B. Foster (eds) *Capitalism and the Information Age: The Political Economy of the Global Communication Revolution*, New York: Monthly Review Press.

Hertog, J.K. and McLeod, D.M. (1995) "Anarchists wreak havoc in downtown Minneapolis: a multi-level study of media coverage of radical protest," *Journalism and Mass Communication Monographs*, 151: 1–48.

Lee, S.I. (2002) "13 KMM men held under ISA," *New Straits Times*, 5 January: 1.

Leong, K.Y. (2002a) "KMM does not exist, militant group suspect tells Suhakam," *Malaysiakini*, 18 June (online), available at www.malaysiakini.com (accessed 18 June 2002).

—— (2002b) "KMM suspects put media on trial in Suhakam inquiry," *Malaysiakini*, 19 June (online), available at www.malaysiakini.com (accessed 19 June 2002).

Loh, D. (2002) "PM questions news report," *New Straits Times*, 6 January: 1.

Loone, S. (2002a) "Gov't rapped for latest ISA arrests, urged to show evidence," *Malaysiakini*, 5 January (online), available at www.malaysiakini.com (accessed 7 January 2003).

—— (2002b) "Try ISA terror suspects in court, says DAP leader at Manila meet," *Malaysiakini*, 12 April (online), available at www.malaysiakini.com (accessed 12 April 2002).

McChesney, R.W. (1999) *Rich Media, Poor Democracy: Communication politics in dubious times*, Urbana and Chicago: University of Illinois Press.

Netto, A. (2002) "Amid arrests, security concerns take a high profile," *Malaysiakini*, 12 January (online), available at www.malaysiakini.com (accessed 12 January 2002).

New Straits Times (2002a) "Weed out the roots," 6 January: 10.

—— (2002b) "Tougher screening for hidden militants," 26 January: 8.

—— (2002c) "Arrests an attempt to cause fear" and "DAP: Charge them," 6 January: 6.

—— (2002d) "Counsel: no plausible reason for client's detention under ISA," 8 June: 8.

—— (2002e) "We underwent Afghan military training, KMM duo tell Suhakam probe team," 19 June: 9.

Reese, S.D. (2001) "Prologue – framing public life: a bridging model for media research', in S.D. Reese, O.H. Gandy, Jr, and A.E. Grant *Framing Public Life: Perspectives on media and our understanding of the social world*, Mahwah, NJ: Lawrence Erlbaum Associates.

Sen, A. (1999) "Democracy as a universal value," *Journal of Democracy*, 10(3): 3–17.

Sigal, L.V. (1986) "Who? Sources make the news," in R.K. Manoff and M. Schudson (eds) *Reading the News*, New York: Pantheon Books.

Stephens, M. (1997) *A History of News*, Fort Worth, TX: Harcourt Brace.
Straits Times (2002a) "Cohesion above all," 8 January: 14.
—— (2002b)
"Should detainees face an open trial?" 26 January: 15
—— (2003) "Opposition MPs back govt's firm action against JI," 21 January: 6.
Tan, T.H. (2002) "Suspected terrorists deserve an open trial," *Sunday Times*, 27 January: 46.
Zulfikar, M.S. (2004) "Fateha.com: challenging control over Malay/Muslim voices in Singapore," in S. Gan, J. Gomez and U. Johannen (eds) *Asian Cyberactivism: Freedom of expression and media censorship*, Bangkok, Thailand: Friedrich Naumann Foundation.

10 Regime, media and the reconstruction of a fragile consensus in Malaysia

Zaharom Nain

Introduction

On 31 October 2003, after twenty-two years at the helm as prime minister of Malaysia, Dr Mahathir Mohamad stepped down. His had been the longest premiership in Malaysia's history. His had also been the most discussed, debated, praised by local commentators and academics, and – less often – criticized and vilified. There had even been talk, fueled by comments made by Mahathir himself, that he would *never* step down. Indeed, the succession process, triggered by Mahathir's "retirement" announcement at the mid-2002 United Malays National Organization (UMNO) General Assembly, has aptly been termed a "slow motion" one (Kessler 2004: 15).

The handing over of power to his deputy, Abdullah Ahmad Badawi, appeared to be smooth and unproblematic. It seemed in keeping with previous transfers of such power in Malaysia. But, as with previous successions, much more had been happening behind the scenes.[1] Indeed, Abdullah was Mahathir's fourth deputy, with three of his previous deputies, Musa Hitam, Ghafar Baba and Anwar Ibrahim, all having had their tenure end under quite acrimonious circumstances. Musa, his first deputy, resigned in 1986 amid increasing disaffection with Mahathir's leadership, which led to the UMNO crisis of 1987. Ghafar, appointed by Mahathir to replace Musa in 1986, was in turn challenged and defeated by Anwar in 1993. Anwar lasted five years and was dismissed by Mahathir in 1998. He was subsequently imprisoned, having been convicted on number of (widely believed to be trumped-up) charges of sexual misconduct and abuse of power.

Be that as it may, when Abdullah took office as Mahathir's deputy, he was widely seen as a Mahathir loyalist who did not quite have Mahathir's charisma and forceful personality. Beside the larger-than-life persona of Mahathir, the staid Abdullah seemed quite colorless. He was burdened by what Khoo (2003b: 5) has described as "the mystique of Mahathir's 'visionary leadership'." Yet at the same time, he was hailed as a "Mr Clean," an incorruptible politician, an individual, it was hoped, who would address the excesses of the previous regime and correct them.

The main problem with this optimistic view of Abdullah is that it quite simplistically assumes that the transfer of power from Mahathir signified a genuine regime change when, in effect, the structures of the existing ruling Barisan Nasional (BN) remain very much intact. Such a view, nonetheless, is quite understandable in a country like Malaysia, where political parties, especially the ruling BN, have become synonymous with individuals more than with ideologies and policies. And this notion had certainly been reinforced under the forceful, authoritarian premiership of Mahathir. As an example, one scholar (Rodan 1998: 140–1) has argued that the "Mahathir factor" played a crucial role in the 1990s in determining how the Malaysian authorities and state-owned companies reacted to international media and journalists. They – like many politicians under Mahathir – took the cue from what Mahathir had to say.

Hence, when Abdullah took over, there was widespread optimism that he would bring a kinder, gentler face to the prime minister's post. In a sense, he was seen as the "good cop" as opposed to Mahathir's "bad cop" image, especially in the context of a nation – particularly the Malay community – that had been rocked by the Asian crisis of 1997, and divided by the Anwar political crisis of 1998 and the subsequent *reformasi* protests of 1998–9.

As far as the Malaysian media were concerned, there was hope that the emergence of a new prime minister would signal greater media freedom, greater transparency by the administration and increasing tolerance for critical commentary in the media. But to understand this hope for change, one needs to look back at how the two decades or so of the Mahathir regime had impacted on the Malaysian media.

Malaysia's media and Mahathir's legacy: the 1980s and 1990s

Much has already been written about the impact of the Mahathir regime on the Malaysian media (see, for example, Gomez 2004; Mustafa 1990, 2002a, 2004; Rodan 1998, 2004; and Zaharom 1994, 2002a). Nonetheless, it is essential that some of the major developments be outlined briefly here, in order to establish the historical context which would help us to more accurately ascertain whether the transition to Abdullah's administration reflects a genuine regime change or simply reflects continuity and more of the same.

Soon after he came to power in 1981, Mahathir introduced policies, such as the privatization policy and Malaysia Incorporated, ostensibly to offset the oft-reported wastage within and by the public sector (see Jomo 1990: 201–20). Under the privatization policy, new media companies – especially radio and television – were created and developed. The majority of these companies were – still are – essentially owned and controlled directly or indirectly by the investment companies of the main component parties of the BN, particularly UMNO, the Malaysian Chinese Association (MCA) and the Malaysian Indian Congress (MIC) (Zaharom 2002a).[2]

158   *Zaharom Nain*

At the same time in the 1980s, existing media laws were tightened and new ones introduced. The Printing Presses and Publications Act (PPPA) was introduced in 1984 to replace the 1971 Printing Presses Act. Even before this, under the 1971 Act, the permit of *Nadi Insan*, a critical newsletter published by local academic K.S. Jomo and friends, had its permit revoked in 1983. In 1986, under pressures imposed by the new PPPA, two other papers, *Mimbar Sosialis* and *The Echo*, ceased publication (Mustafa 2004: 39). The PPPA which, among other things, requires every local regular publication to have a yearly-renewable license or printing permit granted by the then Ministry of Home Affairs, was further amended in 1987, giving the Home Minister immense powers to decide whether a publication can continue to be published. The popularity of video tapes and the spillover of television transmission from neighboring Singapore in the mid-1980s led to the amendment of the National Film Development Corporation (FINAS) Act (1981) in 1984. This amendment broadened the definition of film to include video tapes, video and laser disks and defined the possession of three or more copies of the same film as being involved in film distribution. It also further empowered FINAS officials to legally act on individuals and companies found contravening certain provisions of the Act (Zaharom and Mustafa 2000: 164).

In 1986, the Official Secrets Act (1972) was used to convict two local journalists for reporting a military document deemed "secret" under the Act. Despite opposition by journalists and NGOs, the Act was amended to make it all-encompassing, giving officers of the state almost total powers to deem what is "officially secret." International journalists and media too were not spared in this period. In September 1986, the *Asian Wall Street Journal* was banned by the Mahathir regime for three months and its two Kuala Lumpur-based journalists, Raphael Roy Pura and John Peter Berthelson, were expelled from Malaysia for purportedly publishing news deemed "official secrets" (Chan 1986).[3]

More notoriously, in October 1987, the Internal Security Act (1960) (ISA) and the Sedition Act (1948) were used by the regime to crack down on dissent. The crackdown, known as *Operasi Lallang* (Operation *Lallang* or weed), came at a time when there was a leadership crisis within UMNO. Three newspapers, including the hugely popular English tabloid *The Star*, were closed for an indefinite period because of their coverage of the crackdown. This crackdown proved significant for the Malaysian media. As Wong (2000: 134) puts it:

> Virtually overnight, a tentative culture of inquiry was cowed and eventually disappeared, as a generation of journalists left the trade taking their skills and experience with them. And not all of them were from banned newspapers; there were also refugees from other dailies.

The "taming" of the media notwithstanding, the trend of increasing concentration of media ownership in the hands of companies and individuals closely aligned to the regime, of political interference in media coverage of events, of using the legal apparatus, and of increasing commercialization of media content, continued well into the 1990s.

Studies on the state of the Malaysian media in the 1990s (Mustafa 2004; Loh and Mustafa 1996; Zaharom and Mustafa 2000) have indicated that while commercial media, especially television and radio companies, increased substantially during the decade – from just the one TV3 in the 1980s to three new channels in the 1990s, plus a cable station and a satellite network – most of the companies that were given licenses to operate the different media were invariably those close to the regime.[4] With the rapidly growing media industry and the need for more content, especially for television, the media drifted further into the international market to obtain programs to slot into their programming schedules instead of increasing investment in local productions. The majority of these programs were from the USA, or were produced and marketed by transnational conglomerates with interests in a variety of markets. Hence, while the number of programs has since increased, the types of programs made available remain safe, non-contentious and uncritical.

Aside from the continued commercialization of the media, there were three interrelated developments in the 1990s that are central to our discussion in this chapter. The first is the emergence and development of new information and communication technologies (ICTs) in Malaysia. The second is the persecution of Mahathir's erstwhile deputy Anwar Ibrahim, and, the third being the social and political crisis that emerged from this episode.

The 1990s marked the decade of the Internet in Malaysia, with the development of the Joint Advanced Integrated Networking (JARING) as the country's main Internet Service Provider (ISP) by the government-backed agency, the Malaysian Institute of Micro-electronic Systems (MIMOS). Mahathir was evidently seduced by the potential of ICTs, and in 1996 unveiled the Malaysian Multimedia Super Corridor (MSC) project, which he described as "Malaysia's gift to the world." Unfortunately, much of Mahathir's plans for the MSC and for the digitalization of Malaysia had to be temporarily shelved, due to the Asian financial crisis of 1997–8 as well as to the power struggle that unraveled as he sought to depose his deputy Anwar Ibrahim.

Of course, prior to getting rid of Anwar, Mahathir needed to eliminate Anwar loyalists in strategic and influential positions, including those in the media. Hence, in July 1998, barely two months before Anwar's dismissal from UMNO and from his political appointment and positions, the editors-in-chief of Malaysia's two major Malay-language newspapers, *Utusan Melayu* and *Berita Harian*, widely recognized as Anwar sympathizers and backers, resigned their positions (which effectively meant that they were pushed off the edge). The head of operations of Malaysia's first – and then most popular – commercial television station, the UMNO-controlled TV3,

160   *Zaharom Nain*

soon followed. Mahathir then dismissed Anwar in September 1998, and, subsequently, a couple of weeks later, balaclava-clad and gun-toting police raided Anwar's residence and whisked him away in the middle of the night under Malaysia's ISA. But this was not until after Anwar had gone on a "road show" around the peninsula, professing his innocence and outlining the alleged misdeeds of Mahathir and his cronies to large crowds at public rallies.[5] As Khoo (2003a: 94) describes it: "[T]he severity of Anwar's humiliation and the audacity of his defiance inspired a political and cultural dissent that gave birth to expressions and blossomed on a scale no one could have foreseen."

The virtual decimation of Malaysia's number two political leader and the blatant manner with which he was destroyed laid bare to most Malaysians the fact that

> rights and freedoms which they once took for granted can be so easily taken away, ignored or abused. They have seen how easy it is to misuse the institutions that are supposed to protect our freedom and turn them into tools to repress, silence and curtail that freedom.
>
> (Sabri 2000: 192).

More specifically for the Malay community, the community on which Mahathir's party UMNO depends heavily for support, the episode went against the grain of a deeply held cultural tenet of their race, "a race whose ancient *Annals*, the *Sejarah Melayu*, have decreed that 'if subjects of the ruler offend, they shall not, however grave the offence, be disgraced or reviled with evil words'" (Sabri 2000: 192). It was from this episode that the *reformasi* movement in Malaysia was born and grew to be more than a mere thorn in Mahathir's side. While it began as a response to Anwar's persecution, its demands "quickly moved beyond concern for Anwar's well being to issues such as rule of law, justice for all, curbs on corruption, cronyism and nepotism, repeal of the ISA and other coercive laws, etc." (Loh 2003: 5).

Mahathir – and his regime – did attempt to shift attention away from the street demonstrations that followed to the international arena.[6] The emphasis was on blaming Malaysia's problems on the outside world, referred to as the *penjajah baru* or new colonialists. Taking their cue essentially from Mahathir, the media were quick to blame external forces, such as the international financial system, for Malaysia's woes. This was played up further when the political crisis began and thousands of Malaysians took to the streets of Kuala Lumpur. The first strategy of the media in this instance was to black out images of the demonstrations and all news regarding the demonstrations and rallies altogether. The second strategy was to stereotype the demonstrators as thugs, hooligans, troublemakers, rabble rousers and even as naive individuals influenced by "evil foreigners." Hence, when Al Gore made his infamous speech on 12 November 1998 at the APEC dinner in Kuala Lumpur praising the supporters of the *reformasi* movement as "brave Malaysians," the mainstream media were quick not only to condemn Gore for interference in Malaysia's domestic affairs, but also to link the movement to "foreigners."

The third strategy adopted by the media was to evoke the potential for wide-scale societal violence. Hence, wire reports and images of the ethnic violence particularly in Indonesia were constantly played up by both print and broadcast media. The clear message was effectively: "Let not Indonesia happen here." The fact that the demonstrators on the streets of Kuala Lumpur were multi-ethnic in nature was conveniently disregarded by the media. Of course, the violence perpetrated by the state on the demonstrators was non-existent as far as the media were concerned.

Despite all of these occurrences, Mahathir was not able to shake off the specter of Anwar and the anger felt by many. This was clearly illustrated in the many websites that sprang up following the Anwar episode condemning Mahathir in no uncertain terms.[7] Such condemnations were clearly felt by Mahathir, who was moved to hit back on numerous occasions, an instance of which was in a speech he made at the UMNO General Assembly in Kuala Lumpur on 11 May 2000:

> Use whatever means you can to instill hatred against those who are kind to you. Poison-pen letters, the press, Internet, all these can be used. Call them with (*sic*) disparaging labels because in this way we can incite greater hatred against certain individuals. Label them as "Mahazalim" [most cruel], "Mahafiraun" [most pharaonic]. Do we like tyrants, pharaohs? Of course not. So just hate those who are labeled "Mahafiraun" or "Mahazalim." There is no greater satisfaction than the feelings of hate. Therefore the politics of development is replaced by the politics of hatred. Hate him and vote for me!
>
> (cited in Khoo 2003a: 134)

It is indeed a trifle ironic, looking back at this period, that the new communication technologies which the regime had helped to spread in the country – and which Mahathir had guaranteed his regime would not censor – would be the very technologies (used in conjunction with older technologies, like the photocopier) that were at the forefront of delivering and spreading ideas, messages and meanings critical of Mahathir and his regime.[8]

This predominantly Malay anger against Mahathir was somehow reflected in the 1999 general elections, when the opposition Islamic party PAS made inroads in previously safe UMNO constituencies. In the process, despite blatantly utilizing the "3 Ms" (money, machinery of government, and media), the ruling BN coalition, especially Mahathir's UMNO, lost the east coast state of Trengganu, failed to wrest the state of Kelantan away from PAS, and almost lost another state, Mahathir's own northern state of Kedah. Despite winning 148 out of the 193 parliamentary seats, or 76.7

162   *Zaharom Nain*

percent of the seats, it managed to poll only 56.5 per cent of the popular vote, as compared to 65 percent in the 1995 elections (Loh 2003). Detailed studies indicate that, in terms of voting patterns, the Malay community was split and that Mahathir (and UMNO) could no longer claim to be the champion of the Malays (see Loh and Saravanamuttu 2003).

To sum up this period, the economic and political crises of 1997–8 split the Malay population. The credibility of the mainstream Malaysian media was at an all-time low, with independent figures indicating that the sales of major mainstream papers, such as the *New Straits Times* (*NST*), *Utusan Malaysia* and *Berita Harian* were falling substantially (Zaharom 2002b). Mahathir's leadership was also being questioned by the people, especially given the way he treated Anwar and the heavy-handed manner the regime was treating the *reformasi* supporters. The Islamic opposition party (PAS), on the other hand, was getting more support from the Malay population. The introduction of the Internet into the equation provided – even if briefly – some hope for alternative discourses amid state repression. Apart from the purportedly brutal attacks by the security forces on *reformasi* demonstrators,[9] it is evident that after the 1999 general elections, there was a crackdown on dissent. This helped the regime to curb the expressions of anger, especially among the Malays.

Apart from the shifts discussed above, refinements were also made to minimize dissent in and through more "alternative" media. For instance, there was a clampdown on PAS's twice-weekly newspaper *Harakah*, with its editor and publisher arrested under the Sedition Act for purportedly publishing seditious material. Soon after, *Harakah*'s license was amended by the Home Ministry, reducing its publication to once every fortnight. At the same time, a variety of other pro-*reformasi* publications had their licenses revoked. In addition, a couple of prominent opposition politicians, Karpal Singh of the Democratic Action Party (DAP) and Marina Yusof of *Keadilan*, were also arrested under the same Act during that period. By and large, as it was evident that there was much discontent, the government's reaction was to invoke what is often described as "rule by law" rather than "rule of law."

The regime, PAS and 11 September

The tragic events of 11 September 2001 (9/11) and, to a large part, PAS's response to it, along with previous and subsequent declarations by the Islamic party, somehow helped to alter this scenario. Problems within PAS and its relationship with other opposition parties, particularly the predominantly Chinese DAP, had existed before then. Euphoric about their "success" in the 1999 elections, PAS leaders began talking about their "party of Islam" sweeping through Malaysia's northern states or what has often been called "the Malay heartland." Despite having agreed with the other opposition parties that making Malaysia an "Islamic state" would not be on the agenda, PAS leaders started to talk about creating precisely such a state if PAS came to power. This clearly spooked and annoyed the DAP, the PRM (*Parti Rakyat Malaysia*) and even Anwar's *Keadilan* (Justice) party. Equally important, this alienated a lot of non-Muslims and even "liberal" Muslims, prior to 9/11.

Thus, after the 1999 elections, while it was clear that UMNO had weakened, it was equally evident that PAS could not strengthen its appeal to the non-Muslim population. While there is little doubt that the mainstream Malaysian media played a significant role in demonizing PAS,[10] the party's single-minded pursuit of making society conform to *hudud* did not endear it to many. As one analyst (Ahmad Fauzi 2003: 13) puts it, "PAS serves as a poor embodiment of contemporary political Islam in Malaysia."

When 9/11 occurred, PAS was unlike Mahathir, who condemned the acts of violence but also urged the world to consider the context of such violent acts in order to address the causes. PAS was somewhat ambiguous. There was certainly no official condemnation on PAS's part. In a multi-ethnic, multi-religious country like Malaysia, such a response further raised questions about the nature of a state under PAS. Furthermore, as Ahmad Fauzi's (2006: 110–11) balanced study puts it:

> PAS found itself being implicated with sympathy for and perhaps even direct involvement in terrorism. For example, it never escaped the attention of the mainstream media that activists arrested for involvement with the Mujahidin Group of Malaysia (KMM, or Kumpulan Mujahidin Malaysia, later sensationalized as Kumpulan Militan Malaysia) and the Jemaah Islamiah (JI), both of which were allegedly linked to the Al-Qaeda international terrorist network, were former or active PAS members.
>
> ... after September 11 and the US attack on Afghanistan, emotional outbursts of sympathy for the Taliban and Osama bin Laden's Al-Qaeda network shown by PAS's leadership easily fell prey to the mainstream media.

The tragic events of 9/11 somehow became a godsend for Mahathir and his regime both internationally and, more so, locally. PAS's ambivalent stand on issues of terrorism and its insistence on the setting up of an Islamic state governed by Islamic laws, especially *Hudud* laws, seemed to have worked against it. This was not helped by the arrest, under the ISA, of alleged Malaysian Islamic terrorists linked to PAS, including the son of Nik Aziz Nik Mat, the charismatic PAS member and chief minister of the state of Kelantan.

Mahathir's nurturing of an image of UMNO being the face of a "tolerant Islam" before he retired, on the other hand, appears to have placated the non-Malay, non-Muslim population of Malaysia. In this regard then, it is not surprising that, unfair electoral practices notwithstanding, PAS (and other

164 *Zaharom Nain*

opposition parties such as the DAP and *Keadilan*) suffered badly in the 2004 general elections, losing the state of Trengganu and almost losing Kelantan. However, this should not detract us from the fact that "the *Pak Lah* (Abdullah Badawi) factor" also contributed to the BN's staggering victory in the March 2004 general elections.

Regime change or regime continuity? The media and Abdullah Badawi

Even before he became prime minister, Abdullah Badawi had nurtured a public persona as "Mr Clean." When he became prime minister, he declared that one of the major thrusts of his administration would be a war on corruption (Netto 2004: 2). Some observers have argued that this is part of Abdullah's strategy to distance himself from the excesses of the Mahathir administration. On paper, therefore, it appears that Abdullah aims to be "his own man," as it were, coming out of Mahathir's shadow.

However, other commentators argue that while he may indeed have a different leadership style – more approachable, more diplomatic, less of a loose cannon – from that of Mahathir's, it would take more than such traits to presume a regime change.[11] Developments over the three years since he took office indicate that while he may "speak softer" than Mahathir, the regime that he oversees is really no different. If one looks at Abdullah's dealings and relationship with the media, one could tease out certain factors pertaining to the Malaysian media which point to his regime being no different from Mahathir's. For instance, even before he became prime minister, Abdullah's former press secretary, Kamarulzaman Haji Zainal, was appointed Executive Director of Media Prima Berhad (MPB), Malaysia's largest listed media company. MPB was formed in August 2003 under a restructuring scheme that gives it control over TV3 and NSTP, Malaysia's largest newspaper publishing company. Kamarulzaman also sits on the board of directors of Malaysia's other media conglomerate, Utusan Melayu Berhad (UM), which publishes the top-selling Malay daily *Utusan Malaysia*.

It appears that during the period of transition of power from Mahathir to Abdullah Ahmad Badawi, key decisions regarding the media were also being affected. Prior to the above restructuring exercise, rumors were rife that prominent businessman Syed Mokhtar Al-Bukhary – purportedly an ally of Mahathir's – was attempting to gain control of and merge the two media conglomerates, NSTP and UM. When this did not happen, there was speculation that Abdullah Badawi's people in UM had prevented the merger, mainly to block off any consolidation of power by any particular political group within UMNO, just prior to Abdullah becoming prime minister on 1 November 2003.

UM, by the same token, remains very much in the hands of UMNO. This is quite evident from its board of directors comprising an executive chairman who is a former senator, a member who is an UMNO member of parliament, another who is a former deputy chief minister of the state of Kelantan and an UMNO member, and Mahathir's and Abdullah Badawi's former political secretaries.[12] No sooner had he become prime minister when the editor-in-chief of NST, Abdullah Ahmad (no relation to the PM) had his service terminated because he had become too vocal in pushing for Najib Tun Razak to be made deputy premier. (Ironically, Najib was eventually appointed.) The official line was that the termination was due to Abdullah Ahmad writing a critical piece on Saudi Arabia which, it was asserted, embarrassed both the Malaysian and Saudi governments. In terms of strategic political appointments at least, it appears that Abdullah Badawi's dealings with the Malaysian media are not too dissimilar from Mahathir's.

There are other notable continuities in Abdullah's own history with the media. First, when Malaysia's first independent, web-based daily news portal, Malaysiakini,[13] was raided by the police in 2003, Abdullah Badawi was heading the Home Ministry, which then oversaw the police, the PPPA, and the ISA. Second, he was the minister in charge when he was given signed petitions from more than 900 Malaysian journalists on World Press Freedom Day urging for the repeal of the PPPA. To date, he has done nothing about it. Third, in September 2002, when Mahathir was still prime minister and Abdullah was home minister, who is also in charge of issuing printing and publishing licenses, Malaysiakini had applied for a license to publish a weekly newspaper. Five years on, Malaysiakini still has not got a permit and Abdullah, now in his capacity as prime minister, has stated that a permit will not be given to Malaysiakini for fear that it could threaten national security. In the wake of 9/11 and the global drift towards greater media control, Abdullah's position, while inexcusable, is not surprising.

Draconian controls on the Malaysian media have certainly not been relaxed under Abdullah's administration. As if to establish his credentials as an Islamic leader and to further subdue PAS early in his term, Abdullah introduced the concept of *Islam Hadhari* (Civilizational Islam) – deemed forward-looking and enabling Muslims to peacefully co-exist with other faiths – to Malaysian socio-political discourse. Protecting Islam – and increasingly vocal Malay Muslims – in the wake of post-9/11 anti-Islam sentiments internationally appears to be one of Abdullah's key agendas. Hence, unlike elsewhere, especially where the liberalization of the media has been reversed after 9/11 in a supposed effort to combat terrorism – especially Islamic-linked terrorism – in Malaysia the increasing controls appear to have come about under the pretext of protecting Islam.

Two recent examples clearly illustrate this. First, there is the indefinite suspension in early 2006 of the East Malaysian English daily *Sarawak Tribune* over the reproduction of the controversial Danish cartoons mocking Islam under the PPPA. Subsequently, the evening edition of the Chinese newspaper *Guangming Daily* and an editor in Penang were also suspended for two weeks under the same Act for publishing a photograph showing

166 *Zaharom Nain*

someone reading a foreign newspaper containing the offending cartoons (see Loh 2006; Tan 2006).

The second development followed the disruption of a legally convened forum in Penang on 14 May 2006, to discuss the supremacy of the Malaysian Constitution. The forum, convened by a coalition of non-governmental organizations (NGOs) called Article 11, was the third in a series designed to educate Malaysians about their rights under the Constitution, particularly their religious rights. The first two had taken place without a hitch. But the third was disrupted and effectively stopped by an angry mob of Muslim Malaysians who believed that the forum attacked the position of Islam (and Muslims) in Malaysia.[14] After yet another forum in the southern state of Johor was also disrupted, Abdullah issued clear instructions that there would be no more public discussion of religion, particularly by the Article 11 coalition. However, two public meetings, conducted this time by conservative Islamic groups, were allowed to take place soon after. Both groups aimed at reasserting the dominance of Islam in the light of alleged challenges to the supremacy of the Islamic religion in contemporary Malaysia.

Curbs on content and expression notwithstanding, the commercialization of the media, with little concern for the notion of *public service*, continues unabated under Abdullah Badawi. A new satellite television company, MyTV, started operations in 2005. Changes in form, rather than substance, continue to be the rule of the day. Hence, a newspaper like the broadsheet *New Straits Times* has converted to a tabloid format to bump up its circulation. Other newspapers, in order to push up circulation, have sensationalized violent crime stories.[15] Another English daily, the *Star*, in this regard went one step further by urging for a crackdown on social violence, via a drift towards a "law and order" society through a "rakan cop" (friend of the police) project, arguably a populist legitimization of state violence.

On local television, "reality TV" has taken hold, with local versions of *American Idol* and the like mushrooming virtually overnight. On 28 August 2006, two of the country's biggest "reality TV" programs were aired. These were the live TV3 coverage of the wedding of Malaysian pop diva Siti Nurhaliza and the (again "live") coverage by government-owned TV1 of the break-up of local male pop icon Mawi and his fiancée. These two programs resulted in one of the biggest television ratings battles in Malaysian television history.

On the whole, it is apparent that what we have been seeing in Malaysia since the ascension of Abdullah Badawi in 2003 is far from a regime change. It would be more accurate to suggest that the transition from Mahathir to Abdullah Badawi marked a change in personalities. The actions of the new prime minister thus far suggest that he wishes to "mend fences" with the Malay community, possibly even work out some political pact with PAS. His introduction of the concept of *Islam Hadhari* to the Malaysian public appears to be aimed at establishing his Islamic credentials and at co-opting much of PAS's arguments about the Islamization of Malaysia. Internationally, unlike Mahathir, his diplomatic and measured statements, especially in relation to previously estranged but important trading partners like Singapore and the US, have been hailed by the mainstream media.

As far as media structures are concerned, there has been no attempt at reforming media ownership. This, perhaps, is to be expected as attempts at reforms would not go down well with the current circle of media owners in Malaysia, most of whom are closely linked to politicians and political parties in the BN coalition. Concentration of media ownership – and concentration in the hands of politically affiliated companies, and individuals at that – has been the norm in Malaysia for a long time. Media reform places much importance on the need to disperse ownership, the need to break down monopolies and oligopolies. Going by the experience of more established capitalist economies, there will be much resistance to such reforms. So for the time being, it looks as though, new prime minister or old, it is business as usual in Malaysia.

Notes

1 See Khoo (2003b) for a succinct account of such succession "battles."
2 This pattern of ownership, of course, was nothing new. Political ownership of the Malay press, for example, had begun further back, in the early 1960s (Gomez 2004: 475) when UMNO, under the control of Tunku Abdul Rahman, instituted a takeover of Utusan Melayu Press Bhd to ensure that the company's newspaper would portray his party and administration in a favorable light.
3 However, both expulsion orders were later overturned after legal appeal.
4 The companies that were established included free-to-air television stations, Metrovision (1995) and ntv7 (1998), cable, Mega TV (1995), and satellite TV and radio, Astro (1996). Private radio stations too became rather popular during this period, with stations like Time Highway Radio (1994), Hitz FM (1997), Light & Easy (1997) and Classic Rock (1997) coming on the Malaysian airwaves.
5 See Khoo (2003a: 71–98) for a detailed analysis of Anwar's downfall.
6 Splashed across the pages of mainstream newspapers such as the *New Straits Times* and the *Star* were reports of Mahathir calling on journalists to "focus on their responsibility to society," denouncing "negative reporting," urging "us" to unite, to be one – presumably in the spirit of Malaysia Inc. – in the wake of the present crisis, to ward off "rogue speculators" and other international "evil Others."
7 At their peak, these websites numbered more than fifty, although the quality and credibility of the "news" provided by many of these sites were as questionable as those provided by the mainstream media. Mainly run by amateurs with little or no journalistic training, these sites thrived on rumors and innuendo and had relatively short shelf-lives. Of those that have remained, many owe their continuance to the resilience of their webmasters more than to the quality of their reports.
8 In this regard, it was during this period that Malaysia's first web-based daily news portal Malaysiakini was launched in November 1999. Set up by a few young journalists who had left the mainstream media disillusioned with the state of the Malaysian media, its aim is to provide "independent news coverage, investigative journalism, and in-depth news analysis" (www.malaysiakini.com; accessed 10 September 2002). It would be disingenuous to suggest that the continued

168 *Zaharom Nain*

existence of Malaysiakini and the non-censorship of the Internet by the regime thus far are indicative of a more open or transparent environment. Internet penetration in Malaysia is still quite low and it is clear that penetration and access are still limited to certain classes of citizens in certain urban settings. In mid-2002, 70 percent of Internet subscribers were located in the three main, urbanized states of Selangor, Penang and Johor (see Zaharom 2004).

9 See Sabri (2000) for an eyewitness account of the demonstrations and related events.
10 See, for example, Mustafa (2002b) for an analysis of the demonization of PAS.
11 See, for example, Hector (2003) and Ramakrishnan (2003).
12 Information obtained from www.utusangroup.com.my/bods.html (accessed 20 November 2004).
13 See George (Chapter 9 in this volume) for more details about Malaysiakini's encounter with the authorities.
14 See Mustafa (2006) for a critique of press coverage of the 14 May 2006 Penang forum.
15 The free English language newspaper, *The Sun*, published an extensive feature on this phenomenon on its 14–15 August 2004 issue.

Bibliography

Ahmad Fauzi, Abdul Hamid (2003) "Reforming PAS?" *Aliran Monthly*, 23(6): 11–13.
—— (2006) "The UMNO–PAS struggle: analysis of PAS's defeat in 2004," in S.-H. Saw and K. Kesavapany (eds) *Malaysia: Recent trends and challenges*, Singapore: Institute of Southeast Asian Studies, pp. 100–31.
Chan, T.S. (1986) "The suspension of *Asian Wall Street Journal*: 'national interest' vs 'the role of the press,'" *Malaysian Journalism Review*, 5: 5–7.
Gomez, E.T. (2004) "Politics of the media: the press under Mahathir," in B. Welsh (ed.) *Reflections: The Mahathir years*, Washington, DC: Southeast Asia Studies Program, Johns Hopkins University, pp. 475–85.
Hector, C. (2003) "New face, same body," *Aliran Monthly*, 23(11): 36, 40.
Jomo, K.S. (1990) *Growth and Structural Change in the Malaysian Economy*, London: Macmillan.
Kessler, C.S. (2004) "The mark of the man: Mahathir's Malaysia after Dr Mahathir," in B. Welsh (ed.) *Reflections: The Mahathir years*, Washington, DC: Southeast Asia Studies Program, Johns Hopkins University, pp. 15–17.
Khoo, B.T. (2003a) *Beyond Mahathir: Malaysian politics and its discontents*, London: Zed Books.
—— (2003b) "Who will succeed the successor? Reflections on the Mahathir–Abdullah transition," *Aliran Monthly*, 23(5): 2, 4–6.
Loh, A. (2006) "Deflated dreams," *Aliran Monthly*, 26(5): 8–10.
Loh, F.K.W. (2003) "New politics in Malaysia," *Aliran Monthly*, 23(6): 2, 4–6.
Loh, F.K.W. and Mustafa, K. Anuar (1996) "The press in Malaysia in the early 1990s: corporatistion, technological innovaton and the middle class," in Muhammad Ikmal Said and Zahid Emby (eds) *Malasia: Critical perspectives*, Petaling Jaya: Persatuan Sains Sosial Malaysia.
Loh, F.K.W. and Saravanamuttu, J. (eds) (2003) *New Politics in Malaysia*, Singapore: ISEAS.

Mustafa, K. Anuar (1990) "The Malaysian 1990 general election: the role of the BN mass media," *Kajian Malaysia*, 8(2): 82–102.

—— (2002a) "Defining democratic discourses: the mainstream press," in Francis K.W. Loh and B.T. Khoo (eds) *Democracy in Malaysia: Discourses and practices*, London: Curzon, pp. 138–64.

—— (2002b) "The mousedeer, the Taliban and a sorry state," *Aliran Monthly*, 22(7): 2, 3–5.

—— (2004) "Muzzled? The media in Mahathir's Malaysia," in B. Welsh (ed.) *Reflections: The Mahathir years*, Washington, DC: Southeast Asia Studies Program, Johns Hopkins University, pp. 486–93.

—— (2006) "Flawed reporting," *Aliran Monthly*, 26(5): 16–17.

Netto, A. (2004) "War on corruption: hunting the sharks or ikan bilis?," *Aliran Monthly*, 24(1): 2, 4–6.

Ramakrishnan, P. (2003) "Next change or re-run?" *Aliran Monthly*, 23(9): 2, 4–5.

Rodan, G. (1998) "Asia and the international press: the political significance of expanding markets," in V. Randall (ed.) *Democratization and the Media* (Special Issue: Democratization), 5(2): 125–54.

—— (2004) *Transparency and Authoritarian Rule in Southeast Asia: Singapore and Malaysia*. London: RoutledgeCurzon.

Sabri Zain (2000) *Face Off: A Malaysian reformasi diary (1998–99)*, Singapore: BigO Books.

Tan, L.O. (2006) "The age of uncertainty," *Aliran Monthly*, 26(5): 11–13.

Wong, K. (2000) "Malaysia: in the grip of the government," in L. Williams and R. Rich (eds) *Losing Control: Freedom of the press in Asia*, Canberra: Asia Pacific Press.

Zaharom Nain (1994) "Commercialization and control in a 'caring society': Malaysian media 'towards 2020'", *SOJOURN: Journal of Social Issues in Southeast Asia*, 9(2): 178–99.

—— (2002a) "The structure of the media industry: implications for democracy," in Francis K.W. Loh and B.T. Khoo (eds) *Democracy in Malaysia: Discourses and practices*, London: Curzon, pp. 138–64.

—— (2002b) "The media and Malaysia's reformasi movement," in Russell H.K. Heng (ed.) *Media Fortunes, Changing Times: ASEAN states in transition*, Singapore: ISEAS, pp. 119–38.

—— (2004) "New technologies and the future of the media in Malaysia," in P. Chandran (ed.) *Communicating the Future*, Kuala Lumpur: United Nations Development Programme and Strategic Analysis, pp. 99–116.

Zaharom Nain and Mustafa, K. Anuar (2000) "Marketing to the masses in Malaysia: commercial television, religion and nation-building," in D. French and M. Richards (eds) *Television in Contemporary Asia*, New Delhi: Sage, pp. 151–78.

11 Gestural politics:

Mediating the "new" Singapore

Terence Lee

> Despite its continued reproduction, the authoritarian regime in Singapore is not devoid of tensions and contradictions that require management. Indeed, constant refinements are undertaken precisely for that reason. Thus, instead of asking why democracy has not arrived in Singapore, the question should be: what direction has political change taken in Singapore and how do we explain it?
>
> (Rodan 2006: 3)

On 12 August 2004, Singapore witnessed its second political transition when Lee Hsien Loong – the eldest son of Singapore's elder statesman Lee Kuan Yew – was installed as the nation's third prime minister (PM). In a brief speech delivered at his swearing-in ceremony, Lee promised Singaporeans that his reign as prime minister would see the formation of a "new" approach to governing the nation, one that is marked by greater "openness" and "inclusiveness." As he puts it in the speech that was widely reported in Singapore's national media:

> We will continue to expand the space which Singaporeans have to live, laugh, to grow and be ourselves. Our people should feel free to express diverse views, pursue unconventional ideas, or simply be different. We should have the confidence to engage in robust debate, so as to understand our problems, conceive fresh solutions, and open up new spaces. We should recognise many paths of success, and many ways to be Singaporean. Ours must be an open and inclusive Singapore.
>
> (H.L. Lee 2004: 6)

As long-time observer of the political economy of Singapore Garry Rodan (2006) has warned in the opening quote to this chapter, such promises of openness do not amount to democratic developments. Instead, they point to new directions and strategies that the regime creatively employs from time to time to maintain its grip on power. Along such lines, it is important to recognize from the outset that PM Lee's attempt to widen the scope of what it means to "be Singaporean" is not so much to declare an "open season" under his premiership, but to define the parameters of politics and political participation in Singapore under his charge, and thus mediate the meaning(s) of political transformation in Singapore via a host of creative institutional and gestural initiatives. As Rodan has observed, "it is not the political space of civil society but that of the [People Action Party's] state that is expanding" (Rodan 2006: 4). Rodan contends that political transitions or state transformations in an authoritarian regime like Singapore do not conform to theories of regime change that would typically identify transitional points towards democracy (see O'Donnell and Schmitter 1986; Diamond 2002; Case 2002), but are in effect "regime reproductions" marked by "contemporary refinements to the political regime" (Rodan 2006: 4).

At the most rudimentary level, one could argue that the new prime minister's rhetoric of an "open and inclusive Singapore" is really an attempt to win mass support through product differentiation. Since Lee's predecessor Goh Chok Tong had promised a kinder and gentler style of rule – or the institutionalization of consensus politics – when he took office in 1990, the new prime minister had to adopt a similar tack, but with a new slant. This was all the more necessary given that Goh's terms of engagement were reframed when he felt his authority being challenged in 1994, less than four years after he took office, by a seemingly innocuous political commentary by Singaporean novelist Catherine Lim in the local *Straits Times* daily. The article opined that Prime Minister Goh's promise of a more open, consultative and consensual leadership style had been abandoned in favor of the authoritarian style of his predecessor Lee Kuan Yew (C. Lim 1994a, 1994b). Although Lim was merely thinking aloud and echoing the rumblings of many Singaporeans, she was duly rebuked for "going beyond the pale" (T. Lee 2002). As a consequence, Goh's rule as prime minister (from 1990 to 2004) arguably became best known for the institution and entrenchment of the infamous out-of-bounds markers (or OB-markers), a golfing terminology that is intended to demarcate the parameters of political debate and dissent in Singapore (T. Lee 2002, 2005a). Since the Catherine Lim saga, OB-markers remain the most-cited reason for political apathy among its citizens and the corresponding lack of public discourse on civil society and political issues in Singapore. More importantly, it exposes the PAP government's reluctance to genuinely embrace more liberal modes of political participation, preferring instead for regime reproduction through strategic refinements to authoritarian rule (Rodan 2006: 18).

PM Lee's declaration of greater openness under his premiership could thus be seen as a continuation of PAP's "regime reproduction" initiatives that are intended to steer "change in Singapore down a preferred path of political co-option rather than political contestation" (Rodan 2006: 11). While Goh Chok Tong invoked the Asian values discourse in the 1990s and emphasized "political consensus" through much of his reign, the new premier seems to have developed an early affinity with the rhetoric of "openness." Indeed, a speech peppered with "openness" and other liberal declarations

172   *Terence Lee*

could be seen as amounting to nothing more than a public relations state-ment to project Singapore as a mature, progressive and creative society to the rest of the world. But by using phrases such as "our people should feel free" and "an open and inclusive Singapore," Lee was attempting, on the one hand, to dispel fears that he would return to the dictatorial and authoritarian style of rule that typified his father's reign from 1965 to 1990. On the other hand, by displaying a readiness to engage with "diverse views" and "unconventional ideas" to "open up new spaces," the prime minister was in effect mediating and "branding" his new regime as one that is in touch with the social, cultural and economic realities of the twenty-first century.

As Leo and Lee (2004: 207) have elucidated, this is an "openness" that is deliberately directed at the "remaking and re-branding [of] Singapore as the 'new' smart and creative place to be." What this "new" represents, however, remains hazy and uncertain, especially with regard to the political structures and practices in the city-state. One could observe, for instance, the ways in which the new prime minister has employed the tools of political commu-nication in the form of on-message repetition, rhetoric and other creative strategies widely employed by political parties in more liberal societies from his very first day in office (Esser *et al.* 2000; Lee and Willnat 2006). In public relations critique, such strategies are often subsumed under the con-temporary discourse of "spin," which in political communication involves "the interpretation or slant" placed on an event or a speech with an eye towards promoting and reproducing one's preferred narrative (Esser *et al.* 2000: 213). Although the spread of the media industries, along with the recent rise of public relations as an increasingly indispensable sector, has brought about the ubiquity of "spin," the extent of knowledge about the subject remains marginal in Singapore. As I have suggested elsewhere, this is due largely to a duopolistic media structure as well as a lack of independent media critique and analytical reporting in Singapore (see T. Lee 2005b; Lee and Willnat 2006). In any case, the mainstream media in Singapore prefers to describe this phenomenon as the proliferation of official "buzzwords." As *Straits Times* journalist Ignatius Low has observed with tongue in cheek: "Every now and then, a new buzzword seizes Singapore. In true Singapore fashion, ministers' speeches become peppered with it, it starts appearing in newspaper headlines and the civil service organizes entire workshops to discuss it" (Low 2005).

Employing the rubric of "gestural politics" (T. Lee 2005a), this chapter contends that Lee Hsien Loong's premiership since August 2004 has been typified by the use of language and buzzwords that "seems long on rhetoric but short on content," which reflects an obvious paradox between the state's desire to build a dynamic and creative society while continuing to micro-manage the citizenry (Jones 2004). Such emphases on populist rhetoric and buzzwords like "openness" and "inclusiveness" – cryptic terms that are politically correct and that "sound good" to most people, and can be

Mediating the "new" Singapore   173

invoked repetitively and as liberally as desired (Kumar 1993: 376) – characterizes what I would refer to as "gestural politics" (T. Lee 2005a). Gestural politics occurs or operates when "liberal gestures" in the forms of rehearsed rhetoric, public statements, press releases and, indeed, the propagation of buzzwords by the regime are bestowed with greater discursive powers in shaping perceptions as compared to actual substances or power symmetries (T. Lee 2005a).

While creative strategies utilizing rhetoric, "spin," branding and image-making approaches are not new to modern politics, what is different about the new Lee administration is that it appears to be seeking – somewhat desperately, but no less genuinely – to mediate the reproduction of the PAP regime and its mode of authoritarianism under Lee Hsien Loong via the application of gestural politics. The introduction of new terms or buzzwords is intended to attract Singaporeans to the political cause or issue of the day not by rational argument or persuasion per se, but by its "gestural" attributes – regardless of how mundane or frivolous they may be. After all, this ability to attract and win the political support of the people is the ultimate goal of what Joseph S. Nye (2004) would refer to as a "soft power" approach to Machiavellian politics.

Instead of seeing the Lee administration's overzealous use of buzzwords and other gestures or rhetoric as political "dumbing down," this chapter contends that gestural politics, especially in relation to the tourism sector and the creative industries, is playing – and will continue to play – a major role in the further consolidation of the PAP regime and its political economy in the twenty-first century. The discussion that follows will examine recent applications of such gestures in Singapore: from tourism (re)branding, urban revitalization of the cityscape to the "Great Casino Debate" (from 2004 to 2005), culminating with the bold decision by the prime minister to proceed with the construction of Singapore's first two mega-sized casino complexes. This chapter analyses these events and the ways they have been mediated and communicated to the public, and considers how they impact upon our understanding of political consolidation and regime reproduction in the "new" Singapore.

Creative shifts in gestural politics

Things change fast in Singapore. These days, nightlife stretches to daybreak. And at many pubs, dancing on the bar is actually expected. On the shopping front, new boutiques continue to pop up islandwide, and an ever-growing alfresco dining scene is a treat if you love the tropical outdoors. With thrills like reverse bungee, exciting cabaret acts and so many international concerts, no two visits to Singapore are alike. In fact, your travel guide may already require a reprint.

("Uniquely Singapore" advertisement in *The West Australian*,
19 June 2004: 32)

174   *Terence Lee*

On 9 March 2004, the Singapore Tourism Board (STB) launched "Uniquely Singapore," a new tourism branding to market Singapore as a premier tourism destination, with the primary aim of achieving a target of 7.6 million visitor arrivals for 2004 (STB 2004). This new branding, comprising a range of media advertisements for different global markets, was developed in the wake of the city-state's "recovery" from its economically crippling encounter with the Severe Acute Respiratory Syndrome (SARS) viral epidemic during the first half of 2003. It also coincided with the circulation of broad rhetoric that speaks of a "more open" and "creative" Singapore (Leo and Lee 2004: 205), designed to (re)package the city-state as a vibrant place where local and foreign talents can "live, work, and play" (Lee and Lim 2004: 150). This rhetoric was first articulated, albeit with slight variation, by Prime Minister Lee Hsien Loong when he pledged in his swearing-in speech (cited earlier in the chapter) to widen the "space which Singaporeans have to live, laugh, [and] to grow" (H.L. Lee 2004). As one would expect in a city replete with buzzwords, similar catchcries continue to be echoed by the prime minister as well as other ministers and public servants in Singapore (Low 2005). One of the more recent examples is the release of the PAP's Election Manifesto by Prime Minister Lee Hsien Loong on 15 April 2006 ahead of the 2006 General Elections. Entitled *Staying Together, Moving Ahead*, the very first "vision for every citizen" reads: "[We will] create a future full of opportunities for Singaporeans, with a dynamic economy generating good jobs for all, and a vibrant city which we will all enjoy living in"[1] (PAP 2006: 2).

The STB's new tourism branding is one of several broad-based attempts by the Singapore government to propagate "attractive" images of a "new" and "creative" Singapore (STB 2004). In the "Uniquely Singapore" advertisement cited above, the image of a socially and culturally revitalized Singapore is evident as the nation is presented as a "cool" and "funky" city of excitement and thrills – echoing McCarthy and Ellis's widely publicized cover story in *Time* magazine on 19 July 1999 which presented the city-state as "competitive, creative, even funky" (McCarthy and Ellis 1999). The advertisement was accompanied by a by-line which "instructs" the reader – who is likely to be a prospective visitor – to burn travel guides on Singapore that are old and outdated, defined in the advertisement as any guide book "more than 8 months old." Such inscriptions mark a form of radicalness that is intended to displace old mindsets about Singapore's colorless cultural landscape, its lackluster creative scene, as well as its notoriety as a "police state" (T. Lee 2004).

The fashionable rhetoric of "creativity" – popularized by the Singapore government's declaration in 2002 that it would embrace the global "creative industries" project (T. Lee 2004; Lee and Lim 2004) – has been mobilized to demonstrate to the world that Singapore has become more "open" and "inclusive." The concept of the creative industries has its formal origins in the United Kingdom in 1998 as one aspect of British Prime Minister Tony Blair's economic and political revitalization strategy, and has since been adopted by both the developed world as well as emerging markets in Asia (Flew 2005: 116–17). While the creative industries in Singapore – as it is in the UK and elsewhere – is typically predicated upon the development of a "creative network," comprising the arts and cultural sector, the design sector and the generic media industry, "creativity" has become another buzzword in Singapore to signal its shift into a "new" economy marked by scientific and technology-driven innovation, entrepreneurship and, above all, for Singapore to be seen as a "hip and happening" place for doing business and having fun (Li 2006; Lee and Lim 2004: 150).

While creativity and the creative industries are seen as enlightened and liberating policies, one needs to bear in mind that the overarching intention of creativity and innovation is to boost Singapore's economic capital by attracting talented individuals – many of whom, according to the creative industries discourse, can be described as "bohemian-creative" types (Flew 2005: 126–7). The principle is that the productive energies of such creative individuals would "rub off" on Singaporean workers and generate an increase in the creative industries' contribution to Singapore's Gross Domestic Product (GDP).[2] To this end, the government has begun to liberalize what could be described as the "bohemian fringes" of Singapore culture and society. Some of these publicized changes have included a declared willingness to appoint openly gay public servants to sensitive positions in the civil service, the legalization of "bar-top dancing" in pubs and nightclubs (as captured in the tourism advertisement), the granting of permits for extreme sports such as skydiving and reverse bungee-jumping, and the auto-registration of societies, clubs, and interest groups (Lee and Lim 2004: 150).

Since 2003, the government has also been busy liberalizing the city's nocturnal entertainment scene by allowing 24-hour "party zones" in nightspot districts like Marina South, Collyer Quay/Shenton Way and Sentosa Island, along with a host of established hotels and clubs (Mak 2006: 6; Mulchand and Nadarajan 2003). As Flew (2005: 126–7) points out, a city's "night-time economy," defined as "the range of activities undertaken by tourists and by locals outside of the hours of formal work or study," has become a significant factor in the development of sustainable creative infrastructure and as a potential source of locational advantage in a globalized economy. Regardless of whether one construes these concessions as significant improvements to the creative infrastructure and political condition in Singapore or if these developments are dismissed as mere frivolity, it is likely that more of such gestures will follow in the foreseeable future due to two interrelated reasons.

First, catering to the varied demands of a creative-cum-globalized workforce in a city that aspires to be as cosmopolitan as London and New York, or with vibrant street life in the likes of Tokyo, Seoul or Hong Kong, requires Singapore to become a "a city that never sleeps" – or a city that

176   *Terence Lee*

embraces what is now commonly known as a 24/7 lifestyle (Mak 2006: 6). As Flew explicates:

> [S]uch developments require innovative public policy thinking, that sees activities associated with the night-life of a city, not as a problem for local authorities, but as a both a source of new opportunities for creative industries development, and as part of a *creative milieux* that gives a city or a region a dynamic image, and acts as an attractor to creative personnel in a globally networked new-economy industries.
>
> (Flew 2005: 127; emphases in original).

Second, tolerance to difference, diversity and "acceptance" of alternative lifestyles is now widely regarded as a necessary component of the global innovation and creativity-led new economy. This is a position championed most vociferously by Florida (2002) when he argued that creativity presents itself in intellectuals are other productive workers who are enriched by diverse experiences and perspectives. Prime Minister Lee Hsien Loong displayed an early awareness of such links between tolerance/bohemianism and creativity when his panoramic vision of Singapore included "an expanded space" for Singaporeans to "live, laugh, grow and be themselves" (H.L. Lee 2004). However, the dimension and make-up of this newly liberated "space" – like the invisible boundaries of the OB-markers – are likely to remain cryptic, ambiguous and, for critics, insignificant or frivolous (T. Lee 2005a). Nevertheless, these visionary phrases and terms demonstrate the government's willingness to realign or even slaughter the "sacred policy cows" that are seen to affect global perceptions of Singapore, which are in turn inextricably linked to economic progress and development. While such policy shifts are meaningless to the majority of Singaporeans – and indeed foreigners – who are uninterested in 24/7 nightlife or bohemian and alternative lifestyles, their gestural values are significant enough to "give substance to PAP rhetoric about opening up avenues for political expressions and consensus," regardless of the fact that these policies are not inherently political (Rodan 2006: 4).

Creative phrases and terms introduced by the government in describing the physical remaking of Singapore, especially in the "new downtown" of Marina Bay – a large waterfront plot of land, formed through a massive land reclamation project, that is slated to become Singapore's new city centre by 2010 – has centered around the idea of "creating the buzz of a global city" (L. Lim 2005). In June 2005, Singapore's Urban Redevelopment Authority (URA) unveiled its concept plan for new developments in Marina Bay and announced that it was taking the "Marina Bay" brand abroad to sell Singapore as a vibrant global city with world-class physical and creative infrastructure (Loo 2005). As reported in *The Straits Times Interactive* (the online version of the national daily): "Under the official Marina Bay banner, the URA will pitch the Explore, Exchange, Entertain concept, which sells the idea of a "work, live, play" lifestyle, rather than land or buildings themselves" (Loo 2005). In essence, the government's vision is for Marina Bay to become an iconic representation of a "newer and better" twenty-first century Singapore, which would in turn reflect the dynamism and creativity that one would demand from a leading global city (Lee 2004: 291).[3]

Development projects that have been conceptualized or launched in the Marina Bay area since 2004 have been some of the most breathtaking ever witnessed in Singapore, with various media and marketing superlatives – or "wow" factors designed to dazzle and captivate the public – employed in all news releases and project launches. While Singapore's first "Integrated Resort"-cum-casino complex (discussed in greater detail in the next section of the chapter) is expected to become the most iconic development in Marina Bay, other projects have nevertheless received their share of media attention and limelight. These include: "The Sail@Marina Bay," one of Singapore's tallest and most exclusive residential towers with a unique ship's sail design (Loo 2005); the "Singapore Flyer," a giant observation Ferris wheel which, when completed in 2008, at 178 meters high will stand 43 meters taller than the London Eye, erected on the south bank of the River Thames in London and the source of Singapore's inspiration (Pereira 2005); and three new water-themed public gardens that would occupy about 84 hectares of Marina Bay in total, one of which is envisaged to house a giant air-conditioned conservatory that would allow Singaporeans and tourists a chance to view "flowers that bloom in temperate countries during spring, like tulips, daffodils and chrysanthemums" (H.Y. Tan 2006: 1, 4).

In March 2004, the government informed Singaporeans that it would seriously consider the prospect of building a casino in Singapore with the intention of creating a new tourism-led income stream for the domestic economy (A. Tan 2004; L. Teo 2004). Over the past decade, Asia has become the fastest growing market in casino gaming and Singapore has been looking to exploit its excellent regulatory cachet and transport linkages to draw in more tourist investment and revenue (E.K.B. Tan 2005). Moreover, the Las Vegas-styled glitz of a casino would further the "opening-up" rhetoric, and other like buzzwords, that has consumed the city-state since 2004 and possibly, as some would assert, in the years prior. However, the controversial nature of the announcement – bearing in mind that occasional proposals for a casino in Singapore since the 1970s have been rejected on moral and socio-political grounds, and that the former premier Goh Chok Tong had publicly declared that he would not approve of a casino as long as he was prime minister – meant that the decision would not be as politically straightforward as the authoritarian PAP government would have liked (Ooi 2005: 258). It was therefore necessary to engage the citizenry by gathering feedback and gauging opinions (Koh 2005).

This feedback gathering exercise generated what became known as the "Great Casino Debate" within Singapore, with a sizeable number of Singaporeans

178   *Terence Lee*

participating and airing their views, many for the first time. Indeed, as it has transpired, the "Great Casino Debate" offers one of the most eye-opening and contemporary examples of the extent of policy shifts that have taken place in Singapore since Lee Hsien Loong took office as prime minister. The next section takes a cogent look at the "Great Casino Debate" leading up to the announcement of the government's final decision in April 2005, and considers its impact on the mediation of regime reproduction in Singapore and the extent of political consensus possible under PM Lee.

Opening up new spaces?

[Singapore] cannot stand still. The whole region is on the move. If we do not change, where will we be in 20 years' time? Losing our appeal is the lesser problem. But if we become a backwater, just one of many ordinary cities in Asia, instead of becoming a cosmopolitan hub of the region, then many good jobs will be lost, and all Singaporeans will suffer. We cannot afford that.

(H.L. Lee 2005)

Singapore's Trade and Industry Minister George Yeo was handed the task of declaring Singapore's new state of "openness" when he said in Parliament on 13 March 2004 that the government would be "keeping an open mind" on whether to build a casino in Singapore with the primary aim of diversifying and boosting the domestic economy (A. Tan 2004). As noted earlier, this sparked an animated "Great Casino Debate" in Singapore through much of 2004 and into the first few months of 2005, with the overwhelming majority of the expressed views "polarised along hard-headed, pragmatic-economic arguments on the one hand and on values-morality lines on the other" (E.K.B. Tan 2005; L. Lim 2004). Most religious groups were dismayed at the proposal and voiced strong objections to having a casino in the city-state. In December 2004, a group of citizens calling themselves "Families Against the Casino Threat in Singapore" – or FACTS – began to rally Singaporeans to their cause via an Internet website: www.facts.com.sg (Goh and Sim 2004: 5).[4] As reported on its website, FACTS managed to collect close to 20,000 signatures through an Internet petition which was eventually submitted to the president of Singapore (Ooi 2005: 258–9). While there were many who wrote in support of the proposal – either via the official Feedback channel managed by the Ministry of Trade and Industry (MTI) or the *Straits Times* "Forum" page – most did not even bother to participate, believing that the casino debate amounted to nothing more than a "talkfest" or a public relations exercise (Chia and Li 2005). Even among those who offered their opinions, many remain ambivalent about the government's sincerity in calling for public comments. Nevertheless, by December 2004, MTI had received more than 700 letters, emails and faxes on the issue (Goh and Sim 2004).

Mediating the "new" Singapore 179

In November 2004, at around the mid-way mark of the year-long "Great Casino Debate," Vivian Balakrishnan, the minister tasked with leading the decision-making process, decided to invoke the by now well-rehearsed rhetoric of "openness" by re-framing the discussion into one about the depth of maturity in Singapore society and whether Singapore's should be granted freedom of choice (J. Teo 2004a, 2005b; Ooi 2005: 259). As the minister articulated somewhat candidly – yet strategically – to local journalists:

> [T]he real question which we need to confront is what type of society we are or, to be more accurate, are we now a more mature society than, say, decades ago[?] My own sense of it is Singapore is a much more mature society and, generally, the vast majority of Singaporeans can be trusted to make up their own minds, exercise their choices and act responsibly. The fundamental question is, are we ready as a society to let people make choices of their own, take responsibility for their actions and face the consequences? If we are indeed ready, then we can consider taking more risks in a sense, with new and innovative and radical plans. This issue of an integrated resort with a casino is just one such example.
>
> (cited in J. Teo 2004b)

According to Ooi (2005: 259), by invoking the "freedom of choice" argument, the minister was also making "an indirect reference to whether Singapore should continue as a nanny state or a more open society." The minister was in essence posing a rhetorical question because the answer is an obvious one. But at same time, he was exercising political expedience and opportunism by excluding this same "freedom of choice" argument to other – and indeed, longer-term – "grey issues" such as gay rights, civil society and media, cultural and political censorship, and many others (see T. Lee 2005a). These are all of course issues fraught with different problems (and should be analyzed separately elsewhere), but suffice it to point out here that these do not detract from the fact that if Singapore is indeed a "mature society" as Minister Balakrishnan had posited, then Singaporeans should be given genuine "new spaces" to map out their own social, cultural and political choices. In the spirit of gestural politics, the minister had prudently couched the issue as one of "freedom," where opponents of a casino could simply look the other way and not participate in the discourse. This would in turn give the government the "consensus" it has been seeking to make a seemingly "unbiased" and "informed" decision.

On 18 April 2005, the prime minister announced in Parliament that his Cabinet had decided to proceed with the construction of not one casino, but two mega-size "Integrated Resorts": the first and larger resort in Marina Bay, and the second on the southern resort island of Sentosa. These Integrated Resorts would come with casino-cum-gaming components occupying no more than 3 to 5 percent of the total floor area. This maximum allowable

180 *Terence Lee*

space was couched as a "safeguard" to ensure that the resorts will be seen as family-friendly entertainment venues, and not gambling dens that could be associated with organized crime and other vices. Other gestural measures that would be introduced to protect Singaporeans against the ills of casino gambling include a high entrance fee of S$100 per day or S$2,000 a year and a ban on credit. In addition, PM Lee pledged that those in financial distress, or receiving social assistance, would be kept out. Singaporeans will also be allowed to exclude themselves or their family members (H.L. Lee 2005).

The announcement, as it turned out, was well calibrated and designed to extract maximum media coverage and political mileage. It was in effect an excellent demonstration of the attractive power of gestural politics (T. Lee 2005a). Not only did PM Lee deliver a considered speech in Parliament lasting forty-five minutes, several ministers were roped in afterwards to talk about how the decision would impact positively upon their respective port-folios (Feedback Unit 2005: 64–6). The most notable was Lim Boon Heng, the minister in the Prime Minister's Office and also the secretary-general of Singapore's largest and government-endorsed union, the National Trade Union Congress (NTUC), who declared emotionally that he supported the construction of the "Integrated Resorts" because of the prospect of 35,000 new jobs that would boost the nation's workforce (although the actual number of these jobs going to Singaporeans will remain uncertain until the resorts become operational in 2009 or 2010) (Chia 2005). As Singaporean law academic Eugene Tan predicted prior to the unveiling of the decision in a commentary piece:

> The government will come out a winner regardless whether a casino is built or not. Should the government decide against the gaming compo-nent in the planned integrated resort, the feedback process would be portrayed as a triumph of the Lee Hsien Loong government's con-sultative approach, its decisiveness and resoluteness in policy-making, the political maturing of Singapore society, and an enhancement of the social compact through active citizenry.
>
> (E.K.B. Tan 2005)

In the end, the government's decision to proceed with the casinos enabled it to "have the best of both worlds," notwithstanding that those who partici-pated in the feedback process were "wrong-footed" in that most were doing so on the basis that the plan was for a sole casino or not at all, but never two mega-resorts. Nevertheless, the discourse of gestural politics triumphed as the "Great Casino Debate" – described by Minister Balakrishnan as "the mother of all consultations" (Feedback Unit 2005: 65) – had become a showpiece for the government as it could now lay claims to being open and attentive to public feedback on a major national issue (T. Lee 2005a, 2005c). Indeed, the "Great Casino Debate" was featured in the government's Feedback

Unit 2005 Year Book, entitled *Shaping Our Home: Turning Ideas into Reality*, as a positive example of an "open, transparent, sincere and constructive dialogue" between the government and the people (Feedback Unit 2005: 65). Singaporeans were duly commended for participating in the debate in a rational and constructive fashion, with the Feedback Unit declaring that "the fact that so many Singaporeans had responded so actively to the idea of a casino was perhaps more significant than the final result" (Feedback Unit 2005: 65). In essence, the "Great Casino Debate" invoked the key elements of gestural politics, with gloss and rhetoric taking precedence over consensus in the decision-making process.

The term "Integrated Resort" had been used very sparingly by the Singapore media prior to the decision, but in the aftermath of PM Lee's announcement, the government – and the media – had almost completely jettisoned the less favorable and baggage-laden "casino." This "Integrated Resort" nomenclature brought a new and creative "spin" to the issue. The ills of gambling and its impact on a highly regulated society that was hitherto insulated from a host of contrary vices were backgrounded. In its place, Singaporeans were urged to act with maturity to see the "bigger picture" that included various possibilities. These include *inter alia* foreign investments of at least S\$5 billion for the two resorts, glitzy proposals submitted by global players in the casino-cum-resort business, new iconic structures that would re-shape Singapore's urban cityscape – particularly the Marina Bay area – and create a new buzz as well as a well-publicized promise of new job opportunities for many (T. Lee 2005c).

With a bold affirmation that he would carry the ultimate responsibility for the decision, PM Lee – who had only been in the premier's seat for a little more than eight months at the time of the announcement – displayed a potent mix of candor, political shrewdness and a well-honed ability to apply the principles of gestural politics. Further shoring-up available rationales for his decision, Lee argued that the two "Integrated Resorts" would entice foreign tourists to extend their stay in Singapore, and thus increase tourism takings. It would also, as he has put it, "tip investor mindset toward accepting that Singapore is transforming into a diversified service-based economy," and that it was not receding into a "backwater" (as cited in the opening quote to this section) (H.L. Lee 2005).

In the final analysis, the decision to proceed with the casino had less to do with the quantity or quality of the consultation process than with the structures of a new regime that sees the importance and benefit of utilizing the tools of political communication and of gestural politics to govern a new and more diverse generation of Singaporeans. The "Great Casino Debate" offers a landmark example of gestural politics at play because the decision was made primarily on "gut feel" rather than on empirical substance (T. Lee 2005a: 150). As the prime minister himself admitted in his lengthy parliamentary speech: "This is a judgement, not a mathematical calculation. We see the trends and feel the need to move" (H.L. Lee 2005).

182 *Terence Lee*

This statement is undoubtedly noteworthy for a society premised on the ideology of pragmatism and a nation that has built a "squeaky clean" image globally. Yet all semblances were discarded when the government decided to invoke some elements of public relations "spin" and was prepared to "go for broke" with two mega-resorts that would make news headlines around the business world. The key message that the government was, and still is, trying to send to the rest of the world is that a "new," "open" and vibrant Singapore – a global city with a buzz – is in the making. In doing so, the new Lee administration was effectively mediating the image of a "new" Singapore for domestic and global consumption while concurrently ensuring that its political modus operandi remains unchanged at best, or refined at worst. In fact, the government was successful in ensuring that only the positive attributes of Singapore – including the message that Singapore will soon "open up" to new gaming facilities – are heard and reported around the world (T. Lee 2005c). The corollary is that all other news and reports on Singapore, including its authoritarian mode of rule and its deeply entrenched culture of control, are but distracting noises in the "new" Singapore (Rodan 2004; Trocki 2006).

Conclusion

> Authoritarian regimes are characterised by a concentration of power and the obstruction of serious political competition with, or scrutiny of, that power. The free flow of ideas and information is therefore anathema to authoritarian rule. Almost by definition, authoritarian regimes involve censorship. This doesn't mean, however, that mass media and other publicly available sources of information and analysis are necessarily discouraged. On the contrary, sophisticated authoritarian regimes harness these to propagate their own messages and to promote economic objectives.
>
> (Rodan 2004: 1)

In a book-length study of regime change and transparency in the Southeast Asian states of Singapore and Malaysia, Rodan expressed in his conclusion that there are "different meanings and interests attached to ideas of transparency and – above all else – the political meanings they entail" (2004: 187). Indeed, the very idea of transparency – not unlike the widely held cliché of change being the only constant in contemporary everyday life, a concept well understood by most Singaporeans – can become a double-edged sword. It can be, as Rodan (2004: 187) puts it, sagaciously deployed by various authorities as a technique for "reorganising [state and state-controlled] institutions to insulate them from democratic forces, just as it can to reflect those forces." But while transparency is a much-vaunted virtue in the business and political sectors, it takes on a different persona in the media and creative realms, which is why it is has become highly attractive and politically astute to utilize "feel good" gestures and other creative resources to promote one's own political and economic agendas, just as the new Lee administration has done for Singapore thus far.

This chapter argues that Singapore, described by Rodan (2004: 1) in the above quote as a "sophisticated authoritarian regime," has embarked on a new phase of regime reproduction with a whole-of-government approach, described here as the enactment and practice of gestural politics. Gestural politics involves the invocation of media and creative strategies such as the mobilization of voguish and global/cosmopolitan buzzwords, catchy slogans and other narratives that enables the propagation of one's own and preferred messages (T. Lee 2005a). In the language of public relations and political communication, such approach is better known as "spin," defined quite simply as "the interpretation or slant placed on events" based on the belief that "there is no such thing as objective truth" (Esser *et al.* 2000: 213). This chapter has demonstrated how gestural politics, along with aspects of "spin," has not only been utilized and portrayed in tourism promotion, urban redevelopment and the liberalization of bohemianism, nightlife and the creative industries in Singapore – but indeed in the very mediation of a "new" and creative Singapore.

As more Singaporeans want their voices heard and accounted for by the government in policy making, the ongoing refinement of PAP's rule aimed at ensuring the longevity of the political regime needs to include new strategies to give some substance to its "opening-up" rhetoric (Rodan 2006: 4). Gestural politics can be usefully exploited here because it can exhibit the "liberal gestures of the regime" in words and deeds without necessarily invoking democratic (re)forms and aspirations (T. Lee 2005a: 135). As Singaporean sociologist Chua Beng-Huat (2005) puts it in his socio-political assessment of "Singapore in the next decade," the "new" Singapore of the twenty-first century is likely to be marked by greater liberalization, but not democratization, of the social and cultural sphere.

Gestural terms and strategic applications of buzzwords have the potential to "sex up" the Singaporean economy so that it would produce, as Kenneth Paul Tan (2003: 406) posits, "a fertile, stimulating, innovative and risk-taking climate conducive to success in the new global, knowledge-driven and entrepreneurial economy vital for staying competitive." Both "Integrated Resorts" should attract new and large investments into Singapore, including prominent global casino and theme parks operators.[5] One can expect in the meantime that ongoing news and events pertaining to the development of the forthcoming resorts, and of the entire Marina Bay "new downtown" area, would continue to dazzle and excite Singaporeans, foreign talents and prospective tourists alike. For the PAP government, the employment of gestural politics should ideally translate to a higher percentage of political support via electoral votes. To be sure, the PAP won eighty-two out of a total of eighty-four seats at the General Election of May 2006, securing 66.6 percent of all valid votes cast as Lee Hsien Loong encountered

184 *Terence Lee*

his first election as prime minister (Chua 2006). Rather than risk losing the PAP regime's monopolistic grip on power by embracing democracy and genuine socio-political openness, the new prime minister has chosen to engage in gestural politics by staying on-message and echoing the rhetoric of "openness" and "inclusiveness." With more big-bang media statements in the pipeline, this approach is likely to continue in the lead-up towards the completion of the Integrated Resorts and other flashy physical structures around the Marina Bay and other urban redevelopment precincts. It remains to be seen thereafter whether the "feel good" atmosphere – and accompanying political gestures – will come to an abrupt end. Until then, it appears that the most meaningful way of making sense of the "new" Singapore is via the discourse of gestural politics, where the "liberal gestures" continue to reproduce and mediate an illiberal regime.

Notes

1 It is worth noting that the third vision of the PAP Election Manifesto 2006 reiterates the prime minister's pledge to "foster an open and inclusive society which welcomes diversity, values each individual, and involves all of us in shaping our future" (PAP 2006: 2). For more information on the manifesto, see: www.pap.org.sg/uploads/ap/587/documents/papmanifesto06_english.pdf (accessed 9 September 2006).
2 The key vision of Singapore's Creative Industries Development Strategy is to enable Gross Domestic Product (GDP) contribution of the creative industries to reach 6 percent by 2012 (Creative Industries Development Strategy 2002: v).
3 Although not detailed in this chapter, other plans and strategies that have been, or are about to be, implemented to boost the standing of Singapore as a world-class "global city" include: the embrace of the arts and culture via the "Renaissance City" project (see T. Lee 2004); the development of sports and sporting infrastructure (Yap 2005); and, the introduction of cyber-gaming (or digital/interactive gaming) as a sport cum industry (Leung 2005).
4 The FACTS website became defunct shortly after the decision to proceed with the construction of the casino complexes – or Integrated Resorts – was made in April 2005.
5 The Singapore government adopted a "beauty parade" approach to awarding a contract for the first Integrated Resort development at Marina Bay. By the deadline of 6 April 2006, there were four major bidders vying for the project, most of whom were big-name global casino and theme park players. The final contenders were: Genting International–Star Cruises (Asia-based leisure group); MGM Mirage–CapitaLand (American and Singaporean consortium); Harrah's Entertainment–Keppel Land (American and Singaporean consortium); and, Las Vegas Sands (American casino operator) (Boo 2006). It was subsequently announced in June 2006 that Las Vegas Sands, an American casino operator with Asian experience in Macau, had won the billion-dollar bid to build and operate Singapore's first Integrated Resort at Marina Bay.

Bibliography

Boo, K. (2006) "Marina Bay IR race enters home stretch," *The Straits Times Interactive*, 30 March (online), available at //www.straitstimes.com.sg (accessed 30 March 2006).

Mediating the "new" Singapore 185

Case, W. (2002) *Politics in Southeast Asia: Democracy or less*, London: Routledge.

Chia, S.-A. (2005) "Labour chief: I couldn't say no to 35,000 jobs," *The Straits Times Interactive*, 20 April (online), available at www.straitstimes.com.sg (accessed 20 April 2005).

Chia, S.-A. and Li, X. (2005) "Worthwhile debate or not? It's a toss up," *The Straits Times Interactive*, 23 April (online), available at www.straitstimes.com.sg (accessed 23 April 2005).

Chua, B.H. (2005) "Liberalization without democratization: Singapore in the next decade," in F. Loh and J. Ojendal (eds) *Southeast Asian Responses to Globalization: Restructuring governance and deepening democracy*, Singapore: Institute of Southeast Asian Studies, pp. 57–82.

—— (2006) "GE 2006," *Asian Analysis*, June (online), available at www.aseanfocus.com/asiananalysis/article.cfm?articleID = 958 (accessed 7 September 2006).

Creative Industries Development Strategy (2002) *Report of the Economic Review Committee Services Subcommittee*, Singapore: Workgroup on Creative Industries, September 2002.

Diamond, L. (2002) "Thinking about hybrid regimes," *Journal of Democracy*, 13(2): 21–35.

Esser, F., Reinemann, C. and Fan, D. (2000) "Spin doctoring in British and German election campaigns: how the press is being confronted with a new quality of political PR," *European Journal of Communication*, 15(2): 209–39.

Feedback Unit (2005) *Shaping Our Home: Turning ideas into reality*, Singapore: Government of Singapore.

Flew, T. (2005) *New Media: An introduction*, 2nd edn, South Melbourne: Oxford University Press.

Florida, R. (2002) *The Rise of the Creative Class, and How It's Transforming Work, Leisure, Community and Everyday Life*, New York: Basic Books.

Goh, S. and Sim, G. (2004) "Online petition against casino idea," *Straits Times*, 14 December: 5.

Jones, D.M. (2004) "Contradictions at core of the five-star hotel state," *Australian Financial Review*, 13 August (online), available at www.afr.com.au (accessed 14 August 2004).

Koh, G. (2005) "Casino debate: laying out all the cards," *The Straits Times Interactive*, 14 January (online), available at www.straitstimes.com.sg (accessed 14 January 2005).

Kumar, K. (1993) "Civil society: an inquiry into the usefulness of an historical term," *British Journal of Sociology*, 44(3): 375–95.

Lee, H.L. (2004) "Let's shape our future together," Prime Minister's swearing-in speech, Singapore Government Media Release, 12 August.

—— (2005) "PM Lee's parliamentary speech in full," *The Straits Times Interactive*, 18 April (online), available at www.straitstimes.com.sg (accessed 18 April 2005).

Lee, T. (2002) "The politics of civil society in Singapore," *Asian Studies Review*, 26(1): 97–117.

—— (2004) "Creative shifts and directions: cultural policy in Singapore," *International Journal of Cultural Policy*, 10(3): 281–99.

—— (2005a) "Gestural politics: civil society in 'new Singapore'," *SOJOURN: Journal of Social Issues in Southeast Asia*, 20(2): 132–54.

—— (2005b) "Going online: journalism and civil society in Singapore," in A. Romano and M. Bromley (eds) *Journalism and Democracy in Asia*, London: Routledge, pp. 15–27.

186　*Terence Lee*

—— (2005c) "Going for broke: not one casino, but two integrated resorts," *Asian Analysis*, June (online) available at www.aseanfocus.com/asiananalysis/article.cfm?articleID = 852 (accessed 16 April 2006).

Lee, T. and Lim, D. (2004) "The economics and politics of 'creativity' in Singapore," *Australian Journal of Communication*, 31(2): 149–65.

Lee, T. and Willnat, L. (2006) *Media Research and Political Communication in Singapore*, Working Paper No. 130, Perth: Asia Research Centre, Murdoch University, Australia.

Leo, P. and Lee, T. (2004) "The 'new' Singapore: mediating culture and creativity," *Continuum: Journal of Media and Cultural Studies*, 18(2): 205–18.

Leung, W.-L. (2005) "Cybergaming may gain acceptance as a sport," *The Straits Times Interactive*, 13 September (online), available at www.straitstimes.com.sg (accessed 13 September 2005).

Li, X. (2006) "PAP wants 'hip, happening' image to click with the young," *The Straits Times Interactive*, 27 July (online), available at www.straitstimes.com.sg (accessed 27 July 2006).

Lim, C. (1994a) "The PAP and the people – a great affective divide," *Straits Times Weekly Edition*, 10 September: 13.

—— (1994b) "One government, two styles," *Sunday Times*, "Sunday Review," 20 November: 12.

Lim, L. (2004) "S'poreans split evenly on casino," *Straits Times*, 25 September: 3.

—— (2005) "Yes to two mega resorts: creating the buzz of a global city," *The Straits Times Interactive*, 19 April (online), available at www.straitstimes.com.sg (accessed 19 April 2005).

Loo, D. (2005) "Marina Bay the new brand name," *The Straits Times Interactive*, 22 July (online), available at www.straitstimes.com.sg (accessed 22 July 2005).

Low, I. (2005) "Opportunity knocked," *The Straits Times Interactive*, 20 March (online), available at www.straitstimes.com.sg (accessed 20 March 2005).

McCarthy, T. and Ellis, E. (1999) "Singapore lightens up," *Time Magazine*, 19 July: 17–23.

Mak, M.S. (2006) "Sleepy Hollow," *Sunday Times*, "Lifestyle," 5 February: 6.

Mauzy, D.K. and Milne, R.S. (2002) *Singapore Politics under the People's Action Party*, London: Routledge.

Mulchand, A. and Nadarajan, B. (2003) "Bar-top dancing, 24-hour nightspots now allowed," *The Straits Times Interactive*, 9 July (online), available at www.straitstimes.com.sg (accessed 9 July 2003).

Nye, J.S. (2004) *Soft Power: The means to success in world politics*, New York: Public Affairs.

O'Donnell, G. and Schmitter, P.C. (1986) *Transitions from Authoritarian Rule*, Vols 1–4, Baltimore: Johns Hopkins University Press.

Ooi, C. S. (2005) "State–civil society relations and tourism: Singaporeanizing tourists, touristifying Singapore," *SOJOURN: Journal of Social Issues in Southeast Asia*, 20(2): 249–72.

People's Action Party (PAP) (2006) *Staying Ahead, Moving Together: PAP manifesto 2006*, available at www.pap.org.sg/uploads/ap/587/documents/papmanifesto06_english.pdf (accessed 16 April 2006).

Pereira, M.L. (2005) "Singapore Flyer set to soar in 2008," *The Straits Times Interactive*, 13 September (online), available at www.straitstimes.com.sg (accessed 13 September 2005).

Rodan, G. (1989) *The Political Economy of Singapore's Industrialization: National state and international capital*, Houndmills: Macmillan.

—— (ed.) (1993) *Singapore Changes Guard: Social, political and economic directions in the 1990s*, New York: St Martin's Press.

—— (2004) *Transparency and Authoritarian Rule in Southeast Asia: Singapore and Malaysia*, London: Routledge.

—— (2006) *Singapore "Exceptionalism"? Authoritarian rule and state transformation*, Working Paper No. 131, Perth: Asia Research Centre, Murdoch University, Australia.

Singapore Tourism Board (STB) (2004) "Singapore launches its new destination brand 'Uniquely Singapore'," press release, 9 March.

Tan, A. (2004) "Top-draw resort for southern isles," *The Straits Times Interactive*, 13 March (online), available at www.straitstimes.com.sg (accessed 13 March 2004).

Tan, E.K.B. (2005) "Singapore: to game or not to game?" *Asian Analysis*, April (online), available at www.aseanfocus.com/asiananalysis/article.cfm?articleID = 837 (accessed 16 April 2006).

Tan, H.Y. (2006) "Three new public gardens for Marina Bay waterfront," *Straits Times*, 21 January: 1, 4.

Tan, K.P. (2003) "Sexing up Singapore," *International Journal of Cultural Studies*, 6(4): 403–23.

Teo, J. (2004a) "\$2b fund to make S'pore top tourist destination," *The Straits Times Interactive*, 17 November (online), Available at www.straitstimes.com.sg (accessed 17 November 2004).

—— (2004b) "Investors to be asked to submit resort plans" and "Casino here not a matter of money versus values," *The Straits Times Interactive*, 17 November (online), available at www.straitstimes.com.sg (accessed 17 November 2004).

Teo, L. (2004) "Casino decision in 6 to 9 months," *The Straits Times Interactive*, 20 April (online), available at www.straitstimes.com.sg (accessed 20 April 2004).

Trocki, C.A. (2006) *Singapore: Wealth, power and the culture of control*, London: Routledge.

Yap, K.H. (2005) "Singapore cannot be a global city without sports," *The Straits Times Interactive*, 10 April (online), available at www.straitstimes.com.sg (accessed 10 April 2005).

12 Media and politics in regional Indonesia

The case of Manado[1]

David T. Hill

One of the most visible changes to Indonesian public culture since the fall of President Suharto and his "New Order" in May 1998 has been the increasing diversity of the nation's media. This chapter is an initial attempt to examine these changes at the local level in the perimeter province of North Sulawesi, about 2,000 kilometers from the political epicenter of Jakarta. It explores the impact of a raft of central government policies, collectively dubbed "de-centralization" or "regional autonomy," in North Sulawesi and its capital, Manado. Prior to 1998, with only rare exceptions, studies of the Indonesian media – by both Indonesian and foreign scholars – concentrated on the national media.[2] However, since the post-Suharto deregulation of the media and the dismantling of the repressive Department of Information which had controlled the media centrally, the most dramatic transformation is being driven not from Jakarta but from local media enterprises.[3] At its broadest, this current study of media in North Sulawesi questions whether the collapse of an authoritarian regime and abandonment of media controls axiomatically produce a pluralist democratic media, or whether equally as likely is the capture of the media by particular political interests, for whom media influence – if not control – is a valuable asset in influencing public opinion and electoral outcomes.

Arguing that local governments are potentially more vulnerable than national counterparts to cooption by powerful interest groups, Bardhan and Mookherjee (2000) have noted nonetheless that, provided local media can critically assess local politicians' activities, it can facilitate accountability. Should the local media be incapable of exercising this monitoring role – through lack of competence, resources or political will – the polity comes under increased danger of capture by the local elite. While "democratic consolidation in Indonesia could be undermined by an emerging anti-political atmosphere and a capture of political spaces by quasi-democratic politicians" (Antlöv 2003: 77), in practice the media combines with other contributing factors in such an unpredictable manner that "the extent of relative capture may be context-specific and needs to be assessed empirically" (Bardhan and Mookherjee 2000: 135, in Malley 2003: 105). This chapter attempts just such an empirical assessment of the circumstances in North Sulawesi.

Regional autonomy

In what has been described as "one of the most radical decentralization programs attempted anywhere in the world," in August 1999 the Indonesian parliament passed a package of bills to come into effect on 1 January 2001, devolving a wide range of powers from the central government to the second tier of regional government: that is, the district (*kabupaten*) or municipality (*kota*) rather than the first (provincial) level.[4] Dramatically overturning previous practices, the laws handed districts responsibility for functions as diverse as "education, health, the environment, labor, public works and natural resource management" with the central government retaining only "foreign policy, defense and security, monetary policy, the legal system and religious affairs" (Aspinall and Fealy 2003: 3–4). Its promoters saw devolution of powers to districts as fostering democratization at the level where citizens could most effectively engage in the political process and hold office-bearers accountable. Furthermore, unlike provinces whose boundaries tended to align with ethno-linguistic communities (and, hence, potentially units of ethnic identity), districts were regarded as unlikely to harbor desires to secede from the nation, thus avoiding the threat of national fragmentation (Aspinall and Fealy 2003: 3–4).

In his work on post-New Order politics, Vedi Hadiz has noted that the decentralization process has facilitated the emergence of a fresh constellation of social forces. He argues that

> the range of interests now contesting power at the local level are even more varied than under the New Order. They include ambitious political fixers and entrepreneurs, wily and still-predatory state bureaucrats, and aspiring and newly ascendant business groups, as well as a wide range of political gangsters, thugs and civilian militia.
>
> (Hadiz 2003: 124)

In his analysis, decentralization has triggered sharp competition over control of local institutions between a variety of patronage networks. If this is so, what then does it mean for local media? With media liberalization and decentralization, has *local* patronage and intimidation simply replaced the New Order's previous centralized control?

North Sulawesi as a case study[5]

North Sulawesi's provincial capital, Manado, lies less than 200 kilometers north of the equator, on the west coast of a peninsula which snakes up towards the maritime border with the Philippines. Occupying about 25 square kilometers beside a picturesque bay, it is a sleepy town, ringed by coconut-covered hills and home to a population (in 2003) of around 410,000 (Badan Pusat Statistik Kota Manado 2004: 64). The province's population of just over two million generates a healthy export trade in coconuts, cloves

190   *David T. Hill*

and coffee from a thriving plantation economy. It survived the Asian economic crash of 1997 relatively unscathed, with an annual growth rate of almost 6 percent since 1999. Its poverty rate of 11 percent (2001) was the fourth lowest in Indonesia, and well below the national figure of 18 percent.[6]

In a country that is 88 percent Muslim, Manado (and North Sulawesi generally) is approximately 65 percent Christian. In the central area of Minahasa, Christians constitute 90 percent. While other Christian-majority regions of Indonesia, such as Maluku, have been ravaged by communal conflict since the fall of Suharto, North Sulawesi has a long reputation for stability and order. While inter-communal tensions surface occasionally, close collaboration between religious leaders of all communities and the police have managed to restrain, if not entirely resolve, inter-communal frictions. This makes the region a more attractive destination for domestic and (albeit modest) foreign investment, enhancing its economic resilience (Henley and Tuerah 2003: 4). There is also a deeply rooted tradition of education, encouraged since the mid-1800s by Christian missionaries, and creating a fertile environment for print media consumption.[7]

Historically, North Sulawesi has had a chequered relationship with the central authorities in Jakarta. After Indonesia's independence in 1945, the province was drawn into a regional rebellion against Jakarta from 1957 until 1961. Thereafter the people of North Sulawesi were "among the loyalest supporters of a New Order that offered them a measure of prosperity and self-respect as well as peace and stability" (Henley and Tuerah 2003: 9). It was a loyalty that survived the fall of the New Order, with the former Suharto electoral vehicle Golkar still retaining twenty out of forty-five seats as the largest faction in the provincial assembly in the first post-Suharto elections of 1999 (Henley and Tuerah 2003: 13). Prior to the first direct elections for governor and mayor in 2005, both the North Sulawesi governor and the Manado mayor were Golkar apparatchiks. I shall return later to examine those elections.

Media in Manado

Manado is home to several local newspapers and television stations and more than a dozen radio stations. While radio provides popular music and entertainment programs, it is newspaper and television that appear most directly to set the "news agenda" and (as shall be argued later in this chapter) influence voter inclinations. For this reason, my focus will be on print media and television.

Print media

North Sulawesi's strong local identity encourages consumer loyalty for local media, and locally produced newspapers dominate. Though some of the major Jakarta-based dailies are airlifted to Manado, they hit the news-stands

Media and politics in regional Indonesia   191

well after their local counterparts and their sales are modest.[8] Of these imports, the most popular is the country's largest-selling daily, *Kompas* (*Compass*), which sells about 2,000 copies, a little more than the other national daily *Suara Pembaruan* (*Voice of Renewal*). Subscriptions to such Jakarta papers are rare, with most sales on the roadside, on impulse, depending on headlines. Before discussing their role in local politics, I shall survey Manado's major newspapers and television stations.

Manado Post *and the Jawa Pos Group*[9]

North Sulawesi's largest-circulation, most successful daily paper is the *Manado Post*, part of Indonesia's giant Jawa Pos Group (JPG), based in Surabaya. The media conglomerate began in 1982 when a flagging Surabaya daily paper *Jawa Pos* (*Java Post*) was taken over by an off-shoot of the national *Tempo* newsweekly magazine. The 6,800 circulation daily was transformed into Indonesia's strongest media empire, spanning the archipelago, with interests expanding into print and television. By 2001, the JPG was publishing seventy daily newspapers and fifteen weeklies throughout Indonesia (Jawa Pos Group 2001: 5). While not as diversified outside the media sector as rival media giant, the Kompas Gramedia Group (KGG), the rise of the JPG has been meteoric, with the company not only managing successfully to navigate through the economic crisis of 1997–8, but doubling its revenue in the difficult years between 1998 and 2003.[10]

The pattern of acquisition adopted in Surabaya was replicated around the archipelago. In Manado, for example, in July 1991 the JPG took over one of the city's two struggling dailies, the *Manado Post*, which had first appeared in January 1987 under the editorship of Max Maramis.[11] Maramis had impeccable political connections; he was a former member of Suharto's Golkar party in the regional parliament (DPRD) during the early years of the New Order (1966–71) and former Chair of the provincial branch of the pro-government Indonesian Journalists' Association (PWI) (1978–90). Despite such political credentials, so difficult had it been to establish a newspaper during the Suharto period that he spent nine months waiting in Jakarta for a publication permit to be approved.[12] Under the arrangement with JPG, Maramis retained his formal editorial title, but the enterprise was purchased by Jawa Pos, which injected new staff and revitalized the publication totally, changing a "yellow rag" (*koran kuning*) into a well-produced "paper of record," which was profitable after about five years. Until the national media deregulation in 1998 and the subsequent commencement of new publications in Manado, the *Manado Post* had virtually no competitors, being regarded as the "primadonna newspaper of North Sulawesi" (Parwoko 1995: 13).

The current Managing Editor, Suhendro Boroma, emphasizes that, while covering some national news, the primary brief of the paper is to cover events and issues of local interest, which occupy about 85 percent of the

192   *David T. Hill*

thirty-two-page paper. With a cover price of Rp 2,000 (about 24 US cents), it targets the mid to upper socio-economic strata. The paper claims sales once spiked to about 50,000 for a week (when featuring an exposé about a local "satanic church"), but the more usual circulation claimed (in mid-2004) was about 35,000.[13] The *Manado Post* branched out to establish its own group of publications, including, in Manado, two dailies *Posko* (in July 2000) and *Kosmo* (in July 2002) aimed at the lower end of the market, together with the *Gorontalo Post* in the province of Gorontalo to the south (in May 2000) and the *Malut Post* (*North Maluku Post*) in neighboring Ternate, North Maluku. *Posko*, which claims a circulation of 15,000 to 18,000, is a sensationalist "blood and hormones" tabloid, with the slightly more up-market *Kosmo* not much more than a scandal sheet. Although it initially aspired to be an "urban lifestyle" paper (modeled on *Cosmopolitan*), *Kosmo* failed to find a viable market niche, despite its change in content, selling only about 5,000 copies with a cover price, like *Posko*, of Rp 1,000 (about 15 US cents). By 2005 it had transformed into *Tribun Sulut* (*North Sulawesi Tribune*). Both twelve-page down-market publications, *Posko* and *Kosmo/Tribun Sulut*, used striking front and back page color photos, and a liberal scattering throughout of provocative headings and photos of women to catch attention.

Komentar Group

The tabloid *Harian Komentar* (*Daily Comment*) was established in January 2001 by Jeffrey Johannes Massie, through his company Azravi. His father is a Jakarta-based ethnic Chinese businessman and his mother is Minahasan. Massie graduated in economics from the California State University of San Bernardino, and after returning to Manado he first opened the Global Financial Trading Company and then the newspaper.[14] While he claims to have had no political ambitions at that time, he soon won a seat in the national parliament (DPR-RI) for the Peace and Prosperity Party (Partai Damai Sejahtera, PDS) in the 2004 general elections and subsequently a position on the parliament's influential Commission for Defense, Security, Foreign Policy, Communications and Information. To avoid an appearance of a conflict of interest, he removed his name from the paper's banner, replacing it with that of his father, Sofyan. It is commonly assumed Massie sets editorial policy and *Komentar* provides frequent gratuitous coverage of his activities.[15] His finance company shares the newspaper's small office building and is prominently advertised on *Komentar*'s webpage, which features his photo and a feedback form for people wanting to contact the MP.[16]

In July 2003, Massie opened a down-market stable-mate, *Harian Metro* (*Metro Daily*), which shared *Komentar*'s senior staff and office space. With a price of Rp 1,000 and the motto, "Hot but laid back" (*Panas Namun Santun*), its tone and content may be gleaned from any issue among those I collected during fieldwork in July 2004. For instance, the 29 July edition

Included a blonde bikini girl seductively occupying virtually all of the cover, three women splashed across pages 2 and 3, accompanying a story about posing for *Playboy*, and another article headlined "Raging sex in unique positions" (*"Seks Membara dengan Posisi Unik"*). In September 2002, the *Komentar* group added a twice-weekly tabloid, *Football*. Market taste may be gauged by the fact that their attempt to launch a weekly political magazine, *Politix*, failed, with the publication closing after eight months. By mid-2004, the company claimed *Komentar* had a circulation of 17,500, *Metro* a modest 7,500, and *Football* 10,000.[17]

Global News

In 2002 another new media enterprise opened in an unimposing cramped and dusty office along Manado's Sam Ratulangi boulevard. Under its banner motto, "Bringing Good News" (*membawa kabar baik*), *Global News* is a twenty-page tabloid daily newspaper, in Indonesian,[18] selling for Rp 1,000. Published by PT Metro Post, it is widely believed (and not denied by senior editorial staff with whom I spoke) that the capital to establish and maintain the venture was provided by Mrs Adrianne ("Anne") Frederik-Nangoy, wife of Wempie Frederik, Golkar stalwart and then mayor of Manado. Frederik-Nangoy was herself the Chair of the local Golkar branch. Son Iwan Frederik represented the family in the enterprise as the paper's Deputy General Manager (*Wakil Pemimpin Umum*).

Thus, nearly a decade after the fall of Suharto and the liberalization of Indonesia's media, two of Manado's three daily *news*papers (ignoring the range of largely entertainment publications like *Kosmo* and *Posko*) were either owned by, or under the effective control of, politicians: *Komentar* by a minority party member of the national parliament; *Global News* by the local Golkar chief, married to the Manado's Golkar mayor. Overt political control was more visible in the case of newspaper ownership; television was much more the preserve of business investors.

Television

As was common throughout the archipelago, the local Manado station of the state's national network, Republic of Indonesia Television (TVRI), was in spiraling decline. Located in a large but dilapidated complex on a hill at the edge of town, it was starved of funding from the central coffers. Its Manado staff struggled to produce three hours of local programming daily, mainly news and music videos, with the remainder coming from Jakarta. Formerly the exclusive provider of local TV news, as local commercial competitors emerged in recent years providing a better, more appealing news service, TVRI lost its primacy and much of its audience.

While the number of privately owned *national* television stations has doubled since the fall of President Suharto, there has been seemingly

194   *David T. Hill*

unstoppable growth in the number of *local* stations.[19] By the middle of 2004 at least thirty-four local television stations were broadcasting or seeking licenses to commence.[20] Of these, three were located in and around Manado. While the entire population of Manado falls within the local television broadcast area, no figures are available for actual television audience. As will become evident later in this chapter, despite the absence of audited audience figures, other evidence suggests television's influence on the political inclinations of the constituency may be substantial.

Televisi Manado (TV-M)

The first station, Televisi Manado (TV-M), was established as the Televisi Manado Media Perkasa company in July 2003 and owned by a group of local businessmen, including John Hamenda and Jusak Kereh. The majority shareholder was Hamenda, who as CEO of the Perkasa Group of companies had amassed a fortune from a variety of businesses, particularly agribusiness. Born in the province's northernmost district of Sangir Talaud in August 1957 into a merchant grocer's family, Hamenda was a high school dropout who traded local connections into a substantial business portfolio, including agriculture, manufacturing and real estate interests in Australia and China (Koesoetjahjo 2001).

Owning a local TV station was merely one of a range of his enterprises and one he was no longer able to subsidize when his other businesses struck financial difficulties. The situation was exacerbated by tensions between shareholders over station policy and became unworkable when Hamenda was detained in December 2003, accused of involvement in a multi-million-dollar state bank (BNI) fraud (Hotland 2004). The station was then seized, and placed into receivership, by the Jakarta Public Attorney's Office (*Kejaksaan Tinggi*) on 20 April 2004. In November 2004, Hamenda was found guilty and sentenced to twenty years' jail by a South Jakarta District Court (against which he has lodged an appeal).[21]

TV-M was severely undercapitalized. Without even its own studios, it hired space from the national public radio broadcaster, RRI. Nonetheless, despite such travails, TV-M remained on air. Throughout 2004 it was mainly relaying programming direct from Jakarta's Metro-TV station under a revenue-neutral agreement. This survival strategy worked until other sources of funding were attracted. In late 2004, Victor Koleangan, a member of the North Minahasa Provincial Assembly representing the Indonesian Democratic Party of Struggle (Partai Demokrasi Indonesia-Perjuangan, PDI-P) of then president Megawati Sukarnoputri, briefly entered the fray, getting government permission to assume control of TV-M in what some critics argued was an attempt to use the station to bolster the party's electoral aspirations. Unable to meet staff salaries and faced with a mounting electricity bill, Koleangan withdrew in May 2005.

Media and politics in regional Indonesia 195

Bonifacius Mandalika had been appointed receiver (*penanggung-jawab*) by the Attorney-General's office, responsible for the station's assets. He was both internationally experienced and well connected, having only returned to his mother's city of Manado in 2003 after two decades studying and working in the United States (USA), including a period with the World Bank. His father, Benny Mandalika, was a close friend and business partner of Hamenda in the Petindo Perkasa company, and also held shares in TV-M. Like Hamenda, Benny Mandalika was from Sangir Talaud. After retiring from the military the former major-general had served as Indonesian Ambassador to Papua New Guinea and the Solomon Islands. The family had an interest in resuscitating TV-M.

By this stage the station was broadcasting from what amounted to a garage, with much of its equipment deteriorating and in need of maintenance. Yudie Ardino Kaloh, the Philippines-educated head of Positiva advertising and public relations company, had been producing advertisements and providing other services to the struggling station. Kaloh took over the active management of the station, injected capital, re-scheduled debts, took on new staff and attempted to stabilize the business. Kaloh wanted to purchase TV-M eventually but while Hamenda's legal appeal was underway the company's assets remained frozen under Mandalika's authority, with Mandalika approving Kaloh's involvement.

Officially Kaloh did not own the company but was contracted to supply services to it. His effective control of the station was controversial, however, since he was simultaneously a member of the region's (notionally "independent") Indonesian Broadcasting Commission (Komisi Penyiaran Indonesia Daerah, KPI-D), charged with regulating the industry and adjudicating on both license applications and complaints against licensees. According to the 2002 Broadcast Law (Article 10.1.g) members of the Broadcasting Commission should "not be linked directly or indirectly with the ownership of mass media."[22] Kaloh was, however, able to sustain this apparent contradiction without penalty, not insignificantly perhaps because his father held the influential position of provincial secretary for North Sulawesi (described by one news editor as the second most powerful position in the province after the governor).[23]

TV-M struggled to remain on air. By mid-2005 its agreement with Metro-TV had lapsed and, with about twenty-five staff, it was broadcasting predominantly locally produced programming, on air for about eight hours per day, in two blocks, morning and evening. Viewers tuning in outside its broadcasting hours saw only a test pattern and station logo. Despite economic adversity, staff valued editorial independence and claimed to have strong local audience loyalty. During the July 2005 mayoral elections, the official station policy was to reject any funding from candidates (despite TV-M's grave financial need). Instead they contributed staff and air time to support the election-monitoring program conducted by the National Democratic Institute for International Affairs (NDI) and the inter-community

196   *David T. Hill*

citizens' group, Publika.[24] In July 2005 after the elections, Kaloh decided to economize by ceasing Sunday broadcasting.[25] Unable to stem the losses, by November that year, transmission stopped and the enterprise seemed doomed.[26]

Pacific-TV

The newest Manado station, Pacific-TV (which began broadcasting in October 2003, with its license issued in January 2004), emerged after a management conflict with Hamenda led to Jusak Kereh, one of TV-M's minority shareholders, establishing this rival venture.[27] With an initial investment of approximately Rp 30 billion (approximately $US 3 million) and a commitment to sustain the enterprise for at least three years, Pacific-TV is the dominant local station.[28] In fact, Kereh is now the President Director of the Pacific Televisi Anugerah company, which owns Pacific-TV, while retaining a minority shareholding in the rival commercial station TV-M.

Industry insiders believe Kereh intends to dump TV-M once the legal status of its seized assets is regularized, and focus his investment in Pacific-TV, which boasts new studios and office next to his residence on the outskirts of Manado. In its start-up phase Pacific attracted both dynamic local staff (including some from TV-M) and key mentoring staff from Jakarta stations (though these remained only temporarily). It survived on a mix of local music videos and interactive chat shows. It was still struggling financially in mid-2004, relying very heavily on only a handful of advertisers. In July–August 2004, for example, Top-1 motor oil and Sakatonik health drink ads were repeated invariably during every programming break. By mid-2005, with a more aggressive marketing presence in Jakarta, Pacific had effectively broadened its advertiser base to several dozen firms.

In addition to the regular half-hour local news bulletins, in mid-2004 the station's weekly programming included *Campus on the Move* covering local student activities, the government-sponsored *North Sulawesi Development Priorities*, *North Sulawesi Dimensions* highlighting provincial events, and even *Gabby Tour* (sic), when local pre-teenager "Gabby" took viewers to her favorite tourist and entertainment sites. Of the eighteen hours broadcast daily in mid-2005, several came *gratis* from Voice of America with occasional material from other free international providers (such as Deutsche Welle TV). Pacific produced 60 to 70 percent in-house.[29]

Gospel Overseas Television Network (GO-TV)

A unique addition to North Sulawesi TV was the evangelical Christian broadcaster GO-TV, an off-shoot of the Gospel Overseas Television Network (GOTN), based in Bekasi, on the outskirts of Jakarta. This station broadcasts from the GOTN's Radio 99.15 FM Country Station in the small highland town of Tondano, about 20 kilometers from Manado (Hill 2005).[30]

GO-TV's programming is highly specific. For most of the day, it screens static pictures and biblical verses to a sound track from the radio station. For a couple of hours in the morning and evening, the TV programs are a mix of mainly Christian evangelical broadcasts (such as Rev. John Hartman's English-language sermons interpreted into Indonesian), an English-language GOTN-produced serial *Sheriff John* (featuring Hartman as a "frontier Western" lawman and an Indonesian cast as local townsfolk), and dated American serials like *Bonanza*. Reception in Manado is exceptionally poor, but the station's motivations clearly have nothing to do with profit-seeking. Its emergence provokes questions about the potential consequences of sectarian broadcasters, particularly abutting sites of severe inter-religious conflicts like Maluku and Central Sulawesi.

Fledgling local stations compete for viewers currently against the large array of "national" stations, like RCTI, producing a wide spectrum of slick entertaining programming broadcast by satellite from Jakarta and easily received in Manado. The attraction of local stations lies in their capacity to cover local events and to provide commentary and analysis of local political developments. In this, news and "interactive" or "talk-back" programs are regarded by programmers in the local stations as the most popular (though the absence of any auditing audience figures means such assumptions are untested). Civil society spokespeople and critics of the government provide "good copy" and lively program content for interactive television chat shows. Local media outlets, keen to maximize their comparative advantage, offer a willing forum for such social commentators who feature regularly on a variety of programs.

Despite such advantages, it remains a highly competitive and financially insecure environment for the local stations. Their role, however, takes on fresh importance during periods of heightened local political activity, particularly in the light of changes to the method of determining local political leaders.

Local politics and local media

Under the New Order's highly centralized political system, provincial governors were appointed at the prerogative of the president, and district heads (*bupati*) and mayors were chosen by the Minister of Home Affairs, albeit after a short-list was submitted by the relevant provincial assembly or local council (Rasyid 2003). There was no public input or scrutiny, though "the public could safely predict that Golkar candidates would gain governorships, *bupati*-ships and mayoralties" (Rasyid 2003: 65–6). Between 1999 and 2004, such positions were elected by local parliaments. Since Law No. 32, 2004 on Local Government, governors, district heads and mayors are now directly elected for a five-year term by popular vote, in a procedure administered by the local General Electoral Commission (*Komisi Pemilihan Umum Daerah*, KPUD). Transparent competition for the positions of

198   *David T. Hill*

mayor and governor has potentially exposed personal animosities, internal party rivalries and inter-party political conflicts much more to public view. For voters, it is the local rather than the national media that provides such exposure.

In the lead-up to the 2004 general elections, the State Minister of Communications and Information, Syamsul Mu'arif, was at pains to assure the public that the media were not only bound by their in-house codes of ethics, but were obliged under Article 73 of the 2003 Election Law to treat all election candidates equally (Hari 2004). Such legal requirements were ineffective in Manado, given the substantial interests of local politicians or administrators in the relatively small media industry.

This financial involvement of politicians was particularly evident in the print media. As outlined earlier, of the three major dailies, two had political associations. Of the two commercial television stations, TV-M was controlled by Yudie Kaloh, whose wife ran (unsuccessfully) for Golkar in the 2004 provincial elections and whose father was provincial secretary. While such political links were never foregrounded, and were not necessarily known by the general public, they were relatively easy to ascertain. It is more complex to determine the extent to which such political affiliations influenced media coverage.

Elections represent a major trial of the emerging local media's capacity to navigate the complex political and financial incentives offered to bias reporting. Advertising revenue and unacknowledged payments are manna for a struggling local industry, with election campaigns generating substantial revenue. Candidates (or their parties) paid generously for what the industry euphemistically dubbed *"pencitraan"* or image-making. It is widely accepted within the industry that media outlets adjust their level of coverage of a candidate in accord with the level of financial support paid through either direct advertising or program sponsorship. Cashed-up candidates can buy space or time (and favor) from a media outlet, with no effective control or monitoring. Nor did industry practice require that such material be tagged as political advertising or "advertorial."

North Sulawesi had long been a Golkar stronghold. While its vote had fallen away elsewhere in Indonesia after the overthrow of Suharto, Golkar continued to poll strongly there in the 2004 national elections, garnering 32 percent of the province's votes in the national assembly (DPR) poll. But in what appears to be voter concern with party complaisance, it suffered a heavy defeat in the June 2005 governorial poll gaining only 17 percent, or less than half of the victorious PDI-P's 39 percent.[31] The incumbent governor, academic-turned-politician A.J. Sondakh, was replaced by a popular career bureaucrat, Sinyo Harry Sarundajang, running for the PDI-P on his clean reputation as former interim governor in both the neighboring strife-torn provinces of Maluku and North Maluku.[32]

The defeat of Golkar governor Sondakh was not entirely unexpected. He had been linked to several corruption cases. The most adhesive, known

Media and politics in regional Indonesia 199

locally as "MBH-gate," involved the alleged siphoning off of government funds intended to rehabilitate a former four-star resort outside Manado. In 2003, an assistant to the governor was reportedly "assigned ... by the provincial administration to buy shares in Manado Beach Hotel (MBH) totaling Rp 18 billion (US\$ 1.9 million) from the Indonesian Banking Restructuring Agency (IBRA), the owner of the hotel" (Hajramurni and Rumteh 2004). The press reported that only Rp 6.7 billion was actually paid to IBRA, with the remainder taken corruptly by local officials. Right up to the governorial election in June 2005 the North Sulawesi High Prosecutor's Office and the Corruption Eradication Commission (KPK) continued investigations, which tainted both Sondakh and several provincial councilors. Facing Sarundajang's reputation for competent administration under very adverse conditions, even Golkar's well-heeled electoral machinery was not able to save Sondakh.

In Manado, Golkar was also split by internal rivalries. The Frederiks were facing an assault from local Golkar heavyweight Jimmy Rimba Rogi. Having been elected to the Chair of the Manado Regional Leadership Council (DPD) of Golkar in November 2004, Anne Frederik-Nangoy was ousted when Rogi challenged the validity of the vote (Anon 2004). The move split the party branch. Frederik-Nangoy was subsequently "recalled" by Golkar from the local assembly and, despite claiming to represent "grassroots Golkar" ("*Golkar akar rumput*"), was ultimately expelled from the party. Meanwhile, her husband, incumbent mayor Wempie Frederik, was also beaten by Rogi for the Golkar endorsement in the 21 July mayoral elections. Severed from his party base, and after declining an approach from an Islamic party (PPP), Frederik migrated to the PDI-P ticket, with the local PDI-P Chair as his running mate.

The Manado mayoral election was hard-fought between six pairs of candidates for mayor and deputy mayor. Strongly supported by Golkar national office, Rogi also displayed a political shrewdness by selecting a prominent Muslim leader as his running mate, successfully capturing much of the local Islamic constituency. Rogi won with 30 percent, bringing Golkar's vote back almost to the 32 percent it had achieved in North Sulawesi in the 2004 general election.[33] Jettisoned by Golkar and fighting some lingering rumors about his character, Frederik nonetheless came second with a respectable 27 percent.

Despite the political antagonism surrounding the Frederiks' clash with Rogi, in the assessment of at least one prominent local academic, journalists with *Global News* were generally "professional" rather than flagrantly partisan.[34] While some policy intervention from the owners was taken for granted by academics and activists with whom I spoke, they observed *Global News*' primary benefit to Wempie Frederik's campaign was countering criticisms of him taken up by other media. Industry figures from other electronic and print media generally felt that *Global News* had run a low-key, relatively restrained line. Rather than a crude "gloves off" bias for the

200   *David T. Hill*

mayor, its benefit to the Frederik campaign, they argued, relied on it pursuing a credible reputation as balanced, and therefore able more strategically to maintain base readership while countering criticism of the incumbent appearing in other media.

Similarly, Jeffrey Massie's *Komentar* performed creditably. Realistically, Massie's Peace and Prosperity Party (PDS) had no chance of capturing the mayor's post, though it did field a candidate in coalition with another minor reformist party, the New Indonesian Association Party (Partai Perhimpunan Indonesia Baru, PPIB), and achieved a modest 11 percent. While the paper provided wide coverage of the election lead-up, the tone was moderate. The paper's underlying PDS support was clear, but the spread of candidate coverage was reasonable, and indicative of the paper maintaining a "professional" line on the elections. *Komentar* did not risk alienating its readers with unsubtle bias for a team never likely to win. My reading of the newspaper during this period indicated it was providing satisfactorily balanced, if rather superficial, coverage of platforms and candidates.

Manado's commercial television stations gave extensive coverage to the elections. They covered all candidates in news reports and provided the opportunity for all to appear on their popular interactive talk shows. In the assessment of at least one media specialist at the local Sam Ratulangi University, while not necessarily allocating equal time to all candidates, the stations did cover fundamental policy platforms based on a reasonable professional judgment of newsworthiness and balance.[35] However, additional coverage was generated by candidates' willingness to "sponsor" items for broadcast or provide other financial incentives. Stations virtually never publicly acknowledged this system of "blocking time" as paid political advertising.

The most noteworthy innovation, tried by TVRI in the June governorial election and adopted by Pacific-TV in the mayoral poll, was a marathon live public debate between the candidates. Pacific-TV (together with two radio stations) was paid by the Local Electoral Commission (KPUD) to broadcast all six candidates presenting their policy platforms, answering questions from an expert panel and, selectively, from the floor, over five hours. With an invited audience of about 300, it was a sustained and unique opportunity to use local television to replicate the "town hall meetings" of the past, broadcasting into the surrounding community. Referred to popularly as a "debate" (although candidates did not directly debate or address each other), it provided an opportunity to compare candidates' speeches and responses to questions.

Media influence on voter choice

More comprehensive extended research would be required to determine with greater certainty what influence media coverage may have had over

Media and politics in regional Indonesia 201

voter choice. However, initial findings suggest valuable lines of inquiry. An exit poll undertaken jointly by the National Democratic Institute for International Affairs (NDI) and a local non-government organization, Publika Manado, identified both worrying residues of New Order politics and a striking impact of television upon voter choices.[36]

Of the exit-poll respondents, about 5 percent of those who voted for Rogi attributed it to "money politics," a euphemism which encompasses the exchange of money or other goods in return for votes. Non-government election monitors regarded this as an underestimate of the effect of the widespread dispensing of cash or other gifts immediately prior to polling day – a practice dubbed *"serangan fajar"* (dawn attack) because it is timed to maximize the impact on election morning.[37] Of all the respondents who freely admitted their vote was determined by "money politics," the largest proportion (34 percent) voted for Rogi; only marginally fewer voted for Frederik (at 30 percent). However, as an investigation by the SCTV channel found during the 2004 national elections,

> Like corruption, money politics during campaign periods are not easy to prove, since the candidates or the success teams (i.e. campaign teams) packaged it in the form of "transport money," "fuel costs," daily needs, scholarships, or commonly, donations to "pesantrens" (i.e. religious schools) or certain groups.[38]

The Manado experience would support Malley's observation (made of local parliaments but applicable also to post-2004 direct elections) that "allegations of vote buying mar the election of nearly every governor, *bupati* and mayor" (Malley 2003: 102).

About 10 percent of the total sample claimed there had been intimidation near the polling booths, with about 6 percent complaining of violence. Rogi was accompanied throughout the campaign by black-shirted muscular male "supporters" whose demeanor was quietly intimidating. Even milling outside and in the foyer of the council building in which the Electoral Commission announced the poll results, their presence was obvious, though not actively belligerent.[39] In what may indicate disillusionment with such anti-democratic practices or simply "electoral fatigue" (at the fifth election since April 2004), more than 31 percent of eligible voters chose not to participate (8 percent more than in the governorial election a month previously).[40]

The NDI–Publika survey found nearly 30 percent of respondents indicated TV was the most significant communication medium influencing their voting. It had nearly twice the impact of the "traditional" local determinant, "communication with the candidates' electioneering team" (with only 17 percent). TV's impact surpassed newspapers (12 percent), brochures, posters or banners (7 percent), and somewhat surprisingly was vastly greater than the much more ubiquitous radio (2 percent), presumably because of the latter's concentration on entertainment rather than political news. Of that

202 *David T. Hill*

30 percent who felt TV influenced them most, 13.5 percent attributed this specifically to the televised debate, nearly 11 percent to news coverage and about 5.5 percent to party advertising. While all candidates funded television spots, Golkar had invested an unprecedented amount in TV ads. According to one industry source, Golkar's national office pumped at least Rp 125 million (about US$13,000) per day – or five times the annual official salary of the mayor (not including generous "house-keeping" bonuses) – into Rogi's television ads alone. Rogi also engaged an American-trained Jakarta political consultant to advise on strategy and image-making.

Manado's mayoral elections suggest that local media will play an increasingly influential, if complex, role in grassroots elections throughout Indonesia. Potentially it may be to television rather than print media or radio that aspiring politicians direct their funds – in whatever form such payments might make.

Tentative conclusions

Hadiz's (2003: 124) concern at "the range of interests now contesting power at the local level" needs to be juxtaposed with Bardhan and Mookherjee's assessment that the likelihood of local vested interests successfully hijacking democracy is greatest "where effective electoral competition is lacking, elite interest groups are more cohesive, and the average level of political awareness among voters is low" (Bardhan and Mookherjee 2000, in Malley 2003: 104). The circumstances in Manado may be such as to minimize – though certainly not completely avoid – the likelihood of such capture. In the mayoral elections, there was reasonably effective competition with a field of viable candidates offering voters genuine choice, with the rivalry between the Frederiks and Rimba Rogi illustrating a polarized local elite. Despite the resilience of "New Order" practices of vote buying, voter intimidation and covertly paying media outlets for favorable coverage, there was a robust level of political awareness among voters, supported by a resilient and engaged – if financially weak – local media.

The change from Jakarta *appointing* local officials, such as governors and mayors, to the popular direct *election* of such figures, makes it unsurprising that aspirants for such elected positions would seek to craft the most positive public image through favorable media depiction. They may seek to achieve this by relying more on public relations firms or pollsters to advise on maximizing media profile. They could pursue this through direct ownership, covert payments or blandishments, even through physical intimidation or violence against media workers. There is an inescapable convergence in Manado between political interests and media ownership or control. What is not clear yet is whether this control is sufficient – or is being exercised in such a way – as to pervert the electoral process. While observers might have assumed that the Frederiks' control over *Global News* would have ensured their survival as Golkar-backed mayor and party branch chief, this was not

Media and politics in regional Indonesia   203

to be. While *Global News*' editorial line was pro-Frederik, it would have been counterproductive to promote him so aggressively that the paper lost readership and therefore potential influence. For the politically aligned *Komentar*, the newspaper's link was to a minor party with little likelihood of mayoral success and the paper did not substantially alter that party's performance. In any case, the NDI–Publika survey suggests that, with only 12 percent, the print media had far less influence on voter attitudes than did television with 30 percent; and television remains outside party control.

While the removal of government controls over the media and the devolution of political power to the regions may not necessarily guarantee the growth of a strong and viable democracy in Indonesia amid the complex play of local politics in Manado, there are signs that an emerging local media is, for the present at least, playing a valuable contributory role in that process.

Notes

1 This paper is part of a larger project on "Media in a Post-Authoritarian State: Crisis and Democratization in Indonesia," funded by the Australian Research Council and undertaken jointly with Krishna Sen of Curtin University of Technology, Western Australia (who however, shares no responsibility for the many failings of this particular paper). I express my appreciation to the International Institute for Asian Studies, Leiden, for hosting me as an Affiliated Fellow in November 2004, and the Asia Research Institute of the National University of Singapore where I was a Visiting Senior Research Fellow in 2006, when parts of this paper were written. Thanks also to Abdul Gaffar Karim, Frederik Worang and Marcus Mietzner for comments and suggestions. An earlier version of this paper was published in *South East Asia Research* (March 2007).
2 See, for example, Hill (1994) and Sen and Hill (2000), both of which include some discussion of how the Surabaya-based Jawa Pos Group challenged Jakarta rivals by developing a string of successful local publications. Other exceptions include some chapters in Surjomihardjo (1980).
3 Studies of local media include the Leiden "Indonesian Mediations" project under Professors Arps and Spyer; Hughes (2003); Morrell (2005); Eriyanto (2003); Mirino (2003); (unpublished) research by the Institute for the Free Flow of Information (ISAI), particularly Eriyanto and Stanley, including "Potret Media di Papua 2002" and "The role of media in supporting peace-building and reconciliation efforts in Central Sulawesi, Maluku and North Maluku" (July 2004). Gazali (2000) examines local radio and press during the immediate transitionary period.
4 Law 22 of 1999 devolved political authority while Law 25 of 1999 provided for fiscal arrangements whereby regions retained greater revenue.
5 I thank David Henley of the Royal Institute of Linguistics and Anthropology (KITLV), Leiden, for sharing his unpublished writings and extensive knowledge of Sulawesi during the early phases of this research.
6 On North Sulawesi's rebound from the 1997 economic crisis, see Henley and Tuerah (2003), with statistics on p. 12, citing Badan Pusat Statistik (2002) *Statistik Indonesia 2001*, Jakarta: BPS, pp. 593–5.
7 Schouten (2004) provides a succinct history of North Sulawesi's incorporation into the colonial economy, while the most detailed recent study of the region is

204 *David T. Hill*

Schouten (1998: 113), who notes that in 1860 there were 150 schools for 300 villages in Minahasa.

8 The Jakarta morning *Kompas* arrives in Manado by about 3 p.m. and circulates that afternoon, while the Jakarta afternoon *Suara Pembaruan* arrives that night for sale late night or next morning.

9 An online version of the *Manado Post* is usually available at www.manado-news.com (accessed 15 November 2004).

10 PT Jawa Pos' revenue increased from Rp 156.75 billion (in 1998) to Rp 250.54 billion (in 2003) (Haryanto *et al.* 2004: 25).

11 *Jawa Pos* had initially collaborated with the other Manado daily, *Cahaya Siang* (named after the publication of the 1860s, but with no links to it) as the Surabaya paper's first expansion off Java, but the collaboration collapsed (interview with *Manado Post* Deputy Editor Suhendro Boroma, Manado, 2 August 2004). *Cahaya Siang* then entered into a similar arrangement with the Jakarta-based Media Indonesia Group, but closed within a few years (Parwoko 1995: 12–13).

12 See Parwoko (1995: 80–2). Maramis describes the paper's establishment in "Kisah Balik Manado Post" (celebrating the fifteenth anniversary of the *Manado Post*, 17 January 2001, Hotel Ritzy Manado), obtained from Suhendro Boroma, 2 August 2004.

13 Interview with Suhendro Boroma (2 August 2004). Information provided by Boroma gives the daily circulation as 36,300 copies, of which about 60 percent was in Manado, 5 percent outside of North Sulawesi and the remainder in the province's various regions. However, such data is unreliable since circulations are not audited and publications often exaggerate circulation.

14 Interview with J.J. Massie (Manado, 2 August 2004) who provided an unpublished typescript "Sejarah Singkat Perusahaan" with details of his education.

15 For example, "Peduli Lembeh" (15 October 2005, online) describes Massie very flatteringly as a "*tokoh muda potensial*" (young leader with potential). Available at www.hariankomentar.com/kota05.html (accessed at 15 October 2005).

16 The *Komentar* website is: http://hariankomentar.com. Global Financial Trading's website is www.globaletrades.com/index.html (accessed 15 November 2004).

17 "Sejarah Singkat Perusahaan."

18 For a brief period in 2004, it was published with one page of English- and Chinese-language news, but this ceased by mid-2005.

19 To those national stations broadcasting under Suharto (TVRI, TPI, RCTI, SCTV, ANTV and Indosiar) were added Metro TV, TransTV, Global TV, TV7 and Lativi – all broadcasting nationally by 2005. Under the New Order, several of these stations (such as SCTV and ANTV) were initially granted licenses restricting them to provincial headquarters (Surabaya and Lampung respectively) but all eventually gravitated to Jakarta bases. On TV in Indonesia during the New Order, see Kitley (2000), and Sen and Hill (2000: 108–36).

20 According to Haryanto *et al.* (2004: 56–7; citing Matari dan Riset *Cakram*, edisi khusus televisi, No. 06/2003), there were thirty-four local television stations. Some, such as Bunaken TV (which was Manado's first post-Suharto commercial station but collapsed without a trace within a year), were not actually broadcasting.

21 "*TV Manado* Disita," available at www.liputan6.com/fullnews/76418.html (accessed 10 November 2004).

22 Under the 2002 broadcast law (Section 3, Article 7), the national Indonesian Broadcasting Commission (Komisi Penyiaran Indonesia, KPI) has provincial-level Commissions (Komisi Penyiaran Indonesia Daerah, KPI-D), members of which are "appointed by the Governor on the advice of the Provincial People's Representative Assembly" (DPRD) (Article 10.3). In Manado, several interested

community and professional groups such as the Alliance of Independent Journalists (AJI) protested at the process of determining, and the individuals subsequently appointed to, the provincial Commission. On the Broadcast Law, see Pandjaitan and Siregar (2003).
23 Confidential interviews in Manado (22 and 27 July 2005).
24 Conversation with Bonifacius Mandalika and TV-M's News Director, Mareska Mantik, Manado (22 July 2005).
25 Interview with Yudhie Kaloh, Manado (22 July 2005).
26 Email communication with Mareska Mantik, former TV-M News Director (13 December 2005).
27 Kereh is believed to hold between 20 and 45 percent of TV-M. The station website is available at www.pacifictv.tv/index.php (accessed 12 April 2006).
28 See: "Pacific TV, TV Lokal Kedua di Manado," *Swaranet*, 8 July 2003 (online), available at www.swara.net/id/view_headline.php?ID = 2323 (accessed: 10 November 2004).
29 Interview with Harris Vandersloot, Editor-in-chief, Pacific-TV (25 July 2005). On Voice of America, see www.voanews.com/english/About/Television.cfm (accessed 24 November 2005). On Deutsche Welle, see www.dw-world.de/ (accessed 24 November 2005).
30 On GOTN, see www.gotn-ministry.org/ (accessed 24 November 2005).
31 For provincial, district and mayoral election results, see www.jurdil.org/pilkada05/Content%20Hasil%20PILKADA%20%202005%20%20(by%20date).pdf (accessed 24 November 2005).
32 Defeating nine former generals for the position, Sondakh was the first civilian governor since 1962 (with the sole exception of Abdullah Amu, who served only briefly from 1966 to 1967) (Paputungan 2001: 171–5). Further information regarding the two candidates can be gleaned from Sondakh (2003) and Sarundajang (2005).
33 Confidential interview with a senior television executive, Manado (22 July 2005).
34 Interview with Max Rembang, Sam Ratulangi University, Manado (20 July 2005).
35 Interview with Max Rembang, Sam Ratulangi University, Manado (20 July 2005).
36 The poll sample included about 1,500 (from nearly 200,000) voters. For details, see www.jurdil.org/pilkada05/manadoi.htm (accessed 25 November 2005). I thank Anastasia Soeryadinata of NDI and Ismail Dahab of Publika Manado for their assistance during my observation of the mayoral elections and for sharing their findings.
37 *Serangan Fajar* (Dawn Attack) was the title of a major propaganda film made during the New Order period to highlight the role of then president Suharto in a brief but strategically significant "general attack" (*serangan oemoem*) by Indonesian republican forces wresting Dutch control of the city of Jogjakarta on 1 March 1949. The emotionally loaded term "*serangan fajar*" is now used widely to describe a candidate's showering of material inducements upon electors in the lead-up to an election. On *Serangan Fajar*'s origins and its manipulation by the New Order, see Sen (1994).
38 *Kotak Suara*, SCTV (23 June 2004); also quoted in English in Faisol and Listyorini (2004: 9).
39 Personal observation, Plenary Meeting of the Manado General Elections Commission, DPRD building (26 July 2005). On election day, I observed four separate polling stations for extended periods and noticed no evidence of intimidation, although there was a cluster of muscular males at one station cheering votes for Rogi, such that some voters may have found their obvious partisanship menacing.

206 *David T. Hill*

40 In 2004, there were national general elections in April, followed by two rounds of presidential elections (in July and September), with elections for governor of North Sulawesi on 20 June 2005. Marcus Mietzner makes the point that, considering such demands, the turn-out rate was "very healthy" (personal communication, 30 August 2006).

Bibliography

Anon (2004) "Arianne Nangoy Pimpin Partai Golkar Manado," *Harian Komentar*, 4 November 2004, available at http://hariankomentar.com/arsip/nov04/h1003.html (accessed 15 November 2004).

Antlöv, H. (2003) "Not enough politics! Power, participation and the new democratic polity in Indonesia," in E. Aspinall and G. Fealy (eds) *Local Power and Politics in Indonesia: Decentralisation and democratisation*, Singapore: ISEAS.

Aspinall, E. and Fealy, G. (2003) "Introduction: Decentralisation, democratisation and the rise of the local," in E. Aspinall and G. Fealy (eds) *Local Power and Politics in Indonesia: Decentralisation and democratisation*, Singapore: ISEAS.

Badan Pusat Statistik Kota Manado (2004) *Kota Manado Dalam Angka 2003*, Manado: Badan Pusat Statistik Kota Manado.

Bardhan, P. and Mookherjee, D. (2000) "Capture and governance at local and national levels," *American Economic Review*, 90(2): 135–9.

Eriyanto (2003) *Media dan Konflik Ambon: Media, Berita, dan Kerusuhan Komunal di Ambon 1999–2002*. Jakarta: Kantor Berita Radio 68H.

Faisol, A. and Listyorini, D. (2004) "Feature blocking time in television: violations or not?" *Election News Watch*, Institute Studi Arus Informasi (ISAI) Jakarta, 30 June, 9: 9–12.

Gazali, E. (2000) "Antara Benci dan Banci Terhadap Rezim: Analisis Peran Koran dan Radio Lokal," in Dedy N. Hidayat, Effendi Gazali, Harsono Suwardi and Ishadi, S.K. (eds) *Pers dalam "Revolusi Mei" Runtuhnya Sebuah Hegemoni*, Jakarta: Gramedia Pustaka Utama.

Hadiz, V. (2003) "Power and politics in North Sumatra: the uncompleted *reformasi*," in E. Aspinall and G. Fealy (eds) *Local Power and Politics in Indonesia: Decentralisation and democratisation*, Singapore: ISEAS..

Hajramurni, A. and Rumteh, J. (2004) "Another graft scandal hits South Sulawesi council," *The Jakarta Post*, 25 June (online), available at www.thejakartapost.com/yesterdaydetail.asp?fileid = 20040625.D01 (accessed 15 November 2004).

Hari, K. (2004) "Minister Syamsul pledges TVRI's neutrality in general election," *The Jakarta Post*, 19 February.

Haryanto, I, Laksmini, G.W. and Untung, B. (2004) *Kembalinya Otoritarianisme? Laporan Tahunan Aliansi Jurnalis Independen 2004*. Jakarta: AJI.

Henley, D. and Tuerah, N., (2003) "Twentieth-century crises and their impacts in North Sulawesi," revised unpublished paper presented at Institute of Social Studies/KITLV workshop on 'Comparative social history of economic crises in Indonesia', Leiden, 17 December.

Hill, D.T. (1994) *The Press in New Order Indonesia*, Perth: University of Western Australia Press.

—— (2005) "Wild West TV: televangelism comes to regional Indonesia," *Inside Indonesia*, 82, April–June: 17 (online), available at www.insideindonesia.org (accessed 5 December 2005).

Media and politics in regional Indonesia   207

Hotland, T. (2004) "Adrian to face trial soon for role in BNI scandal," *Jakarta Post*, 8 November (online), available at www.thejakartapost.com/yesterdaydetail.asp?fileid = 20041108.C02 (accessed 10 November 2004).

Hughes, K. (2003) "Re-defining daerah: local press in post New Order Indonesia," unpublished honors thesis, Faculty of Asian Studies, Australian National University, Canberra.

Jawa Pos Group (2001) *Jawa Pos: A proud story* (promotional booklet), Surabaya: Jawa Pos Group.

Kitley, P. (2000) *Television, Nation, and Culture in Indonesia*, Athens, OH: Ohio University Center for International Studies.

Koesoetjahjo, I. (2001) "Australian land sale grounds for optimism," IBonWEB.com, February (online), available at http://articles.ibonweb.com/magarticle.asp?num = 498 (accessed 10 November 2004).

Malley, M.S. (2003) "New rules, old structures and the limits of democratic decentralisation," in E. Aspinall and G. Fealy (eds) *Local Power and Politics in Indonesia: Decentralisation and democratisation*, Singapore: ISEAS.

Mirino, J.W. (ed.) (2003) *Sekelumit Wajah Pers di Papua*, Jakarta: AJI-Papua and Lembaga Studi Pers dan Pembangunan.

Morrell, E. (2005) "What is the news? Criticism, debate and community in Indonesia's local press," *Asian Journal of Social Science*, 33(1): 129–44.

Pandjaitan, H.I.P and Siregar, A.E. (eds) (2003) *Membangun Sistem Penyiaran yang Demokratis di Indonesia*, Jakarta: Warta Global Indonesia.

Paputungan, H. (2001) "Langka, Gubernur Sipil di Sulawesi Utara," in R. Ahmed Kurnia Soeriawidjaja (ed.) *Liputan dari Lapangan: Oknum, Aparat, Prajurit*, Jakarta: NDI.

Parwoko (ed.) (1995) *Almanak Pers Daerah Sulawesi Utara*, Manado: Balai Penelitian Pers dan Pendapat Umum Manado dan Persatuan Wartawan Indonesia Cabang Sulut.

Rasyid, M.R. (2003) "Regional autonomy and local politics in Indonesia," in E. Aspinall and G. Fealy (eds) *Local Power and Politics in Indonesia: Decentralisation and democratisation*, Singapore: ISEAS.

Sarundajang, S.H. (2005) *Pilkada Langsung: Problema dan prospek*. Jakarta: Kata Hasta Pustaka.

Schouten, M.J. (1998) *Leadership and Social Mobility in a Southeast Asian Society: Minahasa 1677–1983*, Leiden: KITLV Press.

—— (2004) "Manifold connections: the Minahasa region in Indonesia," *South East Asia Research*, 12(2): 213–35.

Sen, K. (1994) *Indonesian Cinema: Framing the New Order*, London: Zed Books.

Sen, K. and Hill, D.T. (2000) *Media, Culture and Politics in Indonesia*, Melbourne: Oxford University Press.

Sondakh, A.J. (2003) *Si Tou Timou Tumou Tou (Manusia Hidup Untuk Memanusiakan Manusia): Refleksi atas Evolusi Nilai-Nilai Manusia*, edited by Richard A.D. Siwu and Reiner Emyot Ointoe, Jakarta: Pustaka Sinar Harapan.

Surjomihardjo, A. (ed.) (1980) *Beberapa Segi Perkembangan Sejarah Pers di Indonesia*. Jakarta: Deppen RI and LEKNAS-LIPI.

13 Out there

Citizens, audiences and the mediatization of the 2004 Indonesian election

Philip Kitley[1]

This chapter proposes a new way of understanding Indonesia's citizen-audiences in the context of post-Suharto regime transformation and a fully commercialized media sector which penetrates every aspect of urban social and cultural life. The audience has been crucial to our understanding of communicative processes even if the shaping of radio and television technologies by the challenge of overcoming space tended to place more emphasis on the projection of messages rather than their reception (Shannon and Weaver 1949). In academic research on audiences, however, we can observe a gradual shift away from audiences as (vulnerable) objects of communication processes to ideas of the audience as active, differentiated interpreters (McQuail 1997).

Following the effective establishment of the Indonesian Republic in 1949, broadcasting came under the influence of American theory and scholars – particularly Wilbur Schramm who played a major role in introducing "development communications" and an interest in media effects to Radio Republik Indonesia (RRI) and later Televisi Republik Indonesia (TVRI) (Chu *et al.* 1991). The development communications paradigm and associated ideas of the efficient transfer of socially transformative information was supported in Indonesia by the United Nations and became the official dogma of the Department of Information which was responsible for the expansion of state-sponsored radio and television services. The impulse to control audiences was strengthened by the "coup" in 1965 which led to centralized control of RRI and the newly established television service.

The launch of the *Palapa* satellite in 1976 was another illustration of state authorities' desire to control communications – this time primarily for military purposes, but also for cultural and educational purposes. *Palapa* and its effects were the focus of the largest and most systematic audience research project in Indonesian communications (Chu *et al.* 1991). The study of the impact of *Palapa* on isolated villagers was conceptualized as a longitudinal "experiment" designed to measure the impact of television in viewers' daily lives from 1976 to 1982. Reading the researchers' description of their research questions, it is clear that the experiment was based on the fundamental assumption that television did things to people, and researchers wanted to know how it affected consumption, agricultural practices, adoption of socially transformative practices such as family planning, national language learning and the like. One question inquired into viewers' "use" of television, but there were no questions which expressed interest in what meanings viewers read out of programming, what bored them or what they enjoyed.

American doctoral student Victor Caldarola broke with the information model of development communications and focused on reception of television among Muslim Banjarese in a book-length ethnographic study (Caldarola 1990). In the early 1990s, I studied audience relations by examining fan letters viewers had sent in to TVRI about the popular children's program *Si Unyil* (Kitley 1997). A long-running ethnographic study of the integration and effects of television on a village community in south central Bali, directed by English anthropologist Mark Hobart in collaboration with I Made Bandem of the College of Performing Arts in Denpasar, has produced a wealth of recordings of TVRI arts performances for critical analysis and a developing literature focused on the reception of television (Hobart 1998, 1999, 2000; Hughes-Freeland 1999 [1997]; see also Nilan 2000).

In summary, then, audience research in Indonesia is underdeveloped, and the key research in the field by Indonesian authors reflects quantitative, survey research methods and theories of "vulnerable" or passive audiences which have come under critical scrutiny as theories of encoding/decoding (Hall 1980) and the "active viewer" were developed in a number of landmark studies (Morley 1980; Ang 1985; Fiske 1989; Liebes and Katz 1990; Jhally and Lewis 1992).

The social and political conditions which had influenced the understanding of audiences as targets in a message or text transmission model began to break down in the late 1980s and early 1990s. The new commercial broadcasters tested the waters and began to segment the market, constructing fictions of the audiences and the "segments" their programming and channels supposedly appealed to. The year 1996 was a watershed in the political life of the New Order when an increasingly assertive and competitive commercial television market and print media exposed the brutality of the New Order in crushing student dissent and the popularity of the opposition political party PDI. Since the late 1980s – and later for television (see Sen and Hill 2000) – "the media" has assumed an increasingly central position in the lives of particularly urban Indonesians (ISAI 1997; van Dijk 2001).

The dam burst in 1998 with the resignation of Suharto and the unexpected cancellation of print media licensing requirements and the issue of many new television licenses. Within a few years, five more TV channels were on air, hundreds of new radio stations had been established, and the flood of new magazine titles seemed unstoppable. This media frenzy precipitated two understandable but contrary reactions – enthusiasm from democratically minded citizens who reveled in the longed-for freedom to buy, establish and view whatever they chose, while more politically active

210   *Philip Kitley*

middle-class associations endorsed freedom of information as a strategy in moving Indonesia away from the oppression of the New Order regime. But the changes were also greeted with apprehension by groups which saw the expanded media sector as threatening core national, cultural and religious values. These opposed reactions have combined to produce a new kind of audience in Indonesia, which I call the mobilized audience. "Mobilized" acknowledges the interpretive connotations of the active audience and the various relations viewers form with mediated content, but goes further to name audience relations that involve deliberate practices of answering back or engagement with content to re-frame and re-set representations which misrepresent or misrecognize the activities and values of the social movement. The mobilized audience is intent on reforming and redistributing media power in a contest over meaning.

The mobilized audience can be understood as a relation and a practice; one relation among many that makes up the complex and shifting character of audiencehood. Its forms have emerged from the specific political and media history of Indonesia and the belief that the media, its framing and representations *matter*, something which Indonesians share with many other societies where modern media saturate public communications (Gitlin 2002; Silverstone 1999). The mobilized audience is not confined to Indonesia, but it is likely to perform differently and for different reasons in other places. What is significant about the mobilized audience is that it is a way of performing audiencehood that is shared by a variety of different groups of citizens: the political public or civil society activists; conservative Islamists affronted by what they perceive as media excess; the man and woman in the street caught up in mass political activities such as electoral campaigns; and progressive Muslim teachers who look on the media as a mode of advancing society. The mobilized audience, that is to say, is not ideologically predetermined as left or right: it is a range of relations and ways of behaving that are an outcome of what Gitlin describes as the torrent of mass-produced images and sounds in everyday life that is increasingly a "central element of our civilization" (Gitlin 2002: 118). The mobilized audience can be understood as a tactic of the (relatively) politically and commercially weak, a practice of behaving in a way that is primarily media-oriented, of playing and participating in the media game to complain, promote, critique or provoke media response about an issue or aspect of content that is central to the cultural politics of the affected group. It is a mode of tactically engaging with the cultural politics of representation by inserting the group's interests in the image flow (de Certeau 1984). It is a technology for answering back the media's tendency to subject audiences to its priorities, rhythms and frames.

The practices of the "active audience" are well known: viewers make sure they do not miss favorite shows by time-shifting and recording them for home viewing. They watch repeats and replay recorded episodes, sharing ideas about what the episodes mean to them. They send recordings to

The 2004 Indonesian election   211

friends and share their pleasures. We incorporate images and sequences into our teaching and presentations. We talk about images we love or hate or are struck by. We track our favorite shows and stars through their resonances in magazines, chat shows and celebrity events. We display our interests by wearing our passions on T-shirts or dressing in the style made famous by the show/star/band. We collect the spin-offs, listen to chat shows and sometimes "talkback." We immerse ourselves in the imaginary life of shows by textual poaching, conferencing and the websites that we create. But these are "as if" kinds of conversations because most of the time as audiences we cannot be heard and are not part of the production and circulation of mass media content flows. Because electronic media involve technologies, infra-structures, knowledge, protocols and capital that distance most viewers from directly answering back, audience behavior largely involves practices which map meaning away from the source of production and situate it in more or less private exchanges – with friends, colleagues, fan communities and a vague, virtually constructed "public" on the Web.

However, there are practices which do attempt a more direct engagement with the media as a site of the framing and representation of discourse. Gitlin's "jammers" answer back and deface/re-face billboards, interrupt events at carefully chosen moments, demonstrate in the streets with an eye on maximum media exposure, hack into selected systems to wake them up or rip them off, and may even distribute their own videos to challenge and confront the value system and framing of social and political issues which they resist (Gitlin 2002: 153). There is an extensive literature on relations between social movements and the media which shows that social move-ments think carefully about their relations with mainstream media and the way their movement and its goals are represented (see Carroll and Ratner 1999, Jasper 1997).

By drawing attention to the *mobilized* (rather than the merely active) audience, we draw attention to practices which are consciously performed to re-set mass media representations of political and cultural discourses. This emphasis on the discursive activity involved directs attention to complex interactions between media producers and audiences. It foregrounds the discursive politics of recognition, of the way political and cultural actors see or want to see themselves, and moves away from a one-sided analysis of the relative "power" of the media and its effects *on* the audience.

The mobilized audience paradigm assumes that the mobilized audience is aware of and acknowledges media power and effects and responds in reflexive ways. It is a paradigm which draws together two traditions in media theory which have been held apart. We can say that the engagement of the audience is an effect of perceptions of the significance and signifying power of the media. The mobilized audience paradigm draws production and reception dynamics together, moving away from a dated and one-eyed focus on either an objectified, passive audience in thrall to the corrupting power of the media, or the semiotic power of the active audience, to an

212   *Philip Kitley*

understanding that audiences are relations formed around practices and content, and that the relations include all the familiar interpretive practices of the active audience and more besides – namely, activist practices which involve direct engagement with media production and circulation (Gillard 2002). In Indonesia in 2004, mobilized audiences performed across numerous sites. In this chapter, reference is limited to two empirical cases: the interaction between the election parades in the Jakarta streets and the media and, second, the work of non-government organizations collected together under the banner of "The Media Coalition" (*Koalisi Media*).

Pawai as mobilized audience

Grossberg has argued that "we need ... not a theory of audiences, but a theory of the organization and possibilities of agency at specific sites in every day life (Grossberg 1997: 341). Here Grossberg uses a spatial metaphor in talking about audiences and their agency. In what follows I explore the dispersal of the performance of audiencehood across specific spaces in Jakarta and the projection and representation of that performance in the media. I suggest that one is inherent in the other; that the comportment or the performance of the audience for the media derives from and is directed to its representation on the media. "Being with the media," as Gitlin (2002) writes, is something that has grown over time in Indonesia and other places. It operates at a pre-verbal level like many social practices, and it is not "scripted" so much as recalled from past traditions of parading, renewed and adapted from audience experiences and visual practices that audiences see played out every day across a wide variety of settings (such as sport, politics and national events) at home and internationally. The media circulates a vocabulary of gestures and modes of comportment in public which can be taken up and adapted as required. For instance, the huge street marches in Taipei in September 2006 took the Roman emperors' "thumbs down" as their visual signifier as men and women and children of all ages paraded in the streets, gesturing that Chen Shui Bian "should go." Even at night, aware that it would be better television if the thumbs down could still be seen, the marchers used small torches and swift, downward gestures to show they were not letting up.

The visuality of performance is embodied, often creative and draws in viewers of all ages. Young children riding with their parents on bikes and trucks do not remember the election of five years ago. They have learned or imitated the party victory signs at the pre-verbal stage, just as they learn the gestures of prayer. RCTI's evening program *Seputar Indonesia* on 16 March 2004 showed a father cradling a sleeping child in his arms, waking him and prompting him to wave at the camera when the lens swung in their direction. Children learn from and imitate their parade group, but they also learn from watching themselves and others performing on television and on the streets. It is a recursive, mutually reinforcing set of competencies.

The 2004 Indonesian election 213

In the Indonesian national election campaign which ran from 11 March to 1 April 2004, political parties were scheduled time and space for public meetings and drive-by publicity where their colors, symbols, logos and, most importantly, their supporters displayed themselves in cities and towns across the archipelago. In Jakarta the parties were allocated parade time on the so-called *"jalan protokol,"* the main arteries of the city. *Protokol,* an Indonesian word with Dutch roots, is a signifier closely linked to officially approved modes of deportment and urban segregation. The *jalan protokol* impose and map a grid of power across urban space, channeling the powerful and favored few across the city to centers of influence – banks, five-star hotels, embassies, government departments, national monuments and selected signs of modernity. Turning the streets over to political parties even for the month-long "carnival of democracy" destabilized the protocols of power relations. The twenty-four parties and frequent parades called into question and fragmented the very notion that there was a unitary or agreed protocol, and heralded a political society where the forms of participation are not necessarily consistent with narrowly rationalist forms and principles of association in civic society (Chatterjee 1997: 32).

The street parades or *pawai* that I observed in 2004 were wonderfully colorful, very noisy and frequently playful.[2] The parades have probably grown out of the long, *ramai* (crowded, exciting) foot marches to election venues in 1955 that Feith (1957: 22) describes, and the much more static mass rallies that were part of the first election in the New Order period on 3 July 1971. Ward's (1974) description of the election campaign which began on 27 April 1971 in East Java gives us an impression of mass meetings and set pieces managed by party officials. Golkar introduced something new with its "Safari" – teams of twenty or more popular singers and dancers from Jakarta who traveled to almost every province to entertain electors. In Surabaya, the Safari team led supporters through the city before performing in the Gelora stadium (Ward 1974: 86). Less well resourced parties convened mass meetings which were lively affairs, but there is no indication that the crowds contributed to the event in any other way than just by being there. The spontaneity of mass gatherings of groups, often of unknown affiliations, drawn together under the banner of only newly organized political parties was much harder to achieve in 1971, so soon after the terror of 1965–6.

Descriptions of 1977 election parades are limited, but black-and-white news photographs from Jakarta show that the parades were much more pedestrian, in multiple senses of that term, than 2004, reflecting a time when Japanese motorbikes were rare rather than swarming, the pressure of population in Jakarta was not as great, and the possibility of spontaneous participation in street politics was scary rather than fun (Nas and Pratiwo 2003). Just as Feith noted for the 1955 ballot day, when voters turned out in "good clothes," in 1977 participants wore their own street clothes and paraded on foot, carrying oversize puppet-like figures (*ondel ondel*) and danced with

214   *Philip Kitley*

hobby horses (*kuda kepang*) (Feith 1957). The spatial impact of the parades was understandably limited to the Monas area, reflecting the history of that area as a revolutionary space and the limited transport of ordinary folk in the 1970s (*Kompas*, 31 March 1977: 4). Walking the Jakarta streets is a hot and tiring process.

Significantly, the media were part of these earliest parades in the sense that media personalities such as H. Oma Irama, Harry Roesli, Benyamin, Isak, Kris Biantoro and Ateng were recruited to liven things up (*Kompas*, 7 April 1977: 1). The 1955 Safari tradition, it seems, had taken root. However, the parade stood little chance of seeing itself reflected back through the media – even if someone owned a television set, and very few did. The sole television channel TVRI limited its coverage to three fifteen-minute scripted addresses by party leaders during the campaign. Visual confirmation or mirroring of popular participation was limited to black-and-white photographs in newspapers, which were relatively expensive and read and seen by only a minority. The print and electronic media might have "covered" the parades, but could not – for a range of technical, economic and policy reasons – provide a means or site for any kind of interactive, reflexive witness or construction of the *public's* political identity. That was to come later.

Over time news photographs reveal an increasingly visual, performative and internationally mediatized style to the election parades that now seems clichéd, but was no doubt exciting and emotionally powerful for participants at the time. In 2004, politics and the media were mapped over each other, exemplified best perhaps by PAN leader Amien Rais taking the stage with rock group Fla, borrowing a guitar and pretending he was a rock star to the delight of the Yogyakarta crowd (*Suara Pembaruan*, 15 March 2004). A cartoon in *Kompas* played on the risky meshing of politics and rock, showing a candidate left alone with no one to talk to once the rock group had moved on to provide entertainment for another party (*Kompas*, 29 March 2004). In the 1987 parade, young men shaved their heads to display party logos (*Kompas*, 5 April 1987: 2). In 2004, however, the body painting and hair color of young campaigners was far more playful and inventive. Some young men turned their torsos into roving billboards, displaying messages such as "An informal vote is just" (*Golput Adil*). For some, body art went beyond a display of party logos and messages to a performative and visual style that was abstract and highly creative, while others drew on international tropes such as punk and Spiderman (*Tempo*, 11 April 2004: 30).

In 2004, the parades had assumed an intensely visual and performative style. Urban spaces had been transformed for the campaign. Jakarta had shed its skin and shone with a bewildering variety of posters, slogans, cartoons, billboards and flags that brightened bus shelters and *kampung* walls. Verbal slogans played almost no part in the *pawai* look and practices. Far more important, as we might expect in the days of eleven color TV channels, were the *atribut* – the colors and logos of the twenty-four parties in contention.

The 2004 Indonesian election 215

Everyone had become a jockey, resplendent in their party's colors, all racing up and down Jakarta and other cities' streets in a political carnival. Participants rode a wild variety of vehicles, most numerously motorbikes with streaming flags and open mufflers. Others crowded into trucks sometimes got up as party symbols such as the buffalo of the PDIP (Partai Demokrasi Indonesia Perjuangan, or the Indonesian Democratic Party for Struggle), whose staring eyes and long horns added sculptural flair to the passing parade. Red- and black-painted trucks parading as buffalos were accompanied by a herd of smaller horned riders, noisily keeping up or speeding past the master symbol of the day's parade. Oversize photographs of party leaders such as Megawati (PDIP), Susilo Bambang Yudhoyono (known as SBY; PD) and Amien Rais (PAN) were camera-friendly and extended the parties' advertising reach beyond the ten thirty-second spots per day the Election Commission specified.[3] Riders on bikes and in trucks looked for the video camera along every stretch of the journey, breaking into smiles, flashing their party's number code with upraised fingers, pointing to their T-shirt logos and portraits, calling out to their imagined audience, and swooning just to get on screen as they drove past the TV crews (TV7 2004).

The Peace and Welfare Party chose to differentiate itself from the over-the-top display of their rivals, and mounted parades of colorful but sedate party supporters who made a great show of being courteous to other drivers, not breaking the road rules or messing up the streets by throwing water bottles, flags or other paraphernalia around. Their visual style participated in the whole phenomenon, and only made sense as a representational tactic in the semiotic excess of the *pawai* by being visually and semantically different.

At the end of each party's campaign time, the *pawai* ended up in mass gatherings in open spaces such as the Senayan stadium. The PDIP show that I saw turned the arena into a sea of red, across which huge banners hung down, turning slowly in the heat and water sprays which drenched people on the track but did nothing for those sweltering in the stands. A *dangdut*[4] stage was set up and the bands played to an enthusiastic crowd dancing down in front, begging the hose chief to douse them again so they could keep on dancing. After a while the only spare seats in the stadium, near the VIP box, were taken over by Megawati, who smiled and waved, said things that no one could hear, and departed with cheering ringing in her ears. Once again, speeches were out of the question; it was just a matter of being there, of the leader taking her place in the huge sprawl of the party presence. She and her retinue were the signature authenticating the PDIP canvas that covered the stadium track and seating, the surrounding spaces where weary paraders cooled down under shady trees and the long line of riders still making their way along Jalan Sudirman before they turned into the Gelora Bung Karno, where her father had spoken many times.

The visual impact and the performative style of the campaign over time and space depended, then, on visual awareness, memory and its production

216   *Philip Kitley*

almost day by day as organizers, paraders and the media looped themselves together, especially on television whose news bulletins re-presented, commented on and boosted the parades for participants and the general audience to watch – over and over again. Interviews recorded for television brought the experience of being on camera right into the audience's space. Recording in the open jostle of the parades and meetings meant that interviewees were surrounded by microphones and cameras. When the interviews were broadcast later, many of the lenses appeared to focus directly on the audience, creating a sense for the audience of being continuously on show (RCTI, *Seputar Indonesia*, 16 March 2004).

The Indonesian word *pawai* may be translated as "parade" but the traditional connotations of the word are lost in the English term, which signifies ostentatious display and military ceremonial. *Pawai* signifies linear organization, one thing following another, but a *pawai* is also a cultural practice associated with a joyful coming together, a desire to accompany, witness and join in an activity such as a ritual chant, wedding procession and the like. *Pawai* is inscribed, that is to say, with a sense of fun, of getting out and enjoying something that participants have in common. This sense of something publicly shared is the important subtext of the argument below, that in 2004 the election campaign opened up increased opportunities for citizens to display and witness their part in the expanding space of democratization. It is best understood not simply as an irrational, emotional excess, but, acknowledging the multiple satisfactions of public participation, as a desire to welcome and share in emerging freedoms in ways that drew on and were inspired by long-established cultural practices (Jasper 1997: 84). It was not the first time that this had happened. In 1999, there was a tangible sense of sharing rather than rivalry in the *pawai* activities that crisscrossed Jakarta and other cities. Anyone who participated in the huge gathering of PDIP in front of the Hotel Indonesia in the last days of the campaign was aware of the space that the crowd made for itself, accommodating thousands of fellow citizens without stress or violence, and seemingly without pushing and shoving. In 2004, the atmosphere was similar, but more orchestrated for the media, which had learned from the excitement generated by public enthusiasm for the 1999 election, and scheduled an extensive range of news, comment and talk shows focused on the election.[5]

It is tempting, especially given the local press's use of "*karnaval*" (*Media Indonesia*, 11 March 2003; *Koran Tempo*, 11 March 2003), to interpret the *pawai* as carnival, drawing on ideas of street parades as a "safety valve", or Bakhtin's (1968) analysis of the upside-down logic of street ritual. But the notion of the carnival has historical and cultural associations that are a long way away from Indonesian *pawai*. As well, the critical inverting play that is part of European carnival is missing from the Indonesian *pawai*. In my view, the playfulness and rowdiness are closer to indigenous celebratory practices of *pawai*, and have gained over time their sense of scale and visual style from their imbrications with the camera and television. The election

The 2004 Indonesian election   217

parades are not liminal performances or rituals of rebellion (Turner 1969; Gluckman 1965), but are political rituals that are essentially consensual and closer to Durkheim's "effervescent assembly" (Durkheim 1965).

From day one of the election campaign in 2004, one "live," embodied performance and two more textual performances clashed in the streets, public and imaginary spaces of Jakarta. In the shifting power relations of post-*reformasi* (reform) Indonesia, there was clearly an anxiety about representations of the public in the streets. The political disparagement of the Indonesian masses as too erratic and ignorant to be involved in politics except briefly for the purposes of (highly manipulated) national electoral campaigns has a long history that goes back to elite ideas that the common people were unenlightened and easily led.[6] The mass was resurrected in a persistent, enervating media discourse about the mindless superficiality of the public and the way the noisy and noisome parade of party supporters took over the streets, turning hot tracks of asphalt into ribbons of channeled fun, community and color.

Thus the parades were built around their dispersal across two spatial orders: urban space – the streets, stadiums, halls and sports fields drawn into the campaign – and the ramifying spaces of television, radio and the print media which flicked back and forth across the archipelago, both drawing together and dispersing the political public across the nation. Technologies of satellite news gathering and digital communication patched together parades in Medan and Palembang with parades in Bali and beyond, focusing on the color, the oddities and the noise of display politics. On 16 April, for example, TVRI's *Election Segment* showed snatches of election parades and meetings of five different parties in Batam, Lampung, Ambon, Balikpapan, Jember and Klender in East Jakarta. Later that evening, viewers were shown *pawai* in NTT, the province east of Bali, Golkar's campaign in South Sumatra, party followers dancing at a PPP rally in Batam, a speech in an indoor venue in Jakarta and a meeting in Sleman, Yogyakarta.

The celebration and enthusiasm of the visual coverage was often underscored with commentary which deplored the unruliness of the parades, reading the participants as campaign mercenaries, in it for a few thousand *rupiah* and a T-shirt, undisciplined and reckless in the way they included their young children in the action on the streets, and insincere in the way they enthusiastically boosted one party one day and another party the next (*Media Indonesia*, 15 March 2004; *Koran Tempo*, 12 March 2004). The commentary denigrated the media-consciousness of the crowds, and was irritated by and simultaneously aware of the media-savvy public's obvious understanding of the image-value of their banners, face paint, masks, raucous exhausts and playful tossing around of bottles of drinking water. Alois Agus Nugroho from Atma Jaya Catholic University argued that the 2004 campaigns, despite being supposedly modern, were still "culturally primitive," and that the masses were far more interested in the hurly-burly

218 *Philip Kitley*

of the parades than studying the vision of electoral candidates (*Kompas*, 25 March 2004). PAN candidate Sjaifoel Tanjung discovered this truth the hard way when he asked a small crowd gathered in a sports hall in South Jakarta "Why are you here?" and got the answer "We don't know!"(*Jakarta Post*, 16 March 2004). Communications scholar Effendi Ghazali was equally dispirited, saying that the effort parties went to in putting their flags and banners everywhere they could showed a very old-fashioned understanding of what it took to win an election (*Kompas*, 25 March 2004). But when the streets were relatively empty of supporters, onlookers or both, the media deplored the public's "passivity" and lack of interest in democratic process (*Media Indonesia*, 12 March 2004; *Republika*, 27 March 2004).

For the whole month, media representations tracked back and forth between the perceived excess of the parades and claims about public apathy on those occasions when a crowd failed to turn up for a candidate's speech, or turned out in smaller numbers than expected. At times commentators grudgingly admitted that the public's lack of interest in so-called inside events was understandable, given the emptiness of politicians' speeches and their poor communication skills. Thus we can understand the *pawai* and the media as co-dependents, each in a way the audience of and for the other, each using the other and each schooled by the other in their publicity and image-conscious practices. More significantly, the conflicted discourse registers the dismay and displacement of the elite and new protocols of representation which a far more inclusive public – men, women and children together – has taken hold of and used to reassert their presence, electoral power and pleasure in recognizing and displaying their identity as part of *reformasi* in a way that was hardly imaginable during the New Order when the streets were often "spaces of fear and discipline" (Abidin Kusno 2000).

The injustice of alienating citizens from the public spaces of their cities and of denigrating the form of public participation by stereotypically describing the behavior of *pawai* and rallies as the mindless behavior of the unenlightened mass is an example of what Fraser calls cultural or symbolic injustice: "being routinely maligned or disparaged in stereotypic public cultural representations and/or in everyday life interactions" (Fraser 1995: 71). The public's desire for due recognition and their playful support for a range of parties is best understood as a sign of their interest in being recognized as integral to the whole democratic process rather than as indifference or lack of understanding of the politics of representation. The *pawai* is an activity of political society that depends on media processes, just as much as the powerful elites of civic society depend on press conferences, expert opinion and current affairs shows. As James Jasper puts it, "participating in important historical events, the kind that are reported on the evening news, is a ... profound satisfaction" (Jasper 1997: 82). For Indonesians, this attitude about elections dates back to their first experience of elections, but

The 2004 Indonesian election   219

its form has shifted over time. Feith records that in the first election of 1955, voters felt part of the symbolic construction of the nation and "a sense of participation in greatness" (Feith 1962: 431).

The street parades were involved in the politics of recognition in a way that exhibited the political significance of "the public" as much as the expanded array of political parties. In taking over the streets and using the presentation modes learned from watching sports crowds and globalized media events, political society re-set the parameters of recognition, resisting the elitist discourses of the civic society to exhibit the political significance of the population, the people, the public and their modern forms of political association such as parties (Chatterjee 1997).

Media watch as a mobilized audience

In 1999 four friends with different but well-developed media skills were determined to intervene in the first "free election" since the 1950s (Antlöv and Cederroth 2004: 5). Their objective was modest enough: they simply wanted to remind citizens that the 1999 election presented an opportunity for self-reflection and autonomous decision-making about political representation. The result of their optimism and passion was the "working group" Visi Anak Bangsa (VAB) (The Citizens' Perspective) and a series of public service advertisements on television which caught the mood of the time perfectly. They were immediately popular and the source of tag phrases and regionally inflected ways of insisting that violence must stop and that "we are all entitled to our own political opinions." Five years on, one of VAB's punchlines *"Aku beda, boleh 'kan?"* ("I can have a different view, can't I?") still resonated in a large display advertisement on metropolitan buses. It showed a colored T-shirt amid a string of black-and-white T-shirts on a washing line and carried the caption: "Differences are normal" (*Beda itu Biasa*).

In 2004, VAB and the Institut Studi Arus Infomasi (ISAI) (Institute for the Study of the Flow of Information) formed an umbrella organization, the Media Coalition (*Koalisi Media*), and divided their grant funds among the eleven other groups included in the coalition.[7] All these groups distinguished themselves by intervening in some way in the mediatization of the 2004 election. Here, the focus is on the activities of ISAI as part of a mobilized audience. This analysis of ISAI's activities in 2004 – and analysis of those activities in terms of a mobilized audience – contributes to theorization of democratization processes through an investigation of micro-level activities which, taken together, can be understood as scaffolding larger patterns of change.

As Ariel Heryanto has argued, "a democratic transition in post-colonies is effective when democratization-friendly consciousness, ideas, practices and institutions have already found fertile ground in various forms" (Heryanto 2003: 25). The activities of ISAI and related media-engaged

220 *Philip Kitley*

organizations are part of the fertile ground Heryanto writes of. Taken together, the activities of civil society organizations such as ISAI, VAB, Internews, the Indonesian Media Law and Policy Centre (IMLPC), Aliansi Jurnalis Independen (AJI) (Alliance of Independent Journalists), and many more have signaled reformist principles and practices characteristic of a responsible and more socially responsive media sector in Indonesia. My concern here is to show how the concept of the mobilized audience may be productive in understanding the historical specificities and deeper cultural dynamics of Indonesians' experience of living with the media.

In 2004, ISAI adopted a media monitor role focused on checking television stations' compliance with the regulations agreed between the General Election Commission (Komisi Pemilihan Umum, KPU) and TV stations in February 2004. In 2004, TV stations were restricted to screening one five-minute party political "monologue" for each party and ten thirty-second spot ads per day free of charge for each party throughout the campaign.[8] Parties could book and pay for additional ads, but the high cost of political advertising on TV (since the Commission insisted that commercial rates must be charged) deterred all but the four financially strong parties from significant TV advertising campaigns (*Prospektif*, 22–28 March 2004: 10–29).

In crowded premises at 68H Utan Kayu Street, ISAI established a monitoring program which involved visual coding of public service advertisements, party political spots, free-of-charge party political monologues, blocking time and sponsorship arrangements. The results of the monitoring were released fortnightly during the campaign in press conferences where data handouts were distributed.[9] These press conferences were unexpectedly lively, given the rather dull material that was reported.

The infringements that ISAI documented became the focus of television news items, talk show comment, newspaper reports and payback press conferences where the television channels sought to rebut the charges that they had infringed regulations concerning advertising. The charges about media infringements fed into a disciplinary discourse of campaign misdemeanors that was a feature of the campaign from its outset. *Suara Pembaruan's* headline "The First Day of the Campaign Colored by Violations" was typical (11 March 2004). *Koran Tempo* went further and outlined the 286 violations that police registered on day one of the campaign (13 March 2004). The detailed reporting of violations across the nation was maintained in all major dailies right up to the end of the campaign. Actual violations were underscored with articles about what was lacking in the campaign, absence operating discursively as powerfully as actual infringements in signifying problems with the campaign process. Newspaper headlines such as "Campaign Dialogue Quiet" (*Kampanye Sepi Dialog*, *Koran Tempo*, 25 March 2004) and "Campaign Dialogue So Far Uneducational" (*Kampanye Diaologis Belum Mendidik*, *Suara Pembaruan*, 18 March 2004) lamented unsuccessful debates and meetings between candidates and the public; the empty meeting halls implicitly reminding us of the crowded,

The 2004 Indonesian election 221

lively parades, reinforcing and circulating a view that the public was either not ready or incapable of rational debate, and was most comfortable with the mindless carnival of the parades (*Media Indonesia*, 11 March; *Koran Tempo*, 11 March; *Kompas*, 25 March).

ISAI's claims about media organizations' violations may be read as an intervention into this discourse of democratic immaturity. ISAI's audience activity destabilized the power relations inscribed in the discourse and charged elite institutions with the same irresponsible behavior that the public was accused of daily. ISAI's professional mode in press conferences, where it displayed TV stations' minor infringements in complicated-looking tables, talked about their methodology and cheekily announced the results of its analysis of the "Ten best news reports about the election" for the fortnight, re-framed the discourse of the public's unreadiness for democratic processes and branded elite institutions with the same faults. Television channels were drawn on to the same ground in defending themselves: in denying their infringements of the rules, they committed themselves to the regulatory environment and responsible management of their programming which was ISAI's larger agenda.

I have argued above that specific historical and political circumstances shaped the public's performance of claiming the streets in the election parades. This is equally true of ISAI and its activities, even though a different social dynamic was at work in the politics of ISAI's mobilized audience activities. ISAI was founded in 1994 by a group of well-known media figures as a protest against the summary banning in June 1994 of the respected but critical weeklies *Tempo* and *Editor*, as well as the tabloid *DeTik* (Heryanto 1996).[10] ISAI's monitoring activities and their citations of the ten best news stories can be understood as one of the "novel ventures" which Heryanto considers marked middle-class activism following the media bans in 1994 (Heryanto 2003: 43). Certainly the founders of ISAI were middle-class, public intellectuals, and the personnel who managed the day-to-day activities of ISAI were also middle-class, though less well known than the founders. Most ISAI managers were tertiary educated, and many had had experience as journalists. Heryanto argues that the media industry networks that organizations such as ISAI could draw on contributed fundamentally to the persistence, high public profile and effectiveness of a range of causes pursued by intellectuals after 1994 (Heryanto 2003: 41). "Novel ventures" such as litigation against state authorities, the establishment of an independent professional journalists' association (AJI), the creation of Indonesia's first independent election monitoring body and a general emphasis by civil society organizations on public education about democratic processes and principles of good governance all benefited greatly from media literacies and a clear understanding of the role of the media.

An industrialized media sector reflects and fits into an increasingly globalized circulation of information and media properties. It is also subject to a broader scrutiny and is drawn into transnational regulatory regimes

222   *Philip Kitley*

that serve the interests of multinational media corporations, but can also serve the interests of groups working for greater accountability in media activities. The monitoring activities of ISAI and similar groups in Indonesia are part of a global concern with media practices and draw on best practice and norms of professionalism that are articulated widely in democratic countries and aspiring democracies across the world. What this suggests is that audience research which examines the activities of mobilized audiences in specific circumstances can reveal local events and practices to be an inflection of wider cultural, economic and political processes.

ISAI's mobilized audience role is consistent, then, with its origins in the media. Its tactics in challenging mainstream media using well-established, almost routine practices of monitoring and press conferencing can be understood as the reflexive behavior of media organizations which see their role as contributing to the maintenance of a media environment characterized by principles of freedom of information, respect for public accountability and high standards of journalistic practice. ISAI's mobilized audience activities are closer to conventional audience practices than the parades which can be understood as an exhibitionist mode of comportment derived from and shaped by living with the media. ISAI's audience practice is more textual, an outcome of close reading with a specific audience function or role in mind. It is a process of surveillance, where citizens perform the disciplining function which, following Foucault, we usually link to centers of power (Foucault 1977). In its mobilized audience role, ISAI appropriated the social shaping effects of the media and the disciplinary discourse of campaign violations. It turned the technologies of surveillance back on to the media, adopting the iconic forms and tactics of confrontation which have often been the focus of ideological critique. ISAI uses these public processes and critique quite consciously to disconcert mainstream media channels, publicize their own monitoring practices as a technology of truth, and re-assert the citizen function rather than the commercial function of the media.

The mobilized audience practices described are not limited to concerns over electoral matters. In April 2004, the Aceh News Watch sector of ISAI convened a public seminar and press conference with the title "The forgotten war in Aceh." Speakers discussed difficulties of covering the war and subjected newspaper and television organizations to close scrutiny, arguing that they had taken the easy way out in giving most attention to the election and needed to review their tendency to simplify and sensationalize the war. Close reading and public critique of media was performed by other groups with a similar interest in a socially conscious media environment. The Indonesian Survey Organization (Lembaga Survei Indonesia or LSI) convened an interactive dialogue with Radio Delta on 26 March 2004, at which it invited Radio Delta's audience to phone in their concerns with media coverage during the election. Despite technical problems associated with broadcasting from a noisy meeting room in the Sari Pan Pacific Hotel, LSI's approach organized audience relations around the dominant media discourse

The 2004 Indonesian election 223

and media bias, and re-framed analysis of voter behavior by presenting its careful analysis against the often glib and uninformed assumptions of television talk shows.

The varied audience relations briefly outlined here, situated along a continuum of more or less direct engagement with media texts and production practices, can be understood as part of the "novel ventures" challenging authoritarianism that Heryanto (2003) has described. The ventures are a product of a more competitive and varied market for information, the collapse of corporatist restrictions on journalism practices, lower overheads and the greater flexibility of digital cameras. All these have facilitated the entry of organizations with limited capital, have mobilized audience practices and have challenged mainstream media organizations' capacity to imagine and position their audiences as passive, compliant viewers. Audience research focused on the mobile engagement of audiences with media processes may contribute significantly to understanding the dynamics of social activism and changing forms of cultural critique which often involve and are dependent on recursive or reflexive involvement with the media industry.

Future directions for audience research

My discussion of the concept of the mobilized audience in Indonesia in 2004 is an argument that research should not focus so much on specific moments of audience relations with particular texts, but register and investigate the cultural significance of the shift from a time when television was for most Indonesians a communal, once-a-week event to a time when television sets are "everywhere," in villages and urban households, in restaurants, workplaces, inter-city buses and inter-island ferries. While not discounting text and site specific (at home viewing) audience research (McCarthy 2001: 117), working with an amplified sense of audiencehood and looking for and acknowledging a range of audience practices that derive from and are informed by living with the media will be productive of a culturally and politically inflected understanding of the effects and cultural significance of the media in contemporary Indonesians' lives. As the national television system breaks up into a system of local and regional networks, this approach will enrich our understanding of audiences and audience practices as Indonesians across the nation are increasingly implicated in a reality where the media acts as an important cultural frame and as a site and means for realizing their aspirations.

In the post-Suharto period, there is clearly much more scope for audiences to interact with media producers. The media is a greatly expanded sector at all levels, the highly controlling Department of Information is no more (although a new department, the Ministry of Communication and Information, has been established with more limited powers), there is a progressive Press Act, and interactivity between producers and their audiences is greater than it ever was. Much of the interactivity, however, is still on the terms of the media industry. The dial-in quiz shows, phone-in polling and so on wrap audiences into the genres, rhythms and commercial agendas of media producers. While we can see the *pawai* as a mobilized audience activity that is more independent of the media, in the end *pawai* is performance and display largely structured by media processes. There is, however, some symbiosis here: both are co-dependents and need each other in the construction of the media event. The activities of ISAI and like-minded groups are more interventionist and more constitutive in re-shaping media and cultural relations. Their activities are shaped, however, in reaction to the initiatives of the media sector and depend on inserting themselves into the flow which is managed by the industry. Civil society groups such as ISAI have been very successful in this form of intervention, as has been shown. They are clever about what they do and have the media skills and contacts to make their interventions work effectively. But their opportunities for more extended, less reactive contributions to public debate are constrained by the commercial imperatives of the media industry, a strong commercial television producers' lobby and a newly established regulatory authority, the Indonesian Broadcasting Commission (IMLPC 2003). A further complexity is that the Commission's status is ambiguous given the creation of the Ministry of Communication and Information. This foot-dragging by the authorities is a sign that the media sector and media–society relations in Indonesia are not yet entirely "*post*-Suharto" despite the many changes that have occurred. This investigation of the mobilized audience, understood as relations of interactivity that go beyond a limited understanding of reception, reveals practices of accommodation, intervention and resistance still marked and shaped by official and private sector impatience with public processes of debate and participation in political and cultural life that have the fingerprints of the New Order all over them.

Notes

1 Research for this chapter was supported by Australian Research Council Discovery Grant DP0343059.
2 I observed street parades in Jakarta, Palembang and Medan. The visual style and patterns of behaviour were generally consistent, reinforcing my argument that the *pawai* has shifted from a traditional cultural practice to a pattern of participation that reflects a cultural and political heritage and contemporary, global, modes of media performance and representation.
3 Partai Demokrasi Indonesia Perjuangan (PDIP) is the Indonesian Democratic Party for Struggle; PD is the Democratic Party; and PAN is the National Mandate Party.
4 A popular music genre.
5 Apart from items in news bulletins, election programs included: TVRI's *Gebyar Pemilu* (Election Glance), *Kampanye Dialogis* (Campaign Discussion) and *Debat Parpol* (Political Party Debate); TransTV's *Kilas Pemilu* (Election Brief); MetroTV's *Pentas Kandidat* (Candidates on Show); and, SCTV's *Liputan Pemilu Terkini* (The Latest Election Report).

The 2004 Indonesian election   225

6 Suharto's New Order political machine took the people out of national politics by enacting legislation that forbad political parties to campaign or hold mass meetings except during nominated election periods. The masses were written off as "unenlightened" (*masih bodoh*) and too likely to be distracted by ideologies and ideologues if they were not insulated from politics. This idea was suggested by Nurcholish Majid and enthusiastically promoted by Suharto's political adviser Ali Murtopo.

7 The coalition comprised the Indonesian Media Policy and Law Centre (IMPLC), Yayasan SET, the Institute for the Free Flow of Information (ISAI), Lembaga Studi Pers dan Pembangunan (LSPP), Southeast Asian Press Alliance (SEAPA), Kelompok Kerja Visi Anak Bangsa (VAB) and Jaringan Radio Pemantau Pemilu (JRPP).

8 See Agreement Between the Electoral Commission and the Indonesian Broadcasting Commission Number 12, 2004, No. 002/SK KPI/II/04, 19 February 2004.

9 See Institut Studi Arus Informasi (ISAI) "Hasil Monitoring Berita and Talkshow Pemilu Di Televisi Periode 8–19 and 20–25 Maret 2004" ("Results of Monitoring Election News and Talkshows on Television 8–19 March and 20–25 March 2004") (separate reports).

10 ISAI was founded in 1994 by journalists Goenawan Mohamad, Fikri Jufri, Aristides Katoppo, radio broadcaster Muhammad Sunjaya and scholars Mochtar Pabottingi and Ashadi Siregar.

Bibliography

Abidin Kusno (2000) *Behind the Postcolonial: Architecture, urban space and political cultures in Indonesia*, London and New York: Routledge.

Ang, I. (1985) *Watching Dallas: Soap opera and the melodramatic imagination*, London: Methuen.

Antlöv, H. and Cederroth, S. (2004) *Elections in Indonesia: The New Order and beyond*, London: RoutledgeCurzon.

Bakhtin, M. (1968) *Rabelais and His World*, Cambridge, MA: MIT Press.

Banks, J. (2002) "Gamers as co-creators: enlisting the virtual audience – a report from Net Face," in M. Balnaves, T. O'Regan and J. Sternberg (eds) *Mobilising the Audience*, Brisbane: University of Queensland Press.

Caldarola, V.J. (1990) "Reception as cultural experience: visual mass media and reception practices in Indonesia," unpublished thesis, University of Pennsylvania.

Carroll, W.K. and Ratner, R.S. (1999) "Media strategies and political projects: a comparative study of social movements," *Canadian Journal of Sociology*, 24(1): 1–33.

Chatterjee, P. (1997) "Beyond the nation? Or within?" *Economic and Political Weekly*, 32(1, 2): 30–4.

Chu, G., Alfian and Schramm, W. (1991) *Social Impact of Satellite Television in Rural Indonesia*, Singapore: AMIC.

De Certeau, M. (1984) *The Practice of Everyday Life*, Berkeley: University of California Press.

Durkheim, E. (1965) *The Elementary Forms of the Religious Life*, trans. J.W. Swain, New York: The Free Press.

Feith, H. (1957) *The Indonesian Elections of 1955*, Ithaca, NY: Cornell University Press.

—— (1962) *The Decline of Constitutional Democracy in Indonesia*, Ithaca, NY: Cornell University Press.

226 *Philip Kitley*

Fiske, J. (1989) *Understanding Popular Culture: Reading the popular*, Chapel Hill: University of North Carolina Press.

Foucault, M. (1977) *Discipline and Punish: The birth of the prison*, trans. A. Sheridan London: Allen Lane.

Fraser, N. (1995) "Rethinking the public sphere: a contribution to the critique of actually existing democracy," in C. Calhoun (ed.) *Habermas and the Public Sphere*, Cambridge, MA: MIT Press..

Gillard, P. (2002) "Museum visitors as audiences: innovative research for online museums," in M. Balnaves, T. O'Regan and J. Sternberg (eds) *Mobilising the Audience*, Brisbane: University of Queensland Press.

Gitlin, T. (2002) *Media Unlimited: How the torrent of images and sounds overwhelms our lives*, New York: Henry Holt.

Gluckman, M. (1965) *Politics, Law and Ritual in Tribal Society*, Oxford: Oxford University Press.

Grossberg, L. (1997) *Bringing It All Back Home: Essays on cultural studies*, Durham, NC: Duke University Press.

Hall, S. (1980) "Encoding/decoding," in S. Hall, D. Hobson, A. Lowe and P. Willis (eds) *Culture, Media, Language*, London: Hutchinson.

Heryanto, A. (1996) "Indonesian middle-class opposition in the 1990s," in G. Rodan (ed.) *Political Oppositions in Industrialising Asia*, London and New York: Routledge, pp. 241–71.

—— (2003) "Public intellectuals, media and democratization: cultural politics of the middle classes of Indonesia," in A. Heryanto and S.K. Mandal (eds) *Challenging Authoritarianism in Southeast Asia: Comparing Indonesia and Malaysia*, London: Routledge.

Hobart, M. (1998) "Drunk on the screen: Balinese conversations about television and advertising," paper presented to the Asian Advertising and Media Conference, University of Hong Kong, April 1998.

—— (1999) "The end of the world news: articulating television in Bali," in R. Rubenstein and L.H. Connor (eds) *Staying Local in the Global Village: Bali in the twentieth century*, Honolulu: University of Hawaii Press.

—— (2000) "Live or dead? How dialogic is theatre in Bali?" in A. Vickers, I Nyoman Dharma Putra and M. Ford (eds) *To Change Bali: Essays in honour of I Gusti Ngurah Bagus*, Bali Post and Institute of Social Change and Critical Inquiry, Denpasar: University of Wollongong.

Hughes-Freeland, F. (1999 [1997]) "Balinese on television: representation and response," in M. Banks and H. Morphy (eds) *Rethinking Visual Anthropology*, New Haven and London: Yale University Press.

Indonesian Media Law and Policy Centre (IMLPC) (2003) "Somasi Damai dan Terbuka untuk menjalankan perintah Undang Undang No. 32 Tahun 2002 Tentang Penyiaran, segera membentuk Komisi Penyiaran Indonesia Pusat dan Komisis Penyiaran Daerah di Tingkat Propinsi sebagai partner KPU menyelenggarakan Pemilu 2004 yang jujur, adil, transfaran, damai dan berkualitas" [A peaceful and open legal challenge to the President of the Republic and all provincial governors to effect immediately the substance of Broadcasting Act No. 32, 2002 and establish at the central and provincial levels offices of Indonesian Broadcasting Commission as [which will act as] partners to the General Election Commission in conducting the general election of 2004 in a manner that is honest, just, transparent, peaceful and represents quality practice], 4 November.

The 2004 Indonesian election   227

Institut Studi Arus Informasi (ISAI) (1997) *Peristiwa 27 Juli* [The 27 July Event], Jakarta: Aliansi Jurnalis Independen and ISAI.

Jasper, J.M. (1997) *The Art of Moral Protest: Culture, biography, and creativity in social movements*, Chicago and London: University of Chicago Press.

Jhally, S and Lewis, J. (1992) *Enlightened Racism:* The Cosby Show, *audiences and the myth of the American dream*, Oxford: Westview Press.

Kitley, P. (1997) "Pancasila in a minor key: TVRI's *Si Unyil* models the child," *Indonesia*, 68: 129–52.

Liebes, T. and Katz, E. (1990) *The Export of Meaning: Cross-cultural readings of* Dallas, Oxford: Oxford University Press.

McCarthy, A. (2001) *Ambient Television: Visual culture and public space*, Durham and London: Duke University Press.

McQuail, D. (1997) *Audience Analysis*, Sage: London.

Morley, D. (1980) *The Nationwide Audience*, London: British Film Institute.

Nas, P.J.M. and Pratiwo (2003) "The streets of Jakarta: fear, trust and amnesia in urban development," in P.J.M. Nas, G.A. Persoon and R. Jaffe (eds) *Framing Indonesian Realities: Essays in symbolic anthropology in honour of Reimar Schefold*, Leiden: KITLV Press.

Nilan, P. (2000) "Representing culture and politics (or is it just entertainment?): watching TV in Bali," *Review of Indonesian and Malaysian Studies*, 34(1): 119–54.

Sen, K. and Hill, D.T. (2000) *Media, Culture and Politics in Indonesia*, Melbourne: Oxford University Press.

Shannon, C.E. and Weaver, W. (eds) (1949) *The Mathematical Theory of Communication*, Urbana: University of Illinois Press.

Silverstone, R. (1999) *Why Study the Media?* London: Sage.

Turner, V. (1969) *The Ritual Process: Structure and anti-structure*, Chicago: Aldine.

Van Dijk, K. (2001) *A Country in Despair: Indonesia between 1997 and 2000*, Leiden: KITLV Press.

Ward, K. (1974) *The 1971 Election in Indonesia*, Centre of Southeast Asian Studies, Clayton: Monash University.

Indonesian print media publications

De Tik (tabloid newspaper; banned in 1993, re-published as *DeTak*)
Kompas (daily newspaper)
Koran Tempo (daily newspaper)
Prospektif (business weekly magazine)
Republika (daily newspaper)
Suara Pembaruan (afternoon newspaper)
Tempo (weekly news magazine)

Index

Abdullah Ahmad 165
Abdullah Ahmad Badawi 144, 156–57, 164–67
Aceh News Watch 222
Ahmad Fauzi 163
Al-Qaeda 163
Aliran Online 142, 143, 149
Along the Railway (documentary) 64–65
alternative media: democratic role 140; dominant frames 144–47; explaining difference 147–49; limitations of 149–53; mainstream and 141–44; *see also* insurgent media
Amnesty International 86
Anderson, B. 116
Anwar Ibrahim 156, 159–60
Asian Wall Street Journal 158
audiences: active audience 210–11; future research 223–24; media watch 219–23; theories of 208–9; *see also* mobilized audiences
Aung Pwint 95
Aung San Suu Kyi 85, 88, 90, 91, 97, 100
authoritarian regimes 182–83; bureaucratic-authoritarian regimes 11–13
Aye Htun 96

Baker, C. 131, 135, 151
Bakhtin, M. 58
Bali bombings 139
Bangkok Broadcasting 123
Bangkok Post 124, 131
Bar Girls (film) 77–78
Barisan Nasional (BN) 157, 164
BEC World 123
Beijing 16
Berita Harian 159, 162

Bhumibol, King 122, 127–31
Bin Laden, Osama 152
"Black May" 122, 123
Blair, Tony 174
Boston Globe 135
British Broadcast Corporation (BBC) 96, 100
bureaucratic-authoritarian regimes 11–13
Burma: army control 85–86; British conquest 107; censorship 86–91, 117; constitution 90, 98; economic planning 97–98; elections 100; freedom of expression 85; to independence 98–99; independence 107–8; infant mortality 97–98; international media 96–97; minority language publications 117; national causes 92–93; or Myanmar 101n.1; popular culture 117–19; press freedoms 99–100; state-controlled media 91–96; *see also* Shan insurgency
Burma Journalists' Association 98
Burmese Socialist Program Party (BSPP) 86, 109
Burmese Way to Socialism 99, 109

Campaign for Popular Media Reform (CPMR) 125
CAT (Communications Authority of Thailand) 124
censorship 5–6, 86–91, 182
Central Chinese Television (CCTV): advertising income 52; documentary cinema 37, 56, 61–62; funding 52; investigative programmes 50; management change 54; social issues 52–53; viewing figures 53; as voice of the masses 51

China: audience participation and feedback 53–54, 58; compassionate journalism 34, 36, 46n.3; democracy 44; democratic seeds in documentaries 57–60, 66; documentary cinema *see* documentary cinema (China); editorial division 25–26; global media pressure 54; human rights 31–32, 44; independent film productions 64–65; international media representation 31; journalistic norms 24–25, 28, 36; market forces 52–53; marketization of political management 27–28; media advertising 22; media conglomeration 14–16; media environment 50–52; migrant workers 35–36; newspapers *see* Shenzen press; newsworthy stories 44–45; other voices 33–36; Party Publicity Inc. 12–14, 25–26, 27–28, 51, 53; rural China 34–35, 36–39; rural migrants in cities 41–44; social problems ignored 33; Special Economic Zone (SEZ) 42–43; state subsidies 23–24; television stations *see* Central Chinese Television (CCTV); China Education Television (CETV); urban shadowland 39–41; violent protests 43–44; women's employment 39–41, 42–43; women's groups 35; working sisters 42–43
China Education Television (CETV) 51, 53
China National Radio (CNR) 39
Chinese Journalism Yearbook 15
Chinese Women's Daily 35
Computer Science Development Law 1996 89
conservatism, mainstream media and 147–49
Countries at the Crossroads 2005 7
creative industries 174–77

Danish cartoons 165
The Day We Meet Again (documentary) 61
democracy: alternative media and 151; global media conglomerates and 5; overview 7–8; semi-democracies 140–41; transition 219–20; as universal value 139; world country ratings 7
Democratic Action Party (DAP) 162

Democratic Voice of Burma (DVB) 96
Deng Xiaoping 16, 20–21
development communication 208–9
development journalism 4
documentary cinema (Burma) 95
documentary cinema (China): characteristics of 66; democratic seeds 57–60; film analyses 60–66; redefining 54–57

Economist 134
Election (documentary) 62–63
embedded journalists 4–5
Emergency Provision Act 1950 89
ethnic minorities, abuse of 86
ethno-nationalism 114–15
Exams (documentary) 61–62

FACTS 178, 184n.4
Fateha 143, 144, 145, 148–49, 152
Feith, H. 213, 219
Fire Incident (documentary) 59
Focal Point (CCTV) 37
Freedom House 7
Freedom in the World Country Ratings 1972–2006 7
freedom of expression 31, 72, 85, 86–91
Freedom's Way 110, 111, 113–16
Fribourg Film Festival 75

The General Retires (film) 71
gestural politics 173–78, 183
The Girl on the Perfume River (film) 74
Gitlin, T. 141, 210, 211, 212
Global Fund 98
global media 5, 54, 96–97
Global News 193, 199–200, 202–3
Goh Chok Tong 171, 177
Golkar: advertising 202; local politics 197, 198–99; media control 193; Safari teams 213, 214; voter loyalty 190
Gore, Al 160–61
Gospel Overseas Television Network (GO-TV) 196–97
Grammy 123, 124, 131
Guangming Daily 165–66
Guangzhou 16
Guangzhou Daily Group 14
Guardian 33–34, 134

Harakah 142, 143, 148–49, 162
Harian Komentar 192, 200, 203
Harian Metro 192–93

230 *Index*

Historical Burmese Persons Talk Through Statues (Ko) 88
HIV/AIDS 98
Ho Chi Minh 73
Hong Kong 16
Hong Kong Commercial Daily 26–27
Hong Kong television 52
human rights 31–32, 86, 98
Human Rights Watch 133

indigenous media 111
Indochinese Wars 73, 74, 80
Indonesia: coup 1965 208; cultural imports banned 3; election parades 212–19; elections 197–200, 206n.40, 213, 219; local media 189–97; local politics 197–200; media influence on voters 200–202; media watch 219–23; regional autonomy 188, 189; violent protests 161
Indonesia New order: fall of 188, 209–10; legacy of 201; local politics 189, 197; propaganda films 205n.37; publication permits 191, 209; unenlightened masses 225n.5
Indonesian Democratic Party of Struggle (PDI-P) 194, 215
Indonesian Survey Organization 222
instant noodle films 72, 74
Institut Studi Arus Infomasi (ISAI) 219–23, 224
insurgent media: explanation of 119n.2; history of 107–9; language, print and politics 109–12; market and popular culture 117–19; texts 113–17; *see also* alternative media
Integrated Resorts 179–80, 181, 183–84, 184n.5
Internal Security Act (ISA) 140–41, 145, 150
International Committee of the Red Cross (ICRC) 88
International Federation of Journalists 133
International Monetary Fund (IMF) 75, 97
International Press Freedom Award 95
internet: alternative media and 142, 148–49; restrictions to 89, 91
An Investigation of Chinese Peasants (Chen) 34–35
The Irrawaddy 100–101
Islam Hadhari 165, 166–67
Islamic *jihad* 144

An Itinerant Circus (film) 71
ITV (Independent Television) 123

Jakarta 212–19
Jawa Pos 204n.11
Jawa Pos Group (JPG) 191, 203n.2
Jemaah Islamiyah (JI) 139–41, 146; *see also* alternative media
Jiang Zemin 37
Jiangxi Television 60
Joint Advanced Integrated Networking (JARING) 159

Karlovy Vary International Film Festival 73
Kawn Hkaw 116–17
Khun Sa 113, 114–16, 119, 119n.3
Komentar Group 192–93, 203
Kompas 191, 214
Kompas Gramedia Group (KGG) 191
Koran Tempo 220
Kumpulan Militan Malaysia 147, 163
Kuomintang (KMT) 107

Lee Hsien Loong 170–72, 174, 178, 179–80, 181–82
Lenin, Vladimir Ilyich 55, 57
Literary Works Scrutinizing Committee 87–88
The Little Girl of Hanoi (film) 73
local media 189–97; influence on voters 200–202; local politics and 197–200; monitoring role 188
Low Tide (documentary) 62
Lulu and Me (documentary) 63–64

Magnificent Myanmar 94
Mahathir Mohamad, legacy of 157–62
Malaysia: under Abdullah Badawi 164–67; Constitution 166; elections 161–62; human rights 150, 152; internet 142–43, 159, 161, 167n.7; Islamic protection 165–66; legislation 140–41, 145, 150, 153n.1, 158; Mahathir's legacy 157–62; politically motivated arrests 147; press conferences 149–50; prime ministers 156–57; privatization policies 157; *reformasi* movement 160–62; television 158–59, 166; terrorist arrests 139–41; *see also* alternative media
Malaysiakini 142, 143, 146–47, 150, 152, 165, 167n.8

Index 231

Malaysian Institute of Micro-electronic Systems (MIMOS) 159
Malaysian Multimedia Super Corridor (MSC) 159
Manado 189–90
Manado Post 191–92
Mandalika, Bonifacius 195
Maoism 13
Marina Bay 176–77, 179–80, 183–84, 184n.5
Mass Communications Organization of Thailand (MCOT) 123, 124, 126
Mathathir Mohamad 144, 147, 156
Matichon 124, 127, 131
Media Coalition 219
media piracy 117–18
Media Prima Berhad (MPB) 164
Memories of Dien Bien (film) 74
Minneapolis 142
mobile phones 91
mobilized audiences: explanation of 210–12; media watch as 219–23; Pawai as 212–19
money politics 201
Mong Tai Army (MTA) 113
monitoring 219–23
Moscow International Film Festival 73
Murdoch, Rupert 52
Musa Hitam 156
My Father (documentary) 59
Myanmar Computer Science Council 89

Nanfang Metro Daily 21, 22–23
Nantes Film Festival 75
The Nation 133, 134
National Broadcasting Commission (NBC) 123, 126–27
National Film Development Corporation (FINAS) Act 1981 158
National League for Democracy (NLD) 86, 100
'National Symbols' 114
National Telecommunications Commission (NTC) 127
Ne Min 90–91
Ne Win 99, 109
New Light of Myanmar 93–94, 96
New Straits Times 143, 144, 147, 150–51, 162, 166
New York Times 33–34, 141
news exchange mechanisms 3
night-time economy 175–76
North Salawesi 189–90, 198

Northern Thai language 118
Nostalgia for the Countryside (film) 75–77
NSTP 164
Nugroho, A.A. 217–18
Num Sük Han (Young Warriors) 108–9
NWICO (New World Information and Communication Order) debates 2–3
Nyan Htun Linn 91
Nye, J.S. 173
Nyein Thit 95

objectivity 148
Official Secrets Act 1923 87
Old Men (documentary) 65
Old Mirror (documentary) 60–61
Olympic Games 2008 32

Pacific-TV 196, 200
PAN (National Mandate Party) 214, 215, 218
Panglong Agreement 107–8
Partai Demokrasi Indonesia Perjuangan (PDIP) 215
Parti Islam SeMalaysia (PAS) 141, 144–45, 147, 161–63
Pasuk Phongpaichit 131, 135
Peace and Prosperity Party (PDS) 200
Peace and Welfare Party 215
People's Action Party 171, 174, 183–84, 184n.1
People's Alliance for Democracy (PAD) 122
People's Alliance for Democracy (PAD) 128, 130
post-colonialism 3–4
Printers and Publishers Registration Act 1962 87, 88
Printing Presses and Publications Act (PPPA) 1984 158
Public Relations Department (PRD) 123, 125

Radio Delta 222–23
Radio Free Asia (RFA) 96
Reis, Amien 214
Republic of Indonesia Television (TVRI) 193–94, 209, 216, 217
Review of the Financial, Economic and Social Conditions (MPF, Burma) 97
Revolutionary Council 85–86
Rodan, G. 170–71, 182
Rotterdam International Film Festival 75

232   Index

RTA (Royal Thai Army) radio 125–26
Rural Women Know It All (magazine)
35

Sarawak Tribune 165
SARS 33
Sen, A. 85, 139, 203n.2
September 11th terrorist attacks 144,
163
Seputar Indonesia 212
Severe Acute Respiratory Syndrome
(SARS) 174
Shan insurgency: history of 107–9;
insurgent media 110–12; language,
print and politics 109–10; market
and popular culture 117–19; texts
113–17
Shan State Act 1889 107
Shan State Independence Army (SSIA)
108–9, 110
Shan United Revolutionary Army
(SURA) 110, 111, 112, 119n.3
Shandong Television 61–62
Shanghai 16
Shanghai Television 56, 61, 63–64
Shenzen press: conglomeration 18–19,
19t, 28–29; editorial division 25–26;
management change 19–21;
microcrosm 16–18; monopoly 21–23,
28; overseas expansion 26–27; state
subsidies 23–24
Shenzhen Commercial Daily 18–21, 25, 27
Shenzhen Special Zone Daily 16–21, 24, 25
Shin Corp. 128, 131–33
Sichuan Broadcasting Television Group
51
Singapore: defamation suits 124;
elections 174, 183–84; foreign policy
146; gestural politics 173–78, 183;
Great Casino Debate 177–82; human
rights 150, 152; internet 142;
legislation 140–41, 147; national
security 146; openness 170–72, 174,
178, 179; Shin Corp. sale 128, 131–
33; terrorist arrests 139–41; *see also*
alternative media
Singapore Press Holdings 142
Singapore Tourism Board (STB) 174
Sirindhorn, Princess 130
Socialist Republic of the Union of
Burma 86
Söng Le'o 110, 111, 113–16
Soviet Union 55
spin 172–73, 183

Star 166
State Law and Order Restoration
Council (SLORC) 86, 88, 90, 100
State Peace and Development Council
(SPDD) 86, 92
Straits Times 143, 145, 150, 171
Straits Times Interactive 176–77
street parades 212–19
Suara Pembaruan 191, 220
Suhakam 146, 150
Sukarnoputri, Megawati 215

TAOs (Tambon Administrative
Organizations) 126
Tatmadaw (Burmese military) 86, 93
Televisi Manado (TV-M) 194–96, 200
Television and Video Law 1996 88–89,
96
television ownership 6
Temasek 128, 131–33
terrorism: alternative media 140, 152;
human rights and 152; Islamic
protection 165–66
Thai Post 132
Thai-Rak-Thai (TRT) Party:
corruption 130, 134; privatization
policies 122, 123, 124, 131, 136
Thailand 122–37; anti-Thaksin
campaign 127–33; coup 2006 136–37;
elections 122, 131–32, 133–35; film
genres 129; legislation 133; media
piracy 117–18; media reform 123–27;
Muslim South 130; nationalism 136;
People's Constitution 123, 126; post-
Thaksin 133–36; privatization 123–
24; Shan migrants 117–18
Thailand This Week 128
Thaksin Shinawatra: coup 2006 136–
37; "King whispers" 122; one-party
governance 124; Shin Corp. sale 128,
131–33; Sondhi and the King 127–
31; Thailand after 133–36
Think Centre 142–43, 145–46, 148–49,
152
Tiananmen demonstrations 33
TOT (Telephone Authority of
Thailand) 124
tourism 174–78, 183
transition 2–9
transparency 182–83
TV3 159, 164
TVRI 193–94, 209, 216, 217

U Lu Zaw 89–90

U Nu 99
U Par Lay 89–90
U Win Htein 90, 100
UNESCO 2
United Malays National Organization (UMNO) 156, 157, 158, 159–60, 163–65
Universal Declaration on Human Rights 98
USA 3, 92, 152
Utusan Malaysia 162, 164
Utusan Melayu 159
Utusan Melayu Berhad (UM) 164–65

Vietnam: diasporic gaze 75–76, 77; identity 79–82; legislation 72; liberalization (*Doi Moi*) 70, 73, 82–83; prostitution 77–78; rural Vietnam 75, 77
Vietnam Film Archives 73
Vietnamese cinema 70–83; ethnicity and liberalization 79–82; funding 71; history of 73–75; national male gaze 75–77; private and state-private films 71–72; truth in alleyways 77–78
Vietnamese Communist Party (VCP) 70–71, 72–73
Visi Anak Bangsa (VAB) 219
Vogue 41
Voice of America (VOA) 96

Washington Post 134
We Shall Meet Again (film) 73
Wenhui Bao 15
western bias 3–4
The Wild Field (film) 73
Win Aung 91
World Press Freedom Day 165
World Trade Organization (WTO) 14, 54

Xin'an Evening Post 40–41
Xinmin Evening News 15

Zhu Rongji 51

eBooks – at www.eBookstore.tandf.co.uk

A library at your fingertips!

eBooks are electronic versions of printed books. You can store them on your PC/laptop or browse them online.

They have advantages for anyone needing rapid access to a wide variety of published, copyright information.

eBooks can help your research by enabling you to bookmark chapters, annotate text and use instant searches to find specific words or phrases. Several eBook files would fit on even a small laptop or PDA.

NEW: Save money by eSubscribing: cheap, online access to any eBook for as long as you need it.

Annual subscription packages

We now offer special low-cost bulk subscriptions to packages of eBooks in certain subject areas. These are available to libraries or to individuals.

For more information please contact webmaster.ebooks@tandf.co.uk

We're continually developing the eBook concept, so keep up to date by visiting the website.

www.eBookstore.tandf.co.uk